# BRITISH HYMN BOOKS
# FOR CHILDREN, 1800–1900

# Ashgate Studies in Childhood, 1700 to the Present

*Series editor: Claudia Nelson, Texas A&M University, USA*

This series recognizes and supports innovative work on the child and on literature for children and adolescents that informs teaching and engages with current and emerging debates in the field. Proposals are welcome for interdisciplinary and comparative studies by humanities scholars working in a variety of fields, including literature; book history, periodicals history, and print culture and the sociology of texts; theater, film, musicology, and performance studies; history, including the history of education; gender studies; art history and visual culture; cultural studies; and religion.

# British Hymn Books for Children, 1800–1900

## Re-Tuning the History of Childhood

ALISA CLAPP-ITNYRE
*Indiana University East, USA*

ASHGATE

Published by
Ashgate Publishing Limited
Wey Court East
Union Road
Farnham
Surrey, GU9 7PT
England

Ashgate Publishing Company
110 Cherry Street
Suite 3-1
Burlington, VT 05401-3818
USA

www.ashgate.com

**British Library Cataloguing in Publication Data**
A catalogue record for this book is available from the British Library

**The Library of Congress has cataloged the printed edition as follows:**
Clapp-Itnyre, Alisa, 1967–
    British hymn books for children, 1800–1900: re-tuning the history of childhood / by Alisa
        Clapp-Itnyre.
        pages cm. — (Ashgate studies in childhood, 1700 to the present)
    Includes index.
    ISBN  978-1-4094-5430-4  (hardcover)  —  ISBN  978-1-4094-5431-1  (ebook)  —
ISBN 978-1-4724-0701-6 (epub)
    1. Hymns, English—19th century—History and criticism. I. Title.
    BV312.C53 2015
    264'.230830941—dc23

2015011124

ISBN: 9781409454304 (hbk)
ISBN: 9781409454311 (ebk – PDF)
ISBN: 9781472407016 (ebk – ePUB)

Printed in the United Kingdom by Henry Ling Limited,
at the Dorset Press, Dorchester, DT1 1HD

*To Annetta May Itnyre, the empowered child singer in my life*

# Contents

*List of Figures*                                                                      ix
*List of Tables*                                                                        xi
*Permissions*                                                                         xiii
*Acknowledgements*                                                                 xv

Introduction: Re-Tuning the History of Childhood with Chords and Verses    1

1   Creating Communities of Song: Class and Gender in Children's
    Hymn-Singing Experiences                                                         15

2   Re-Writing the History of Children's Literature: Three Periods of
    Children's Hymnody                                                                   55

3   Complicating Child-Adult Distinctions: "Crossover" Children's
    Hymn-Texts and Tunes                                                                89

4   Staging the Child: Agency and Stasis for Children in Art and
    Hymn-Book Illustrations                                                            139

5   Reforming Society: Missionary, Bands of Hope, and Bands of
    Mercy Hymns                                                                          181

6   Resurrecting the Child: The Cult of the Deathbed, Hymns of Faith,
    and Children of Life                                                                 227

*Works Cited*                                                                          269
*Index*                                                                                  295
*Hymn Index*                                                                          303

# List of Figures

1.1 "Lord, I have passed another day." From [Lucy Wilson], *Short and Simple Prayers, with Hymns, for the Use of Children* (1844). Courtesy of King's College Library, Cambridge University. 27

1.2 Frontispiece to *The Sunday-School Union Hymn-Book*, 20th edition (1835). Courtesy of The Angus Library and Archive, Regent's Park College, Oxford University. 39

2.1 Frontispiece to Ann and Jane Taylor's *Hymns for Infant Minds* (1809). 2nd edition (1810). Courtesy of The Lilly Library, Indiana University, Bloomington, Indiana. 68

3.1 "Christ the Lord is risen today." From *The Methodist Sunday-School Hymn & Tune-Book* (1879). From the author's collection and in the public domain. 112

3.2 "Abide with me." From *Hymns Ancient and Modern* (1861). From the author's collection and in the public domain. 120

3.3 "Father, in high heaven dwelling." From *The Young People's Hymnal: Edition with Tunes* (1896), H. Elliot Button, ed. From the author's collection and in the public domain. 125

3.4 "One day, dear children, you must die." From *Accompanying Tunes to the 'Hymns for Infant Children'* (1862), John B. Dykes, ed. Courtesy of Andover-Harvard Theological Library, Harvard Divinity School. 127

3.5 "Holy, holy, holy." From *The Children's Hymn Book* (1878), [Mrs. Carey Brock, ed.]. From the author's collection and in the public domain. 130

4.1 Frontispiece by H. Anelay to *Texts and Hymns Selected for Children* (1857), H. J. Sturge, ed. From Internet Archive. 148

4.2 Frontispiece to *Hymns and Poems for Very Little Children* by Hon. M. E. L. [Margaret Elizabeth Leigh Child-Villiers, Countess of Jersey, 1849–1945] (1875). Courtesy of The Lilly Library, Indiana University, Bloomington, Indiana. 153

4.3     Hymn No. 1, "A General Song of Praise to God." From
        *Divine and Moral Songs for Children by the Reverend Isaac
        Watts DD*, Pictured in Colours by Mrs. Arthur Gaskin (1896).
        Courtesy of The Lilly Library, Indiana University,
        Bloomington, Indiana.                                          155

4.4     Magic lantern slide to verse 2 of "I think when I read that
        sweet story of old." Courtesy of the Kent Museum of the
        Moving Image.                                                  162

4.5     Isaac Watts's Song No. 28, "Lord, how delightful 'tis to see."
        From *Divine Songs Attempted in an Easy Language* (London,
        c. 1800). Courtesy of The Lilly Library, Indiana University,
        Bloomington, Indiana.                                          176

4.6     Isaac Watts's Song No. 28, "Lord, how delightful 'tis to
        see." From *Divine and Moral Songs*, illustrated by C. W. Cope,
        engraved by John Thompson (London, 1848). From Internet
        Archive.                                                       177

4.7     Isaac Watts's Song No. 28, "Lord, how delightful 'tis to see."
        From *Divine and Moral Songs* (London, 188-). Courtesy of
        University Library, University of Illinois at Urbana-Champaign.  178

5.1     Hymn No. 10, "The Golden Rule." From Watts's *Divine Songs
        for Children* (London, 1802). Courtesy of The Lilly Library,
        Indiana University, Bloomington, Indiana.                      191

5.2     "The Voice of the Helpless," Song No. 65. From *Songs of Happy
        Life: For Schools, Homes, and Bands of Mercy*, compiled by
        Sarah J. Eddy (London, 1st edition, 1897). From Internet Archive.  221

6.1     "Abide with me" magic lantern slide. Courtesy of the Kent
        Museum of the Moving Image.                                    234

6.2     "There is a happy land." From *The Methodist Sunday-School
        Hymn and Tune-Book*, 1879. From the author's collection and
        in the public domain.                                          251

6.3     "Vital Spark of Heavenly Flame." From *The Sabbath-School
        Bell* (1856). Courtesy of the University of Michigan Library
        (Music Library).                                               260

# List of Tables

1.1    Percentages of Popular Hymns in Three Classes of Hymn Books    52

3.1    The 25 Most Frequently Appearing Hymns in Nineteenth-Century Children's Hymn Books    90

3.2    Turn-of-Century Reflections on Most Popular Victorian Hymns (adult selection)    96

3.3    Hymns Found in All of Five Prominent Adult Nineteenth-Century Hymn Books: Anglican, Methodist, Baptist, Gospel, and Church of Ireland (alphabetical)    97

3.4    The 25 Most Frequently Appearing Hymn Tunes in 30 Nineteenth-Century Children's Hymn Books with a Separate Tune Index    116

5.1    Most Frequently Appearing Songs or Hymns in 12 British Band of Hope Songbooks, 1860–1899    202

# Permissions

I would like to thank the following for permission to reproduce, in revised form, these works:

A small portion of Chapter 1 has appeared as "Community in Children's Hymn-Singing" in *Victorian Review*, Spring 2015.

Chapter 2 first appeared as "Nineteenth-Century British Children's Hymnody: Re-Tuning the History of Childhood with Chords and Verses," published in *Children's Literature Association Quarterly* 35.2 (2010): 144–75. Reprinted with permission by Johns Hopkins University Press; copyright 2010 Children's Literature Association.

A majority of Chapter 5 appeared as "Reforming Society: Missionary and Bands of Hope Hymns for Children" in *"Perplext in Faith": Essays on Victorian Beliefs and Doubts*, edited by Alisa Clapp-Itnyre and Julie Melnyk, Newcastle upon Tyne: Cambridge Scholars Publishing, 2015. Published with the permission of Cambridge Scholars Publishing.

Various analyses of hymns first appeared in "Writing for, Yet Apart: Nineteenth-Century Women's Contentious Status as Hymn Writers and Editors of Hymnbooks for Children," *Victorian Literature and Culture* 40.1 (March 2012): 47–81.

# Acknowledgements
## "I Love to Tell the Story"

I hope that the writing of any book is a "labor of love" for the writer but I feel incredibly fortunate that at least this book project was so for me. For one, I grew up singing hymns and was one of those children I discuss in the book who found hymn texts inspirational and hymn tunes quite infectious. This was in the American United Methodist tradition where "When morning gilds the skies" and "How great thou art" were still, in the 1980s, powerful congregational standards. My childhood favorite was "I love to tell the story," appropriately enough a nineteenth-century British hymn, although I did not realize it at the time. In fact, I realized at a young age the flexibility of text and tune when my father, the Rev. Jon M. Clapp, one of the ministers at Clarkston (Michigan) United Methodist Church, would challenge the congregation by selecting a text to be sung to a tune on another page. Scouring the hymnal's metrical index, I soon found out how he could do that. I even enjoyed singing an occasional hymn for the congregation in four-part harmony with my younger sister Amy Clapp, mother Karen Clapp, and father, such as "It is well with my soul." Hymns continued to be an important part of my life, sung at the Bay View Association of the United Methodist Church in Petoskey, Michigan, during summer vacations there; and then a vital part of student-led Midweek services of the Wesley Foundation at the University of Illinois, Urbana-Champaign, during graduate school. I am still blessed to be in a neighborhood in Richmond, Indiana, where two nearby churches toll out hymns twice a day—and quite a few nineteenth-century favorites such as "Nearer, my God, to Thee" at that. I realize I am of a dwindling number of people who can still claim to be surrounded by hymns, let alone so appreciate them, but it gives me an affinity with nineteenth-century children which helped in the writing of this book. And such societies as the Hymn Society in the United States and Canada, and the Hymn Society of Great Britain and Ireland, whose conferences I have enjoyed presenting at and simply attending, also give me hope that I am not quite as alone in my love of hymns as I first thought.

Secondly, research for this book has given me some wonderful memories with my family. My daughter, Annetta, grew up during the writing of the book, from age 4 to 13, and if not sharing my love of hymns quite as much as me, still demonstrates an insatiable desire to sing seemingly every minute of the day. Further, she always listened to my stories about hymns and even learned about a dozen to sing, alone or with friends, so I could record them and have hymn illustrations for my various professional presentations. She and my husband Ron Itnyre have allowed me an immense amount of uninterrupted time these nine years to write. Ron also helped me create and navigate the Excel database that became crucial to my data collecting and consequently to some of my major claims. My mother-in-law, Elizabeth Itnyre, gave me a quiet retreat at her farmhouse in northern Illinois whenever we visited and where some of my best work was written. My aunt Joanne Close has generously named herself the "biggest fan" of my scholarship. My musician-sister Amy and I have had some wonderful discussions about the hymn tunes I discuss, and for her careful reading of Chapter 3, I thank her. Likewise, my brother-in-law David Salmonson has kindly shown unflagging interest in the progress of the book. They, niece Rebecca, and nephew Andrew have also granted me quiet time for writing during vacations to the family cottage on Lake Louise, Michigan, an inspirational place to read and write. The kids have also reminded me of the unbounded energy for singing and playing residing in childhood. Learning how to sing a nineteenth-century-children's favorite, "I think when I read that sweet story of old," in sign-language with my niece Becca and the others, so as to be able to perform it in 2009, is an especially sweet memory for me. And I especially want to thank my wonderful mother, Karen Baird Clapp, for her steadfast support and love, for this project and in life.

Annetta and Ron have also accompanied me on three trips to England for research purposes, always understanding my need to be in libraries and not sight-seeing with them, although this was hard for Annetta as a 4-year-old tourist. For various other conference and research trips to the UK—the biannual Music in Nineteenth-Century Britain conferences, for example—my sister, and then mother and father accompanied me, too, and I will never forget hearing hymns and choral works sung at St. Martin's in the Field, Westminster Abbey, Christ Church Oxford, and Durham Cathedral with them. I know the power of hymns, in fact, because my dear father, now suffering from dementia, can still call up the tune and most of the words to many a hymn, like "Holy, holy, holy," whenever I start to sing it with him. Though he has not been able to edit this book as he did all my college papers, I still use his three-point approach to sermon-writing, quite unconsciously, in almost everything I write, as the structure for most of my chapters will attest.

Finally, this book project put me in contact with some extremely knowledgeable and kind people in the field, both personally and professionally. I have enjoyed researching or attending conferences together with colleague-friends Natalie Ziarnik, Joanne Passet, Elaine Bearden, and Emily Cody. I have Nancy Faus Mullen, personal friend and editor of the *Hymnal: A Worship Book* (1992) to thank for talks about hymns and for first inviting me to speak at the Hymn Society in the United States and Canada in 2011. My daughter's piano teacher, Caryle Bailey, discussed and recorded hymn tunes for me to use in presentations and on the website. And my "Writing Buddies"—fellow faculty at Indiana University East including Drs. Daron Olson, Cathy Ludlum Foos, Ron Itnyre, and Paul Kriese—and I have met weekly to encourage each other's scholarly writing even amidst our teaching obligations.

I also have a long list of colleagues to thank for reading chapters of this manuscript: Jill May and Robert May, professors of children's literature and history, respectively, at Purdue University, Jill being my first mentor in the field of children's literature in 1997; Margaret Thomas Evans and Laverne Nishihara (English) and Jessica Raposo (music) at IU East; Laureen Tedesco (English) of East Carolina University; Charles McGuire (music) of Oberlin College;

Christina Bashford (music) of the University of Illinois, Urbana-Champaign; Lisa Surridge (English) of the University of Victoria; Laura Vorachek (English) of the University of Dayton; Margaret Mackey (children's literature editor) at the University of Alberta; Louise Van Dyke, Fellow of the Hymn Society; and Emily Cody, graduate student (English/animal studies) at the Ohio State University. Julie Codell (art history) at Arizona State University and Cynthia Huff (English) at Illinois State University both gave invaluable leads to books on art history and on diary repositories in the UK, respectively. Well-known hymnologist J. R. Watson invited me to my first Hymn Society of Britain and Ireland conference in 2010 and shared conversations about hymns. Finally, Joss Marsh (retired, English, IU Bloomington) and David Francis first introduced me to the fascinating world of the magic lantern, then shared hymn slides from their own collection. In fact, many of the aforementioned colleagues I have either met at, or served together on the Board of, the Midwest Victorian Studies Association, and for the 20 years of support and collegiality of this organization, as well as several chances to share my research, I am deeply indebted. Its treasurer Julie Melnyk (English, University of Missouri) early on shared her research on women's hymnody; I just co-edited a volume on Victorian religion for Cambridge Scholars with her and thank her (and them) for permission to republish a part of Chapter 5 from that volume.

I am especially thankful to Laureen Tedesco, a friend from the Children's Literature Association (ChLA), who believed in this project long before I thought anyone else did and encouraged me to continue despite initial discouragement. I am appreciative of Kate Capshaw for first publishing what is now Chapter 2 in the *Children's Literature Association Quarterly*. And I also have the ChLA to thank for a Faculty Research Grant in 2009 which helped support my second research trip to England. My home institution, Indiana University, has also been incredibly generous in granting me three New Frontiers in the Arts and Humanities Fellowships and two Overseas Conference Grants to research and then disseminate this scholarship. I am grateful for my affiliation with Indiana University, the IU Lilly Library archives, and the impressive collection of Isaac Watts's *Divine and Moral Songs for Children*, nineteenth-century editions, which it houses. Because of the help of Lilly librarians (Rebecca Cape, Isabel Planton, and Zach Downey, in particular), I have been able to view most of them and then been granted permission to publish quite a few of their images at almost no charge when reproduction of the English versions I had originally used was too expensive.

My own campus, Indiana University East—Associate Vice-Chancellors Mary Blakefield and Ross Alexander, in particular—has likewise been extremely supportive, awarding me various Summer Faculty Fellowships, Research Grants, and two sabbaticals to cover some of the cost and time needed for this project. As Director of the Honors Program there since 2010, I have been surrounded by helpful honors students, several of whom were not only willing but eager to assist with some of the legwork and data-input of this project: Patricia Finley, Terri McGunegill, Holly Walls, Ian Holt, and Jessica Baker. Another Honors alumna, Deidra Purvis, came on as my course assistant in fall 2014 so I could work on the final revisions. At IU East, too, I want to thank Marcia Sloan, interlibrary-loan librarian, for countless hours spent acquiring much-needed primary and secondary sources.

I also express gratitude to librarians in the UK without whom I would not have been able to carry out this research project. Peter Horton at the Royal College of Music gave unlimited access to use and photocopy what were to become key hymn books in my initial study, while Claire Welford, Rare Books Superintendent of Cambridge University Library, helped tremendously in finding and photocopying vital temperance and illustrated hymn books, even helping me with details over email three years later. To other librarians and library staff whom I will not be able to name by name I give whole-hearted, if general, gratitude: at the British Library; the Bodleian Library, Oxford; Cambridge University Library; the National Archives, London; the Wesley Chapel and Museum, London; Durham University Library (Fred Pratt Green Collection); the University of Manchester (John Rylands Library); and the University of Cardiff Library, Wales.

My undergraduate professors at Oakland University, Michigan, Drs. Jane and Robert Eberwein, first introduced me to the pleasure of research and continue to support my scholarly endeavors. I am especially honored to have worked with Nicholas Temperley, world-renowned hymnologist, as a doctoral student at the University of Illinois and now am grateful for his reading of several chapters, help with sources, and encouragement of the entire project, even as he continues to add important monographs to the field himself. And finally, I thank Claudia Nelson who went well beyond the duties of a series editor in reading almost every chapter of this manuscript and giving astute and encouraging comments for all of them. I thank her, Ann Donahue, Alyssa Berthiaume, Stephanie Peake, and others at Ashgate for their interest in publishing this study and then for a very pleasant publishing experience.

For one week in June 2015, Dr. Jessica Raposo, music professor at Indiana University East, and I held a "hymn camp" for 17 auditioned young singers, boys and girls, ages 8–13, at Central United Methodist Church, Richmond, Indiana, teaching them close to 20 of the hymns I discuss in this book, which were then professionally recorded. I am grateful to Jessica for undertaking this project with me and especially to these young singers for giving a week of their summer break to learn these old hymns so enthusiastically and then singing them so beautifully. It was an emotional closure to this nine-year project for me to witness how adults and children might still come together to enjoy the inspiration and beauty of hymns. With thanks to my institution for providing the website and Dr. Greg Weber for building it, I am pleased to invite the reader to the following webpage to actually hear the voices of these children singing many of the hymns I will closely explicate in this study: http://www.iue.edu/hss/research/clapp-itnyre/childrenshymns.

It is because of all these people listed above that I am finally able to share with scholars and laypeople alike the vast, unexplored world of children's hymn singing, which was clearly a powerful and pleasurable experience for many Victorians.

*Alisa Clapp-Itnyre, Richmond, Indiana*
*July 2015*

# Introduction
# Re-Tuning the History of Childhood
# with Chords and Verses

The Victorian period was *the* age of the child. One out of three people during the era was under 15 years of age.[1] Victorian society was a society of children, and, more importantly, it was arguably the first society to define "childhood" in completely new and separate terms from adulthood. Children became dominant in literature and a major concern for social reformers. This was the era of Oliver Twist and Alice in Wonderland, of Walter Pater's "The Child in the House" and Elizabeth Barrett Browning's "The Cry of the Children," an era to idealize the child and mobilize for its relief from poverty and labor practices. The "Cult of the Child" as a slogan may not have been coined until the 1880s, but a cult was in practice well before then.[2]

Childhood studies has become a vital scholarly arena in which to consider children's history; as scholar Sally Shuttleworth pointedly asked in 2004, "Is it now time to add age, and more specifically childhood, to the triumvirate of class, gender, and race?" (107). She and other scholars, particularly in history and literature, have responded in the affirmative, pointing to the nineteenth century as that in which childhood was first acknowledged, or, more accurately, constructed apart from adulthood. Philippe Ariès, in his seminal *Centuries of Childhood: A Social History of Family Life* (1962), argued that medieval society saw little difference between children and adults; that it was only the modern era that created a new distinction between children and adults especially through education.[3] Useful maxims have furthered the distinction of the Victorian era, as with Judith Saltman who, in the *Riverside Anthology of Children's Literature*, writes, "If the

---

[1]  See Pamela Horn, *The Victorian Town Child*, 3.

[2]  This now-famous phrase came from an 1889 essay by poet Ernest Dowson while an inaugural scholarly study was that by George Boas, *The Cult of Childhood* (1966), although Marah Gubar notes how few pages he actually devotes to the Victorian era whose authors (Charles Dickens, Lewis Carroll) have now become synonymous with the term (viii–ix).

[3]  Ariès has been much contested since the 1960s: see Lloyd de Mause, ed., *The History of Childhood* (1974), Edward Shorter, *The Making of the Modern Family* (1976), and Lawrence Stone, *The Family, Sex and Marriage in England 1500–1800* (1977); Linda A. Pollock in *Forgotten Children* (1983). Hugh Cunningham, in *Children and Childhood in Western Society Since 1500* (1995), gives a useful overview of childhood-history scholarship (3–18). In "Childhood Histories" he summarizes the scholarship up to 2004, suggesting that histories in the last decade have split into two groups: history of ideas about childhood, and life of a child in a particular place or time. Significantly, almost all studies listed here or discussed by Cunningham prioritize the nineteenth century as one of immense change in constructing childhood.

Puritans discovered *the child*, then the Victorians discovered *childhood*" (4; her italics). Her assessment not only highlights Puritans' unique focus on children in order to train them in godly living, but also suggests another immense ideological shift by the Victorians in expanding and even idealizing the years of childhood. As Hugh Cunningham describes the Victorian ideology: "At its heart was a reverence for, and a sanctification of, childhood which was at total odds with the Puritan emphasis on the child as a sinful being," such that the child himself became "godlike, fit to be worshipped, and the embodiment of hope" (*Children and Childhood in Western Society* 72).

Perry Nodelman, Jack Zipes, and Karín Lesnik-Oberstein, among others, have reminded us of the power struggles at the heart of defining "the child" against "the adult" in our own century.[4] This power struggle is particularly acute in the context of Victorian society where, again, much scholarly attention has been placed. David Grylls points to "the curious paradox, the chief distinguishing characteristic, of Victorian parent-child relations," that adults could shower children with both "cloying affection" *and* "fierce discipline and a brooding suspicion of sin" (23). C. John Sommerville also suggests that this period of "the greatest glorification of childhood" coincided with "the greatest exploitation of children" by adult society (160). Recognizing the immense class divide between "children who formed the backbone of industrialization and those whose pampered lives rested on that labor," he yet suggests that even upper-class children might experience adult manipulation "disguised as kindness" (160). Child-labor reform leading up to the Education Act of 1870[5] helped to enforce legally a period of childhood for the working classes: as Eric Hopkins argues, not only did childhood "transform" during the nineteenth century but "part of the transformation was the extension of childhood itself, in that at the beginning of the nineteenth century, starting work at so early an age brought an enforced end to infant irresponsibility and the start of a lifetime of earning a living; whereas by 1900 this climacteric had been postponed to the age of twelve at the earliest, and for many till the age of fourteen" (vii). Yet this late-century acknowledgement and extolment of childhood, as paralleling the Golden Age of children's literature, has also been challenged by such scholars as Marah Gubar who reveals resistance to the cult by many late-century writers (Carroll, Nesbit, Barrie, etc.), who, instead of exploited children, used the trope of adult-child collaboration as they created savvy, empowered children in their novels and plays (*Artful Dodgers: Reconceiving the Golden Age of Children's Literature*, 2009). Claudia Nelson even demonstrates Victorians' consistent blurring of adult and child altogether (*Precocious Children and Childish Adults: Age Inversion in Victorian Literature*, 2012). As all these arguments attest,

---

[4]    See Nodelman's *The Hidden Child* (2008), Zipes's *Sticks and Stones* (2001), and Lesnik-Oberstein's *Children's Literature: Criticism and the Fictional Child* (1994), for instance.

[5]    The Factories Act of 1844 which, among other reforms, limited the work-day to 12 hours, while the Factories Act of 1878, together with the Education Act of 1870, prohibited labor for children under 10 and required their attendance at state schools instead. These will be considered at greater length in Chapter 1.

defining Victorian childhood is tenuous at best, Monica Flegel suggesting that the uneven conclusions of various scholarship of the nineteenth century stem "in part, from the instability of its object—childhood itself" (*Conceptualizing Cruelty* 13).

Somewhere between labor and play, between austere didacticism and idyllic scenes of childhood, between the adult and the child, resides a facet of children's nineteenth-century culture that has rarely been examined but could help us come to a greater understanding of that childhood: children's hymnody. Alongside the Evangelical and Oxford revivals of the first half of the century and even during the Crises of Faith of later decades, hymns proliferated. Hymns have been defined as "pure song in praise of God" (Blessington 495) or, more specifically, could be termed sung religious poems, urging Christian ideals of praise, repentance, and moral conduct upon their audience, adults as well as children. Hymn singing permeated Victorian children's lives, not just in churches and chapels on Sundays as might be the experience for children today, but throughout the week in schools and in the home. Children were furnished their own liturgical, hymn-singing spaces: in working-class Sunday schools, in middle-class children's services, and as part of upper-class boarding-schools. By the late 1870s, one hymn editor was able to write that "Hymn-singing has found its way into nearly every family circle; the Sunday School has been largely developed within the Church of England; Children's Services have multiplied; Guilds, Bands of Hope, and kindred societies have been formed in hundreds of parishes; and the demand for hymns suited to the young, on all subjects within the range of their interests, is becoming daily more and more urgent" (*The Children's Hymn Book*, 1878, [ed. Mrs. Carey Brock], iii). Children wrote about hymn singing in their diaries, writers incorporated them into children's scenes in their novels, and adults of the twentieth century reflected upon hymn singing's influence on their Victorian youth. Hymns touched all aspects of nineteenth-century childhood, all denominations, classes, locales, equally for both genders.

The number of hymns being published was in response to the century's theological fervor, fueling it, too, for the youngest of citizens. Hymn books for children flourished as readily as did religious tracts and literature. Ministers and mothers, trained composers and factory workers, all wrote hymns for children, publishing them in church periodicals, original books of hymns, or as part of hymn compilations. The hymn-book genre especially disseminated hymns in a versatile way: as Isabel Rivers and David L. Wykes write, "Hymns were originally sung by congregations from a dictated text ('lined out' by a clerk), but the printed hymn-book transformed the ways in which they could be used. They could be shared by other congregations in public worship, families could sing them together at home, and individuals could learn them by heart, quote them in their journals, and recite them on their deathbeds" (*Dissenting Praise* 2).

This was especially true for the children's hymn book which came into its own during the century. Susan Tamke shows that children's hymn books outnumbered hymn books of any other single category during the era, the most popular sometimes running into a hundred editions ("Hymns for Children" 19). Samuel J. Rogal, in *The Children's Jubilee: A Bibliographical Survey of Hymnals for*

*Infants, Youth, and Sunday Schools Published in Britain and America, 1655–1900*, identifies almost 800 children's hymn books published from 1800 to 1900 in Britain and America. The British Library catalogues over 350 children's hymn books of the century (in its *General Catalogue of Printed Books* and *Catalogue of Printed Music*) still extant in their collections (including various editions of the same hymn book).

It could also be argued that the children's hymn book as a separate hymn book was almost exclusively a genre of the nineteenth century. Originating in the eighteenth century with Isaac Watts's *Divine and Moral Songs, Attempted in an Easy Language for the Use of Children* (1715), yet followed only by a few other notable hymn books for children throughout that century (Charles Wesley's *Hymns for Children, and Others of Riper Years* [1763], Christopher Smart's *Hymns for the Amusement of Children* [1772], for example), it was not until the nineteenth century that the genre exploded in consonance with religious revivals. The publication of these hymn books continued into the Edwardian era, but generally twentieth-century hymn books for children dwindle, often eclipsed by general hymn books with a children's section and slowed by a growing secularization of society. For example, the British Library's collection of children's hymn books published in the twentieth century is about half the size of that from the nineteenth century, visibly decreasing in number every decade.[6] Similarly, periodicals known to print hymns turn to secular songs even by the turn of the century.[7] The children's hymn book is thus a genre peaking in the nineteenth century.

Despite their centrality to Victorian life and book history, however, children's hymn books have received scant recognition in the scholarship of the period, being noticeably absent in the scholarship of Evangelical literature and children's literary history. Some of this is intentional; in his classic study of children's literature, F. J. Harvey Darton (1932) defined "children's books" as those works written "to give children spontaneous pleasure" and therefore excluded anything "purely moral or didactic" (1); he thus points to the year 1744 (the publication date of John Newbery's first book) as commencing the era of children's literature. Darton's definitions disavow the possibility of didactic literature still causing pleasure, a theory I will test with children's hymns, and also soundly ignores Watts's *Divine and Moral Songs* (1715) of 30 years earlier. More recent children's literature scholarship and anthologies, bringing into view the full realm of didactic and religious literature for children of the eighteenth and nineteenth centuries,

---

[6]    Tallying the number of children's hymn books in both *The British Library General Catalogue of Printed Books* and *The Catalogue of Printed Music in the British Library*, I count 371 vs. 176 publications between the two centuries. I also track a gradual increase throughout the nineteenth century, climaxing in the 1850s and 1870s (64 and 57 books, respectively) but remaining high throughout the first decade of the twentieth century (42), though dipping down to only a dozen or so publications by the 1960s and 70s. I realize these are not complete lists of all published books.

[7]    Looking at *The Girl's Own* Annual, for example, I found hymns scattered throughout issues of the 1880s, in about an equal proportion to secular hymns, but by the end of the century, the secular (particularly love) songs clearly dominate with only an occasional hymn.

now acknowledge *Divine and Moral Songs* but ignore the wealth of other hymns and hymn books for children yet peaking alongside the religious tracts and stories of the nineteenth century.[8] Social historians likewise pass over the context of hymn singing altogether or give only passing, pejorative gestures to "dull routines of hymn singing and Bible reading" (Hopkins 134).

When children's hymns are acknowledged, it is primarily in the context of hymn studies. Yet, here they often face harsh critique. Susan S. Tamke did important work in the 1970s in recovering hymns for consideration in a literary context. Her *Make a Joyful Noise Unto the Lord* (1978) contains an entire chapter on hymns for children. Yet she describes these hymns as being chiefly "dark and pessimistic warnings" or exceedingly "sweet and gentle" (87), concluding that:

> Children were taught to be passive—to be submissive, humble, and obedient, to deny their individual impulses. At the same time, they were taught to be vigorously active—to struggle mightily against temptation and sin and for truth and a better world … This conflict in role models, between the demands that a child be both submissive and aggressive, must have created a great deal of tension and psychological confusion for young adults. (90)

Noted hymnologist Erik Routley, in *A Panorama of Christian Hymnody* (1979), devotes one article to hymns for children, speaking of the "fatal habit of Victorians" which was to litter their hymns with the word "little"—"and what child wants to think of itself as little?" (124). Likewise, Lionel Adey, writing one of the first systematic studies of children's hymns based on economic stratification (Sunday Scholars to Privileged Youth) in *Class and Idol in the English Hymn* (1988) ultimately judges hymns based on their aesthetic deficiency, finding most late-century hymns to be "inferior fuel" and in "poetic decline" (Adey 157, 148). Ian Bradley, in his comprehensive study, *Abide with Me: The World of Victorian Hymns* (1997), does not even devote a full chapter to children's hymns, only about five pages, noting the "whole cult of childhood innocence" they represent but also their "powerful images and metaphors" as having a profound impact on all classes of children (49). J. R. Watson, writing a significant study of English hymnody in *The English Hymn: A Critical and Historical Study* (1997), limits his comments

---

[8] Consider such important scholarship of eighteenth- and nineteenth-century children's literature by Meigs, Eaton, Nesbitt, and Viguers, *A Critical History of Children's Literature* (1953); Gillian Avery, *Nineteenth Century Children* (1965); Margaret Nancy Cutt, *Ministering Angels* (1979); Ruth K. MacDonald, *Literature for Children in England and America from 1646 to 1774* (1982); J. S. Bratton, *The Impact of Victorian Children's Fiction* (1981); Mary V. Jackson, *Engines of Instruction* (1989); Samuel F. Pickering, *Moral Instruction and Fiction for Children, 1749–1820* (1993); Patricia Demers, *Heaven upon Earth* (1993); Ruth B. Bottigheimer, *The Bible for Children* (1996); Judith Plotz, *Romanticism and the Vocation of Childhood* (2001); Briggs, Butts, and Grenby, *Popular Children's Literature in Britain* (2008); Lynne Vallone, "A humble Spirit under Correction" (1992); and Carolyn Sigler, *Wee Folk, Good Folk* (diss., 1992). Hymns are conspicuously absent, except for occasional references to Watts, and Anna Laetitia Barbauld's *Hymns in Prose for Children* (1781) whose works are not sung (verse) hymns.

on children's hymns to only a handful of pages (within a chapter titled "Different Traditions"), summing up the state of children's hymnody thus:

> The idealized view of childhood … is only one of the problems facing those who would write for children in the nineteenth century. There is an uneasy condescension in many of the hymns, a simplifying of the gospel so that it sounds trite, and at the same time a cloying sentimentality…. Apparently oblivious of the problem, hymn-writers turned out children's hymns in vast numbers, and reprinted them with enthusiasm in collection after collection. (507)

He concludes that "[t]o anyone attempting to recover the hymn as a subject for serious critical study they are an embarrassment" (Watson 508).

Admittedly, there is some truth to the dour reputation of children's hymns. Watts saw hymns to be sung "with *Grace in the Heart*" but also "to teach and *admonish one another*" (his italics, 72, *Divine and Moral Songs*, 1807 edition), which he does quite effectively when referencing Hell and damnation to the sinful throughout many of his Divine Songs. Likewise, Charles Wesley, the other pillar of Protestant hymnody, focused on fire-and-brimstone theology in his hymns for the young. As these critics also suggest, it is true that, on the other end of the century, many hymns prevailed which now seem saccharine and sentimental to us. Children's hymnody has become associated either with rote Evangelical didacticism drilled into children attending Sunday schools, or syrupy sentimentality as they consistently sang about themselves as "little" and "meek." Children could be seen as caught in the middle, required to sing the ideologies of competing adult views.

However, I argue that it is time for a reassessment of children's nineteenth-century hymns. Assuming a cultural significance and an unacknowledged diversity of hymns of this period, I will pursue three main themes in this study: 1) children's hymnody was a genre integral to the fabric of Victorian childhood experience; studying hymns gives a fuller picture of children's daily aesthetic and intellectual opportunities than hitherto explored; 2) children's hymn singing was a context for immense empowerment of Victorian children, thus complicating our understanding of the child-adult power binary supposedly at play in Victorian society; and 3) children's hymn-book production intersected with major aesthetic movements of the period, from the peaking of Victorian hymnody to the Golden Age of Illustration, and its inclusion in such scholarly discussions will only deepen our understanding of the aesthetic network for children and adults. From the heaps of castigation and didacticism perceived of hymns, an empowered child singer emerges.

This book, then, proposes to show the many ways that a study of children's hymns alters our understanding and appreciation for child empowerment. Marah Gubar challenges the notion of children as "artless beings devoid of agency" (32) and demonstrates that, in certain fiction, "children can resist and reconceive the scripts handed to them by adults, participating not only in the production of narrative, but in the drafting of their own life stories" (38). Similarly, I argue that children's hymnody provided another space for agency and creativity. For one, children and youth were often collaborators, too, in the hymn-writing process. Diaries and autobiographies of the period reveal children writing and parodying hymns in their creativity and play. Routley even acknowledges that "our hymns are so frequently the work of young people" and names three hymn writers all under the age of 18: Joseph Grigg wrote "Jesus, and shall it ever be?" at age 10; Isaac Watts wrote "Behold the glories of the Lamb" at age 16; and John Milton wrote "Let us with a gladsome mind" at age 16 (*Hymns and Human Life* 243–4).

Furthermore, the very act of singing allows for creativity and agency. Victorian society presumably coined the adage that children "should be seen and not heard," yet singing surely allowed the child to be heard. Individual subjectivity is further inscribed to the child singer through musical interpretation and physical response: children may sing faster, louder, out of tune, with personal inflections, with passion and animated hand-gestures, with distraction and ambivalence, even with insolence and rebelliousness. Children could in fact negotiate the controlled world of hymn singing with their own voices, using their singing to express the inexpressible, to defy without defiance. Too, *en masse*, their voices would outnumber the adults, a singing army of controlled yet uncontrollable minions. Victorians often encouraged the physical dynamic of hymn singing, even the rebellion implied by "marching," as when James Currie, editor of *Infant School Hymns and Songs with Appropriate Melodies* (1865), instructs "either marching or manual movements ... [Hymns] are intended to be acted as well as sung" (5). Helping the child remember the hymns, physical gestures and bodily movements also enabled children to be *actively* praising, playing, and pretending. I therefore challenge the notions that hymns could not "give children spontaneous pleasure" (Darton 1) or that they simply taught passivity and submission (Tamke 90).

Finally, the content and variety of children's hymn-texts, rather than confusing a child, complimented their intellect and discernment. Indeed, children's hymn books put the debate about "the child" in high relief. After all, in children's hymn books, intricate issues of theology (content) and poetry (form), both typically kept within the domain of adulthood, are conveyed to those of younger years and comprehension. Adults' desire to disseminate complex Christian values to the young often necessitated new approaches to hymn writing and book editing. In negotiating this, hymn writers and editors were not simply debating the most appropriate approach to hymn writing, but were *defining "the child"* within their hymns.

As such, an analysis of children's nineteenth-century hymns participates in the larger debate about children's literature as written by adults. Perry Nodelman sums up this situation thus:

> all children's literature is written across what must inevitably be perceived to be a gap, written for and often about a group to which the writer does not belong. Thus, the concept that allows children's literature to exist at all is in itself binary and oppositional. It requires an adult writer different from and in many ways opposite to the child reader implied (and perhaps especially ... in terms of knowledge). It requires that the adult intermingle with the childlike but remain finally separate from it. ("Pleasure and Genre" 11)

Thomas Travisano further describes this binary: "a dialectic confrontation between the claims of childhood and the opposing claims of adulthood may be ever-present, and a tug-of-war across the divide in consciousness between author and reader may act itself out on every page, pulling the child forward into adulthood and pulling the adult back into a world of child-experience that the adult may pride himself on having grown beyond" ("Of Dialectic and Divided Consciousness" 28). As Nodelman further explores in his book *The Hidden Adult*, children's texts operate for both a "child" audience and an "adult" audience, regardless of age: "the presence of knowledge that a text invites its readers to know but pretend not to know seems available to the readers of all ages" (210). Ultimately, Laura C. Berry acknowledges:

> Although it constitutes a recognizable and familiar social category, as does "gender" or "race" or "class," "childhood" is unique because the child occupies a position that homogenizes rather than fragments the social community. Simply put, everyone can lay claim to membership, at least for a time, in the community of children, because everyone must have been a child. The necessary fact of childhood changes the way that this particular subject position functions socially. (4)

All of these theories come to bear on a study of children's hymns which were almost exclusively written by adults for children, often for very didactic reasons. Yet such writing invoked the adults' awareness and even experience with their own childhoods. Rather than polarizing, children's hymns reflect shared adult-child interests and understanding of complex social, theological, and eschatological concerns. Power struggles went hand in hand with ways in which nineteenth-century adults democratically shared hymns with children.

Ultimately, this study will entertain the power of hymn singing consciously and unconsciously given to children by adult hymn writers and editors, and the power also wrested back by the singing children. If adults had anxieties for the agency of music given and taken by children, this did not stifle a century's worth of children's hymn-book publication and hymn singing.

*******

Chapter 1, "Creating Communities of Song: Class and Gender in Children's Hymn-Singing Experiences," then, provides an historical overview of the contexts in which nineteenth-century children were exposed to hymns. I explore these contexts from the perspective of class, acknowledging the different, and separate, ways in which the working classes, middle classes, and upper classes would have sung hymns. Though all classes might have experienced hymns in church, other contexts were bifurcated: working and impoverished classes sang hymns in Sunday schools and Ragged Schools, the middle classes at home and late-century children's services, and the upper classes at home and, for boys, the public schools. Gender, too, is an important consideration as girls were expected to become leaders of hymn singing in the home. Despite the ways in which class and gender differentiated hymn-singing experiences for children, I show the many common hymns all classes were singing; hymns could be said to have become a common language for all Victorian children. Thus, class-based communities were created in conflict with one another, but hymnody's innate communal qualities certainly united children across the century.

The second chapter, "Re-Writing the History of Children's Literature: Three Periods of Victorian Children's Hymnody," defines three basic stages of children's-hymn history during the century: Evangelical, Tractarian, and Romantic. Confronting the notion that such trends reflected either heavy-handed didacticism or simple sentimentality, I will suggest ways in which hymn writers appealed to children's higher abilities. This can be seen, first, with hymn singing's responsive and physical qualities highlighted especially in the early, Evangelical era. In reaction to the Evangelicals' simple language and concepts, though, Tractarian and also Methodist hymn writers of mid-century write with the difficult language and severe concepts of adult hymns. By late in the century, Romantic hymn books, despite the increasingly saccharine qualities of text and tune, nevertheless appeal to the child's expanding theological appreciation by exposing children to a myriad of different approaches and theologies. That is, a child could not be intellectually "simple" to browse through and understand the complexity of religious doctrines conveyed in late-century hymn-book compilations. Thus, in these hymns, perceived to be didactic and doctrinaire, lay great empowerment of children through music's physical agency, "adult" approaches to hymn writing, and the intellect required to negotiate through theologically disparate texts. Placing this in the context of children's literary history, I suggest how an awareness of hymns necessitates a reassessment of that history.

The third chapter, "Erasing Child-Adult Distinctions: 'Crossover' Children's Hymn-Texts and Tunes," looks closely at the most popular hymn-texts and tunes of the day, investigating the reason why so many adult hymns exist in such high numbers in children's hymn books. In fact, hymns show interesting crossovers in that youthful concepts (of storytelling, for example) frequently appear in adult hymns, while adult concepts and rhetoric carry over into children's hymn books. Ultimately, adults were "lowered" to the level of children in the acknowledgement that both have similar interests and fears, needs for stories and assurance of divine comfort. Yet the tunes especially "raised" the child's intellect in asking him/her to read challenging music and to follow the shifting of texts to different tunes. Tunes were the great equalizer of age-distinctions, and by the Victorian era, newly written tunes were engaging and challenging adults and youthful singers alike. All this suggests the fluidity of adult-child ideologies and aesthetics throughout the century and deconstructs the notion of a definitively "child hymn."

In the fourth chapter, "Staging the Child: Agency and Stasis for Children in Art and Hymn-Book Illustrations," I consider the illustrations in hymn books and their intersection with the Golden Age of Illustration (the 1860s), the Golden Age of children's picture-book illustrations (especially the 1870s), and the late-century cult of the child in high art. Illustrations in hymn books sometimes reflected the technical strides of the former and the vibrancy of the latter, picture-book movement. However, only in the context of the magic lantern hymn slides of late century did hymn images succumb to objectifying children, particularly little girls, a trend found in high art of the era. In fact, overuse of stock images showed moments of adults displacing the child in these children's hymn books, and use of new color and engraving techniques created high-end hymn books whose images catered to readers of privilege. However, in their fiscal and social conservatism, hymn-book editors never eroticized the child. Instead, images of singing children contrasted with the stasis of such high-art images. These considerations of age, class, and gender will inform a close look at 20 Victorian-illustrated reproductions of Isaac Watts's classic 1715 *Divine and Moral Songs for Children* to conclude this chapter.

As I will demonstrate in Chapter 5, "Reforming Society: Missionary, Bands of Hope, and Bands of Mercy Hymns," not only were children the objects of reform throughout the century but were, more importantly, the agents of reform. Missionary, Bands of Hope, and Bands of Mercy organizations relied upon children to spread the word of the gospel, of temperance, and of kind treatment of animals, respectively. Empowering children, the Bands of Hope and Mercy hymns pushed children past the rhetoric of difference and elitism found in missionary hymns to acknowledge sameness and personal culpability, even sameness on a species level. Empowered child singers emerged from all these organizations and effectively enacted "reverse reform" as children transformed the adult world around them.

The final chapter, "Resurrecting the Child: the Cult of the Deathbed, Hymns of Faith, and Children of Life," tackles the century-long eulogy of The Child, that is, the cultural invoking and sentimentalizing of deaths of real and fictional children, exaggerated even beyond the statistics of child mortality rates. Hymns prepared the child to meet their Heavenly home in maudlin terms but also in comforting, Christian terms that appeared to reassure real children who faced death. As I recognize the dying child in this adult-created posture, from visual to musical expression, I simultaneously create the binary of the "live child," the record found within the literal pages of hymn books through marginalia and cover inscriptions. Further, children often showed a healthy witticism with hymn lyrics, rewriting and revising to suit their own sense of "theology." Finally, examining the brief record of children's diaries, I reveal the important ways that hymns entered their lives and, quite honestly, comforted their deaths.

I ultimately argue that nineteenth-century hymns created an empowered child singer. What I will not do is idealize hymns in as problematic a way as has been done of the children who sang them. I will acknowledge, for example, classist and especially racist tendencies in hymn-texts (chapters 1 and 5, respectively). I will probe ways in which children could mentally rebel during hymn singing (Chapter 2) or at least become oblivious to theological doctrine in their enjoyment of the tune (Chapter 3). I will note the eliding of the child for the adult in hymns (Chapter 2) and images (Chapter 4). Finally, I will consider sentimental and maudlin hymns alongside the criticisms of the children who sang them (chapters 2 and 6).

Nevertheless, it is essential that we begin to study children's hymns within an interdisciplinary context. Hymn singing was an important cultural institution which both divided and *united* the classes of Victorian society; too, hymns were used systematically during reform movements to give children a voice, both phenomena needing attention by social historians. Clearly, too, hymns participated in the theological debates of the century, disseminating Nonconformist, Tractarian, even Broad-Church ideologies, important to the religious historian. I especially consider the network of aesthetics combining to create the children's hymn book: specifically, their texts, their tunes, and their illustrations. Hymn-texts, truly a form of nineteenth-century children's literature worthy of study, created a space of child-empowerment through various strategies, intended or not, to present difficult theology and poetry to the youngest generation. Victorian hymn composers insisted upon adult-like musical proficiency even of the young, but also assume mutually favorite tunes of both children and adults; with its continuities with the "adult" hymn tradition, then, children's hymnody cannot be divorced from current scholarship of Victorian hymnody. Likewise, the art historian of child studies might consider how hymn-book illustrations often defy the passivity of children, showing them in adult-like postures of privilege. Closely looking at these three components of text, tune, and image in chapters 2, 3, and 4, respectively, I not only hope to show an empowered child singer but also show the sophisticated aesthetic systems in which hymn books engaged that singer. And as I participate in various fields of study, I wish to prove that our traditional marginalization of children's hymnody outside the fields of literature, musicology, art history, even history, makes those fields of study incomplete.

*******

This study is based on extensive archival research at major library collections in the United Kingdom: the British Library; the University College London Library; the National Archives; the Royal College of Music Library; the Bodleian Library, Oxford; the Cambridge University Library; the John Rylands Library Special collections (including the Wesley collection) at the University of Manchester; the Pratt-Green Collection of hymn books at Durham University; and the Library of the University of Cardiff, Wales. Nearly exhausting these collections of their children's hymn books, I have ultimately examined over 200 children's hymn books of the century. As part of my methodology for this project, I catalogued the over 16,000 hymn titles found in 100 of these nineteenth-century children's hymn books with indices in order to determine the most frequently appearing titles. This will allow me to make claims about the popularity of a text and to assume that it was being sung more frequently and thus was more influential than other titles. Examination of diaries and autobiographies tend to confirm these conclusions, as do contemporary lists of favorites (Stead's *Hymns That Have Helped*, for instance) and other hymnologists' lists (as by Lionel Adey).

Given my past exploration of literary-musical texts, in *Angelic Airs, Subversive Songs* (2002), readers may be surprised by the dearth of literary focus in this study. I recognize, indeed have written about in this previous work, just how much such authors as Elizabeth Gaskell, George Eliot, and Thomas Hardy, among other writers, have referred to hymns in their works. Their references to *children's* hymn singing, however, are more limited. For this current study, I content myself with some intentionally chosen literary epigraphs to each chapter which allow me some space for literary explication. Instead, the children's hymn book now becomes my literary focus and I shift from fictional analysis to poetic explications, from literary scholarship to a wide expanse of historical connections.

The complexity of the topic also means that parts of the larger study have needed to be left out of this book. I point in particular to an earlier study on women hymn writers and hymn-book editors, "Writing for, yet Apart: Nineteenth-Century British Women's Contentious Status as Hymn Writers and Editors of Hymnbooks for Children," that was published in *Victorian Literature and Culture* in 2010. In it, I consider how women as moral educators of the young were empowered to teach and to write hymns and hymn books for children. They were very successful, in fact, in reaching out to and engaging young singers, although this success also diminished their own empowerment, aligning them with their child audience which seemed only to confirm the already existing social and legal links women had with children. Ultimately, though, I argue that many hymn-book editors, such as M. A. Woods, and hymn writers, such as C. F. Alexander, utilized numerous poetic strategies for recouping assertiveness and self-identity as women within this genre for the young, most notably by co-opting the postures of an anonymous, omnipotent God; the meek, glorious Christ; or the Holy Spirit abiding in human domestic details, for themselves. Thus, though I appear to do less with women's hymn writing for the young, I am acutely aware of the sexist conditions of both the writing and publishing of hymns. I also have done less with the long-term impact of hymn singing on adults later in life, but am currently studying Patrick Brontë's own Sunday school hymn book and hymn sheets to consider how his theological choices for children's hymn singing would influence his famous daughters' poetic and hymn output. Neither of these studies fits the scope of this book, however, and I modestly hope that those interested will look for them in other places.

Due to space, this study must be restricted in other ways, too. I realize, for instance, that many children's hymns were first printed, or reprinted, within periodicals, as I have noted in *Peter Parley's Annual* (London, 1840s), *The Children's Friend* (ed. W. Carus Wilson; Kirby, Lonsdale; 1848), *The Sunday Magazine* (London and Edinburgh, 1860s), *The Child's Companion and Juvenile Instructor* (London: Religious Tract Society, 1870s), *The Boys Own Paper* (London, 1879–1890s), *The Girl's Own Annual* (London, 1880s), and other periodicals I researched.[9] But I have chosen to limit this study to the hymn books themselves, their publication histories, editing choices, and paratexts (illustrations, covers, etc.). Candy Gunther Brown writes that while periodicals featured contention and novels reflected the novelists' values, "hymns embodied the shared convictions

---

[9]    American periodical volumes I examined include: *Boston Observer, and Religious Intelligencer* (Boston, 1830s); *Journal of Christian Education, and Family and Sunday-School Visiter* [sic] (New York, 1840s); *Youth's Casket and Playmate: A Magazine for Boys and Girls* (Boston, early 1860s); *The Sunday School Teacher* (Chicago, 1860s–1870s); *Our Young Folks* (Boston, 1860s–1870s); and *St. Nicholas* (ed. Mary Mapes Dodge, 1870s). Many printed hymn-texts and/or scores, especially prior to the 1870s.

and experiences" of their culture (in Noll and Blumhofer 195); I might add, too, that religious periodicals printed the latest hymn favorite, not necessarily those that would become permanent preferences, and sermons mirrored the pastor's personal theologies, while favorite hymns reflected a whole culture's theological values. Furthermore, I have consciously limited this study to Protestant hymn books mainly published in England, thus needing to exclude the hymn history particular to Scottish, Welsh, and Irish Protestants, although I discuss important hymn writers of these traditions as relevant. Further, Irish and English Catholics had their own traditions of children's hymns divergent enough from the Protestant religious history and theology I present here that I recommend a separate study of Catholic children's hymnody, though I do consider High Church hymnody quite extensively.

I have also researched around the United States where I have found an abundant assortment of both British- and American-published children's hymn books. Therefore, where germane, I point to the many similarities I have found between British and American children's hymn-singing experiences and texts and will occasionally use an American example. Thus, though American hymn books have not been considered for most of my major claims and data collection, I highlight the transatlantic nature of this book. I will discuss continuities whenever relevant: temperance and the Bands of Mercy movement clearly being transatlantic movements, for example. Scholars remind us that many children's books in America in the late eighteenth century and after were pirated from English books given the lack of international copyright laws (Larson 11); antebellum American hymn books frequently consisted of British eighteenth-century hymns (Gallagher in Noll and Blumhofer 240). I have found this phenomenon borne out in the many children's hymn books with both English and American editions, and certainly with common hymns in their contents. As one example, of 118 hymns in *Sunday-School Hymns and Tunes* (New York, 1877), 84 were by British hymn writers. For all these reasons, though I focus primarily on English-published hymn books and children's diaries, I suggest the implications on American childhood history as well. But I also acknowledge that the American hymn tradition had influences such as camp-meeting and Gospel hymnody that make its qualities and hymn favorites somewhat different. Even the American Moody and Sankey gospel hymns, though beloved by late-century British audiences, never rose to the surface in my data collection and therefore will receive minimal treatment here.[10] I consequently refer the reader to other scholarship on the American hymn tradition.[11]

---

[10]    Evangelist Dwight L. Moody and musician Ira D. Sankey led revivals in America in the late 1860s, inspiring Britons through tours in 1873–1875. The movement was buttressed by singable, sentimental congregational hymns as found in various *Gospel Hymns* volumes (1875–1883). Philip Bliss, Daniel Whittle, William Doane, and especially Fanny Crosby contributed powerful hymns to the movement. See Hindmarsh's and Blumhofer's essays in Noll and Blumhofer; and Wilhoit in Clarke, 97–116.

[11]    See, for example, the essays in *Sing Them Over Again to Me: Hymns and Hymnbooks in America*, edited by Mark A. Noll and Edith L. Blumhofer (2006); Candy Gunther Brown's *Word in the World: Evangelical Writing, Publishing, and Reading in America, 1789–1880*;

In 2014 I made a final return trip to England to research children's diaries, attempting to hear from children themselves what hymns had meant to them. Sally Shuttleworth reminds us of the difficulties in recovering the actual voices of children "where part of the constituency is not only pre-literature, but also pre-verbal" (108). Indeed, the record is sadly lacking in nineteenth-century children's diaries, and to date I have only recovered about 25. But what I have discovered is that even in these few journals, hymn singing was clearly a vital part of children's lives. Children write about family get-togethers and graduation ceremonies enhanced by hymn singing, about ship rides where hymns are sung on deck, about parading around the house singing hymns. Children debate the use of hymns, cite their own and their friends' favorite hymns. Hymns were more easily understood than sermons, more quickly memorized than school-teachings. They were pivotal to conversion and recited for comfort on children's family members' deathbeds, and even their own. These stories will be detailed further in Chapter 6.

Though children rarely wax sentimental about their hymns, one adult woman, Lucy Larcom, recalling her girlhood in the 1820s, devotes an entire chapter to the influence of hymns ("Chapter III: The Hymn-Book"), opening thus:

> Almost the first decided taste in my life was the love of hymns. Committing them to memory was as natural to me as breathing.... I think more gratefully now of the verses I learned from the Bible and the Hymn-Book than of almost anything that came to me in that time of beginnings. (*A New England Girlhood Outlined from Memory* [1889] 58, 66)

Lucy grew up in a New England Puritan community yet enjoyed the religious teachings as they came through hymns, which challenges our traditional exclusion of didactic literature as "enjoyable" children's literature. Further, the fact that she can call up these feelings 65 years afterwards attests to their staying power. Finally, these hymns are some of the few things she recalls from her youth with such pleasure, which proves their ability to speak to both old and young, to the adult Lucy as well as the child Lucy.

Lucy's story is a demonstration of why it is critical that children's hymns be examined in the context of children's nineteenth-century experience. This book opens up such an examination.

---

June Hadden Hobbs's *"I Sing for I Cannot Be Silent": The Feminization of American Hymnody, 1870–1920* (1997); and Mary DeJong's "'I Want to be Like Jesus': The Self-Defining Power of Evangelical Hymnody" and "'Theirs the Sweetest Songs': Women Hymn Writers in the Nineteenth-Century United States." Heather D. Curtis specifically examines American children's hymns in "Children of the Heavenly King: Hymns in the Religious and Social Experience of Children, 1780–1850" in *Sing Them Over Again to Me*, 214–34. Though briefer, her study verifies many of the topics of this present study as relevant to American children's hymn books, from reform hymns to illustrated hymn books.

# Chapter 1
# Creating Communities of Song: Class and Gender in Children's Hymn-Singing Experiences

… "This is the last night that we shall sleep here, dears, in the house where we were born," she said quickly. "We ought to think of it, oughtn't we?"

They all become silent; with the impressibility of their age they were ready to burst into tears at the picture of finality she had conjured up, though all the day hitherto they had been rejoicing in the idea of a new place. Tess changed the subject.

"Sing to me, dears," she said.

"What shall we sing?"

"Anything you know: I don't mind."

There was a momentary pause; it was broken, first, by one little tentative note; then a second voice strengthened it, and a third and a fourth chimed in in unison, with words they had learnt at the Sunday-school—

> Here we suffer grief and pain,
> Here we meet to part again;
>> In Heaven we part no more.

The four sang on with the phlegmatic passivity of persons who had long ago settled the question, and there being no mistake about it, felt that further thought was not required. With features strained hard to enunciate the syllables they continued to regard the centre of the flickering fire, the notes of the youngest straying over into the pauses of the rest.

—Thomas Hardy, *Tess of the d'Urbervilles* (1891), ch. 51

Thomas Hardy's scene here depicted illustrates one very common space for song: a working-class home, without luxury of piano to keep children's untrained voices from straying off pitch or over rests, in which family members sing a hymn that they learned in Sunday school. Even the hymn they sing, Thomas Bilby's 1832 "Here we suffer grief and pain," a popular hymn (in 24% of children's hymn books during the century, to be discussed further in Chapter 6), registers a reality of poverty and vulnerability to death, which reflects more directly the precariousness of their situations than would be the case had it been sung by members of higher classes. Yet, when they are called upon to sing *something*, it is a

Sunday school hymn that comes most quickly to mind for these young children, creating, if only briefly, a family community before homelessness and tragedy permanently divide them.

Indeed, hymns are, by their very nature, communal. *The Oxford Dictionary of the Christian Church* defines hymns as "Sacred poetry set to music and sung in the course of the services of the Church ... to express doctrine or the devotion of individuals" (681). That is, hymns are sung by a society of singers, in contrast to individual solo performances; furthermore, they are sung among amateurs, in contrast to concert or operatic choruses. For these reasons and others, they are an aesthetic uniting all singers, children included, who come together to express and affirm common Christian doctrine.

Just as certainly, though, a child's class situation would predispose him to certain communal experiences with hymns much different than those of peers in other economic strata. In fact, a child's class status would define singing opportunities, aesthetic and leisure availability, school options, even the duration of childhood itself. As Anna Davin points out, for working-class children, "Work and responsibility were not the separate province of adults, but co-existed with [a child's] growth, with play and with school; they anticipate full adulthood by many years" (85). Eric Hopkins demonstrates that the greatest transformation of childhood also related to work, given that work responsibilities curtailed childhood around the age of 6 early in the century, and delayed it until around age 12 by the end (vii). For many historians, then, a focus on class difference is imperative to understanding nineteenth-century childhood.[1] Children's hymn books, as I will argue, are both the rule and the exception to Victorian children's class stratification: though the contexts for singing hymns would have been predicated on class demarcations, hymns touched all economic strata, from children of opportunity to children at risk.

Lionel Adey details, in his book *Class and Idol in the English Hymn* (1988), how religious communities were likewise predicated on class segregation; based on Charles Booth's studies of late century, he suggests the following generalities: the most impoverished citizens were usually attracted to Primitive Methodism; skilled workers and lower middle class were often Baptist; skilled, lower, and middle classes populated the Wesleyan Methodist chapels; middle class and wealthy manufacturers were found in the Congregationalist congregations; while generally the middle, wealthy, and aristocratic populations were found in Anglican parish churches and cathedrals (5–13). He subsequently divides their hymn books into the Learned (Anglican, Congregational, Presbyterian) and the Popular

---

[1]   See Anna Davin, *Growing Up Poor: Home, School and Street in London, 1870–1914*; Eric Hopkins, *Childhood Transformed: Working-Class Children in Nineteenth-Century England*; C. John Somerville, *The Rise and Fall of Childhood*; Linda A Pollock, *Forgotten Children: Parent-Child Relations*; Hugh Cunningham, *Children of the Poor: Representations of Childhood since the Seventeenth Century*; and Pamela Horn, *Children's Work and Welfare, 1780–1880s*.

(Baptists, Primitive Methodist) traditions,[2] suggesting implicit class difference in the hymn tradition. Children's hymn singing is, likewise, stratified, as he further demonstrates. Concerned with the "class conditioning" found in various hymn books for children, Adey creates five categories based on class in which to consider hymn books; those for: 1) "nursling and infant scholars" (of the literate classes); 2) "the submerged child" (orphanages, Ragged Schools, etc.); 3) "the average child" (the child in National, church-based schools); 4) the Sunday school child (working class); and 5) "privileged youth" (upper class in boarding schools) (chapters 7–11, respectively). These are useful categories. However, in this chapter, I will expand and challenge his conclusions in some ways. Firstly, gender is a consideration that must be made in addition to class. Secondly, I will suggest that not *all* children's hymn books can be divided up so easily since many hymn books were much more inclusive in their intended audience (for middle-class home services *and* Sunday schools, for example) and in other ways defy categorization. Most importantly, I will argue that though the context for singing certainly differed among classes, more often than not, their hymns did not, a distinction that Adey does not make. In short, though Adey's class categorization is useful and influenced my own, the breadth of my study is larger,[3] my approach is different, and my conclusions diverge significantly.

This chapter, then, will explore the traditions of children's hymn singing throughout the century from a class standpoint, as class imposed spatial limitations on childhood experience, from home to school. In order to simplify the complex nature of Victorian society to discuss their hymn use, I will organize and analyze the context for hymns within three arenas: 1) upper-class public (boarding) schools; 2) middle-class homes and churches; 3) working-class National, Sunday, and Ragged Schools; and, finally, contexts for the most vulnerable: foundlings, orphans, children working in cottages and factories.[4] Each class had privileges (or lack thereof) which affected their access to hymns, whether it was the privilege of public schools (where hymns were sung in the chapels) open mainly to the upper classes or the availability of a piano and home services enjoyed primarily in middle-class homes. Using a variety of children's hymn books—for home, school,

---

[2] Specifically, Adey defines the Learned tradition as "The educated congregation, which learned its religion at boarding-school and university rather than Sunday-school or back-street chapel" and which "sang more of social national service, perceiving work as vocation or fulfilment," while the "Popular" hymnals of Baptists and Primitive Methodists "convey feelings ranging from crude apprehension of Judgment and hell-fire to Dionysian jubilation" due to hard times in life (2–3). I can appreciate some of these conclusions but will point out hymn books' inclusivity of denominationally different themes as well.

[3] Adey's surveys of children's hymn books use fewer hymn books (21 in one study, six in another [146, 170]), whereas I examined over 200. His individual chapters, therefore, tend to consider a very limited pool of hymn books from which he generalizes.

[4] I am using traditional class divisions such as those put forth by Richard Altick (in ch. 2 of *Victorian People and Ideas*). Specifically, he uses the terms "aristocracy," "gentry and middle classes," and "the lower orders."

Sunday school, Ragged School, orphanage, even factory—I will consider how contexts for and content of hymns varied immensely between classes.

Ultimately, though, I will suggest that even in those hymn books meant for the darkest of fates lay empowerment and encouragement for young singers, creating empowered child singers in all classes. Furthermore, the experience of hymn singing itself cut across the class divide, while a body of hymns became a common language between rich and poor children of the century. Being a communal act, hymn singing created class-based communities, but a larger Christian community of child hymn singers was clearly intended by hymn writers, editors, and teachers. In many ways, then, hymns mitigated class distinctions, creating a space for song for many generations of children.

## Part I
## "The image of Thy godhead here":
## Hymns for the Upper Classes in Public-School Hymn Books

Philippe Ariès argues that the modern era was predicated on a new distinction between children and adults mainly due to education that necessitated a transition period between the two, an unfortunate segregation that created rigid and insular education: "[t]he school shut up a childhood which had hitherto been free within an increasingly severe disciplinary system, which culminated in the eighteenth and nineteenth centuries in the total claustration of the boarding-school" (413). This is a generalization of European education but in fact does bear out the typical rigidity of boarding experiences that had existed since the eleventh century for the British upper classes. After preparatory schools, nobility and gentry sent their sons ages 13 and over to one of seven historically prominent public schools (usually boarding schools): Charterhouse School, Eton College, Harrow School, Rugby School, Shrewsbury School, Westminster School, and Winchester College.[5] Daughters, of course, were home-schooled by governesses, self-taught, or superficially educated at finishing schools.

By the second half of the nineteenth century, private boarding schools had become extremely sought-after institutions for sons of the affluent and, traditionally Anglican, families of prestige from the aristocracy and, increasingly, upper middle classes. Public schools generally utilized a classical education, "heavy with anachronism" (Altick 254), to which modern subjects such as mathematics and

---

[5]     English public schools were "public" in the sense that they were open to all religions, were outside the home, and were under public (not private) management. They were all-male schools with boys entering from preparatory schools at the age of 13, either by examination or competitive scholarship (Weinberg xi). Many headmasters were denied "public school" designation for their schools by the Clarendon and Taunton Commissions of the 1860s (Weinberg x). Led by Edward Thring, headmaster of Uppingham, those excluded schools then formed the Headmasters' Conference (now the Headmasters and Headmistresses' Conference which includes the "original" seven as well). See Ian Weinberg, *The English Public Schools* (1967).

science were slow in coming. Thomas Arnold's attempt to modernize Rugby's curriculum was offset by his moral-building agenda (soon labeled "muscular Christianity"), leading to "the cult of games" as "end rather than a means," which accrued much criticism (Altick 253).

Religious-aesthetic opportunities such as hymn singing were a part of these various home and school contexts, though unevenly. Upper-class young women would generally learn, sing, and play hymns in a domestic context. (As this is true of middle-class girls as well, I will expand on this discussion in the next section.) Wealthy boys, though hearing and singing hymns at home, would also have encountered them in public schools. However, this opportunity came about slowly. William John Cooper Green, in a thesis on music education in the public schools,[6] shows the insufficiency of actual music education at the public schools prior to the 1830s, it being considered too effeminate, "the preserve of foreigners," and "unsuitable in the education of a nobleman" (qtd. in Green 11). When the Public Schools Commission of 1864 made recommendations about expanding the classical curriculum, music was one subject recommended for inclusion (Green 25). Despite these recommendations, music organizations were gradual in coming, being of little interest to the boys more focused on the increasing attention to sports. So, according to Green, "provision for music in the 'Great' public schools in the middle of the nineteenth century was at best patchy, often neglected, and frequently strenuously neglected" (33).

Integrating hymn singing into school chapel services, if not curriculum, fared a bit better in Anglican-affiliated institutions (Green 22). Various headmasters individually began to emphasize music through choral and hymn music: Edward Thring at Uppingham in the 1850s;[7] S. A. Pears at Repton; Dr. Percival at Clifton College (who compiled the school's first hymn book in 1862, then took his ideas to Rugby in 1878); and Dr. Butler at Harrow in the 1870s through mid-1880s (see Green 45–50, 75–6). By late in the century, due to the Commission's recommendations, changes in attitude towards music, and "the conviction that school songs and hymns could have a tremendous impact on the minds of young men," most public schools began to institutionalize vocal music into their social and religious life such that by late century it would have been "unusual for a school not to have a chapel choir" (Green 107–8). By 1897, an article on "Music in the Public Schools" describes the public school chapel choir typically singing a short

---

[6]   See Green's *The Development of Musical Education in the Public Schools from 1840 to the Present Day*, Durham theses, Durham University, 1990. Available at Durham E-Theses Online: http://etheses.dur.ac.uk/6281/. Green mentions hymn singing but does not identify or discuss the hymn books or specific hymns being used.

[7]   Edward Thring was brother to the hymn writer Godfrey Thring, author of *A Church of England Hymn Book* (1880). Not surprisingly, Godfrey Thring's hymns (e.g., "Again Church's year hath run," "Watch now, ye Christians, watch and pray," and "We all had sinned and gone astray") figure prominently in *Hymn-Book for the Use of Uppingham and Sherborne Schools* (1874). For more about Godfrey, see Benjamin A. Kolodziej, "Godfrey Thring: Victorian Hymnwriter of the *Via Media*" in *The Hymn* 64.2 (2013): 29–37.

service every weekday and two on Sundays, boys joining "either by compulsion or voluntarily" (qtd. in Green 112). This led to debates on whether anthems and hymns of the chapel service should be sung exclusively by the trained chapel choir or by the congregation of boys. Harrow led the way in privileging congregational hymn singing: "The congregational character of the service at Harrow has often struck visitors ... The hymns are familiar. The singing is in unison ... [I]t induces the largest number of boys to feel themselves partners in the devotions and supplications of public worship. And I do not know any school chapel in which divine service is so general, so heartfelt, so inspiring" (qtd. in Green 114–15). That is, hymn singing began to be used specifically for its communal quality, making the boys feel as "partners in the devotions."

Public school writers suggest hymn singing to be a vital part of public school life of the period. Thomas Hughes shows Tom Brown, after his initial day's adventures at Rugby, being inspired by hymns at his first chapel experience with the Doctor (Thomas Arnold): "As the hymn after the prayers was being sung, and the chapel was getting a little dark, he was beginning to feel that he had been really worshipping" (*Tom Brown's School Days*, 1857, 141).[8] Scholar Jonathan Gathorne-Hardy, himself a student at Bryanston School, Dorset, suggests that hymns, even more than school songs, played a vital role in rallying school spirit, linking all public schools together:

> ... public schools had their own corpus of song, great simple stirring songs that echo down the 19th century and on into the 20th century. ... Hymns bound the public schools together: Wesley's "Jesu, Lover of my soul," Cowper's "God moves in a mysterious way"; perhaps best known of all, Augustus Toplady's famous "Rock of ages cleft for me" ... Many headmasters and masters wrote hymns, and one can quite often detect hymn themes or treatments in English composers of a certain generation as thousands of public school Sundays and assemblies stir in their subconscious—in Vaughan Williams (Charterhouse) particularly.... (*The Public School Phenomenon* 144–5)

Significantly, hymns "bound the public schools together" and inspired such famous graduates as the composer Ralph Vaughan Williams.

It is not surprising to find that many of the public schools issued their own hymn books. These included *Hymns for the Chapel of Harrow School* (1855, also of 1881), *Hymns for the Use of Rugby School* (1857, also of 1876), *Hymn-Book for the Use of Wellington College* (1860), *Psalms and Hymns for the Use of Clifton College* (1863), and *Hymn-Book for the Use of Uppingham and Sherborne Schools* (1874), while *The Public School Hymn Book* (first edition 1903) was published by the collective Committee of the Headmasters' Conference. By late century, when girls' high schools were established to parallel boys' public schools,

---

[8]    See John R. Reed ("The Public Schools in Victorian Literature") and Jenny Holt (*Public School Literature, Civic Education and the Politics of Male Adolescence*, ch. 2) for more about Hughes and other public school literature. It is notable that Arnold supported an enlarged hymn book for Rugby during his tenure there (Gillman 279).

many compiled their own hymn books. For instance, Clifton High School, founded in Bristol, 1877, to compete with the local Clifton College, used *Hymns for School Worship* (London, 1890), as "compiled by M. A. Woods, Headmistress of the Clifton High School for Girls" (a hymn book now held at the Bodleian).

In his chapter "Privileged Youth," Adey laments the "prestige," "generation lag," "secluded," "manly," "competitive," and "egocentric" nature of public-school hymns (158, 159, 161, 161, 165, and 166, respectively). Despite late-century secularism, however, Adey believes that public school hymns were "at once more profound and less distorted by jingoism or sentimentality than was to be found in the hymnody of their contemporaries at Sunday or elementary school" (174). I would suggest a few clarifications to this assessment. Analyzing some of the same and some different hymn books as Adey, I see three main qualities to emphasize: a much greater diversity of hymns than Adey suggests. Despite his claims that "the Evangelical tide receded" (174), Evangelical hymns *are* retained in hymn books. Hymns reveal a sense of "prestige" and "egocentrism" but also evidence humility. Finally, all hymn books demonstrate overlaps with Sunday-school hymn books and century-long hymn favorites.

Harrow and Rugby hymn books are representative of many public school hymn books. First to note is their Anglican focus: solemn hymns unfettered with emotional (Evangelical) fervor, categorized around the Book of Common Prayer and its divisions of the church year: Advent, Christmas, Epiphany, Lent, Easter, Whitsuntide, All Saints' Day. Additional hymns for each of 14 saints' days (St. Philip, St. James, etc.) reflect High Church influence (e.g., Harrow School [1881] and Wellington College [1860]).[9] Yet, one can note a change of theology as the editions progress: *The Hymns for the Chapel of Harrow School* (with six editions between 1855 and 1908) begins with fairly dark hymns of Evangelical fervor which, though retained in the 1866 edition, would be excised by the fourth, 1881 edition: "Dark River of Death" (Hymn 141), "All, all is vanity below" (144), and "Affliction is a stormy deep" (210), for example. On the other hand, *Hymns for the Use of Rugby School* of 1876 prints almost verbatim the various hymns of the earlier, 1857 hymn book, *Psalms and Hymns for the Use of the Congregation of Rugby School Chapel*. Clearly psalm singing is losing favor (a phenomenon to be discussed in my Chapter 3)—"Psalms" are dropped from the title, although they are still integrated throughout the later hymn book—but almost all the older hymns are kept intact along with the many newer hymns added to the 1876 edition. The Rugby hymn book therefore lends itself to a close study of the continuity and change of public school hymnody of the era.

*Hymns for the Use of Rugby School* (1876) follows the Anglican Book of Common Prayer, opening with hymns for Morning, Evening, and Sunday, then moving into seasons of the ecclesiastical calendar from Advent through Trinity Sunday. It ends with hymns for general praise, topics which reflect a later-century positivism: Praise, Prayer, Faith, and Hope. Five hymns reflect the public school's classical heritage in being older Latin hymns, although these were not found in

---

9    Chapter 2 will examine High Church characteristics in greater detail.

earlier editions or those at Harrow. Occasional hymns also reflect some of what Adey refers to as "egocentric" qualities, given the high privilege of most of the boys in attendance who would be uttering the first-person sentiments, as in Hymn 310, "O Love, Who formedst me" by German Angelus Silesius (1624–1677) and translated for English consumption by Catherine Winkworth:

> O Love, Who formedst me to wear
>> The image of Thy Godhead here … (v. 1, line 1–2)
> … On me Thy choice has gently laid … (v. 2, line 2)
> … Thine ever, only Thine to be. (last line of every verse)

Self-focused sentiments, of being in God's specific image, of being God's choice, are certainly Christian concepts said of all humanity, yet these lines take on added import in this upper-class context. It is not surprising to find this hymn in the Anglican hymn book *Hymns Ancient and Modern* (1861) and *Hymns for School Worship* (1890) for Clifton girls. The hymns missing from these hymn books are also significant: "Here we suffer grief and pain," discussed above, is *not* found in here or in any public school hymn book in my study. Instead, 60 pages are devoted to the topic of Praise, the largest section in the book, for indeed these young men had much for which to be grateful.

In fact, one notable hymn in Rugby's "Praise" section is Hymn 193, by Thomas William Jex-Blake, headmaster during the printing of this hymnal (from 1874–1887):

> Lord, we thank Thee for the pleasure
>> That our happy lifetime gives,
> The inestimable treasure
>> Of a soul that ever lives;
> Mind that looks before and after,
>> Yearning for its home above,
> Human tears, and human laughter,
>> And the depth of human love; (v. 1)
>> *******
> For the thrill, the leap, the gladness
>> Of our pulses flowing free;
> E'en for every touch of sadness
>> That may bring us nearer Thee;
> But above all other kindness,
>> Thine unutterable love,
> Which, to heal our sin and blindness,
>> Sent Thy dear Son from above. (v. 2)

Each verse opens with what might be the stereotype of public school life: their "happy lifetime" free from physical wants (v. 1); "the pulses flowing free" during sports (v. 2); the "early wise" of their privileged education (v. 3). Yet Jex-Blake takes each moment of privilege and exacts a task from his youthful singers: to pursue "the depth of human love" (v. 1); to value "Thine unutterable love, / Which [was sent] to heal our sin and blindness" (v. 2); and to work for "Thee, and not [for] men":

> Teach us so our days to number,
>     That we may be early wise;
> Dreamy mist, or cloud of slumber,
>     Never dull our heavenward eyes;
> Hearty be our work, and willing,
>     As to Thee, and not to men,
> For we know our soul's fulfilling
>     Is in heaven;—not till then. (v. 3)

Moving them from selfish pursuits to core Christian values, he also reminds them of their sin and acknowledges the "sadness" and "human tears" which even they, despite wealth and social advantage, will experience.

This humility is highlighted in other hymns as well: for example, "every fault that lurks within; / Every stain of shame glossed over" will be noticed by God; that "All our powers / Vain and brief are borne away" (Hymn 8), "laden with my sin … so vile I am … Evil is ever with me; / Yet on mine ears the gracious tidings fall" (Hymn 97), both hymns new to the 1876 edition, suggesting less an early-century Evangelical hold-over than a late-century humbleness. In Anglican, especially High Church fashion, most hymns are rhetorically demanding and rarely talk down to, let alone mention, their youthful audience. Still, mention is made of Jesus bringing "Thy children to Thy knee" (Hymn 49), the need for all persons to be "Simple, teachable, and mild, / Humble as a little child" (Hymn 250), and, most personally, in second person: "Pitying, loving Saviour, / Hear Thy children's cry" (Hymn 252) … all ways to remind the boys of their youth and humility. A 1903 edition of *The Public School Hymn Book* perhaps explains this multiplicity of approach, the book attempting to give "adequate utterance for the emotions and aspirations—the joys and sorrows, the hopes and regrets—of boys of very different ages" (Preface).[10]

Though social issues are not addressed significantly in these hymns, mission work is alluded to, Heber's "From Greenland's icy mountains" being a popular inclusion (six of seven public school hymn books I examined). Consider also "Forth in Thy name, O lord, we go, / Our daily labour to pursue; / Thee, only Thee, resolved to know / In all we think, or speak, or do" (Hymns 8) or "For all we love, the poor, the sad, / The sinful, unto Thee we call" (Hymn 32 in *Hymns for the Chapel of Harrow School* [1866]), which may have inspired, or reflected, the various home mission work launched by public schools at mid-century. Thring of

---

[10]    *The Public School Hymn Book* (1903, reissued c. 1918) reveals not only continuity with previous collections (severe hymns of sin, Latin texts) but also new trends: a longer, "brighter" section of Christmas hymns and some very current hymns: James Russell Lowell's "Once to every man and nation" (Hymn 232) and Walter Chalmers Smith's "Immortal, invisible" (Hymn 320), neither found in many children's hymn books of the nineteenth century but generally popular in adult books well into the twentieth.

Uppingham, a pioneer of public school mission work, for instance, established a mission for his school in London's East End in 1869, and William Law inspired boys at Harrow School to minister to the workers in the laundries and brick-kilns of Notting Hill, West London (Scotland 104, 111, 113). Encouraging former pupils of the schools to reside in their mission district, public school reformers hoped to Christianize the district, teach self-improvement, and provide alcohol-free entertainment (Scotland 110). Boys were encouraged to visit the districts they sponsored and often these were organized in the form of music, chapel choirs giving concerts or groups of boys entertaining with music and drama (Scotland 125).[11] No doubt a hymn or two was included.

These public school hymn books actually have much in common with the young women's counterpart in song, the 1890 *Hymns for School Worship* compiled by M. A. Woods for the Clifton High School for Girls: stately hymns, of a diverse theological background, with little mention of children directly. If anything, Woods emphasizes the high-class, mature nature of her students by writing that the book is not intended for children only; indeed, she has purposely selected hymns with a "special seriousness" and difficult language hoping that her compilation will be not simply a "schoolbook only" but become "a personal companion and friend" later in life (v). Too, she seeks a "somewhat higher literary standard" as complement to the literary appreciations of her young readers, and in the book she has included poems by Sir Philip Sidney, Edmund Spenser, Ben Jonson, John Milton, and even the American Henry Wadsworth Longfellow, as counterparts to standard hymns by hymn writers such as Thomas Ken, Harriet Auber, Horatius Bonar, and John Mason Neale. Her female students, then, will be expanding their literary as well as theological experience through hymn singing.

A final, and important, point to make about these hymn books is that, despite personally written hymns by headmasters and other marks of exclusivity, they show much continuity with other hymn books across the century, from working-class Sunday school to middle-class home hymn books. For example, six hymns found in both Harrow and Rugby hymn books of (almost) all editions are Tractarian John Keble's "Sun of my soul"; Anglican Henry Francis Lyte's "Abide with me"; Anglican Charlotte Elliott's "Just as I am"; Anglican Bishop Heber's "Holy, holy, holy"; but also Calvinist Augustus Toplady's "Rock of ages"; and Methodist Charles Wesley's "Love divine, all loves excelling." These hymn writers' theological diverseness already belies doctrinal entrenchedness, and the fact that these hymns were some of the most popular inclusions in all hymn books of all economic persuasions cannot be overemphasized.

In short, public school hymn books reflect their audience's elite status and avoid addressing social change. On the other hand, they do challenge their singers mentally with mature rhetoric and literary prowess, and on a personal level, often encourage outreach, gratitude, and personal humility.

---

[11]   For more on public school missions, see Nigel Scotland's *Squires in the Slums: Settlements and Missions in Late-Victorian London* (London, 2007), ch. 5.

**Part II**
**"I with so many comforts am blest":**
**Hymns for the Middle-Class Child**

Generally speaking, about a quarter of British families could be considered middle class by 1867 (Horn, *Town Child* 19). Middle-class education was yet academically limited throughout the first part of the century, while even in the second half, schooling for the middle classes "remained chaotic with schools varying widely in quality" (Horn, *Town Child* 32). As with the upper classes, middle-class young girls were mainly educated in the home with a focus on reading, music-playing, sewing, and home management, while young boys would be sent to grammar schools, proprietary schools, or private homes where, once again, curriculum was narrowly focused on the classics (Altick 254). A series of laws—the Grammar Schools Act of 1844 and the Endowment Schools Act of 1869—expanded curriculum and led to a more institutionalized form of secondary education later in the century. Further, young women's educational opportunities increased with the creation of their own grammar schools and colleges.

Within these varied contexts of Victorian middle-class schooling—school, home, church—hymn singing was firmly entrenched. Few hymn books appear to have been published specifically for middle-class educational institutions, probably because more general children's hymn books would have been used. Also, private pupils would simply have been included in family hymn-sings. Certainly a main context for upper- and middle-class children's hymn singing would have been the home where hymn books, pianos, and leisure time would have been available. Indeed, middle-class leisure could be demonstrated by ownership of pianos and whole families available for daily service. Hymn singing would have formed a main part of home devotionals, part of the daily or weekly routine, shown by such titles as *Morning and Evening Hymns, for Every Day of the Year, for the Family and Church, with Appropriate Music* (ed. John Smith, Glasgow, 1857); *The Family Hymn-Book: A Selection of Five Hundred Hymns and Spiritual Songs for Social and Domestic Worship* (1864), and *The Home Hymn Book: A Manual of Sacred Song for the Family Circle* (ed. Hawkins, 1885).

This devotional training began young, the "Infant Hymn Book" being a common genre intended for the youngest children. Ann and Jane Taylor's *Hymns for Infant Minds* (1809) was the most famous of a genre that also included *Hymns for Infant Children* (1852) and *Infant Amusements: or, How to Make a Nursery Happy* by William H. G. Kingston with a "Hymns" section (London, 1867). Their language was simple and direct in educating children aged 3 through 5 in both theological and moral precepts: "Where is the holy Jesus? He lives in heaven above … / Once He came down from heaven, / And became a little child" (Taylors' Hymn 8). Yet class privilege slips out even for the smallest of children, as in the Evening Hymn in *Infant Amusements*:

> But many little children poor,
> Have not a place to go;

And many hardships they endure,
    Such as I ne'er did know. (v. 2, 160)

To which the simple conclusion is gratitude, not aid:

My dear mamma, I'll thank you oft
    For this, my nice warm bed;
And for my pretty pillow soft,
    Where I can rest my head. (v. 3)

Ann and Jane Taylor's *Hymns for Infant Minds* will also occasionally slip into middle-class assumptions of childhood: the child's "Praise for Daily Mercies" includes "The food I eat, the clothes I wear, / Are all bestow'ed by thee" (Hymn 46), and "I with so many comforts am blest" (Hymn 66), words hard to mouth if one were starving and homeless. Also, hymns espouse the class structure without ever questioning it: "Alike the rich and poor are known, / The cultur'd and the wild; / The lofty monarch on the throne, / And ev'ry little child" … with uncomfortable alignments between poverty and wildness (Hymn 50). Acceptance, not alteration, of the status quo is the theme in C. F. Alexander's famous "All things bright and beautiful":

The rich man in his castle,
    The poor man at his gate,
God made them, high or lowly,
    And ordered their estate. (v. 3)

This controversial verse is lamented by critics today (Watson, *English Hymn* 431; Lenti 34), and for this reason, removed from most twentieth century hymnals that include the hymn.

Often hymns were to be simply—and arduously—memorized, in the home context as well as at school: note titles such as *Hymns for the Young Selected for the Purpose of Being Committed to Memory* (c. 1839) and *Hymns for Children, Selected with a View of Being Learnt by Heart* (1856). A typical child's mental capacity was such that a "tolerably diligent Scholar will learn the contents of both [hymn books—Watts and another] in one year," according to the editor of *The Sunday-Scholar's Companion* (1822). No doubt some children begrudged this arduous task; celebrated American conservationist John Muir, who grew up in a strict Calvinist household in Dunbar, Scotland, wrote about the physical and mental pains of memorizing hymns and biblical texts "by heart and by sore flesh" (John Muir Birthplace Museum, Dunbar, Scotland). Yet others seemed to like the challenge: young Lucy Larcom found it so easy to memorize hymns that "[b]efore I was five I had gone beyond the stipulated hundred" (*New England Girlhood* [1889] 67). Verse was especially valuable in memorization and reinforcement of religious truth: as one writer of hymn books, Benjamin Rhodes, insists in his 1787 preface: "Children of taste (especially those who have a good ear) are much more pleased and affected with verse, than prose—receive any sentiment sooner, when delivered therein, and retain it longer" (6). By mid-century, this zeal to memorize

48    SHORT AND SIMPLE PRAYERS,

HYMN.

Lord, I have passed another day,
    And come to thank Thee for Thy care ;
Forgive my faults in work and play,
    And listen to my evening prayer.

Thy favour gives me daily bread,
    And friends who all my wants supply ;
And safely now I rest my head,
    Preserved and guarded by Thine eye.

Look down in pity, and forgive
    Whate'er I've said or done amiss ;
And help me, every day I live,
    To serve Thee better than on this.

Now while I speak, be pleased to take
    A helpless child beneath Thy care,
And condescend, for Jesus' sake,
    To listen to my evening prayer.

" Now while I speak, be pleased to take
    A helpless child beneath Thy care;
And condescend, for Jesus' sake,
    To listen to my evening prayer."
                                                                        D

Figure 1.1    "Lord, I have passed another day." From [Lucy Wilson], *Short and Simple Prayers, with Hymns, for the Use of Children* (1844). Courtesy of King's College Library, Cambridge University.

seemed to have run its course, and some adults, such as Henry Bateman, author of *Sunday Sunshine: New Hymns and Poems for the Young*, regretted the "ofttimes sad sigh with which a child has looked at the selected Hymn, with its six or seven verses, and peculiar metre" (vii). He therefore wrote uniform hymns so that "the eye sees at a glance the whole task; and it is known that every day or week as it comes, has nothing harder to be acquired than the last" (*Sunday Sunshine* vii).

Other times hymns were read aloud during home devotionals. One mother-author (Lucy Wilson) advises other parents in the preface to her anonymously published *Short and Simple Prayers, with Hymns, for the Use of Children* (1844): "The writer usually conducts the evening devotions of her own beloved little group according to the following plan. After the reading, verse by verse, of some simple portion of the Scriptures, or a Bible Story … and the repeating or singing of a hymn, she endeavors to recall to the remembrance of her children, the providential occurrences of the day" (6). Using prayers and hymns written by adults, she says, is essential: "When children make use of their own expressions *only*, there is a danger of their prayers becoming desultory or familiar; while a short form serves to fix and concentrate, as it were, the attention, and to direct it more entirely to those glorious Gospel truths, which, if not at the time fully comprehended, are still likely, by this means, to be indelibly imprinted on the infant mind" (7). Notable is the struggle between allowing the child free rein of his/her expression and the desire to implant, even if without comprehension, the ideals of the faith. Themes within the included hymns reflect an awareness of sin and the importance of gratitude, often coupled with overt awareness of middle-class comfort. One hymn included in this mother's hymn book, notably from the Taylors' *Hymns for Infant Minds*, opens:

> Lord, I have passed another day
>> And come to thank Thee for Thy care
> Forgive my faults in work and play,
>> And listen to my evening prayer. (v. 1, 48)

This hymn, accompanied by a picture of a child kneeling at a canopied bed with a curtained window and plush chair, admits the comforts she enjoys (see Figure 1.1):

> Thy favour gives me daily bread,
>> And friends who all my wants supply;
> And safely now I rest my head,
>> Preserved and guarded by Thine eye. (v. 2)

Still this child is not without reproach:

> Look down in pity, and forgive
>> Whate'er I've said or done amiss;
> And help me, every day I live,
>> To serve Thee better than on this. (v. 3)

Faithful living, not always social awareness, constituted the frequent theme of such hymns.

As this author also attests, many middle-class women took their role of spiritual leader seriously, religious training falling to middle-class mothers, or governesses in wealthier homes. Women were trained in music, but were also seen by society to be ideal religious guides to the young. Mrs. E. R. Pitman, author of *Lady Hymn Writers* (1892), expressed this point: "Somehow it needs mother-love to interpret divine love to the little ones" (281–2). Other writers also give a special charge to mothers and daughters to perpetuate the domestic, moral community through hymnody. Sarah Stickney Ellis, in *Daughters of England* (1843), describes a reprobate brother brought back to emotional health as his sister plays hymns on the piano: "She knows the power of music [and] … Her brother knows it well. It is the evening hymn they used to sing together in childhood, when they had been all day gathering flowers. His manly voice is raised … Once more the parents and children, the sister and the brother, are united as in days gone by" (61). Because the "daughter of England" has "made religion her stronghold" (214), she is able to transform others, re-creating the hymn-singing community of childhood at the piano. Alice Pollock, who grew up as a wealthy child in Wiltshire in the 1870s, recalls her mother playing hymns on the harmonium, both before breakfast with prayers and on Sunday evenings (41, 43). When she grew older, she was expected to play for the household, although she recounts an awkward moment when she forgot the repeat of the hymn "Great God, what do I see and hear" and caused the maids to sing to the wrong notes (*Portrait of My Victorian Youth*, 1971). The evening service and hymn singing could be a high point of the day, as one mother rhapsodizes: "When the hour arrived, we summoned our household, and sang a hymn in full chorus" ending with a short sermon and prayer: "Well, indeed, might it be a prayer of thanksgiving!" (*My Children's Diary*, 1824).

Writing hymns or compiling hymn books for their young charges, women thus entered the public sphere in powerful, if often anonymous, ways.[12] Of this first example, Mary Lundie Duncan, daughter, then wife, to Anglican ministers, wrote 23 hymns for her own children. After she died in 1840, her mother published some of them in a *Memoir* and then *Rhymes for My Children* (1842) (McCutchan 447). Of the second role, hymn-book compiler, consider *The Christian Mother's Hymn Book* (1855), compiled by a "Christian Mother," never named, a common publishing practice for women wanting anonymity for their faithful actions. She published it "in the hope of aiding the Christian parent in the fulfillment of the anxious and solemn trust which is more especially committed to her" (iii). Acknowledging that many hymns are chosen for their "simple and pleasing style," she states that "language of faith and experience" is not excluded either (iv), dividing her hymn book into two parts, one for young children, one for those in "advanced years and intelligence" (v). This editor's hymn book is filled with the standard hymns of mid-century: Wesley's Easter favorite, "Christ, the Lord, is risen today" (Hymn 191), the missionary hymn by Reginald Heber, "From Greenland's icy mountains" (Hymn 166), and the singable "There is a happy land" (Hymn 40), as well as classics by Charles Wesley ("Gentle Jesus, meek and mind," Hymn 7), Isaac Watts ("I sing the almighty power of God," Hymn 56), and the Taylors ("This is a precious book indeed," Hymn 94), most of which were being sung in Sunday schools. Notice, too, similar hymns in the public school repertoire including Methodist Charles Wesley's "Jesus, Lover of our souls," Anglican Charlotte Elliott's "Just as I am," and Calvinist Augustus Toplady's "Rock of ages."

The hymn book's middle-class audience is occasionally implied, yet never assumed, as in another familiar hymn of the century, "Happy the home when God is there," by Henry Ware (1846) (often sung to the tune of St. Agnes):

> Happy the home, when God is there,
>    And love fills every breast ... (v. 1)
>        *******
> Happy the home, where prayer is heard,
>    And praise is wont to rise;
> Where parents love the sacred word,
>    And live but for the skies. (v. 3)

Though this might be called the stereotypical middle-class hymn, there is nothing that precludes a home of *any* economic status portraying these Christian attributes, of love, prayer, and parental oversight, save for the economic fortune to own a

---

[12]   Please see my article "Writing for, yet Apart" for a thorough discussion of women hymn-book editors, their anonymity, and other single-hymn writers such as Duncan.

home, money to own a hymn book, and the leisure to sing the hymn. Though more frequent in home hymn books, it was included in at least two Sunday school hymn books in my study (*Sunday School Hymn Book*, 1871, and *Sunday School Hymnal*, 1892). In conclusion, occasional hymns (such as those just mentioned) carried overt ideological weight, but others such as "Happy the home" could be universal in their implications.

Not addressing social difference or change directly, home hymns had a social influence mainly on the larger family circle itself, Alice Pollock's example above being a reminder that the "family circle" could include servants and visitors among those influenced by hymns. Henry Bateman notes how quickly the dissemination of hymn ideologies may carry "[w]here mothers or sisters are engaged during the week in teaching the young child to repeat, with proper emphasis, and with understanding, the few verses which every father will gladly listen to on the coming Sunday from the lips of his loved little one; ... [A]nd relatives or friends who may be by, will listen readily to the short and simple Hymn which a child is pleased to say" (*Sunday Sunshine*, 1858, viii). So, too, interestingly, would this dissemination carry to the servants of the family, as "when the nurse up stairs, or any servant of the house, lends a willing ear to the pleasant voice that repeats it again and again during the passing week" (viii). It was perhaps for this reason that hymns like Alexander's which extolled the status quo were so germane.

It remains to be speculated what children themselves thought of these family hymn-sings. One man, Thomas A. Lamont, living as a boy in a Methodist parsonage in America in the 1870s, reflects: "when we had relatives or friends visiting us ... my mother would play a hymn on the old square rosewood piano ... and we would stand up and join in the singing before Father offered the brief final prayer. But normally we would rush out to get in as much play as we could before dark" (*My Boyhood in a Parsonage* 33). The inspiration described by adults may not always have been realized by the children intent on play. However, a cold drawing-room or tea-room could yet be warmed by hymn singing, as another boy growing up in rural Goudhurst, England, in the 1890s recalls: "The drawing-room was of all places perhaps the least cheerful ... On Sundays, in the winter, it is true, the family ... stood round the American organ to sing, before we children were sent to bed. Peopled like this with a fire and a song the place was quite transformed" (*The Small Years* 51). Or when his uncle played hymns on the piano, "[t]he music went softly on, filling the room as gently as the lamplight" (108–9). Thus, most middle- and upper-class children would first learn and appreciate hymns in the home as taught by mothers, sisters, and governesses, sung by family and servants alike. As all these various examples also suggest, home communities and family relationships could be solidified by communal hymn singing.

It hardly needs mentioning that the other space where hymnody had influence upon upper- and middle-class children was in worship; churchgoing was integral to Victorian culture and of course "[r]egular worshippers would naturally take their children to church or chapel" (Hopkins 151). This does not exclude the working-class child, either. Despite Victorian concerns that "workers have no religion" (Friedrich Engels, qtd. in Hopkins 147), Hopkins reminds us that if one of two Victorians attended worship (according to an 1851 census), there was "substantial working-class attendance," particularly in the countryside and among the Primitive Methodist chapels (Hopkins 148–9). Nevertheless, Hopkins suggests that working-class children were more engaged in religious education through Sunday schools than adult church services (151). Furthermore, churchgoing was a vital, outward sign of respectability for all proper classes. And, for better or worse, more of the extant hymn and memoir record chronicles upper- and middle-class churchgoing, so I turn to it in the rest of this section.

One aspect that both upper- and middle-class children recall about church was its monotony. Forrest Reid remembers being taken to Chapel for the first time by his Low Church governess and his "surprise and indignation" at finding the experience "dismal, noisy" (18–19): "Sunday became to me a veritable nightmare, casting its baleful shadow even over the last hours of Saturday. I hated Sunday, I hated church, I hated Sunday School, I hated Bible stories" (19).[13] Similarly, Victorian Sundays were "apt to give a mental shiver to people of long memories" (Hughes 57), tempered as they were by the Sabbatarian traditions of abstinence, deprivation, contemplation, and religious focus. Molly Hughes, worshipping at St. Paul's, London, in the late 1860s, writes of "the long walk" and "those long services" (58) but that she relished the music of the Cathedral, if not the hymns: "No footling sentimental hymns, but Te Deums, Psalms, Creeds, Introits, and Kyries that intoxicated us" (Hughes 58). Majestic music could enliven the lengthy services. And divorced from the service per se, church activities could enliven the whole week; writing of the Wesleyan Chapel of King's Cross, London, in the 1890s, Frank Kingdom called it the "social center around which our family interests revolved" and the "recreational center where our good times were held" (94), no doubt including some hymn-sings. Hymns could even offer solace to some children during the church service itself, as for Lucy Larcom living in America: "I was told to listen to the minister; but as I did not understand a word he was saying, I gave it up, and took refuge in the hymn-book, with the conscientious purpose of trying to sit still … and sometimes I learned two or three hymns in a forenoon or an afternoon" (58). Probably due less to the location (New England) than the era, the 1820s when Evangelical fervor was high and other childish entertainment was much more limited, Lucy's love of hymns yet suggests that to some, the joy of learning hymns at church, even *memorizing* them on one's own, could overcome doctrine and dreariness.

One change in various churches by the second half of the century that relieved many of the bored children just mentioned was the institution of "children's services"—children's own separate "children's church"—which was recognized as a necessity to keep fidgeting children occupied during the main service. As one hymn-book editor in 1865 explains:

---

[13]    Luann Walther notes the ways that adults re-constructed their Victorian childhood, often taking extreme views, of wretchedness or paradise. I therefore qualify that some of these comments are not strictly children's authentic views. See Chapter 6 for actual children's experiences. Most children note going to church on Sunday mornings, working-class as well.

The task of maintaining order and attention in church among young children throughout a long service of which a great part is necessarily beyond their comprehension, has long been felt an arduous and unsatisfactory one; and it may be accepted as a cheering token of the increased interest taken by the Church in the welfare of her younger members, that the desirableness of special arrangements for children's services is becoming more generally recognized. (*The Children's Liturgy and Hymn Book* iii)

By 1897, this innovation was described as an "urgency" especially felt in the Anglican churches where an "increasing number of the clergy" made "special arrangements for children's services in addition to the ordinary services of the day" (*Children's Service Book*, Preface to the Second Edition). Too, in some parishes children were "publicly catechising in the presence of the congregation" (Preface). Admittedly, the children's services still employed a great deal of sitting and listening, sprinkled with some participatory activities, as the following "Service for Children; with 50 Hymns" (Manchester, 1894) suggests:

Opening Hymn
Minister and Children: Responsive Reading of the Beatitudes
Lesson, Address, and/or Catechism
Psalm (sung)
Thanksgiving in unison
Lord's Prayer
Benediction
Hymn

As this service outline reveals, hymns were integral to the children's services, many hymn books being published in the last half of the century to meet these needs: *The Children's Hymnal and Christian Year; for Use at Children's Services* (ed. C. H. Bateman, 1872); *The Children's Service Book with Hymns, Litanies, Carols, and Prayers for Public and Private Use* (ed. M. Woodward, 1889); and *A Service Book for Church and School* (ed. George S. Barrett, 1891).

Of one, C. H. Bateman's *The Children's Hymnal and Christian Year*, it is useful to note that although many of its hymns appear to be original and some were clearly tied to Anglican liturgy ("Eight days amid this world of woe" for the Circumcision of Christ, No. 13), many others were popular hymns found in other denominational hymn books: Calvinist ones such as Toplady's "Rock of ages," seasonal ones such as Wesley's "Come, Thou long-expected Jesus," poetic ones such as Harriet Auber's "Our blest Redeemer, ere He breathed," and classic ones such as Thomas Ken's "Awake, my soul, and with the sun." As befits the mood of the late century (to be discussed in the next chapter), some took a "speaking down" approach to children, as with C. F. Alexander's popular "We are but little children weak":

We are but little children weak,
Nor born to any high estate;
What can we do for Jesu's sake
Who is so high and good and great. (v. 1)

As the third verse acknowledges, "We need not die; we cannot fight"; and as it ends, the child is made to ask, "What can we do for Jesu's sake?" The answer is given in the fourth verse:

> … There's not a child so small and weak
> But has his little cross to take,
> His little work of love and praise
> That he may do for Jesu's sake. (v. 4)

It is no wonder that at least two children of the time period remember detesting this hymn. One, a Mary MacCarthy who lived in London in the 1880s, vividly recalls being forced to sing the hymn when a visitor requested it during the evening hymn-sing: "Oh, why did we have [to sing] 'We are but little children weak'?" she remembers bitterly crying to her mother later that night (*A Nineteenth-Century Childhood* 23). Another boy of 1880s London also later reflects in his autobiography: "If churchmen only knew the minds of children … they could never have compelled them to sing: 'We are but little children weak,' with a strangled resentment against a religion which, like Blake's poem, exalted meekness and mildness. Little children are tough customers," and that he preferred to see Jesus as "the First of Heroes" (L. E. Jones 26). This boy specifically resented the rhetoric of "meekness" as offensive to both his gender and his age. It is a valid point, further problematized by the hymn's wide popularity (18% of children's hymn books), in home and Sunday school hymn books alike. Given that Jesus was frequently described as "meek," Alexander no doubt meant this as a complimentary posture for children, whether they registered it or not.[14] Too, the empowerment given to children, of middle-class work with social implications ("His little work of love and praise / That he may do for Jesu's sake") had some staying power. Nevertheless, it was expunged in later service hymn books, such as the 1898 *Children's Service Book*.

In short, middle-class hymns had moments of class-conceit and callousness, even condescending lyrics for the middle-class child. Nevertheless, a home filled with hymn singing or a church service with hymns specifically for young people created important communities for middle-class children of the era, uniting them with their youthful peers across society.

## Part III
## "'Tis the song of those oppress'd":
## Hymns of the Working and Impoverished Child

If there was ever a child who needed the solace and grace offered by hymns, it was the working-class child of the Victorian period. The Industrial Revolution

---

[14]    C. F. Alexander and her famous hymn book *Hymns for Little Children* (1848) are given much greater treatment in my "Writing for, yet Apart" where I further develop a feminist argument of her use of the diminutive with children.

created a need for small bodies and cheap labor to work in factories, mines, and cottage industries. Soon, working-class children were laboring more arduously than perhaps at any time prior: comparisons with slavery even fueled the rhetoric (Horn, *Children's Work* 15).[15] One immense difference between working- and middle-class children in the first half of the century was the amount of time devoted to schooling. Indeed, working children felt not only their poverty but the educational privilege denied them. As a child worker in the pottery industry of the 1830s,[16] Charles Shaw recalls, "I knew other children so differently placed to myself, who could go to school every day, who never wanted food, who never wore shoes with the toes out, nor jackets with elbows out. They had bright homes in which they could laugh and sing and play. I hardly ever saw my home except on Sundays, for I only slept there during the nights … Was there any guardian angel watching over me? God knows" (*When I was a Child* 61). This child noticed not only his lack of a "bright home" and chances to "sing and play" but also his lack of "school every day."

As reflected in the Benthamites' catchphrase, "the March of the Mind," many reformers worked towards expanding schooling for all citizens in the hopes that a more educated workforce, not overworked children, would improve the national economy (Altick 247). Too, reformers eventually realized it was more prudent to educate than punish young criminals; Jeannie Duckworth asserts that "removing young children from the streets and putting them into schools in a well-organised manner was the main factor in reducing the juvenile crime rate as well as improving the country's work force" (ix). Initially, though, most educational reform came about for religious edification through various church-based institutions. As early as 1808, the Dissenting churches supported a British and Foreign Schools Society; by 1811, the National Society for the Education of the Poor in the Principles of the Established Church in England and Wales was established, both of them to educate working-class children in reading, writing, and arithmetic for a small fee. Often using the monitorial system developed by Andrew Bell in India, these schools were able to educate hundreds of students because children of more advanced learning taught those of lesser in a top-down approach (Novo 241). Yet both competed for government funds in support of their schools. They also competed theologically such that "sectarian disputes and rivalries … bedevil[ed] elementary education" (Horn, *Schoolchild* 2). Dame schools charged a fee to teach children in front parlors of private homes often with few books and no desks; other dame

---

[15]   For more about child labor in the nineteenth century, see Horn, *Children's Work*, ch. 2; Davin, *Growing Up Poor*, pt. 3; Cunningham, *The Children of the Poor*, chs. 3 and 7; Sommerville, *The Rise and Fall of Childhood*, ch. 5, and, for the American situation, *Pricing the Priceless Child*, chs. 2 and 3. An especially useful first-hand analysis of child workers in agriculture, straw plait trade, silk industry, papermaking, brickmaking, and chimney sweeping in Hertfordshire, based on surviving records and testimonials, can be found in Eileen Wallace's *Children of the Labouring Poor*.

[16]   See F. S. Schwarzbach, "Twelve Ways of Looking at a Staffordshire Figurine," for an in-depth cultural study of the pottery industry, including its effect on child workers.

schools might simply be taught during the work-day of cottage industries, the children working while the Bible was read and paying part of their earnings for this schooling (Novo 241). Infant Schools, established by Samuel Wilderspin in the mid-1800s, catered to the smallest children, ages 4–7.

English working-class parents, having to pay for "day" schooling and to find the time for working children to attend, often preferred the free Sunday schools which met only on Sundays when children were available. The first one is attributed to Robert Raikes, who established a school in Gloucester in 1780, and they quickly spread throughout the country owing to the renewed Evangelical spirit of the late eighteenth and early nineteenth centuries. Thomas Walter Laqueur, in his *Religion and Respectability: Sunday Schools and Working Class Culture, 1780–1850*, further identifies three specific objectives for their establishment throughout the century:

> For some, the new institution was an instrument for the moral rescue of poor children from their corrupt parents, thereby at one stroke insuring the happiness of the little ones and the regeneration of society. Others saw in the schools primarily a means of spreading the Word of God, an end valuable for its own sake. Thirdly, a new, soft, kind, more optimistic and sentimental view of children and childhood induced benevolent men and women to direct their attentions to the young. (4)

The Sunday School Movement cut across denominations, from Dissenting to Anglican to Quaker.[17] Clearly, these denominational schools emphasized a religious curriculum; the need to read was in order to read the Bible. In fact, debates persisted throughout the century as to whether teaching writing and mathematics was both too secular and too much "work" for a Sunday. Some Sunday schools worked around this rule by adjusting their meetings, and bearing in mind their working-class audience: one Methodist Sunday school advertised that children "are taught to read, to commit to memory their Catechism, portions of God's Word, Hymns, etc. And in addition to this, two evenings in the week are devoted to teaching the higher classes Writing, and the first Rules in arithmetic, to qualify them for the different stations in life to which Providence may call them" (*Hymns to be Sung at City Road Chapel* hymn sheet, November 27, 1825). This set of eight Sunday schools boasts having "received" about 30,000 children since their inception in 1798. Indeed, Sunday schools steadily grew, Laqueur estimating their enrollment to be 2,099,611 by 1851: 12.5% of the population, 56.5% of those between 5 and 15, and 75.4% of working-class children between those ages (44).

Notably, public schools and state-run national schools segregated the sexes, which resulted in different curriculums (see Davin 142–53), but Sunday schools

---

[17] Laqueur identifies six main national Sunday school organizations: the Sunday School Society (interdenominational, est. 1785); the Sunday School Union (mainly Dissenting; est. 1803); the Sunday School Association (predominantly Unitarian, est. 1833); the Methodist Sunday School Union (Wesleyan, est. 1837); the Sunday School Institute (Church of England, est. 1843), and the Society of Friends First Day School Association (Quaker, est. 1847) (33).

were almost always co-educational (*Hymns to be Sung by the Children ... Frome*, 1813, lists 105 boys and 110 girls in their Sunday school). On the other hand, there was a large gulf between the classes: if the middle classes sponsored Sunday schools, they infrequently taught at them, teachers mostly coming from the working classes themselves (Thorne 135). Another problem was that working-class church attendees—both adults and Sunday scholars—were relegated to free seats in the gallery apart from the rented pew seats for the more privileged in Congregational churches, for example. Perhaps due to this divide, reformers struggled throughout the century to keep their Sunday scholars as church attendees once they became adults (Thorne 117).

If Sunday schools met the educational needs for working children in urban and agrarian communities, Ragged Schools catered specifically to impoverished urban children who lacked work and were thus available for day schools but too "ragged" for them. To provide for their education, Ragged Schools were established in London and across the country, the Ragged School Union set up to oversee this work in 1844. Ragged Schools were intended for children "as yet unreached by any other institution, an urban group brought into existence by the rapid and unplanned growth of England's larger cities" (Schupf 162). They were for the children of parents with the most menial of jobs or no jobs at all, providing meals and clothing in addition to education. By 1852, 41 towns had Ragged Schools, 110 schools existing in London alone (Horn, *Victorian Town* 82).[18]

Universal education was slow in coming but the 1870 Elementary Education Act (also known as the Forster Education Act after its sponsor) finally provided state-supported, national education to all children in both England and Wales; the Education Act of 1880 made this schooling compulsory for children ages 5 to 10. The above schools—National, Ragged, and Infant—were eventually incorporated into state schools run by a local board. This initiative was generally supported by the churches.[19] Of course wealthier children continued to attend public and denominational schools (Novo 243). Despite early resistance from working classes, these acts were "landmark" legislation in providing "cheap and efficient universal elementary education" (Shea 31).[20]

---

[18]    For more on educational opportunities, see Laqueur, Altick, Schupf, Pierce and Pierce, Horn, *The Victorian and Edwardian Schoolchild* and *The Victorian Town Child*, Davin, pt. 2; Shea, Hopkinson, Galbraith, and Hunt.

[19]    See Smith, *Methodism and Education 1849–1902* (1998) for in-depth analysis of the role of the Wesleyan Methodist church, and J. H. Rigg in particular, in support of the Education Act (ch. 3).

[20]    The compulsory nature of these schools was not only resisted by many working-class parents but was hard to enforce (see Auerbach, "Some Punishment Should Be Devised"). Parents in rural areas such as Hertfordshire who depended upon their children's labor also defied the law or sent their children to school irregularly (see Wallace 43–7). Taking children ages 3–5 out of the home was also controversial (Davin 118). With compulsory schooling, Ragged Schools moved to charitable operations, the last closing in 1906 (Davin, footnote 5, 218).

Notwithstanding the various shortcomings in all aspects of English education in the nineteenth century, without a doubt all institutions increased literacy of the working classes throughout the century. The Society for the Promotion of Christian Knowledge (SPCK), the Religious Tract Society (RTS), and the Sunday School Union (SSU) disseminated many educational publications.[21] Horn credits the Sunday school movement for "the upsurge in children's periodical literature ... Tracts, books, testaments and Bibles were distributed in tens of millions to Sunday scholars" (*Victorian Town* 163).

What authors neglect to include in their studies of educational-religious publications, though, are the many children's hymn books also used in Infant Schools, Sunday schools, National schools, and state schools throughout the century. For example, hymn books were designed specifically for national schools as we see with *Easy Hymns for the Use of Children in the National Schools* (1850) as published by the Society for the Promotion of Christian Knowledge.[22] Most hymns are standard (by the Taylors, for example), so it is interesting to note other titles unique to this hymn book which address head-on the economic status of its audience: "Some think it a hardship to work for their bread" (Hymn 20) or "Some poor little ignorant children delight" (Hymn 22), as the Christian message is brought to comfort—if not alter—their situations of struggle. Other hymn books were written specifically for the Infant Schools, such as *A Selection of Hymns and Poetry for the use of Infant Schools and Nurseries* (Elizabeth Mayo, 1838) and *Infants' Songs for Home and School* (Wesleyan Methodist Sunday School Union, 1876), of the simpler rhetoric discussed earlier.

Until the 1860s, most hymn books contained only the texts to hymns; children would be taught about a dozen tunes to which the text could be sung, separate tune books being printed with tunes mostly for teachers. As the century progressed, musical education was promoted in schools. In their Preface to *The Child's Own Tune Book* (1846), George Hogarth (arranger) and John Curwen (editor), the latter the champion of the Tonic Sol-fa system in schools, advised: "Teach the tunes to as many as can be gathered into Bible classes or special singing meetings, held in the course of the week ... Teach by pattern. Sing to the children a short phrase of the tune, while they attentively listen ... Sing a few choice hymns and tunes well, and often" (ii–iii). Chapter 3 will examine music education more fully, but here we see the desire to ingrain in children's heads a few tunes to use with the various hymns they will sing in school or meetings.

---

[21]  For background on the RTS and SPCK, see J. S. Bratton, 32–52, and Goldstrom, 11–13. See Aileen Fyfe, "Commerce and Philanthropy: The Religious Tract Society and the Business of Publishing," for analysis of the RTS as a philanthropy and business.

[22]  A few other state-sponsored, day-school hymn books published prior to the Education Act that I found include: John Yates, *Harrington-School Hymns* (Liverpool, 1818); A. D. Thomson and W. Sugden, *The Training-School Song-Book* (Glasgow, 1849); John Ellerton, *Hymns for Schools and Bible Classes* (1859); and, probably for board schools: Emma Mundella, *The Day School Hymn Book* (London, 1896); and [E. H. Mayo Gunn, ed.], *School Hymns* (London, 1891).

Even after state-wide Board Schools were established, Adey conjectures that "children in both church and secular schools can be presumed to have sung at least one hymn per school service" (*Class and Idol* 120). While children at church-sponsored schools would have continued to use their denominational hymn books, those at the more poorly funded Board Schools were probably learning hymns off of blackboards or wall charts (Adey 120).

Without a doubt, though, Sunday school hymn books dominate the genre for working-class children, the schools creating an enormous demand for material that taught reading and religious principles (Routley, *Hymns and Human Life* 253). Early in the century, hymns were used throughout the day: Joseph Benson writes in the preface to his 1806 hymn book that a variety of hymns are needed for "the regular worship usually performed in Sunday Schools ... [as well as] that used in other Schools which are wont to be opened and concluded with singing an hymn and with prayer morning and evening every day; not to mention the daily worship which children attend in pious families, and in stated or occasional meetings" (*Hymns for Children and Young Persons* iii). Children might enjoy the singing, yet the space where they sang could reflect grim reality. Sunday and Day schools were very often held in dark, cold basements of churches (Hopkins 139), and early on, a tight rein on students, even during singing, seems typical. An image in an 1835 Sunday school hymn book (*The Sunday-School Union Hymn-Book*) shows students facing a head teacher who leads the group singing. Boys appear to be separated from girls by a half-wall and walled in on their other sides by male teachers standing at the end of each row. All children are dutifully reading their books, many with awkward leg positions as if they have been standing for an extended period (see Figure 1.2). Yet they may have enjoyed the singing as a change of pace, a pleasing activity amidst the grim circumstances.

Many denominations published their own Sunday school hymn books. The Methodist Sunday schools were extremely prolific throughout the century, their 1879 *Sunday School Hymn Book* considered a classic of children's hymn books (Julian 223), to be discussed in Chapter 2. SPCK, RTS, and the SSU also contributed a variety of hymn books, such as the *Sunday School Union Hymn Book Consisting of Devotional Hymns for the Use of Sunday Schools* which went through many editions early in the century: 1826 (5th ed.) and 1835 (20th ed.), for example. Other hymn books were individually published by conscientious churchmen and women: William Gadsby's *A Selection of Hymns from Various Authors for the Use of Sunday Schools* (1836); T. H. Gregg's *The Sunday-School Hymnal* (1870); and Henry John Betts's *The Children's Hosannah: A Selection of Upwards of One Hundred and Twenty Hymns, Adapted for Sunday School and Family Use* (1858). Editors and publishers were acutely aware of the expense of such books for the working-class child: wrote Betts, "Every Sunday Scholar who can read ought to have a hymn book; the price of the hymn book, therefore, should be within every scholar's means. Hence, no apology can be needed for the issue of a PENNY *Sunday School Hymn Book*" (Preface; his emphasis). By tightly printing several hymns per page, Betts is able to offer 124 hymns in a 3 × 4.5-inch, thin hymn book.

Figure 1.2    Frontispiece to *The Sunday-School Union Hymn-Book*, 20th
              edition (1835). Courtesy of The Angus Library and Archive,
              Regent's Park College, Oxford University.

Of these selections, Gadsby's *A Selection of Hymns from Various Authors for
the Use of Sunday Schools*, represents an early-century Evangelical hymn book:
many hymns focused on sin ("Poor sinners dejected, of comfort debarr'd," Hymn
23, etc.), some Calvinistic references to the Elect ("Election is a truth divine,"
Hymn 48), Last Judgment ("Ye that die without repentance," Hymn 169), and
death ("Death has his millions slain," Hymn 160). Significantly, several hymns
address the economic situation of their singers, like Hymn 196:

> Though young in years, and very poor,
>     Exposed to trials great,
> If I am led to mercy's door,
>     God's mercy to entreat. (v. 1)
> He will not my poor cry despise,
>     Nor spurn my humble plea;
> My prayer he'll hear and send supplies
>     And guide me night and day. (v. 2)

Other, passing references also take on double meaning given the situation of these
young singers: "Poor, helpless, sin-sick souls / Who on the Lord rely" (Hymn 198)
or "Where'er thou hast the work begun, / Give them new strength the race to run"
(Hymn 199). In the "Prayer for the School" (Hymn 199), though, hope is given
that "this school with fervent pray'r / [Can] ... pierce the skies, and reach thine
ear" (v. 1), that unified prayer and "glorious [songs of] praise" (v. 3) could bring

about transformation, spiritual at least. These hymns were, notably, not found in any other hymn books of my study.

Gregg's *The Sunday-School Hymnal* (1870) is a very typical Sunday school book of mid-century, representing some continuities with earlier Evangelical texts and also more Romantic attitudes of the late century, as will be explored in Chapter 2. Over half of its contents are popular hymns found in many similar Sunday school hymn books: classic Evangelical hymns like Wesley's "Gentle Jesus, meek and mild" is here (Hymn 10), Toplady's "Rock of ages" (Hymn 43), "Here we suffer grief and pain" (Hymn 15), and John Mason Neale's "Jerusalem the golden!" (Hymn 23). As the titles suggest, attention is focused on the sin and misery of this life, with golden rewards in the next, themes perhaps purposely angled at those suffering so much in this world. Its hymns focus specifically on children: its use of the first person and the common adjective "little," personally invite the child to admit faults, give up personal authority, and seek divine intervention. However, their economic suffering is placed solely in the context of desire for the next world, as all children sing the popular hymn, "There is a happy land, far, far away" (Hymn 49).

Because Sunday schools were financed almost entirely on the generosity of patrons, special services and the annual anniversary celebration were held as fundraisers for the schools (anniversary walks as well, to be discussed in Chapter 5). Children sang the hymns they had learned for a larger audience of parents and middle-class patrons; one hymn sheet, for the Wesleyan Sunday Schools, Doncaster, for Sunday, April 30, 1848, for example, notes that hymns will be "Sung by the Children" and that the "Schools are supported by voluntary contribution" (*Wesleyan Sunday Schools*, 1848). These hymns are almost always focused on children ("Lord, teach a little child to pray" opens this particular service), but the context of fundraising is never far from their singing either, as Hymn 1 in *Hymns to be Sung by the Children of the Sunday School, at the Methodist Chapel, Frome* (Sunday, May 30, 1813) exemplifies:

> Guardian guides of innocence,
> Almoners of providence,
> Hither turn your eyes, and view
> Infant hands held out for you …

Even the hymn sheets themselves are sold "and the profits applied to the support of the School, which depends on subscriptions, donations, and an annual public collection" (*Hymns to be Sung* 2). So hymns served many purposes in the Sunday schools.

Though Sunday schools were distinct from grammar schools in being co-educational, "Boys' Brigades," founded in 1883, were special opportunities given to Sunday school boys ages 12–17 for "the advancement of Christ's kingdom among Boys, and the promotion of habits of reverence, discipline, and self-respect, and all that tends toward a true Christian manliness" (qtd. in Laqueur 249; see also Horn, *Schoolchild* 152–6). These militaristic organizations, growing to over

11,000 boys by 1888, utilized hymn books to galvanize their cause, such as *The Boys' Brigade Hymnal* (London, n.d.). Though ever-popular hymns such as "Abide with me" (Hymn 1), "Christ the Lord is risen today" (Hymn 11), and "Rock of ages" (Hymn 87) are found, *The Boys' Brigade Hymnal* also touts many muscular Christian hymns as well: "Courage, brother! Do not stumble" (Hymn 16), "Fight the good fight" (Hymn 23), and "Soldiers of the cross, arise" (Hymn 92). An organization created specifically for girls in 1875 through the Anglican Church, the Girls' Friendly Societies, aimed to help working-class girls avoid out-of-wedlock pregnancies by giving them a Christian society and middle-class mentors. The Anglican *Children's Hymn Book* (1878) contains two hymns in its Girls' Friendly Society section to inspire young women: "Oh, grant to each before Thee now / A meek and lowly heart, / That like another Mary, we / May choose the better part" (v. 1 to Hymn 338). These are rare moments of gendered hymns, however.

Whether for the companionship, the hymn singing, or simply the break on Sundays, Sunday schools were loved by many working-class children. Charles Shaw, the child potter-laborer quoted above, writes that the Sunday school "leavened my life from my sixth to my tenth year … [T]he influence of the Sunday school stood me in good stead … Sunday brought sweetness into my life, and lifted me out of the demoralising influences of the working days" (8–9). Too, when their dire situation is brought to the attention of the young Durbeyfield children, in the chapter's epigraph, it is a Sunday school song which comes first to mind to express, and perhaps soothe, their trepidation.

Finally, Ragged Schools relied upon hymns with their focus on literacy and Christian education. Two hymn books are of note in the Ragged School genre, both published in 1848 when the movement was beginning: *Ragged School Hymns by a Ragged-School Teacher* (1848) and *The Ragged-School Hymn Book* by John Kendrick Pelly (1848). In fact, despite their common publication date, they actually represent diametrically opposed approaches to teaching Christian virtues to the most impoverished. At one extreme is *Ragged School Hymns by a Ragged-School Teacher*. Perhaps his or her teaching experience embittered this teacher to the realities of street children, for the topics are dark: "Against Wickedness," "Death, Judgment, and Eternity," "*Duty* of Kindness" (my italics), and "Forgiveness: Its Value." When the teacher addresses the social structure, it is always in the context of depravity and sin, as in Hymn 13:

> Have I any cause to envy
>> Persons who are rich and high?
> No, for they are often wretched,
>> Far less happy e'en than I.

The second verse than uses the parable of Dives and Lazarus to promote the position of the poor (Luke 16:19–31):

> See that sinner cloth'd in purple,
>> In a palace richly fed;

> At his gate a tatter'd beggar
>     Humbly craves a piece of bread;
> Look again; the rich man's treasure
>     Has been taken all away,
> But the poor has found in heaven
>     Joys that never can decay. (v. 2)

The poor shall reap their reward but must wait for it in heaven. Wealth does not protect a person from death or the final Judgment, as Hymn 14 highlights:

> Why should I envy those who have
>     More money or more clothes than I?
> These cannot keep them from the grave,
>     Or help them when they come to die. (v. 1)

Money cannot protect the rich from final Judgment: "No earthly gold, or house, or land, / Can purchase their acquittal there" (v. 2). These hymns work to build up children against the "laughs and sneers" of others since "I've a mighty Friend above" (Hymn 40) and if others "have hurt *you*, do not hurt them again" (Hymn 39; original italics).

But the hymns also make unfortunate assumptions about the Ragged School student ("Look upon the young and thoughtless … Though they now be poor and needy," Hymn 95), sometimes on a severe level ("For whosoe'er his brother hates / Must have a murd'rer's mind, / And Satan with impatience waits / His guilty soul to bind," Hymn 49). Hymn 100, "The Barren Tree," initially tells the story of the "tree whose leaves were bright and green, / But fruit it would not bear" as presumably a parable about rich dressings belying the productivity of the person; yet by the fourth verse, the hymn condemns the singers themselves for not being productive:

> Attend, ye young, and trifle not,
>     Worse evil you must share,
> Eternal fire will be your lot,
>     If fruit *you* do not bear. (v. 4; my italics)

In short, this hymn editor encourages the young, underprivileged singers to see past material privilege yet is also concerned for the serious sins they may commit because of their poverty.

The second editor, John Kendrick Pelly, displays a kinder attitude towards his youthful charges, perhaps because he was himself a Sunday Scholar. Writing a Preface to his "Fellow Labourers," the Teachers, he explains his goal of providing hymns "such that the most depraved and degraded might sing with freedom and safety," possibly in direct reference to the above types of hymns (iii). To make every child feel comfortable singing the hymns, he encourages teachers to substitute "girl" or "child" whenever he has used the word "lad." He urges hymn books to be provided for every child "that they may not only have them to sing with at school, but that their parents, brothers, sisters, and young companions may have the opportunity of hearing the words repeated at home" (v). He thus attempts to make a connection between the schools and the home environment, that learning hymns could offer inspiration in both contexts. Further, given that most Sunday school books would have been shared and kept at the school, Pelly's desire that every child have their own book is a magnanimous gesture: in the Preface, he urges the child singers to "take very great care of it [the hymn book] ... learn at least one hymn every week ... and pay very great attention to the suitable tunes that are sung to each in this *your own Hymn Book*" (vii; his italics). To children who owned very little, this book would have been quite a gift.

It is therefore no surprise to feel the joy in these hymns penned by Pelly himself (iv), as in Hymn 30: "Though I am poor, I have a soul, / Riches can never buy ... Though poor, though very poor, I may / Behold his [God's] smiling face." Hymn 44 expounds upon this love available to all:

> Little children, black or white,
>     Every sinner, young or old,
> Ragged children we invite
>     To the dear Redeemer's fold. (v. 1)

This Redeemer is much more appealing than in the previous hymn book:

> See his arms are open'd wide,
>     And the smile is on his face;
> Can you from him turn aside,
>     And refuse his offer'd grace? (v. 2)

For children perhaps without the opened arms, either at home or at work, this image of Christ would be very attractive. Given that this is a hymn of praise, Pelly does not question the economic system which places children in such abject poverty. For example, note the lines in Hymn 45 that almost move in that direction as I insert in brackets:

> ... And grant that all our youthful race,
>     May meet before his throne
> ... And each poor child from sin [not poverty] set free
> ... Is cloth'd in righteousness [not literal clothes].

Thus, this hymn book offers to a destitute child an open-armed Savior, a Heavenly Love, and other emotional comforts. That it does not do more to satisfy the child's physical needs is perhaps too much to ask of a book in 1848, as child labor evils were just beginning to receive public attention and resulting legislation.[23]

---

[23]   Ashley's Mines Commission, exposing atrocities of child labor in mines, was published in 1842; Elizabeth Barrett Browning's poetic response came out in 1843. Various Factory Acts limited hours for children (1833, 1844, 1847, 1850, and 1857), but it was not until the Factory Act of 1878 which actually prohibited labor in all trades for all children under 10 years old ("A Web of English History," www.history.co.uk).

Other hymn writers, aware of the struggles of overworked children, attempted to include all children when writing and compiling hymn books. For instance, concerned for children in the cottage industries, Rev. Joseph Jones published *Cottage Verse: A Collection of Hymns and Spiritual Songs; Chiefly Intended for the Use of Cottagers and Young Persons* (1852). This clergyman writes the book "with an especial regard to cottagers, children, and young persons of the labouring classes," urging these intended readers to "store their memory with Psalms, and Hymns, and Spiritual Songs" (vi). Given that children were exploited in spinning, lacemaking, straw plaiting or weaving cottage industries, he treats spirituality only as an opiate to social inequity. Indeed, children would have sung or recited these hymns *while working* within the cottage, plaiting straw, etc.[24] The hymns are therefore to provide comfort, not question child labor itself, and are fairly standard hymn inclusions: "Christ the Lord is risen to-day" and "From Greenland's icy mountains."

A much more socially engaged hymn writer, writing before the horrors for child factory workers were well known, published the *Hymns for Factory Children, Original and Paraphrased* (Leeds: T. Inchbold, 1831) because he/she was "grieved at the afflictions of others" (A2). Leeds, a major industrial town of the nineteenth century, would have seen its fair share of overworked child laborers in the factories. This anonymous writer, "a sincere friend of suffering Humanity," like Pelly, wrote many of his/her own hymns for them. In these, little children are allowed to express discontent at their lot:

> Encourag'd by thy word
> > Of promise to the poor,
> Behold an infant, Lord,
> > Wait at thy mercy's door.
> No hand, no heart, O Lord, but thine,
> Will help or pity, wants like mine. (Part 2, Hymn II, v. 1)

In the final couplet, the child points an accusing finger at those without "hand" or "heart." In fact, despite the title "Hymns for Factory Children," the hymns are actually addressed to the factory owners, and poetic images relate their "iron-hearts" and "breasts of steel" to the literal pieces of factory machinery. Twelve years before Elizabeth Barrett Browning's "Cry of the Children," this anonymous hymn writer penned works of similar indignation and power:

> 'Tis the song of those oppress'd
> > 'Neath the iron-grasp of pow'r,
> Vexed on earth, despis'd, distress'd,
> > By the lordlings of an hour. (Part 1, Hymn II, v. 2)

From lordlings, the factory owners become murderers:

---

[24]   See Wallace, *Children of the Labouring Poor*, 54–9, especially, for more about cottage industries.

'Tis the song of infants dead,
  Crush'd beneath the *murd'rous wheel*;
For *Heaven's Christ* could pity them,
  Tho' *Earth's Christians* could not feel. (v. 3; original italics)

These are powerful words urging social action, and the pity is that their influence was limited both in locale and time. Few hymn books published later on took up the social indignation of this writer.[25]

The final, perhaps most desperate, situation for a child was that of being orphaned. Institutional aid originated in the late 1600s to mid-1700s to minister to homeless children through both church and private charities. Anglican charity schools, often supported by SPCK, not only took in orphans but taught them to sing, first psalm-tunes, later hymns, which eventually led to orphan choirs being featured on charity-sermon Sundays to elicit funds directly from parishioners (Temperley, *Music of the English Parish Church* 104–5, 133–4). Their walks to a well-known cathedral like St. Paul's for such a Sunday service became legend, and certainly can be seen as an important precursor to Victorian children's public hymn singing and the confidence in children to master hymns and even anthems.

Private charities also responded to the need. The Foundling Hospital of London was established in 1739 by Thomas Coram, and used art and music for fundraisers, with support from the painter William Hogarth and composer George Frideric Handel. Such hospitals utilized hymns as part of their chapel services and, in this context, several hymn books were published, such as *Psalms, Hymns, and Anthems, Sung in the Chapel of the Hospital for the Maintenance and Education of Exposed and Deserted Young Children* (1760, 1797). Amidst general hymns on sin and suffering, notable in this book are two hymns addressing explicitly the sin and suffering of orphans, and I linger in the eighteenth century for a few minutes in order to make comparisons with orphan hymns of the next century. In "A Hymn for the Children of the Foundling Hospital," child singers are made to mouth these words:

Left on the world's bleak waste forlorn;
  In sin conceiv'd, to sorrow born;
By guilt and shame foredoomed to share
  No mother's love, no father's care. (1774 edition, v. 2)

The opening "Foundling's Hymn" likewise paints a bleak and unminced portrait:

When Parents, deaf to Nature's Voice,
  Their helpless Charge forsook
Then Nature's God, who heard our cries
  Compassion on us took. (v. 2)

---

[25] I am grateful to the librarians at the John Rylands Library at the University of Manchester, particularly Mr. Peter Nockles, who, during my visit to the library in October 2006, went to great lengths to procure and later send a copy of this rare hymn book to me.

Clearly God "still their Wants [supplies]" (v. 3), but other hymns address the patrons who might also supply aid, as in "Father of mercy, hear our prayers":

> Each hand and heart that lends us aid,
>     Thou dost inspire and guide,
> Nor is their bounty unrepaid
>     Who for the poor provide. (v. 2)

Indeed, the children often performed concerts to elicit donations, so such songful appeals were vitally important to sustain the hospital. Likewise, the young women of the Magdalen Hospital were often asked to sing at fundraisers; unlike innocent children, "there were risks involved in having them too openly displayed to the public view," and thus the young women "sang from behind a grill" (Temperley, "The Hymn Books" 240). During the 1770s, their "singing of psalms, hymns, and responses ... became a great attraction to London society, mentioned in several guidebooks and memoirs" (Temperley 242), suggesting the value and also exploitation of women and children in these institutional practices.[26]

*A Collection of Hymns and Psalm Tunes: Sung in the Chapel of the Asylum for Female Orphans* (1820), also known as *Horsley's Asylum Hymns*, brought this musical attention to orphans into the nineteenth century.[27] William Horsley (1774–1858) was a composer and organist at the Asylum Chapel, and the hymn book contains a handful of hymns he himself composed for the children ("our little performers" [Preface]) to sing. One such hymn, "In early years by parents left," is of note:

> In early years by parents left
> Forlorn on life's tempestuous wave
> Of hope's reviving dawn bereft
> Thy mercy, Lord! Alone could save [repeat].

Clearly focused on the goodness of God who alone can save, this 1820 hymn is still more about finding inner peace than social outrage. Still, its tone is more hopeful than those of the late-1700s Foundling Hymns:

> Cherished by beams of brighter ray
> To thee our grateful hearts we'll raise

---

[26]   See Temperley, "The Hymn Books of the Foundling and Magdalen Hospital Chapels," 221–57, for a historical and musical analysis of hymns in the Foundling and Magdalen hymn books.

[27]   Founded in Lambeth, South London, in 1758, specifically for girls, the Asylum for Female Orphans, together with the Magdalen Asylums, attempted to prevent prostitution "by receiving and affording the protection to the deserted and orphan children of the poor" (qtd. in "Mogg's New Picture of London," 1844, from *The Dictionary of Victorian London* online, accessed June 2013). Other asylums established around England and Ireland mainly became prison-like sweatshops.

    And strive to consecrate each day
    With deeds of love and hymns of praise [repeated].

The orphans singing such "hymns of praise" might find much-needed solace.

    The Foundling Hospital continued into the nineteenth century, and as part of the admittance custom, a distinguishing token was required of parents: "monograms, childrens' caps … [or] forms of scraps" all faithfully recorded by the hospital (*The History and Objects of the Foundling Hospital with a Memoir of the Founder*, by John Brownlow, 1881). John Brownlow recorded each object, many of which are poems and verses of the lower classes themselves, youthful parents who are leaving their child forever. Their anguished verses balance the accusing tone of the printed hymn books just quoted:

    Pity the offspring of a Youthful pair,
    Whom folly taught, and Pleasure did Ensnare,
    Let the poor Babe, its parents' fault atone
    Stand you its friend, or else it is undone! (qtd. in Brownlow 51)

Others are parents' simple blessings, much more positive and affirming than the hymns written by others:

    Go gentle babe, thy future life be spent
    In virtuous purity, and calm content;
    Life's sunshine bless thee, and no anxious care
    Sit on thy brow, and draw the falling tear.

Rather than describing the child as a curse to the country, they suggest his/her great usefulness, if well-attended in its infancy:

    Thy country's grateful servant may'st thou prove
    And all thy life be happiness and love. (51)

In contrast to the bleak, accusatory, and unsympathetic hymns often penned for foundlings, these poems suggest the true contriteness, agony, and yet hope of the parents themselves.

    In my research these, alone, are the only complete hymn books to be published for foundlings and foundling hospitals. By the Victorian era, the rhetoric changes to "orphans" and attention appears to turn towards general hymn books which would include individual sections or hymns on behalf of the orphan: for example, "O Thou the helpless orphan's hope" is found in both the 1839 *Hymns for the Young Selected For the Purpose of Being Committed to Memory* (ed. Dorothy Thrupp) and the 1869 *A Book of Praise for Home and School* (ed. S. D. Major); two "Orphans Hymns" appear in the *Portsmouth Sunday School Hymn Book* (Andrew Preston Peabody, 1840); "We are not orphans on the earth" is found in the 1854 *The Children's Hymn Book*; "The Orphan Child" appears in *The National Hymns and Hymn-Writers* (Charles Rogers, 1861); *The Children's Hymn Book* (1878) features three hymns in a section "For Orphans"; and "Holy Father, throned on high," another hymn about orphans, is found in the 1885 *Home Hymn Book* (ed. H. P. Hawkins).

These hymns continue the maudlin approach of eighteenth-century hymns, but the sin of parents and child is now almost completely excised. For instance, the *Portsmouth Sunday School Hymn Book* uses the "Hymn for the Children of the Foundling Hospital," quoted from the 1760 Foundling Hospital hymn book, above, verbatim in the first verse in its "The Orphan Hymn" (No. 142):

> Attune the heart to mournful strains;
> Of wrongs and woes the song complains;
> An orphan's voice essays to swell
> The notes, that tears, by turns repel. (v. 1)

However, it significantly alters the second verse, already quoted, which labeled the child as "in sin conceiv'd, to sorrow born," instead altering the verse thus:

> Left on the world's wise waste forlorn,
> *To suffering and to sorrow born.* (v. 2; my italics)

This puts the sorrow in the world in general, not as a consequence of their parents' sin. Neither are the parents condemned, as in the original version where the child is "By guilt and shame foredoomed to share / No mother's love, no father's care." These lines instead become:

> No guide before my steps to tread
> Above no friendly shelter spread. (v. 2)

In this revision, society is answerable to its charges, for failing to provide a "guide" or "friendly shelter."

By late in the century, such orphan hymns become sentimental, for example reflecting on the pathetic figure of "a hapless orphan child" who lies all alone in the woods at night and whose appeals to God are met by his death. Only then can he escape hunger and grief:

> Thus spoke the child, and moan'd and wept;
> Then 'neath the pallid moonbeams slept;
> An angel's hand it was that shed
> The dews of slumber o'er his head;
> And when he woke the night was gone,
> Hunger and grief away had flown,
> From that poor orphan child.
>
> (v. 2, "The Orphan Child," *The National Hymns* 1861)

A late-century orphan hymn, "Holy Father, throned on high," in the 1885 *Home Hymn-Book*, contains similar sentiment but also a generous outpouring of Divine love not necessitated by death: "Fold us in Thine arms of love" (v. 1) … "This shall be our joy and peace" (v. 4). It also is more generous to the absent parents who, admittedly, may be absent by death, not desertion: "Those, the dearest and the best, / In whose love our lives were blest, / Now no longer here" (v. 2). "E. J.," Edith Jones, contributed this hymn (Hymn 359) to the *Home Hymn-Book*, focusing on those set apart from society (Clapp-Itnyre, "Writing for, yet Apart" 58). Indeed, she set herself apart in only using her initials. This bears witness to the fact that often anonymity was a conscious choice, as she purposely aligned herself, perhaps, with those forgotten not by choice: the nation's orphans.

Adey places hymns for orphanages, Ragged Schools, and charity schools in the same category: those for "the submerged child," describing the hymns as oscillating from "harsher" and "unctuous," to "dramatic" and "tear-jerking" (113). In the sense that these children were beyond the average Victorian's notice, they were, perhaps, "submerged," but they were also well represented by philanthropists and clergy, who attempted to aid these less fortunate children both physically and spiritually. If the words of hymns are often bleak, judgmental, or mawkish, there is evidence that at least a few of the hymn writers, coming from the "submerged" classes themselves, both in class (Pelly) and gender (E. J.), did feel the pain of children: their poverty, hunger, overwork, lack of family and care.

## Part IV
## "*We* thank Thee, Lord, for this fair earth": Hymns for All Children

If the previous sections show the divisive context of hymn singing during the nineteenth century, I end this chapter by arguing another facet to children's hymn singing; that this aesthetic, perhaps more than any other available to children of various classes throughout the century, even toys and games,[28] had the potential to unite them. Hymns spoke to all genders, classes, situations, and denominations. Hymn writing was an important outlet for women, and I examine elsewhere the immense contributions that women made as hymn-book editors, hymn-book writers, and hymn writers; C. F. Alexander is one notable example, among many, whose *Hymns for Little Children* (1848) impacted the entire century and are still sung today; the Taylors, to be examined in Chapter 2, were considered equal to Watts in their day. The hymns themselves also remained, for the most part, genderless. Occasional hymns would address girls and boys separately, such as Boys' Brigade and Girls' Friendly Society hymns (also some temperance hymns, to be discussed in Chapter 5). Illustrations would also emphasize gender roles undelineated in the hymn lyrics (as I will discuss in Chapter 4). Yet Sunday schools themselves included both sexes, and though middle-class, domestic musical opportunities may have been gendered, as described above, the actual

---

[28]    For other examples of classism and imperialism imbedded in children's aesthetics and play, see Teresa Michals's "Experiments before Breakfast: Toys, Education, and Middle-Class Childhood" in Denisoff, 29–42; and Megan Norcia's "Playing Empire: Children's Parlor Games, Home Theatricals, and Improvisational Play."

hymns themselves address both boys and girls without distinction, enabled by their tendency to speak in first and second person. This is unlike children's fiction which J. S. Bratton has been able to divide into "Books for Boys" and "Books for Girls" (in *The Impact of Victorian Children's Fiction*), so intent were publishers on appealing to perceived gendered interests and literary genres (see also the "Manly Boys and Rosy Girls: School Stories" in Demers, *A Garland from the Golden Age*), a phenomenon leading up to *The Boy's Own* and *The Girl's Own* periodicals premiering in the 1880s. This segregated reading phenomenon was not to be found in the children's hymn-book tradition.

Further, the class stratification of society was challenged in many ways by the children's hymn tradition. Instead, the hymn genre drew writers and composers from all classes. Lower-middle-class mothers such as Mary Lundie Duncan and teachers of Sunday schools such as Jemima Thompson (later Luke), frequently wrote a hymn or two for their young charges, while men of modest means such as John Fawcett and Thomas Bilby tried their hand at hymn writing: in these four cases, their hymns become the great children's favorites "Jesus, tender Shepherd, hear me," "I think when I read that sweet story of old," "Children of Jerusalem," and "Here we suffer grief and pain," respectively. Further, hymn-tune composition enticed working-class men and professionals (merchants, doctors, politicians, and of course clergy) alike, who, as self-taught musicians, produced many popular tunes of the era (see Bradley 143–5). Of one example, the very popular "Diadem" tune used for Edward Perronet's "All hail the power of Jesus' name" was written by James Ellor, an 18-year-old hatter and amateur composer, who took his 1838 composition to the hat-making factory where friends were working, and they used Tonic Sol-fa to piece together the parts, enthusiastically singing the new tune (McCutchan 208). It went on to become a very popular, rousing tune to this text, especially during the American gospel era (Noll 53). Not all hymns, therefore, were being used as religious propaganda from the rich to the poor but were being written by those working in modest circumstances themselves.

In fact, hymn-book publishers for children cast a wide net to audience and usage, as seen simply in their subtitles: *Original Hymns: Adapted for Social Prayer-Meetings, Missionary Services, Sunday-Schools and Christians in General* (1828); *The Children's Hymn Book for Use in Children's Services, Sunday Schools, and Families* (1878); *Songs of Love and Mercy for the Young: A Hymn Book for Children's Services and Sunday Schools* (1878); or *The Epworth Hymnal: Containing Standard Hymns of the Church, Songs for the Sunday-School, Songs for Social Services, Songs for the Home Circle, and Songs for Special Occasions* (1885). No hymn-singing occasion is left out, suggesting not only a pragmatic marketing strategy, but also that hymns crossed many social divides: from school, to home; from adult social services to children's church services; from middle-class prayer meetings to working-class Sunday schools.

Significantly, then, hymnody connected children of all classes, having the potential to bring them all comfort, whether surviving the dark conditions of a child laborer or institutionalized orphan, or the childhood traumas in middle-class and upper-class homes and schools. Other cultural experiences would further divide children, such as literature, which depended on literacy and book-ownership, and art, open only to those with means to pay for tools or exhibition fees. In contrast, all children had access to hymn books and sang them in similar contexts, from church to school.

Further, they all sang many of the *same* hymns. Various hymns analyzed in this chapter for classist implications were yet selected by editors of a variety of other hymn books. For example, Winkworth's "O Love, Who formedst me to wear," seemingly popular to public school audiences, was yet found in two non-public school, late-century hymn books of my study (*Young People's Hymnal* [1896] and *The Children's Service Book* [1897]). The Taylors' "Lord, I have passed another day," noted as a middle-class-conscious hymn, was also found in two working-class hymn books of my study: Elizabeth Mayo's *A Selection of Hymns and Poetry for the Use of Infant Schools and Nurseries* (1838) and a church school's *Collection of Sacred Music for the Use of Schools* (1849). Of another example, C. F. Alexander writes to the humblest of orphans ("Who deems himself quite desolate, / Left in the world alone?") in her Hymn 32 of *Hymns for Little Children* (1848), a standard middle-class hymn book.

Beyond these specific hymns analyzed in this chapter, we must recognize that a high number of popular hymns, many still sung today, infiltrated hymn books of all class types. Examining the various hymn books of my study that clearly fall into class designations through their titles—upper-class public school hymn books (seven), middle-class "home" hymn books (six), and working-class Sunday school hymn books (16)—I totaled frequently appearing hymns in each (see Table 1.1).[29] Many of these will be the focus of future chapters because of their popularity. For now, we can note class trends. Some inclusions, or lack thereof, are not surprising because of age differences: simple favorites such as the Taylors' "I thank the goodness and the grace," written for the youngest of children and found in Sunday school and home hymn books, are lacking from any public-school hymn book whose singers were older boys. I noted earlier the absence of Bilby's "Here we suffer grief and pain" from any public school book which is found in 44% of Sunday school hymn books, Thomas Hardy demonstrating its popularity there.

However, many other hymns cross class lines with startling ease. High-class Anglican favorites were common to public school hymn books—John Keble's "Sun of my soul," Reginald Heber's "Holy, holy, holy" and his missionary hymn "From Greenland's icy mountains" (86–100% of these selected hymn books)—but these were also found in high numbers in Sunday school hymn books of various denominations (31–50%). Sentimental hymns often associated with middle-class home life—like Jemima Thompson Luke's "I think when I read that sweet story of old"—are found in abundant numbers in Sunday school hymn books (63%). Hymns of sin and redemption often found in Sunday school literature—Charles

---

[29]    I note that Adey's lists of hymns found in the four public school hymnals, Appendix V, 263–70, show similar reoccurring titles.

Table 1.1      Percentages of Popular Hymns in Three Classes of Hymn Books

| Title | Public School (7) | Home (6) | Sunday School (16) |
|---|---|---|---|
| "I thank the goodness and the grace" (Taylors) | 0% | 71% | 50% |
| "Here we suffer grief and pain" (Bilby) | 0% | 57% | 44% |
| "Sun of my soul" (Keble) | 100% | 43% | 34% |
| "Holy, holy, holy" (Heber) | 100% | 14% | 31% |
| "From Greenland's icy mountains" (Heber) | 86% | 71% | 50% |
| "Hark, the herald angels sing" (Wesley) | 71% | 71% | 56% |
| "Rock of ages" (Toplady) | 100% | 29% | 44% |
| "When I survey the wondrous cross" (Watts) | 100% | 14% | 25% |
| "I think when I read that sweet story" (Luke) | 0% | 71% | 63% |
| "Nearer, my God, to thee" (Adams) | 71% | 43% | 34% |
| "Awake, my soul, and with the sun" (Ken) | 100% | 57% | 44% |
| "Jesus shall reign where'er the sun" (Watts) | 57% | 29% | 50% |

Wesley's "Hark, the herald angels sing," Augustus Toplady's "Rock of ages," and Isaac Watts's "When I survey the wondrous cross"—are yet favored in high quantities in middle-class and upper-class hymn books (71–100%). All children knew the classics by Thomas Ken (e.g., "Awake, my soul, and with the sun," 44–100% of hymn books) and Isaac Watts (e.g., "Jesus shall reign where'er the sun," 29–57% of hymn books) because they were found in all of their hymn books. Finally, "We thank Thee, Lord, for this fair earth" (this section's epigraph) was found in public school hymn books (e.g., the 1876 Rugby hymn book and the 1903 *Public School Hymn Book*), middle-class hymn books (e.g., *Hymns and Chorales for Schools and Colleges* [1892] and *Children's Service Book* [1897]), and Sunday school books (e.g., the 1879 *Methodist Sunday School Hymn Book* and Winters' *Sunday School Hymnal* [1897]). Because of their general popularity it is quite safe to say that this handful of hymns and many others were known to most Victorian children who yet sang them in varying contexts. It truly was the communal "*We*" who did "thank Thee, Lord, for this fair earth."

In fact, it is their inclusive language which allowed hymns to move so fluidly between class contexts. Conspicuously, these above hymns are relatively free of the class markers identified within various hymns in this chapter, especially in their universal exhortations of praise and supplication incumbent upon all humanity.

Further, the first person offers an inclusivity unbounded by class, a universality and a personal invocation to all who sing the hymn whether alone ("I") or communally ("we"). One can note this subjective, first-person language simply in the titles just given. As Julie Melnyk writes, "hymns are communal ... because of their essentially communal subjectivity" ("Congregational 'We'" 151).[30] The communal nature of first-person plural creates inclusive language, interspersing God's grace to all singers, of any class, denomination, gender, age, or circumstance. Furthermore, through the use of first-person singular, hymn writers invited singers to speak only of themselves, to feel included in the singing without gender or class implications. I will return to a discussion of point of view in future chapters; for now, I emphasize that between language and the universal supplication for grace, hymn-texts thus leveled class barriers.

The critical mass of recent historical research about childhood of the nineteenth century has importantly refocused our attention on class and gender in this context; that "how it was experienced by particular children depended as much on their sex as on class, education, respectability or any other factor" (Davin 217). What a study of hymns exposes, however, is that though children's lives were stratified, their hymn experience was not. Hymns became a common language for children to express theological doctrine, Divine love, human sin, heavenly joys, and childish wonder. Even as their schooling and spaces of worship segregated children across the nation, hymns united them in common quests for life's meaning and purpose.

---

[30]  See Melnyk's unpublished study, "The Congregational 'We': Women's Hymns and the Poetry of Community," 150–52. Melnyk considers the Victorian hymn writer's shift to the communal "we" from the Romantic poet's "I," a change not always appreciated by contemporary clergy John Keble and Christopher Wordsworth. For my purposes, singular and plural are less important than the first-person nature of hymns which thus avoids naming gender or talking *about* another as in the third-person point of view.

# Chapter 2
# Re-Writing the History of Children's Literature:
# Three Periods of Children's Hymnody

... Esther said, "Suppose we say some hymns" ... [and] whispered to herself the beginning of the evening hymn. It was very comforting to say

Keep me, O keep me, King of kings,
Under thine own Almighty wing.

"You are saying hymns, though I asked you not! You are very cross, Esther, I don't like you at all," and [Eddie] pushed her away from him ... Poor Esther!
—Charlotte Yonge, *Leonard, the Lion-Heart* (1856)

Traditionally, scholars of children's literature have described the nineteenth century as one of immense, and linear, progression. As Gillian Avery explains: "In eleven decades ... the world of the juvenile novel changed from a place where all childishness was exorcised, to one where the child was supreme and the adults only shadows" (226). A classic study of historical influences on children and their reading, *A Critical History of Children's Literature* (ed. Cornelia Meigs), defines the literature of the era of 1840–1890 as consisting mainly of fairy tales, nonsense fiction, and adventure stories. The authors fail to address religious works, though, when suggesting the "Widening Horizons" offered to the auspicious late-century child. Patricia Demers divides her two anthologies of children's literature at the year 1850 and argues that, prior to this date, the literature focused on stern instruction while, after this, the literature became one "whose unashamed *raison d'etre* was to give pleasure to children. The Golden Age had dawned" (*From Instruction to Delight* xi).[1] Indeed, the history of childhood and children's literature in nineteenth-century Britain is often shown to be an awakening consciousness, a Romantic dawning, not only to the joy of childhood but the freedom and innocence of children, Alice rising triumphantly after decades of Goody Two-Shoes. As children's literature evolved to reflect changing views of childhood, Evangelical didacticism gave way to Romantic idealism at the end of the century. Largely, the differences being transmitted concerned the ideologies for the child reader, even

---

[1]  Consider this general view found in mid-twentieth-century histories by Avery (1965), as well as in more recent works, such as Penny Brown (186, etc.). Jackson and Demers (*Heaven upon Earth*) even end their commentaries on religious works in 1839 and 1850, respectively. Standard textbooks (*The Riverside Anthology, Literature and the Child*, 4th ed., and *The Broadview Anthology of Victorian Literature*), among others, also subscribe to this view.

*of* the child reader, changing from a concern for the "little sinner" to an exaltation of the pure child.

Recently, critics have begun to dismantle this linear history of children's literature and the late-century "cult of the child," most notably Marah Gubar (*Artful Dodgers: Reconceiving the Golden Age of Children's Literature*) who argues that Golden Age fiction and theater texts "interrogated Romantic ideas about childhood rather than simply affirming them" (209). Aware of the power relations in this "cult"—innocent, passive children dominated by reverential yet manipulative adults—Golden Age authors portrayed both innocent and empowered children, suggesting a willingness to acknowledge children as "precocious actors, authors, editors, and collaborators" and a "hope that the authority of adults does not obviate the possibility that the children can enjoy a measure of agency and creativity" (Gubar 209).

I would suggest, though, that Golden Age fiction and theater are not the only spaces where an empowered child emerges. Situated at a crossroads between the flourishing genre of religious tracts for children and the grand tradition of English hymnody, both of which would culminate in the nineteenth century, children's hymns are vital to our understanding of the era's childhood experiences. Along with religious tracts and Bible stories, hymns taught many generations of children about human sin, Christ's atonement, the love of the omniscient Father, the heavenly afterlife, and other Christian ideals. Notably, studies of nineteenth-century children's literature have consistently neglected this important subgenre.[2] Yet nineteenth-century children's hymns are not only important in understanding the century's theological beliefs and appreciating its poetic output for children, but also a means by which we can, and should, re-examine the changing constructions of childhood during an age of religious and social reformation. An awareness of children's hymnody would help, for instance, in realizing that religious didacticism did not disappear after 1850, for the proliferation of hymn books for children actually increased through the end of the century. In fact, Samuel J. Rogal's bibliography of children's hymn books lists 169 books published between 1800 and 1849, and *597* between 1850 and 1900 (xxxv–xxxvii).

Further, its roots in the hymn tradition give children's hymnody unique qualities which, in fact, temper traditional views of literary history, suggesting a more nuanced understanding of religious literature for children during this century. For one, hymns were uniquely a sung tradition, which had important implications, especially for the early century's Evangelical phase, traditionally seen as a time of preaching to passive learners. Though adults still preached in these hymn books, children were not submissive readers but were singers, physically and mentally involved in the creation of song. The active agency

---

[2]   For scholarship of eighteenth- and nineteenth-century children's literature, see Avery; Jackson; Bottigheimer; Bratton; Brown; Cutt; Demers; Meigs; MacDonald; Pickering; Shavit; Knuth; Paul; Grenby; and Vallone. Hymns are conspicuously absent, except for occasional references to Watts and Anna Laetitia Barbauld's *Hymns in Prose for Children* (1781).

afforded to children was actually emphasized through various strategies of early-century hymn writers. Secondly, taking into account denominational difference and revival interrupts a linear approach to literary history. For instance, the Oxford Movement of mid-century contributed hymn books which, rather than portraying children as either sinful or sinless, de-emphasized the child's qualities altogether and spoke to children as "little adults," paradoxically erasing *and* empowering children in many ways. Thirdly, late-century hymn books very much subscribed to the Romantic view of childhood, hymn books fixating on the "littleness" and innocence of children. Unexpectedly, these hymn books also engaged them with a plethora of challenging theologies. This was because, unlike other literature of the era, hymn books were often compilations of many writers' hymns; in becoming multi-voiced, hymn books took on a fluidity of authorship which presented quite an ideological banquet for the discerning child.

Given that all hymns for children were written by adults for their edification, I am especially intrigued with the interplay between "the adult" and "the child," the elusive boundary between the two, and the results when the former attempts to define and control the latter through writing. Perry Nodelman, among many critics, reminds us that all children's literature is, inevitably, "written for and often about a group to which the writer does not belong" ("Pleasures" 11). Therefore, children's literature is a concept that "is in itself binary and oppositional" since the writer of the text will always be in opposition to the reader for whom he/she writes (11). Karín Lesnik-Oberstein acknowledges the resulting danger in children's literature: "Amusement is not only a force of liberation and pleasure for children but also a concept applied to 'children' and 'adults' as a means for the adult to satisfy a will or need to have the knowledge and control of children's desires, will, and consciousness through voluntary, spontaneous surrender" (76). That children may have appropriated the dictums and art of the adult hymn writer, yet invested the performance of the hymn with their own energy, suggests a breaking down of the binary analyzed by Nodelman. To the extent to which the child is empowered beyond the means of the adult, Lesnik-Oberstein's theory that "the child comes within the adult again" also needs reconsideration, for the child singer does not "come within the adult" but is just as living a presence as the adult hymn writer.

Hymn writers for children, even in the eighteenth century, seemed very aware of the child-adult binary and took intentional stances as they, too, debated the definition of childhood. Isaac Watts's pioneering hymn book for children, *Divine Songs Attempted in an Easy Language for the Use of Children* (1715), begins with an awareness of the child's separate and simpler identity, while John Wesley, 80 years later, argued for writing with adult language and concepts. Together, Watts's and Wesley's comments set the stage for another century's worth of debate on the definition of childhood as seen in various children's hymn books of the nineteenth century.

A study of hymns aptly demonstrates the child's place in society as very much an invention by adults, with a noticeable oscillation occurring throughout the century between Watts's "child-like" and Wesley's "adult-like" templates. Nevertheless, without completely negating identifiable trends in nineteenth-century children's literary history—early-century religious didacticism changing to a Romantic sensibility by late century—a study of children's hymnody shows cracks in the continuum. The sung tradition, denominational difference, and multi-authored collections of hymnody are nuances that color our appreciation of nineteenth-century religious literature, signifying, ultimately, many empowering moments for the child reader/singer. Taking seriously this "crossroads" between children's literature and religious hymnody, in this chapter I will position hymns within both the literary and religious developments of the era. Using both literary and theological explication of key hymn books, I will historicize children's hymnody of the nineteenth century into three distinct phases: the early, Evangelical (Dissenting and Low Church) phase represented by Ann and Jane Taylor's *Hymns for Infant Minds* (1809); the mid-century Oxford (High Church) Movement seen with Isaac Williams's *Ancient Hymns for Children* (1842); and the late-century, Romantic ideologies of the child and Broad-Church liberalism best seen in hymn collections such as *Golden Bells* (1890). Our understanding of children's literature can and should be "re-tuned" with this prolific, yet understudied, genre of the century.

## Part I
## Eighteenth-Century Debates about the Child:
## Watts and Wesley

Puritan, minister, and poet, Isaac Watts (1674–1748) was revolutionary in being "the first composer of original hymnody in the Calvinist tradition" (Wolosky 215). This is no small feat, given that John Calvin had given clear injunctions against any hymns not using biblical texts verbatim (215). Watts incurred criticism yet defended his hymns on spiritual and aesthetic grounds (Marshall and Todd 31–2). Indeed, his "Joy to the world" and "O God our help in ages past" (both 1719) remain extremely popular to this day. Watts wrote one hymn book for children: *Divine Songs Attempted in an Easy Language for the Use of Children* (1715). This book (later titled *Divine and Moral Songs for Children*) uniformly surpassed all other eighteenth-century religious poems for children in its immense popularity. These poems were ground-breaking in their unique focus on "the child"; as Harry Escott writes, "There was nothing even approaching them in content, delightfulness and versification … [T]hey were, despite their being written in an age that understood little of child life, children's praises—not songs *about* children, but praises written *for* them" (216; his italics). Watts's awareness of the child's separate identity is evidenced even in the title, suggesting that children needed a different language from their parents. Unlike writers of harsh Calvinist poetry, Watts encouraged delight as part of edifying religious truths: as he states in the Preface, "There is something so amusing and entertaining in rhymes and metre, that will incline children to make this part of their business a diversion" (Preface, vi). Additionally, the distinctiveness of poetry is pivotal in that it is "longer retained in memory, and sooner recollected. The like sounds, and the like number of syllables, exceedingly assist the remembrance" (vi–vii). Though writing poems, Watts very much had the act of singing in mind: "to sing one in the family, at such time as the parents or governors shall appoint," he writes (vii). Thus he has "confined the verse to the most usual psalm tunes" (vii).[3] The retention rendered by music is especially powerful in that "a song running in the mind, may be an effectual means to keep off some temptation, or to incline to some duty, when a word of Scripture is not upon their thoughts" (vii). According to Escott, it was exactly Watts's ear for verse and meter that set his hymns apart: "Almost all his themes are paralleled in puritan children's books, seventeenth-century devotional verse, and in some Anglican manuals of moral and religious instruction. Watts's originality and supremacy lie in the masterly way in which he manages his versification, and in its metrical variety" (213).

Admittedly, much of Watts's book bears the stamp of his age in its didacticism.[4] Watts reinforces traditional Christian theology in his verses "Praise to God for our Redemption" (Song III) and "Praise for the Gospel" (Song VI) but endorses specific Puritan precepts, too, about original sin and hell. Like his predecessors, Watts often "scares" the child into obedience with his rhetoric: "'Tis dangerous to provoke this God: / His power and vengeance none can tell; / One stroke of His almighty rod / Can send young sinners quick to hell" (Song XIII). The theme of childhood death, as found in James Janeway's *A Token for Children: Being An Exact Account of the Conversion, Holy and Exemplary Lives, and Joyful Deaths of Several Young Children* (1672), for example, is found in Watts's Song X, among others: "There is an hour when I must die, / Nor can I tell how soon 'twill come; / A thousand children, young as I, / Are called by death to hear their doom" (Song X). Such warnings are, of course, to discourage sinful behavior. Sins have their own mildly admonishing poem, including: "scoffing and calling names," "swearing and taking God's name in vain," "idleness and mischief," "pride in clothes," and "complaining." Yet, as Demers and Moyles write, "unlike his predecessors ... his poetry gently softens the Christian message of repentance and gracefully attenuates the stress on fire and brimstone" (*From Instruction* 61).

---

[3]   The hosannas sometimes printed at the end are specifically labeled with a corresponding musical meter (e.g., "Hosannah to King David's Son" is labeled in Long Metre, 88.88, four lines of eight syllables). Once their popularity was established, composers wrote and published books of music scores to accompany each of Watts's poems: for example, see Benjamin Jacob's *Dr. Watts' Divine and Moral Songs* (London, c. 1806; owned by the University of Illinois Music Library).

[4]   The ideologies expressed in Watts's lyrics are, notably, a product of *early* eighteenth-century thinking; as Watts biographer Harry Escott shows (11), arguing a debt to seventeenth-century Calvinist writings for children, including John Bunyan's *A Book for Boys and Girls* (1686) and James Janeway's *A Token for Children* (see Escott 208–12). However, Escott also points out the Anglican influence upon Watts, namely the "catechetical character of some of Watts's songs" (212). For more on Watts, see Escott; Benson; Rogal, "Isaac Watts"; Davie and Stevenson; Shaw; Demers and Moyles; Meigs; and my own unpublished manuscript, "'And Teach the Babes to Sing': The Power of Music in Isaac Watts's *Divine and Moral Songs for Children* (1715)."

What is also original in *Divine and Moral Songs* is Watts's construction of the child. If Calvin wrote that "Infants themselves bring their owne damnation with them from their mother's wombe … Yea, their whole nature is a certain seed of sinne, therefore it cannot but bee hatefull and abominable to God" (qtd. in Escott 201–2), Watts's verses notably open with the lines, "The eternal God will not disdain / To hear an infant sing. / My heart resolves, my tongue obeys, / And angels shall rejoice / To hear their mighty Maker's praise / Sound from a feeble voice" (Song I). Here is the Lockean influence, of constructing children as valuable, active, and purposeful.[5] Specifically, Watts highlights children's pure singing in contrast to the sin of adults: "Children a sweet hosanna sung, / And blessed their Saviour's name; / They gave Him honour with their tongue, / While scribes and priests blaspheme" (Song XIII). Singing is thus an active, potent way for a child to respond to his Maker.

Ultimately, Watts provides a distinctive approach in writing to the child, stating: "I have endeavoured to sink the language to the level of a child's understanding … [and] have designed to profit all" (Preface, viii). Through first-person perspective and active verbs, Watts empowers children: "I sing the wisdom that ordained / The sun to rule the day …" (Song II). Using first-person narration and simple language, though, can sometimes create a scenario where the child must berate herself: "Why should I love my sport so well, / So constant at my play; / And lose my thoughts of heaven and hell, / And then forget to pray?" (Song XXIV). Yet songs such as "The Ant, or Emmet" ask the child to think on an ethical and symbolic level when considering the industriousness of a creature children notice but often abuse: "We tread them to dust, and a troop of them dies, / Without our regard or concern … But I have less sense than a poor creeping ant, / If I take no due care for the things I shall want, / Nor provide against dangers in time" (Moral Song V). Watts caters to a child's concern, then builds it into an analogy of godly living, teaching difficult concepts of sin in the process.

It is significant that the other pillar of English hymnody,[6] Charles Wesley, should take up this debate concerning the child. Yet the founders of Methodism, Charles and his preacher-brother, John Wesley, would be critical of Watts's attempt to fit the language and viewpoint of children within hymns, of writing "down to them." In his *Hymns for Children, and Others of Riper Years* (1763), Charles Wesley is clearly writing to the child of, as his subtitle reads, "riper years." John Wesley succinctly and clearly identifies their contrasting approach when adding a preface to a new edition of his brother's hymn book:

---

[5]    John Locke's *Some Thoughts on Education* (1693) would usher in a new view of childhood of the eighteen century. He wrote that children should not be "hindered from being children, nor from playing and doing as children … They love to be busy, change and variety are what they delight in; curiosity is but an appetite for knowledge, the instrument nature has provided to remove ignorance" (qtd. in Demers and Moyles 77).

[6]    As musicologist Robert Stevenson points out, Watts and Charles Wesley are still the most common eighteenth-century English hymn writers in Lutheran, Presbyterian, Methodist, and even Catholic hymnals (Davie and Stevenson 23).

There are two ways of writing or speaking to children; the one is, to let ourselves down to them; the other, to lift them up to us. Dr. Watts has wrote [sic] in the former way, and has succeeded admirably well, speaking to children as children, and leaving them as he found them. The following Hymns are written on the other plan: they contain strong and manly sense; yet expressed in such plain and easy language, as even children may understand. But when they do understand them, they will be children no longer, only in years and in stature. (John Wesley, Preface to *Hymns for Children*, March 27, 1790)

To implement this theory, Charles Wesley rarely addresses the child directly in his hymns. He refrains from differentiating between an adult or child reader. As in his adult hymn books, Wesley's *Hymns for Children* engage weighty theological subjects, from praises to God (Hymn 1), to the "Creation and the Fall of Man" (2), to "the Redemption of Man" (3), all in the first three hymns. All follow the general Wesleyan creed as found, for example, in Hymn 13: "Unassisted by thy grace / We can only evil do; / Wretched is the human race, / Wretched more than words can show, / Till thy blessing from above / Tells our hearts that God is love." Children are not immune to this evil. Even when hymns occasionally take their point of view, they are clearly fallible: "Almighty God, to thee I cry, / Assist a child's infirmity" (Hymn 10) or "Why should our parents call us good, / And poison us with praise, / When born in sin, by Nature proud, / And void we are of grace?" (Hymn 58). Still found in nineteenth-century hymn books, specific hymns ask "And am I born to die?" (Hymn 59) and "Am I only born to die?" (Hymn 64). Hell's fires do not spare the child: "We shall with many stripes be beat, / The sorest judgment feel, / And of all wicked children meet / The hottest place in hell" (Hymn 48, v. 8). These are harsh Christian precepts used to challenge, even frighten, children. Still, Wesley softens his tone in a section entitled "Hymns for the Youngest," which contains the most frequently excerpted Wesleyan hymn for children during the nineteenth century, "Gentle Jesus, meek and mild / Look upon a little child / Pity my simplicity / Suffer me to come to Thee" (Hymn 72), originally published in John and Charles Wesley's 1742 *Hymns and Sacred Poems*. Though acknowledging the young, Wesley still relies upon lofty rhetoric, as in the second verse: "Fain I would to Thee be brought / Gracious God, forbid it not / Give me, O my God! A place / In the kingdom of Thy grace."

Notably, few of Charles Wesley's children's hymns were ever in the same league with his extremely powerful adult hymns, "Hark, the herald angels sing," "Christ the Lord is risen today," and "Jesus, lover of my soul." Not quite written either for adults or for children, Wesley's hymn book missed its mark altogether,[7] while Watts's hymn book never lost currency throughout the nineteenth century.

---

[7]  As Julian writes of Wesley's attempts for children, "The work was never very popular, and with the exception of 'Gentle Jesus, meek and mild,' has hardly a hymn in it known to modern collections outside the Wesleyan body" (221). Indeed, my own survey, where I tabulated most frequently appearing hymns in representative hymn books throughout the century, showed "Gentle Jesus" to be only in the top 40 throughout the nineteenth century; by the early twentieth, it had slipped to 102.

Yet, together, Wesley's and Watts's two philosophies reveal the complex ideology of the child found in these early hymnals: the child should be considered innocent and open to new ideas while the ideas presented should change the child's natural innocence into an "adult" understanding of human sins and the resulting need for Christian restraint and obedience. This debate would carry into the nineteenth century but, as I will demonstrate, their influence held sway at different times during the century, Watts appealing more to early- and then late-century children's hymn writers; Wesley influencing hymn movements of mid-century.

**Part II**
**The "Active Child":**
**Evangelical Hymn Books, 1809–1840**

As an outgrowth of Wesleyan Methodism that became the social manifestation of the Dissenting and Low Church movements, Evangelicalism held ideological sway primarily during the first half of the nineteenth century, with immense influence not only on religion, but on the politics, moral beliefs, and even culture of the time.[8] As Richard Altick succinctly explains, "Evangelicalism was concerned less with doctrine and the forms of worship than with the way men should live, and much less with life for its own sake than as a preparation for eternity" (165). Sunday schools—"the infrastructure for much Evangelical and Dissenting pressure group politics" (Laqueur xiii)—created a sudden need for religious literature. This literature came in the form of Evangelical tracts, chapbooks,[9] and books

---

[8]  By leading the Methodist movement to revitalize the Anglican church of the eighteenth century, the Wesleys effectively instigated the Evangelical movement which blossomed well into the nineteenth century. By then, the Methodists became the largest of the Dissenting (or Nonconformist) sects to exist in opposition to the Church of England, though Evangelicalism influenced a revival within the Church (the so-called "Low Church" movement). Nonconformists also included Baptists, Presbyterians, and Congregationalists (descended from the Puritans or Calvinists). Increasing rapidly throughout the first three decades of the nineteenth century, Nonconformity had surpassed the Anglican church in numbers by the 1840s (Helmstadter, "Orthodox Nonconformity" 69). The basic doctrinal beliefs of the Evangelical movement included "the need for conversion, the authority of the Bible, the immediacy of an individual's relationship to God, the assurance of salvation, and the necessity of social involvement and activism" (Melnyk, *Victorian Religion* 185–6). For nuances between moderates and extremists, though, see Boyd Hilton, *The Age of Atonement*, ch. 1. By late century the number of Nonconformists fell and "relative to the total population, membership began to decline from the 1880s" (Rivers and Wykes 12).

[9]  Chapbooks, or penny histories, were small, cheaply printed books made by folding several sheets into quarters (or more), resulting in eight to 16 pages, often illustrated with woodcuts, and usually sold for a halfpenny or penny. Though publishers first featured unsavory stories and fantastic tales in chapbooks, eventually religious publishers followed suit and published Christian stories, poetry, and hymns in chapbooks (Watts's *Divine Songs* was frequently published as a chapbook in the early nineteenth century). For more about chapbooks, see Shavit 158–76; Jackson 67–70; Knuth 3–4; and Demers and Moyles 77–8.

published by the Religious Tract Society (RTS), the Society for the Preservation of Christian Knowledge (SPCK), and the Sunday School Union (SSU), among other organizations (as explored in Chapter 1). Writers of these religious tracts and verses, the "Sunday School Moralists" (Demers and Moyles 186), included Anna Laetitia Barbauld (*Hymns in Prose for Children* [1781]), Sarah Trimmer (*Fabulous Histories* [1786] and various works through the posthumous publications of 1812–1819), Hannah More (*The Shepherd of Salisbury-Plain* [1795] and other works through 1825), and Mary Sherwood (*The History of the Fairchild Family* [1818–1847], contributions to *The Youth's Magazine*, and other works). More's establishment of the Cheap Repository Tracts in 1795 created a cheap market to compete with chapbooks and broadsides such that sales of religious tracts, pamphlets, and books escalated in the ensuing decades: "Thus, out of religious tracts emerged a new model of the children's system—that of the commercially successful religious story" (Shavit 172). The didactic and overtly religious stories of More and her contemporaries influenced the next generation of Evangelical writers "whose work contributed substantially to nineteenth-century tract literature for children [of] … explicit and topical preaching" (Demers, *A Garland* 135): for example, Maria Louisa Charlesworth (*Ministering Children* [1854]) and Charlotte Maria Tucker (or "A. L. O. E."; *Precepts in Practice; or Stories Illustrating the Proverbs* [1858]), among many other works). Hesba Stretton was a key writer for the Religious Tract Society (*Little Meg's Children* [1868], etc.) and continued to publish up until 1900, though the Evangelical influence would dwindle by 1870 (Cutt 180).

Evangelical literature thus dominated children's literature of the early nineteenth century, becoming, according to Margaret Cutt, "a calculated part of the Evangelical determination to reform and convert the nation and eventually the world" (20). Further, the message of much of the tract novels of the day was one of "controlled piety" in which children learned restraint and resignation (Cutt 20). Early-century tales, as bound by Tract Society stipulations, kept to simplistic teachings, "assuming the reader's ignorance or immaturity" (Cutt 185). Children's hymns of the Evangelical era complement religious tracts and prose in their overt didacticism, the expounding of fundamental Christian principles of human sin, Christ's atonement, and the heavenly end.

Where they diverge, I will argue, has much to do with the innate qualities of their respective genres. Vallone stresses "the *form* of Evangelical/religious fiction as promoting a vigorously ideological program of social control by attempting to prescribe and regulate the 'nourishment' upon which children feed" (75). Though this point is not meant by Vallone, I would draw attention to the form of tract literature as written works meant for reading which physically promoted control and restraint: a subdued child bent over the book or tract, reading. Penny Brown suggests that early-century fiction inculcated passivity also through its child-adult posturing: "the child [was] the passive recipient of instruction, seen almost exclusively from the viewpoint of the adult narrator" (186). Specifically, writers contrived dialogues in which the "child's inquisitiveness is artificially manipulated by the author to lead to the desired educational outcome, often beyond the limits of credibility" (Brown 14). As Knuth concludes, Evangelical writers "conveyed little optimism about children" and "den[ied] them zest and possibilities" (31).[10]

One could use Barbauld's *Hymns in **Prose*** (my emphasis in bold) to illustrate this point. Doubting "whether poetry ought to be lowered to the capacities of children ... for the very essence of poetry is an elevation in thought and style above the common standard," Barbauld instead chose to share religious sentiments in prose, intending them still "to be committed to memory, and recited" (Preface, iv–v). Their memorization would be made more challenging if one agrees with Watts that rhyme, meter, and tune aid such attempts. Even the imagery of music is denied the fictional child when "birds ... warble" yet children "open [their] lips in His praise" to speak; clearly, "we ... can praise Him better" (Barbauld, Hymn II). Through Barbauld's frequently used tactic of question-answer hymns, in which the adult narrator asks and answers the questions, the reading child learns very literal, straightforward messages. Even the figurative is elucidated for the child: "But who is the shepherd's Shepherd? ... God is the shepherd's Shepherd" (Hymn III). Children appear unable to recognize even what Rousseau would argue was innate, the beauty of nature: "Come, and I will show you what is beautiful. It is a rose fully blown," says the adult leader (Hymn IV). When the child is allowed a voice in rare dialogues, he is presented as naïve:

> [adult] Child of reason, whence comest thou? What has thine eye observed? ...
>
> [child, presumably] I have been wandering along the meadows ... the fields were bright with summer, and glowing with beauty.
>
> [adult] Didst thou see nothing more? Didst thou observe nothing besides? Return again, child of reason, for there are greater things than these.—God was among the field; and didst thou not perceive Him? ... (Hymn VI)

Whereas natural beauty was being taught in Hymn IV, the presiding adult has changed the question in Hymn VI such that the child is in the wrong again: here, this adult speaker denies the astute observations of the child in favor of didactic interrogation. Thus, though Vallone states that these hymns were "written for the young child ... in a form which celebrates harmony and beauty" (75), the hymns themselves do not seem to celebrate the child.[11]

---

[10]    We can see this tactic in Mrs. Sherwood's *The History of the Fairchild Family* (vol. 1, 1818) where adults manipulate the dialogue and scenes to teach children lessons through often gruesome stories (of a brother murdered, of a child burned to death). Notably, each chapter ends with a hymn and even despite a few harsh hymns of Watts's ("Almighty God, thy piercing eye," Hymn XIV), their overall effect is to interject gentler, more inclusive messages where adults and children sing and learn together, often through adult hymns (e.g., "O God our help in ages past," Hymn XX).

[11]    See Vallone's full argument in "A humble Spirit under Correction," 72–95. I am clearly taking a more critical approach towards this hymn book than Rod McGillis in "Editor's Comments: That Great Writer in the English Language" (163).

I will argue that hymns, in contrast to prose Evangelical literature of the day, generally convey more confidence in, and "zest" for, their child singer. For one, poetry by its nature allows for more interpretational space than literal prose: imagery replaces the concrete; questions may be metaphorically answered, or not answered at all; and speakers can be anonymous. Further, in singing, both the child's mind and body can respond to theological lessons of repentance, gratitude, and praise, rather than mentally and silently receiving such ideas through reading and recitation. Hymn writers, both consciously and unconsciously, empowered children in the daily, zestful singing of hymns.

While there was a dearth of hymn-book publications between Watts and the end of the century (Barbauld's being a possible exception), the children's hymn book as a genre exploded in the next century due to Evangelical reform, the Sunday school movement in particular, and the increase in hymn singing as a liturgical practice in all denominations. Yet these hymn books still demonstrated a debt to Isaac Watts in their attempt to make serious doctrine "simple" for the child reader. For instance, the editor of *The Sunday-Scholar's Companion; Being a Selection of Hymns, From Various Authors, for the Use of Sunday Schools* (1822) shows concern about other hymn books (potentially referring to those by the Wesleys) which "contain a large proportion of Hymns, unintelligible in their language to the youthful understanding." The editor further criticizes hymns that "breathe the mature experience of eminent Christians, and which … ought never to be found upon the thoughtless tongues of our Pupils generally" (Preface, A2–3). Instead, in this book, "poetry has necessarily, in some instances, been sacrificed to simplicity; yet, it is hoped, without degenerating to coarseness" so as to more ably reach the child audience (A3). Likewise, in *A Selection of Hymns and Poetry for the Use of Infant Schools and Nurseries* (1838), a hymn book compiled for the Model Infant School, King's Cross, London, Elizabeth Mayo (anonymous in the first edition) indicates that "the desire of the Committee [is] that the pleasure children so generally find in verse should be early consecrated to the Lord" such that "lighter pieces" have been included to instill "a grateful perception of the wisdom and goodness of the Creator" (iii–iv). Very Evangelical in content, her rhetoric of "pleasure" and "lightness" suggests a child-based approach. Watts's theories thus dominated early-century hymnody.

Watts's most important successors were Jane and Ann Taylor who published their *Hymns for Infant Minds* in 1809. This hymn book aptly illustrates the basic approach of Evangelical hymn books and their constructions of the child. Daughters of a Congregational minister, the Taylors wrote a series of books for children, mostly middle-class, including *Original Poems* (1805), *Rhymes for the Nursery* (1806), and *Original Hymns for Sunday Schools* (1812). Julie Melnyk, in her unpublished study, "The Congregational 'We': Women's Hymns and the Poetry of Community," points out the opportunities for women hymn writers during this period: "Religious writing had long been socially-acceptable, even socially-approved for women, and British women hymn writers enjoyed a certain equality of treatment in the 'marketplace' for hymns" (5). Jane and Ann Taylor would begin a tradition of women's contributions to hymnody, children's hymnody being especially linked to female nurturing.

Yet, to even attempt another hymn book for children when Watts's book was still at the height of its popularity indeed suggests some daring. In an apologetic yet confident "Advertisement" to the first edition of *Hymns for Infant Minds*, initially published anonymously, the two sisters justify their book:

> The "Divine Songs" of Dr. Watts, so beautiful, and so universally admired, almost discourage, by their excellence, a similar attempt; and lead the way, where it appears temerity to follow. But as the narrow limits to which he confined himself excluded a number of useful subjects, the following Hymns, though with much diffidence, are presented to the Public. (iii)

Its own success suggests that their confidence—not the so stated "diffidence"—was well founded. Indeed, its success is staggering: 22 editions by 1830, 35 editions by 1844, 52 editions by 1877.[12] The most popular hymns continued to be printed in hymn books up until the end of the century. In my study, the most popular hymns were "Great God, and wilt thou condescend / To be my Father and my Friend" (Hymn V),[13] appearing in 25% of children's hymn books throughout the century, and "I thank the goodness and the grace" (Hymn I), appearing in 23%. About a handful held solidly in the 12–17% categories (e.g., "A sinner, Lord, behold I stand," "How long sometimes a day appears," and "This is a precious book indeed"). A few less common hymns could even be found in later hymnals: one hymn rarely anthologized before—"How kind in all His works and ways"—found appeal to editors of an 1895 hymnal while eight of the 70 Taylor hymns lingered in early twentieth-century hymnals.

The Taylors' hymns were popular because they so well addressed their child reader, possibly as young as the nursery age. Their preface delineates this intent, asserting the purpose of adapting "evangelical truths to the wants and feelings of childhood, in language which it understands ... with the sacrifice of poetry to simplicity, wherever they stood opposed." Their opening hymn takes up this "simple" approach, while also stamping the English, Christian status

---

[12]  Their popularity and influence are shown in the number of hymns reproduced in other hymn books throughout the century, with at least two pirated copies that I have discovered: the 1821 *Hymns for the use of the Providence Sunday Schools Selected from Various Authors* which reproduces many of the Taylors' hymns and uses their preface verbatim; and an 1842 American chapbook, *Infant Hymns, designed for Young Children by Dr. Watts*, which actually consists of six hymns by the Taylors. Further, the 1810 copy of *Hymns for Infant Minds* I am using, now held at the Lilly Library, Indiana University, Bloomington, contains a handwritten poem in its cover, "To Ann and Jane," written by James Montgomery, himself a famous hymn writer ("Angels from the realms of glory," etc.). His intense praise for these "minstrels" who have brought "unborn millions" to God shows his own literary debt to them.

[13]  I am using the second edition, 1810, and the Roman numerals refer to its numbering system.

of its audience: "I thank the goodness and the grace / Which on my birth have smil'd / And made me, in these Christian days / A happy English child" (v. 1). The rest of the book engages in similar early-century Evangelical ideological leanings, teaching of morality, sin, and the afterlife, much as Wesley's book did.

Yet it follows Watts's approach in bringing these challenging topics "down" to the comprehension of a child. One tactic is to use first-person narration, though often as confessionals. The child reads, "Lord, I confess before thy face / How naughty I have been" (Hymn IV) and "There's evil, that I never knew / Before, within my breast" (Hymn XV). The Taylors also rely on visual imagery. For instance, Christ's redemption on the cross is vividly delineated to induce guilt and gratitude from the child, as in Hymn XXV: "See! the blood is falling fast / From his forehead and his side! / Listen! He has breath'd his last! / With a mighty groan he died!" (v. 3). Using vivid descriptions, the Taylors help the child to "see" the blood and "listen" to the groans of Christ. Culpability is cast on all humans, including children, now in second person: "You were wretched, weak, and vile; / You deserv'd his holy frown" (v. 5). Yet Jesus forgives: "But he saw you with a smile, / And to save you hasten'd down" (v. 5). To those not embracing the redemptive nature of Christ, God is truly an angry God, a scare tactic for children: "And those who dar'd to disobey / Be dragg'd before thine angry eyes!" (Hymn XXXV, v. 1). Given the tenuousness of life at this time, the Taylors write "A Child's Prayer in Sickness" (Hymn XLI), "A Hymn of Praise for Recovery" (XLII), even a hymn "For a Dying Child" (XLV). When a mother dies, the child voices extreme guilt: "Oh! If she would but come again, / I think I'd vex her so no more" (XXXI; see frontispiece image, Figure 2.1). The dying child is yet reminded of the glorious purity of his final home: "O take this guilty soul of mine, / That now will soon be gone, / And wash it clean, and make it shine, / With heav'nly garments on" (XLV, v. 4). All sentiments are consistent with the Congregational upbringing of the Taylors as inherited from Calvinist theology.

Again, their literary approach remains consistent with Watts's child-focused one. Their lessons are those relevant to the young: hymns on "The way to cure Pride" (Hymn XXI), "Against Impatience and Anger" (XVI), "On attending Public Worship" (XIX), "Against Selfishness" (LVII), and the like. Hymns use dialogue: Hymn XXI is written in the form of questions and answers, clearly labeled "Child" and "Mama," presumably to allow for two voices: "Tell me, Mama, if I must die" to which the "Mama" austerely replies, "'Tis true, my love, that you must die; / The God who made you, says you must; / And every one of us shall lie, / Like the dear baby, in the dust" (vv. 1, 3). Clearly, the Taylors intend to use "great plainness of speech" (see their epigraph), as Watts had encouraged, language that is clear and unnuanced, as seen also in one of their more popular hymns, "The Bible" (Hymn VIII):

> This is a precious book indeed!
> Happy the child that loves to read!
> 'Tis God's own word, which he has giv'n
> To shew [sic] our souls the way to heav'n! (v. 1)
>
> *******

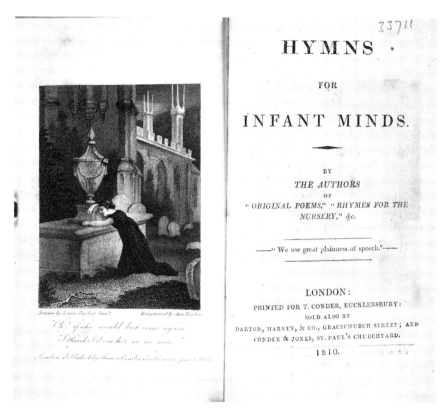

Figure 2.1      Frontispiece to Ann and Jane Taylor's *Hymns for Infant Minds*
                (1809). 2nd edition (1810). Courtesy of The Lilly Library, Indiana
                University, Bloomington, Indiana.

> It tells us how the world was made;
> And how good men the Lord obey'd:
> There his Commands are written, too,
> To teach us what we ought to do. (v. 2)

Simple couplets and iambic tetrameter underscore uncomplicated concepts of "good men" obeying the Lord, and biblical texts teaching us "what we ought to do." Other poems invoke simple ABAB rhymes and iambic pentameter to keep the hymns singable and easily memorized.

Simple verse, perhaps, but this does not imply a "simple" child, not when children are associated with the great and mighty: "The poorest child, the greatest king, /Alike must humbly own" (Hymn X). Though God's "condescension" to a child is emphasized repeatedly (a term used not less than 10 times in these hymns), the Taylors use the nineteenth-century religious denotation of the word, as a courteous "affability to one's inferiors" (OED, 2nd ed.), and never to diminish the worth of the child: "But what a condescending King! / Who, though he reigns so high, / Is pleas'd when little children sing, / And listens to their cry" (Hymn LI).

Even the question/answer approach of so many hymns, though overtly didactic, empowers the child voice, not necessarily when he/she is parroting back well-worn theology but when it becomes apparent that the little child is finally answering her own questions, in contrast to Barbauld's child reader who never does. Take these various examples, as when the child asks, in the fairly popular Hymn XXII, "Among the deepest shades of night / Can there be one who sees my way?" and then answers the question and completes the rhymes with: "Yes;—God is like a shining light, / That turns the darkness into day." The child of faith answers with great assertion, "But where is Jesus?—Is he dead? / O no! he lives in heaven above" (Hymn XLIX). In poetry, the child answers his question: "Lord, what is life?—'tis like the bow / That glistens in the sky: / We love to see its colours glow; / But while we look, they die" (Hymn LV). Rote answers, perhaps, but with enough poetic imagination (to compare life to a rainbow), poetry (double rhymed ABAB), and confidence ("Yes") to give further appreciation of the "sinful" child who may be in more control of his own rescuing than always recognized. This point is highlighted when comparing the hymns, many by the Taylors, with the catechisms given directly before each, in the 1859 *Soft Showers on the Opening Bud*. Here, straight questions with rote, unimaginative answers are provided, such as (adult) "When Pilate asked what evil he had done, did they tell him of any?"; (child) "No they only said, 'Crucify him.'" The Taylors' subsequent hymn ("When, for some little insult given") is quite a breath of fresh air: dogma directed at the young and also poetically pleasing in comparison: "Dear Saviour, may I learn of thee / My temper to amend, / But speak of that pardoning word for me / Whenever I offend."

This empowerment further derives from the inherent genre of hymnody. Written in verses of four lines of tetrameter alternating with trimeter, the Taylors' hymns meshed easily with common-meter tunes (86.86, alternating eight- and six-syllable lines). Teachers and parents would be able to pick a well-known tune, then lead their choristers through a hymn in *Hymns for Infant Minds* through music.[14] Though Hymn XVIII refers to "learning my hymns to *say*" (my italics), even more hymns refer to their being sung (Hymns II, VII, IX, XIX, XXX, LI, LXV, and LXIX). Hymn XXX describes "An Evening Hymn for a Little Family":

Now condescend, Almighty King,
    To bless this little throng;
And kindly listen while we sing
    Our pleasant ev'ning song. (v. 1)
We come to own the Pow'r divine
    That watches o'er our days;

---

14   Some of the Taylors' hymns can be found to specific tunes in hymn books: for example "I thank the goodness and the grace" is set to "Cherubini" in the 1843 *Juvenile Harmonist* (Hymn 9), while "A sinner, Lord, Thy gracious call" and "When little Samuel woke" are set to "Dunfermline" and "Adoration," respectively, in *The Methodist Sunday-School Hymn and Tune-Book* (Hymns 273 and 215).

> For this our feeble voices join
> 　In hymns of cheerful praise. (v. 2)

Music captures the ear of the condescending King and elicits blessing therewith. The quality of the singing ("feeble") is not as important as the intent of the praise ("cheerful").

In fact, the great agency of singing can threaten hymn-texts' transparency, causing some anxious moments for the Taylors. In a fairly common hymn anthologized from their hymn book (13% of children's hymn books in my study), the Taylors lament "Against Wandering Thoughts": "Yet foolish thoughts my heart beguile; / And when I pray, *or sing* [my italics], / I'm often thinking, all the while, / About some other thing" (Hymn IX, v. 2). Along with prayer, singing can be deceptive, hiding inner, un-Christian thoughts, the Taylors acknowledge. Unlike silent prayer, though, singing can be further deceptive in that its text is usually counterfeited from another source, in contrast to prayer which is thought to be spontaneous and original. The child singer well knows that an adult (like the Taylors) has created a text to tunefully repeat, and may rebel against the act, at least in thought, or even, theoretically, through the musical expression (through personal dynamics, facial expression, etc.). The Taylors, in Hymn XX, have the child repeat, "From early infancy, I know, / A rebel I have been," with the potential to grow worse ("I fear I grow in sin").[15] Ironically, music allows the space for these tendencies to become more masked—or more manifest—during the act of singing, the very form Taylors use to incite the children to holiness.

I end with a close look at their most famous hymn in hymn books throughout the century, "Great God and wilt Thou condescend" (Hymn V) in which many of these qualities become apparent. The first verse invokes the condescension of God to children:

> Great God, and wilt thou condescend
> To be my Father, and my Friend?—
> I a poor child, and thou so high,
> The Lord of earth, and air, and sky!

Through empowering first-person perspective, the child forms her own question, distinguishing the "poor child" from the omnipotent God, "Lord of earth, and air, and sky," as a child would comprehend the Divinity. The alliterative terms "Father" and "Friend" qualify this omnipotence, though, with familial tenderness. The former persona is further explored in the next stanza:

> Art thou my Father?—Canst thou bear
> To hear my poor imperfect pray'r;

---

15　Consider other hymns in which the Taylors express anxieties for children's covert rebellious tendencies: IV ("Forgive my … wicked thoughts"); XI ("Pride / Loves deep within the heart to hide"); XII (to "conquer what is wrong? / Then look within"); XVII ("folly dwells within").

Or stoop to listen to the praise
That such a little one can raise?

The question continues, "Art thou my Father?—Canst thou bear…?" This verse then invokes the medium of singing as a conduit up ("praise … raise") to this Father. The lisping of the "p's" ("poor," "pray'er," "praise") further shows the imperfection of the "little one's" praise, as reasons why "thou" might *not* listen. In the next stanza, the child answers her question:

Art thou my Father?—Let me be
A meek, obedient child to thee;
And try, in word, and deed, and thought,
To serve and please thee as I ought.

The next two stanzas also begin, "Art thou my Father" as the child ultimately confirms her "Father" and, despite her self-deprecating assonance ("meek, obedient"), determines her own course of *action*: "to serve and please thee"; "depend / Upon the care of such a friend" (v. 4), determining even at the last, "To be thy better child, above" (v. 5). The child has been empowered to answer her question, to create the gentler Father-figure she desires,[16] and to chart her own, Christian course. Simple verse in AABB couplets and iambic tetrameter lends itself to singing and, indeed, this hymn was found in as late as the 1894 *Hymns for Children with Opening & Closing Services*, suggesting how singable it continued to be.[17]

The Taylors' hymn book represents but one influential hymn book among many published through the 1840s.[18] Various other hymn writers also held to a Wattsian approach to hymnody: very moral, didactic, yet simple approach to

---

[16]    Bottigheimer examines the image of God in children's Bibles, suggesting the "new gentleness read onto God's character" in eighteenth- and nineteenth-century Bibles, though "an angry God" image "had loomed far too large … simply to disappear" (63).

[17]    One tune to which it is set is "Holley" (in *The Methodist Sunday-School Hymn and Tune-Book*, 1879, Hymn 70). A tune in E-flat major, its harmonies are generally created by thirds. Its third line ascends up the scale to a C5 (C above middle C), perhaps to reflect, in the first verse, "Thou so high" in contrast to the "poor child" represented by an F4 and E4. Due to the repetition of music, however, this same ascending scale also highlights the various actions of the child: "deed and thought" (v. 4) and "to do and be" (v. 5).

[18]    Other hymn books of early decades that reflect theological seriousness told through a simpler approach include: *The Sunday-Scholar's Companion* (1822); John Mann, *Original Hymns: Adapted for Social Prayer-Meetings, Missionary Services, Sunday-Schools and Christians in General* (1828); *The Sunday School Union Hymn Book* (1835); William Gadsby, ed., *A Selection of Hymns from Various Authors for the Use of Sunday Schools* (1836); Elizabeth Mayo, *A Selection of Hymns and Poetry for the Use of Infant Schools and Nurseries* (1838); [Dorothy Ann Thrupp, ed.], *Hymns for the Young Selected for the Purpose of Being Committed to Memory* (1839); Jane E. Leeson, *Hymns and Scenes of Childhood or A Sponsor's Gift* (1842); Cecil Frances Alexander, *Hymns for Little Children* (1848); and [Miss Harrison, ed.], *The Weston Hymn Book for Children* (1849).

children's hymn books. They hoped to rescue the child from sin and damnation amidst undemanding poetry and imagery. Still, the tradition of singing suggested at least *a space* for the child's active, even rebellious, possibilities against Evangelical ardor.

## Part III
## The "Adult Child":
## Mid-Century Tractarian and Methodist Hymn Books for Children

A linear approach to children's literature of the nineteenth century suggests the dwindling of Evangelical texts and an increasing embrace of Romantic, Blakean views of the child, culminating in the "Golden Age" of children's literature by the end of the century. Acknowledging children's hymnody in this equation, though, reminds the scholar of several bumps in the road, moments when the focus on children disappeared altogether, namely, when Watts's philosophy of child-like simplicity was replaced by Wesley's philosophy of speaking "up" as to an adult. Two such periods also coincided with denominational upsurge and revival: the Oxford Movement and the peaking of the Methodists mid-(nineteenth)-century. Both Protestant groups created a plethora of children's hymn books in order to inculcate new generations of followers away from the Established Church. As C. John Sommerville writes, "It is never long before movements realize that future success will depend on attracting the younger generation" (108). Hymns were one way for religious movements to reach their youngest recruits.

The first instance was the Oxford Movement of the 1830s and 1840s, which urged High Church, Anglo-Catholic focus on ritual, tradition, and the authority of the church.[19] It is notable that even as the movement was gaining momentum with the publication of *Tracts for the Times* (1833–1841), by John Henry Newman and others, various "Tractarian" children's hymn books were also being conceived and published. Indeed, "if Tractarian children were to sing hymns at all, new ones had to be written; for, to express the formulas of the new school, there were no English hymns to be had," points out early twentieth-century hymnologist John Julian (222), confirming Sommerville's above observation and suggesting hymns' specific ability to reach the young.

The Yonge family, neighbors to Tractarian leader John Keble, contributed to this upsurge in Tractarian publishings. Its most famous member, novelist Charlotte

---

[19]     Begun in 1833 with John Keble's "National Apostasy" sermon, and associated with many middle-class academics from Oxford University, the Oxford Movement urged a revival within the Church of England based on church authority and tradition, honoring the church's Roman Catholic roots. Various High Church leaders, including John Henry Newman, published *Tracts for the Times* from 1833 to 1841, leading to the term "Tractarianism." For helpful overviews of the different sects and states of religion in the Victorian era, see Melnyk, *Victorian Religion*, and the various essays in Paz, *Nineteenth-Century English Religious Traditions*.

Mary Yonge, is sometimes referred to as the novelist of the Oxford Movement because her novels so often convey the ideals of High Church Anglicanism within their social and domestic settings, "spreading the faith in fiction" (*Oxford Dictionary of the Christian Church* 1506). Yonge does so through her focused portrayals of children and domestic scenes where, significantly, "pious middle-class families [consist] of active but generally docile youngsters" (Demers, *A Garland* 167). Within these contexts, Yonge frequently refers to church music; fiction such as *Henrietta's Wish; or, Domineering* (1850), *The Daisy Chain* (1856), and *Leonard, the Lion-Heart* (short tale, 1856) frequently reference hymn singing as shown in the epigraph to this chapter. In *Henrietta's Wish*, for example, music is associated with various holy days (81, 94, 114, 214), the carolers sing on Christmas Eve (94), and the characters read hymn, biblical, and poetic reflections (215, 229, 199, 266, 288) such as Keble's important collection of meditative poems, *The Christian Year* (1827) (262).

It is significant, however, that we rarely see Henrietta's family *sing* hymns, and that Esther clearly suggests *whispering* hymns to her brother in *Leonard, the Lion-Heart*, metaphorical battles even ensuing with the suggestion (see epigraph). Indeed, Keble's poems, though made into hymns by others (such as the famous "Sun of my soul," to be discussed in Chapter 3), were intended to be read only. This approach to hymnody affected children's hymn singing as well. Charlotte's mother, Frances M. Yonge, anonymously edited[20] a children's High Church hymn book, *The Child's Christian Year* (1841), a volume to which Charlotte herself contributed (Charlotte M. Yonge Fellowship online). Clearly meant to imitate Keble's famous work in title and approach, its hymns are referred to as "religious poetry" and encouraged to be "read," thus eschewing the relationship with music (1, 3). Keble is even used as preface-writer where he addresses the importance of "preparing another generation for something like a revival of Discipline" to be "trained up in the tone of the ancient Church" (Preface). He re-defines the "Hymn" against earlier attempts "both in doctrine and manner very unworthy of that sacred name" (probably referring to the simplicity of Watts and emotionalism of Evangelical hymns).

Perhaps most importantly, the book reflects the divergent approach of Tractarian hymn books in treating the child audience as adult-like, needing great intellect even to comprehend the profound verse. Thus, these hymns diverge at once from Evangelical hymns and even from Tractarian fiction if Charlotte Yonge's fictionalized "docile" children are the example; indeed, Yonge reportedly viewed "intellectual hubris [as] a sin" (Knuth 41). Yet as the Preface to *The Child's Christian Year* reads: "The first impression on looking over this little book, will probably be that the hymns are too difficult ... [Yet] It should likewise be considered that such subjects cannot be lowered to the level of childish minds without more

---

[20]   Please see my "Writing for, yet Apart: Nineteenth-Century Women's Contentious Status as Hymn Writers and Editors of Hymn books for Children," 50–59, for an extensive discussion of the restrictions and yet subtle, re-inscribed power of anonymous women editors of children's hymn books.

or less of irreverence ... In the school for which the hymns were collected, they have been found useful in leading to questions and explanations" (3). So, like the Evangelical hymnists, difficult topics of sin and death are included, but now these are not couched in the simple, "childish" rhetoric of Watts. As one example, the Christmas Day hymn reminds children of women's "doom" in childbirth as descended from Eve: yet "Mothers no more their pangs shall blame, / By which the world's Redeemer came" (v. 3). Though an important message for Yonge, perhaps, this is certainly not the tactic of Watts for children.

Neither do Tractarians disguise their antipathy for Watts. An Anglican clergyman, Tractarian leader, and follower of neomedievalism, John Mason Neale wrote his original *Hymns for Children* (1842, 1844, and 1846) with the express desire "to free our poor children from the yoke of Watts" (Neale viii). Also known for his translation of hymns from Latin and Greek, his much-praised "Jerusalem the golden!," a translation of Bernard of Cluny's work, was an immensely popular inclusion in hymn books for children yet was a serious poem without reference to children (to be discussed more in Chapter 6).

Though either Yonge's or Neale's hymn books would repay close analysis, I turn to one final, and important, hymn book for children of the Oxford Movement that also reflects the above characteristics, Isaac Williams's *Ancient Hymns for Children* (1842). Labeled by Tractarian scholar G. B. Tennyson as "the third of the Tractarian poetic triumvirate [with Newman and Keble]" (138), Williams contributed two tracts to the Tractarian series. Tract 80, "On Reserve in Communicating Religious Knowledge," was taken as direct criticism of Evangelical emotionalism, a volatile controversy which would deprive Williams of Keble's seat as Oxford Professor of Poetry in 1841. Williams would go on to write a number of Tractarian devotional books, such as *The Altar* (1847), but no scholarly attention has been given to his *Ancient Hymns for Children*.[21]

In contrast to Taylors' *Hymns for Infant Minds*, Williams's hymn book was directed, most probably, to an older, middle- to upper-class, educated child audience (as Julian argues about Yonge's hymn book, 222). It points to the past, as the title indicates, to timeless lessons of Christian belief, rather than the morality lessons characteristic of the Taylors. Further, these are translations, as opposed to original hymns, though Williams still relies on original poetry and creativity in his work. His stated objective was to select hymns that seemed "the most easy and suitable for children," altering as needed "for that purpose" (Preface). Notably, though, he has translated hymns from an older Latin text which he had also mined for an adult hymn book, *Hymns translated from the Paris Breviary* (1839),

---

[21]     G. B. Tennyson's *Victorian Devotional Poetry: The Tractarian Mode* (1981) is a pivotal book in reconsidering Tractarian poetry, which Tennyson defines as "devotional" rather than "religious" poetry, a term he considers too imprecise. See chapter 5, which closely analyzes Williams's Reserve tract and Gothic-revival poetry. More recently, *Victorian Poetry* devoted an entire issue to Tractarian poets (vol. 44, no. 1, Spring 2006, guest-edited by Kirstie Blair and Emma Mason). None of these works mention Williams's hymn book for children.

further suggesting that there was very little specifically for children in this new collection.[22] In fact, the word "children" is only used in the title and in one hymn ("Christ leaving His Apostles"). Williams's selections, as well as the content and form of the hymns themselves, suggest a Wesleyan view of children. Williams addresses them as adults who are able to embrace the challenges of Tractarianism.

In terms of content, this book engages in various High Church theologies. This is obvious even from the title page, which shows a priest in High Church robes. Within the book itself, rites of the church year are paramount, many hymns pertaining to holy days: Christ's Birth, the Epiphany, the Crucifixion and Ascension of Christ, and Whit-Sunday. Its approach, too, is very much High Church intellectualism in contrast to Low Church emotionalism. Indeed, Tractarian writings may strike the "modern reader as less religious and more literary than their Evangelical counterparts" (Melnyk 24). As the architect of the doctrine of Reserve—encompassing reverence, mystery, and analogy as well as reticence (Tennyson 142–3)—Williams crafts hymns full of subtlety and imagery.

One example is his hymn "Christ crucified" in which Christ's sacrifice is rendered more figurative and poetic than the literal vividness of the Passion found in Evangelical hymn books such as that by the Taylors: "The sorrows of the Crucified, / The wounds of Him that died; / Him, who a willing victim came / To die a spotless Lamb" (33). Told in symbolism ("spotless Lamb"), the literal "wounds of Him" are unemotionally portrayed. This High Church approach explains the focus on saints—St. Stephen and St. John the Evangelist—whose own tragic deaths are similarly cloaked in figurative language: "Death, kind angel, watching nigh, / Sweetly clos'd his tranquil eye" ("St. Stephen" 19). Figurative language, of course, challenges the comprehension of children more comfortable with the literal. Frequent allusions to the sexual organs of divine figures—the Virgin's womb, Christ's circumcision—also indicate a more mature audience. Similarly, Williams avoids moments that would traditionally be rendered child-like—such as a nativity scene laden with animals, seen in the popular Christmas hymns "The Friendly Beasts" (from the twelfth century) and "Away in the Manger" (attributed to Martin Luther). Williams's own nativity hymn, "Christ in the Manger," instead re-directs the literal imagery of beasts to the figurative Sheep: "From dark foes that seek Thy sheep, / Sacred Shepherd, save and keep" (16). Children are encouraged to think beyond the comforting nativity to the unsettling Crucifixion, from literal animals to the figurative Lamb.

In fact, the hymn book makes only two mentions of childhood. One appears in "Christ leaving His Apostles," in which "Little children" are told "not [to] fear" as they prepare for death themselves since "He shall hence before you go, / And take you with Him to dwell" (47–8). The other is given in response to the famous scripture from Matthew 19:14: "Suffer little children to come unto Me; for of

---

[22] Tractarian hymnists such as Williams and John Neale researched medieval Latin hymn books, such as the *Paris Breviary*, offering translations of these as a "new" hymnody for the High Church to differentiate their hymnody from the "overly emotional" hymns of the Low Church. See Benson, 492–506, and Temperley, 251, 262–6, among others.

such is the kingdom of heaven." Instead of focusing on Jesus bidding children to him during his life, as Taylors and other popular hymnists of the period did (Jemima Thompson Luke's "I think when I read that sweet story of old," etc.), Williams reflects upon the murder of the Innocents during Old Testament times, with a therefore awkward, even inappropriate, concluding stanza: "Jesu, born of Virgin's womb … Sing we glory unto Thee" (26).

The last line reminds the reader that singing is part of praise to the Maker, yet this is one of the few references to singing, oddly, in this, a "hymn book." Another reference to raising the communal voice in worship makes clear in the successive lines that this is about prayer, not singing (61). Only angels sing, in the hymn "The Sabbath of Heaven," since we, as "exiles," can lift only a "feeble strain" (66). The awkward meters of these hymns further confirm that their inclusion is more for meditation than singing. Spondees are frequent, awkward stresses begin lines, while a variety of meters can be found in one single hymn: tetrameter, trimeter, and dimeter are all used in the hymn "Christ ascended" (41). Such hymn-texts would be difficult to sing to existing common-meter tunes or other patterned tune meters. It is no surprise, then, that I found none of these hymns in any later hymn books of the century.

One close look at a hymn puts these many characteristics in high relief. "To the Holy Spirit" (45–6) is a medieval hymn translated by Williams based on John 14:26: "The Comforter, which is the Holy Ghost, whom the Father will send in my name, He shall teach you all things." Rather than focusing on the concept of teaching, or the personal Father, as the Taylors might have done to appeal to children, the hymn writer instead focuses on the more difficult concept of the Holy Spirit. Williams himself uses obscure vocabulary in his translation for children, beginning with the term "Paraclete" as a lesser-used term for the Holy Spirit:

> Come, Thou creating Spirit blest,
>     And be our guest;
> And fill the hearts which Thou hast made
>     With Thy sweet aid.
> Thou who are call'd the Paraclete,
>     From Thy blest seat,
> The living fount of light and love,
>     Come from above. (lines 1–8)

Approach is formal ("Thou" and "Thy") and rhetoric is adult-centered ("creating Spirit blest" and "living fount of light"). Likewise, metaphors are diverse and even mixed, the Spirit at once being a "guest," an aid-giver, and a "living fount." The Spirit gives strength to "our flesh's infirmity" (line 15)—a common trope in these hymns—in order to ward off "the foe's assaultings" (line 17). The concept of the Trinity is invoked (line 25) and also unpacked a bit:

> May we by Thee the Father know,
>     And Son below;
> And Thee, the Spirit, come from both. (lines 21–3)

Williams writes "up" to his audience in mature language and concepts, with another formal invocation ("May we by Thee") and proposes a more difficult concept of a Spirit which "comes from both" a Father and a Son. This is in contrast, for instance, to C. F. Alexander who explains the Trinity in simple terms in her *Hymns for Little Children* (1848), Hymn 3: "We are little Christian children ... We believe in God Almighty, / Father, Son, and Holy Ghost."

Ultimately, Williams the hymn writer encourages "Praise aye be done," though this is still not the praise of singing, which is reserved for the Spirit alone to inspire those stumbling in speech:

> And layest on the untutor'd tongue
> The Spirit's song. (lines 11–12)

As these sample lines show, its poetry is atypical of earlier children's hymns in its awkward enjambment between lines and exceptionally short second lines (iambic dimeter). Its meter alternates between iambic ("And fill the hearts which Thou hast made") and trochaic ("May the foe's assaultings cease"), with the meter literally crumbling in some lines ("Thou that in sevenfold power dost stand"), further distancing it from standard, uniform hymns of the era. With short and frequently inconsistent metrical lines, this poetry would be tricky to sing to existing hymn tunes, too, and thus the child's voice is silenced for all but the most creative and determined of child singers. In short, the difficult concepts of the Trinity and challenging terminology ("Paraclete"), together with peculiar meters, would be beyond many children's comprehension and musical ability, though they also complimented children, to think more like an adult.

It might be tempting to credit the educated, upper-middle-class audience intended for these hymns for their mature, intellectual quality. However, these Tractarian children's hymns are strikingly similar in approach, if not content, to those of the lower- to middle-class Methodist movement already discussed: both write to the child as "an adult." Writing of both the Oxford and Methodist movements, in fact, Temperley says that though "later regarded as being opposed to each other ... [they] had much in common, and taken together added up to an Anglican revival" (*Music* I: 204). One continuity was their construction of the child within their revivals, with the child often blurring with the adult as hymn writers attempted to reach both generations with religious reformation. Certainly this was true of Wesley's own hymns, according to John Wesley's clearly stated principles of not writing "down" to children. Early Methodist hymn books such as *Hymns for Children and Young Persons* (Joseph Benson, 1806) followed suit by rarely even addressing the child. Various Methodist hymn books of mid-century continued this Wesleyan philosophy, even as the Methodist church broke into various sects.[23] These included the *Primitive Methodist Sabbath-School Hymn*

---

[23] For a comprehensive examination of Methodism and its various splinter sects during the nineteenth century, see Davies, *A History of The Methodist Church in Great Britain*, vols 2 and 3.

*Book* (1864), the United Methodist Free Churches' *Sunday-School Hymns* (1870), and, perhaps the best-known of children's hymn books in the Methodist tradition, *The Methodist Sunday-School Hymn and Tune-Book* of 1879, published by the (main) Wesleyan Methodist conference.[24] Differences in style and doctrine appear in these three representative Methodist hymn books: the Primitive Methodists especially favored "stirring melodies" and choruses (Benson 276), seen with the rousing chorus "Beautiful gates of pearly white / Beautiful temple, God its light!" of Hymn 278. Given their close mid-century publication date, one can also note doctrinal differences in that the Primitive Methodists give as subject-categories "Repentance," "Death," and "Judgment"; the Free Methodists showcase a similar atonement theology: "The Fall of Man," "Sin," and "Death and Judgment." In contrast, the Wesleyan Methodist features a section on "Repentance," then quickly moves to "Faith," "Confidence and Joy," and "Service," revealing a more guilt-free, socially driven doctrine. Yet a common trait is that they all include a separate section on "Early Piety" ("Infant Classes" in the Free Methodist) because the overall content of their hymn books is not always so child-centered.

The 1879 *Methodist Sunday-School Hymn and Tune-Book* is a case in point. A quick examination of the hymn book gives the sense of an adult hymn book, containing hymns about "adults" ("Let all men praise the Lord," Hymn 16), with convoluted syntax ("Come, Holy Ghost, our hearts inspire, / Let us Thine influence prove," Hymn 195), or known to be written for the adult tradition ("All hail the power of Jesu's name," Hymn 184). One must wade through the first 50 hymns before finding any mention of children (in Hymn 58, which refers to "infant tongues"), and look specifically to the "Early Piety" section to find an abundance of child-focused hymns ("Happy the child whose youngest years," Hymn 228, and "I am Jesus' little lamb," Hymn 230). Though the profusion of adult-centered hymns in a children's hymn book is a phenomenon to be explored at length in Chapter 3, I would point out here how this hymn book also anticipates the anthologies of hymns of late century, to be discussed next, which embrace many approaches to hymns, child- and adult-centered. Indeed, the 1879 *Methodist Sunday-School Hymn and Tune-Book* is vast: 575 hymns, such that child-centered and adult-centered hymns mingle freely in this book. Across the page from "All hail the power of Jesu's name" sits "Little children, praise the Saviour" (Hymn 186). Standards by Watts, the Taylors, and other child-centered writers are found, even outside the "Early Piety" section: Watts's "I sing the almighty power

---

[24]     Other Sunday school hymn books published by sects of the Methodist Church include: *Hymns for Children and Young Persons* (Joseph Benson, 1806), *Sunday School Hymn Book for Children* (Hugh Bourne, 1822), *A Collection of Hymns for the use of Wesleyan Methodist Sunday School* (1827), *Wesleyan Methodist Sunday-School Hymn-Book* (1857), *Methodist Free Church Sunday School Hymns* (1860), *Methodist New Connexion Juvenile Hymn Book* (1862), *Methodist Scholar's Hymn Book* (1870), *Primitive Methodist Sunday School Union Hymn Book* (1879), *Wesleyan Methodist Sunday School Hymn Book* (1879), and *Methodist Free Church School Hymns* (1888). For a complete list see *School Hymn Book of the Methodist Church* (London, n.d.), xi.

of God" (Hymn 35), Taylors' "I thank the goodness and the grace" (Hymn 55), and Mary Lundie Duncan's "Jesus, tender Shepherd, hear me!" (Hymn 491). Leaning towards an adult-centered approach, then, the 1879 Methodist hymn book yet exhibits qualities of late-century, heterogeneous anthologies. It is this quality, possibly, which prompted Julian to call this publication "first in merit of any collection for children yet made" (223).

In short, various hymn books especially of mid-century—Tractarian hymn books such as Williams's and various Methodist hymnals—disavow the "childness" of children and address them as adults, as both Wesley and then Keble encouraged (strange theological bedfellows indeed). This move at once complimented the intellect of and empowered children (notably in contrast to Charlotte Yonge's disapproved intellectualism). Yet this approach also effectively effaced children at times, disavowing any child-like difference between them and the adults sharing the hymns. Acknowledging these movements erases the common wisdom about the smooth transition of the Evangelical child to the Romantic child of late century.

**Part IV**
**The "Astute Child":**
**Late-Century Hymn Books**

There is much about the late-century hymn tradition for children that coincides with Golden-Age literature. The Romantic Child of Rousseau, then of Blake and Wordsworth, built up momentum throughout the nineteenth century, reaching its height in popular culture by the last decades of the century,[25] affecting writers and hymn writers alike. Blake was pivotal in envisioning an "innocence" alongside "experience," in placing "Infant Joy" along with "Infant Sorrow," and initiating the cult of the child in which their sorrows and joys, welfare and play—not guilt and blame—were suddenly worthy of poetry and protection. This "Romantic child" persisted and overcame earlier views of the errant child: Gillian Avery writes that early-century tract books defined the child as sinful and very aware of that sin, whereas late-century texts are "the first presentation of children as virtually sinless" (81). As Penny Brown notes, early portrayals suggested that a child was a "product of Original Sin ... burdened by the innate depravity of mankind" while later in the century this view is replaced by "a version of the 'innocent' child, a symbol of purity and grace" (43). The Golden Age of children's literature as ushered in by Lewis Carroll's groundbreaking *Alice in Wonderland* (1865) made late-century literature significantly different than earlier eras. The works of Edward Lear (*Laughable Lyrics*, 1877), Robert Louis Stevenson (*A Child's Garden of Verses*, 1885), Rudyard Kipling (*Jungle Book*, 1894–1895), E. Nesbit (*The Treasure Seekers*, 1899), and Kenneth Grahame (*Wind in the Willows*, 1908),

---

[25]   "Romanticism" refers to the early nineteenth century in English poetry and the entire century in music history, but is used by many children's scholars to refer to the later nineteenth century. See Cunningham 69; Lundin 45; Knuth 74.

among many others, are written about and for children at ease in exploring the world around them, quite apart from the strictures of parents and school.

Hymn books followed suit. Though religious didacticism did not disappear, clearly in late-century hymn books, joyfulness overtakes the sullen doctrines of early and mid-century, as even the titles suggest: Henry Bateman's *Sunday Sunshine: New Hymns and Poems for the Young* (1858) provides an early example of this change, to be followed in the 1870s through the 1890s with *Songs of Gladness: A Hymn Book for the Young* (1871); George Coward, Jr.'s *The Child's Book of Praise* (1871); *Songs of Love and Mercy for the Young* (1878); and *Golden Bells; or, Hymns for our Children* (1890).[26]

Even without Romantic titles, late-century hymn books' doctrines reveal similar optimism and intentional focus on the child. For instance, M. A. Woods, "Head Mistress of the Clifton High School for Girls," in 1890 compiled *Hymns for School Worship* in order to provide for common and school worship, which she describes as "bright rather than sad, simple rather than complex, devotional rather than doctrinal or didactic" (Preface, v), making direct attacks against both Evangelical approaches and Revivalist rhetoric. Similarly, H. K. Lewis, in his *Little Children's Hymns and Songs* (1895), directly challenges Wesley's precepts in his Preface: these hymns are "selected for children *as they now are*, rather than for *what they may become*"—with "facts and truths which children may be able to grasp, and suitable as expressions of the love and gratitude, the hope and joy, of children under Christian training" (3; his italics). A new hymn book had been born, reverting back to a Wattsian vision of the child while taking on a "brightness" all its own.[27]

Indeed, if Evangelicals saw children as needing religious education because of their sins, Romantic hymn writers saw children as needing religious education simply to rejoice in their happiness and purity, the debt to Rousseau and Blake observed on every page of these books. Hymns in these hymn books speak of children as "little friends of Jesus" (in "We are little children"), "lambs to His fold" ("I think when I read that sweet story"), "happy children, / Robed in snowy white" ("If I come to Jesus"), and "the Saviour's lambs" ("Come, little Children").

---

[26]   Late-century American children's hymn books exemplify this penchant for ebullient, even alliterative, titles even more obviously: *Golden Shower* (Chicago, 1862), *The Prize for Our Sunday School* (Detroit, 1870), *The Sunny Side* (New York, 1875), *The Voice of Joy* (Cincinnati, 1882), *Green Pastures* (Cleveland, 1886), *Winnowed Songs for Sunday Schools* (New York, 1890), *Echoes of Zion for the Sunday School* (Moultrie, Ohio, 1891), and *The Seed Sower* (Toledo, 1897). Hymns themselves tend to exemplify this brighter theology infused with the American gospel hymn-singing tradition. I am grateful to the University of Michigan Music Library for the opportunity to peruse these.

[27]   It should be noted that late-century publishers continued to publish Watts's *Divine Songs*, although the illustrations often belie the severe doctrine, to be discussed in Chapter 5. At least one edition (*Childhood's Songs of Long Ago*, New York, 1897) excised entire hymns of this nature, praising the "delight" Watts gave to the "youthful mind" while criticizing his "method of expression" as being too "forceful" (10), revelatory of both late-century delight in the child and divergence from harsher Evangelical doctrine.

Without completely obliterating the need for redemption by Christ, these hymns show children to be closer to Christ than adults.

Further, the child's distinction—his bodily smallness—now earns praise, so much so that "little" becomes a positive trope, as seen even in the lines quoted above. H. K. Lewis's *Little Children's Hymns and Songs* (1895) uses the term unfailingly when mentioning children (in Hymns 26, 32, 49, 57, 60, 69, 81, 95), even extending to all things connected with children, as in "A little daisy" (98) or "A little tiny bird" (60). Sentimentality follows in many of these hymn books as found in *Hymns and Rhymes for Children by the Daughter of a Clergyman* (1871): "Be kind to little Johnny Bell ... He never saw his mother's face ... Blind Johnny all the children love; / He's in the holy keeping too" (46), or "Mother,— I'm dying now ... Never beside your knee / Shall I kneel down again at night to pray" (from "It must be sweet in childhood to give back" 221). It would be these various approaches which no doubt prompted modern-day critic J. R. Watson to complain about hymn books' "uneasy sentimentality" in which children must "respond to ideas of themselves as 'little' and 'tiny,' and to nature as full of sweet little children" (*English Hymn* 509–10).

This smallness and sweetness perhaps came at a cost. In literary portrayals of children, one might note the passivity that often cripples children's abilities to think logically or persevere through trials. Alice, throughout her adventures in Wonderland, demonstrates this side of Romantic childhood: not wonderment but bewilderment. Robert Polhemus praises Carroll's ability to take us backward to "early years, early pleasures ... [to] shrink the essence of authority to a child's scale, diminish the threatening urgencies of society, [and] make jokes of them" (*Alice in Wonderland* 366–7). Yet very often the joke is on the child. Alice is constantly confused: "I ca'n't explain *myself*," she confesses to the Caterpillar (*Alice in Wonderland* 35), "I don't know of any that do," she admits to the Duchess (48), and "I don't know what you mean," she acknowledges to the Mad Hatter (56). As in the real world, the adults she meets constantly remind her of her artlessness: "You don't know much," the Duchess tells her (48), and when Alice claims a "right to think," the Duchess retorts, "Just about as much right ... as pigs have to fly" (72). If the Romantic child is liberated to explore, she is not liberated to think.[28] It is no surprise that Lissa Paul refers to the Romantic period as one of "innocence, ignorance, and separation from the world" which suspended "thinking [and] knowing" (3).

A challenge to this portrayal of the period's children as innocent and ignorant, though, is to consider the form typically taken by late-century hymn books: anthologized collections, which really did require children to think. Rather than containing original hymns written by one or two authors, most often hymn books

---

28    Note other critics' views on Alice, from U. C. Knoepflmacher, who sees Alice as "still close enough to childhood to wean herself from the infatuation with empowerment she has derived from the world of her Victorian elders" (184), to Marah Gubar, who sees Carroll as "poking fun at Alice" in order to amuse and form a relationship with his young readers (116), who "never allows his heroine to evolve into a full-fledged creative agent" (124).

were becoming collections of hymns by a myriad of hymn writers, named and unnamed, all with differing views of children. By extension, because of advances in printing techniques that made larger hymn books possible, late-century hymn books were expansive, so that *everything* is included. Evangelical hymns sit next to Tractarian hymns in sacred grab bags, so that hymn books embrace differing, even conflicting, theological standpoints. This enabled teachers and children to seek whatever personally appealed to them. Children would need to contemplate the divergent theologies unveiled in these hymn books.

This awareness alters our perceptions of late-century "childhood" in two ways. For one, our appreciation of children's literary history is altered: as Heather D. Curtis notes when studying a similar trend in American hymn books for children, "Although it is possible to discern a general liberalizing trend in attitudes toward childhood during the antebellum period … this theological progression was not as linear in practice as it may have been in theory. Hymns such as Isaac Watts's 'Solemn Thoughts of God and Death' … were printed in the same hymnals and magazines that pictured children as innocent 'lambs'" (216). That is, the diversity of hymns still residing in late-century hymn books represented childhood more ambiguously than commonly thought, as both sinful *and* innocent.

Further, children can no longer be seen as completely "simple" and "innocent" when they are expected to understand and appreciate the complex and diverse theologies represented in these hymn books. And given the religious climate in the second half of the century, there was much to ponder, Darwinian theory and the ensuing Crisis of Faith forever changing religious ideals. In many ways, these later-century children's hymn books represent the ideologies of the Broad Church as initiated by "liberal, educated, theologically progressive" Anglican clergy who believed the church should be "broad enough to encompass almost all Christians in Britain" (Melnyk, *Victorian Religion* 30), and broad-minded enough to accept scientific challenges to traditional faith.[29] For example, Broad Church hymn writer John Ellerton, who published his edited *Hymns for Schools and Bible Classes* in the publication year of *Origin of Species*, 1859, seems to suggest this very melding of science and religion in the hymns he selects. Such verses as: "With grateful hearts the Past we own; / The Future, now to us unknown, / To Thy great wisdom we commend, / Who seest, from the first, the end" (Hymn 20) suggest a Divine presence (who "seest") yet within a world evolving on its own,

---

[29]    Altick refers to the Broad Church movement within the Anglican Church as "the nineteenth-century heir to the Latitudinarian tradition, with its moderate skepticism and indifference to sharply defined dogma and prescribed forms" which remained "undisturbed by Darwinism; they [its clergy] took it in stride and suggested ways in which … Christianity did in fact find it possible to come to terms with the implications of biological evolution" (207–8). Albert Edward Bailey names about 10 well-known writers of hymns to be associated with the Broad Church, including Alfred Lord Tennyson, William Walsham How, John Ellerton, and John Addington Symonds (see Bailey, *The Gospel in Hymns*, ch. 14). Identifiable Broad Church hymns appeared in children's hymn books in increasing numbers after 1870.

a "Future … unknown." Notably, his Christmas hymn contrasts with those of the Tractarians Yonge and Williams, less doctrinal and more joyous: "O sing Alleluia, / Bright chorus of angels, O fill ye the courts of heaven with song! / Sing ye, *All glory / To* God *in the highest*" (Hymn 17, his italics).

It is no surprise, then, that a theological, even national, variety is to be found in *Hymns for Use in the Sunday School and the Guild and at Children's Services in the Congregation* (1891), which contains many hymns by contemporary literary authors, from the Unitarian William Gaskell to the Broad Church poet Tennyson (his "Great God, who knowest each man's need") to the agnostic Thomas Carlyle (his "So here hath been dawning / Another blue day; / Think wilt thou let it / Slip useless away?"). Included too are a number of American writers—William Cullins Bryant, Henry Longfellow, Oliver Wendell Holmes, James Whittier, and Julia Ward Howe. Consequently, children were empowered as consumers, thumbing through hymn books to procure whatever hymns they found most appealing amongst such variety, even in the face of adult selection at school or home. As one example, Lucy Larcom, in *A New England Girlhood* (1889), recollects such discrimination even at age 5: "Some of them [hymns] were so prosy that the words would not stay in my memory at all, so I concluded that I would learn only those I liked" (59). An empowered child singer, certainly!

In no book do these characteristics better reveal themselves than with the hymn collection, *Golden Bells; or, Hymns for our Children* (1890), published by the Children's Special Service Mission.[30] It suggests trends typical of the late nineteenth century much in contrast with those individually written and translated texts discussed earlier. For one, containing no fewer than *628* hymns (text only), *Golden Bells* is comprehensive. Hymns as far back as Thomas Ken's 1674 "Awake, my soul" (Hymn 487) are included, but so too is the very recent "Rescue the perishing" (1870) by American hymn writer Fanny Crosby. It includes well-known titles, such as "Hark, the herald angels sing" (Hymn 56), and those not found elsewhere ("Can it be true?," Hymn 215, among many others). The hymn book comprises hymns clearly for children, such as Albert Midlane's "There's a Friend for little children" (Hymn 358), and others originally intended for adults, such as Wesley's "Christ the Lord is risen today" (Hymn 133). Influential hymn writers such as Watts and the Taylors are represented, but so too are authors known only for one hymn, such as Jemima Thompson Luke and Henry Francis Lyte. Here is found a complex array of denominational viewpoints: the Calvinist Augustus Toplady ("Rock of ages," Hymn 130), Dissenting minister Edward Perronet ("All hail the power of Jesus' name," Hymn 19), as well as Anglican minister Reginald Heber ("Holy, holy, holy," Hymn 3) and Tractarian leader John Keble ("Sun of my soul," Hymn 493).

---

[30]    As of 1966, *Golden Bells* was still in print (Allen 153). Cecil J. Allen points out that in 1926 a new edition of *Golden Bells* was produced which contained fewer children's hymns, a trend continuing into the second half of the twentieth century when a newer hymn book, *Hymns of Faith*, was added (1964) with even fewer children's hymns, "striking" given that the C.S.S.M is "an organization for children and young people" (153). Allen thus suggests the child-adult quandary is still rampant in modern hymn books.

Still, its title and the title hymn, "Golden Bells, their sweet chimes ringing," suggest this to be very much a Romantic hymn book in its "sweetness" and happy tenor. Further sections exude cheerful sentiments simply in their titles: "God in Creation, Providence, and Grace," "The Birth and Childhood of Jesus Christ," "The Life and Miracles of Jesus Christ," "Joy and Peace in Believing," etc. A quick glance at the first lines, only, of hymns found in the latter section, for instance, unfailingly shows uplifting sentiments: "Grace! 'tis a charming sound" (Hymn 275); "Joy! Joy! Joy! There's joy in the presence of the angels" (Hymn 277); "Oh, what a Saviour—that He died for me" (Hymn 277); and "O Happy day! that fixed my choice / On Thee" (Hymn 279). The editors' notable usage of exclamation marks is in stark contrast to earlier books which rarely used them, conveying a child-like intensity of emotion projected by these hymns (as with "Oh, what a Saviour—that He died for me!").[31]

Admittedly, the section entitled "The Redemption by the Blood of Christ" includes more Atonement theology and bloody details of the Passion: "Redeemed! How I love to proclaim it!" (Hymn 119) and "There is a fountain filled with blood" (Hymn 118). Others give the message of the Crucifixion in terms for a child, as in C. F. Alexander's "There is a green hill far away" from her 1848 *Hymns for Little Children*: "We may not know, we cannot tell, / What pains He had to bear" (Hymn 101). Others specifically indict children, as in "Children, you have gone astray" (Hymn 163) and "Oh, think not, dear children, because you are young, / No blood of atonement you need" (Hymn 165). But others stress late-century optimism: amidst hymns of Passion we find Anna Bartlett Warner's classic "Jesus loves me! This I know" (Hymn 92) and Fanny Crosby's gospel favorite "To God be the glory! great things He hath done!" (Hymn 120). Amazingly, in a section entitled "Easy Hymns for Young Children," the hymn "Little ones of God are we, Therefore we His praise repeat" (Hymn 551) literally sits across the page from "I'm not too young to sin, / I'm not too young to die" (Hymn 561).

The plethora of differing hymns is thus crucial in appreciating what late-century hymn books were suggesting of children, allowing them to sift through various theologies and views of themselves, investing in their intellectual competency so as to determine their own religious sensibilities, a phenomenon true of most late-century hymn books.[32]

---

[31]     Children were/are wont to add exclamation marks to reflect their energy; in her 1876 unpublished diary, I counted no less than 12 exclamation marks used by 12-year-old Mary Smith to show her enthusiasm for a favorite meal. Courtesy of Lilly Library, Indiana University, Bloomington.

[32]     Other hymn books that I studied which follow these general patterns include: Henry Bateman, *Sunday Sunshine: New Hymns and Poems for the Young* (1858); J. H. Wilson, ed., *Hymns for Children* (London, 1866); George Coward, Jr., *The Child's Book of Praise* (1871); *Hymns and Rhymes for Children by the Daughter of a Clergyman* (1871); *The Sunday School Hymn Book* (1871); *Songs of Gladness: A Hymn book for the Young* (1871); *Children's Hymns* (1873); *Children's Hymn and Chant Book* (1873); Claudia F. Hernaman, *Child's Book of Praise* (1873); *Children's Hymns with Musical Directory and School*

Further, in contrast to the Taylors' concern for "sinful" singing and Williams's avoidance of singable hymns altogether, the hymns in *Golden Bells* encourage singing without reservation, using common meter and other standard meters to fit with a variety of tunes, and invoking appealing refrains to encourage singing ("God is love!" in Hymn 46, for example).[33] In the opening section on "Praise and Worship" alone, 22 (of 24) hymns mention singing, "gladsome music" (Hymn 1), or "happy songs" (Hymn 17), singing children being central to that praise (consider "children, sweetly sing," Hymn 7; "joy-bells ringing, children singing," Hymn 15; and "Hosanna! Be the children's song / To Christ, the children's King," Hymn 22). Children's participatory roles empower them: singing hymns engages their own voices and emotions while exploring various theologies challenges their intellect. If music is a powerful means to physical *and* mental inspiration, then children have clearly gained that power in these hymns.

I end this section with a close examination of one hymn, of the 628 found in *Golden Bells*, chosen because of its popularity and relative newness: "Hushed was the evening hymn" or "The Child Samuel" (1857). Found in the hymn book's section on "Consecration and Love to the Saviour," this hymn (Hymn 305) nestles among bright hymns ("I feel like singing all the time," Hymn 304) often focused on Jesus ("More like Jesus would I be," Hymn 303), though the section preceding contained seven somber hymns "Confessing Christ." Once again, the variety of moods is notable.

This particular hymn was written by Rev. James Drummond Burns of the Free Church of Scotland as part of a book entitled *The Evening Hymn* (1857), which contained original hymns and prayers for every evening of the month. "Hushed was the evening" became the most famous, appearing in one-fifth of the hymn books I tabulated. By the 1870s, Arthur Sullivan had written a tune for it, "Samuel," first published with the text in *Church Hymns with Tunes* (1874) (McCutchan 447). In many ways, the hymn represents the latter half of the century in its sentimental appeal to follow the faith of a child. Based on 1 Samuel 3:1–18, the hymn references this narrative of the boy Samuel who one night is chosen by the Lord to hear His message, God purposely overlooking the sleeping priest

---

*Prayers* (1876); Lawrence Tuttiett, *Original Hymns for Younger Members of the Church* (2nd ed., 1889); *Hymns for the Little Ones* (1890); M. A. Woods, *Hymns for School Worship* (1890); *School Hymns: A Book of Praise for Teachers and Scholars, Guilds, Christian Bands, Christian Endeavor Societies, etc.* (1890); *Hymns for Use in the Sunday School and the Guild and at Children's Services in the Congregation* (1891); *282 Hymns and Melodies for School and Family Use* (1893); *Hymns for Children with Opening and Closing Services and Songs and Hymns for Bands of Mercy and of Hope* (1894); *Hymns and Bible Songs for Use in Sunday Schools* (1895); H. K. Lewis, *Little Children's Hymns and Songs* (1895); M. Woodward, *The Children's Service Book and Appendix, with Hymns, Litanies, Carols, and Prayers for Public, Private and School Use* (1897); *Sacred Songs for Children of All Ages* (1900).

[33] Tune editions of *Golden Bells* such as c. 1926 contain delightful tunes for singing: "Diademata" (Elvey), "Morningside" (folk tune), "Alleluia" (S. S. Wesley), "Alford" (Dykes), etc.

Eli nearby. Burns sets the scene with vivid descriptions, building in intensity, to appeal to a child reader. The tune written by Sullivan, with intentionally placed non-harmonic tones, adds intensity to the scene (see, for example, *Golden Bells* with tunes [c. 1925]). The hymn opens:

> Hushed was the evening hymn,
>     The temple courts were dark,
> The lamp was burning dim
>     Before the sacred ark:
> When suddenly a voice divine
> Rang through the silence of the shrine.

Written in iambic tetrameter with iambic pentameter refrains, in ABABCC rhyme schemes, the poetry of the stanza is more complex and interesting than the Taylors' simpler poetic approach, already demanding more poetic appreciation of the child singer. As this first stanza shows, the "voice divine" becomes the central character of this drama, even before Eli ("The old man, meek and mild") and Samuel ("The little Levite") are introduced in verse 2. It is this voice and the divine calling which therefore become paramount in the story. Further, when the Divine chooses the little boy over the wise priest, Burns emphasizes this privilege shown to the child:

> And what from Eli's sense was sealed
> The Lord to Hannah's son revealed. (v. 2)

Burns concludes the story here, turning to lessons for his contemporary audience:

> Oh, give me Samuel's ear!
>     The open ear, O Lord,
> Alive and quick to hear
>     Each whisper of Thy word … (v. 3)

Burns appeals to his audience to hear the "voice divine" in their own experiences, using active terms to represent this state of being "open," "alive," and "quick." Burns then appeals to the emotions:

> Oh, give me Samuel's heart!
>     A lowly heart that waits …
> By day and night, a heart that still
> Moves at the breathing of Thy will. (v. 4)

Injunctions here to have a "lowly heart," to move to "Thy will," and, later, to possess "a sweet unmurmuring faith," and be "obedient and resigned" all suggest the Evangelical ideals of passive resignation to the Divine will. However, the last verse portends ideals of late-century. For one, Burns, after appealing to the reader's ear and heart, petitions the reader's *mind*:

> Oh, give me Samuel's mind!
>     A sweet unmurmuring faith … (v. 5)

This "sweet," silent faith yet requires a mind to direct it, very much consonant with the need for faithful *thought* in utilizing hymn-book collections of the day and digesting the various theologies therein presented. Secondly, Burns reminds his readers—adults and children alike—that a child's insight is supreme:

> That I may read with child-like eyes
> Truths that are hidden from the wise. (v. 5)

Burns has idealized "child-like" insight even over the apparent acumen of grown-ups, a child view able to comprehend truths that even "the wise" cannot fully digest. Indeed, children's hymnody of the end of the century required both reading with insight and singing with strength, "child-like" as Burns now envisions "the child" to be. By 1911, hymnologists Charles Nutter and Wilbur Tillett, claimed that "No poet has made more effective and beautiful use for devotional purposes of the familiar Scripture story of the child Samuel than has the author of this hymn" (352). Indeed, Burns's hymn heralds the ideals of "the robust and authentic" child appreciated especially by those of the next, Edwardian era (Knuth 96).

## Conclusion

In conclusion, there is a discernible oscillation of child-centered, Wattsian, Evangelical hymn books; to adult-centered, Wesley-influenced mid-century hymn books; back to Watts-inspired, late-century, Romantic hymn books. Hymn writers thus reflect the little-studied ambiguity of clearly defining the child during the "age of childhood": the Victorians hardly discovered "childhood" when "the child" disappeared altogether at times. Additional stereotypes, of the "tractable Evangelical child" and the "innocent Romantic child," break down when considering the rhetorical and musical agency offered Evangelical hymn singers and the theological discernment required of Romantic child singers. Even the literary images we may associate with these various periods of history—of Barbauld's emboldened hymn reader, of Charlotte Yonge's thoughtful songsters, and of Carroll's clever child-heroine, for example—need contextualizing within the hymn tradition's empowered child singers. I thus emphasize the need for "re-tuning" our understanding of children's literary history by including hymnody whenever we study religious and secular children's texts of the period.

# Chapter 3
# Complicating Child-Adult Distinctions:
# "Crossover" Children's
# Hymn-Texts and Tunes

The little attenuated voices of the children brought to her ear in distinct utterance the words they sang without thought or comprehension:

> Lead Kindly Light, amid the encircling gloom
> > Lead Thou me on.

… Once that she had begun to cry for she hardly knew what she could not leave off for crowding thoughts she knew too well. She would have given anything in the world to be as those children were, unconcerned at the meaning of their words because too innocent to feel the necessity for any such expression.…

—Thomas Hardy, *Far from the Madding Crowd* (1874), ch. 56

"The object of this Collection," wrote Mrs. Carey Brock, the editor of the *Children's Hymn Book* (1878), "is to provide a Hymnal for the young, in which, whilst a high standard of excellence and a healthy religious tone are preserved, every hymn shall be, as regards the sentiments conveyed and the expressions used, within their possible experience, and, as far as may be, within their comprehension" (Preface, iii). It is a conclusive claim, and one made by many other children's hymn-book editors throughout the century, that the hymn book will meet a need for children, whether in terms of a child's "sentiments," "experience," or "comprehension." Even the titles of children's nineteenth-century hymn books, though varied in their terminology for "the young," nevertheless convey a conscious effort on the part of the writers and editors to create a separate liturgical space for young parishioners: *The Infant-Hymnist* (1831), *The Juvenile Harmonist* (1843), *The Child's Own Hymn Book* (Curwen, 1851), *Hymns for the Little Ones* (1868), *The Little Chorister* (1890), and *The Young People's Hymnal* (1896). Though theological approaches varied in these many hymn books, as shown in Chapter 2, clearly a new market had been established by the dissemination of so many hundreds of hymn books and thousands of hymns for children throughout the century.

It is surprising, therefore, to examine those many hymns appearing in children's hymn books of the era, surprising because so many are clearly not children's hymns. Table 3.1 shows a list of the 25 most common hymn titles I calculated from

100 hymn books of various publishing dates, denominations, and approaches.[1] If, as I argue in Chapter 2, a "child-centered hymn" can be defined as that which uses simple language, literal images, and basic meter and rhyme, then only nine of the top 25 qualify.

Table 3.1    The 25 Most Frequently Appearing Hymns in Nineteenth-Century Children's Hymn Books

|  | Percentage in 100 hymn books | Title (alphabetical within same percentages) | Date | Author |
|---|---|---|---|---|
| 1 | 46% | I think when I read that sweet story of old | 1841 | Jemima Thompson Luke |
| 2 | 43% | Awake, my soul, and with the sun | 1674 | Thomas Ken |
| 3 | 42% | Sun of my soul, Thou Saviour dear | 1827 | John Keble |
| 4 | 41% | From Greenland's icy mountains | 1823 | Reginald Heber |
| 5 | 40% | Hark! The herald angels sing | 1739 | Charles Wesley |
| 6 | 38% | There is a happy land | 1843 | Andrew Young |
| 7 | 36% | Let us with a gladsome mind | 1623 | John Milton |
| 8 | 33% | Holy, holy, holy, Lord God almighty | 1826 | Reginald Heber |
| 9 | 33% | Rock of ages, cleft for me | 1776 | Augustus Toplady |
| 10 | 31% | All hail the power of Jesus' name | 1779 | Edward Perronet |
| 11 | 31% | Glory to Thee, my God, this night | 1695 | Thomas Ken |
| 12 | 31% | Jesus shall reign where'er the sun | 1719 | Isaac Watts |
| 13 | 29% | Abide with me, fast falls the eventide | 1847 | Henry Francis Lyte |
| 14 | 29% | I sing the almighty power of God | 1715 | Isaac Watts |

---

[1]    When I examined American children's hymn books of the century (on a smaller scale, about 25), the following six were also near the top: "Nearer, my God, to thee," "Rock of ages," "All hail the power of Jesus' name," "Awake, my soul," "Holy, holy, holy," and "Abide with me." The list also includes Samuel Francis Smith's "My country 'tis of thee," Joseph H. Gilmore's "He leadeth me," and Fanny Crosby's "Blessed assurance," all American hymn writers.

| 15 | 28% | Our blest Redeemer, ere He breathed | 1829 | Harriet Auber |
| 16 | 28% | When I survey the wondrous cross | 1707 | Isaac Watts |
| 17 | 26% | I heard the voice of Jesus say | 1846 | Horatius Bonar |
| 18 | 26% | Nearer, my God, to thee | 1841 | Sarah Flower Adams |
| 19 | 25% | All people that on earth do dwell | 1561 | William Kethe |
| 20 | 25% | Around the throne of God in heaven | c. 1838 | Anne Shepherd |
| 21 | 25% | Great God, and will Thou condescend | 1810 | Anne & Jane Taylor |
| 22 | 25% | Just as I am, without one plea | 1834 | Charlotte Elliott |
| 23 | 25% | Lo! He comes with clouds descending | 1758 | Charles Wesley |
| 24 | 25% | Lord, dismiss us with Thy blessing | 1774 | John Fawcett |
| 25 | 25% | There's a Friend for little children | 1859 | Albert Midlane |

If one defines a child's hymn further as one that actually names or addresses children, then the list drops to four. Admittedly, the most popular, found in 46% of the hymn books, is clearly a children's hymn: "I think when I read that sweet story of old," by Jemima Thompson Luke (1841), which appropriately reflects on the biblical story of Jesus and children, from Matthew 19:14, in straightforward language and concepts:

> I think, when I read that sweet story of old,
>     When Jesus was here among men,
> How he call'd little children as lambs to his fold,
>     I should like to have been with him then.
>                     (v. 1, Hymn 5, *Juvenile Harmonist*, 1843)

The other three hymns addressing children from the top 25 include "There's a Friend for little children," "Around the throne of heaven," and "Great God, and wilt thou condescend." In 25% of hymnals, "There's a Friend for little children" by Albert Midlane (1859) describes the allures of heaven—the "Friend" (v. 1), "rest" (v. 2), "home" (v. 3), "crown" (v. 4), "song" (v. 5), and "robe" (v. 6)—all awaiting little children "above the bright blue sky"; its simple language, repetitive structure, and appeal to children throughout justify its inclusion in so many children's hymn books. Similarly, Anne Shepherd's 1830s "Around the throne of God in heaven," also at 25%, invokes a heaven where singing and brightness are also portrayed, but where she specifically imagines children:

Around the throne of God in heaven
    Thousands of children stand;
Children, whose sins are all forgiven,
    A holy, happy band,
      Singing glory, glory, glory. (v. 1, Hymn 98, *The Weston Hymn Book*, 1849)

Also appearing on the list are those hymns by the popular author team for children, Jane and Ann Taylor, whose "Great God, and wilt Thou condescend" (25%) and "I thank the goodness and the grace" (23%) are both from their *Hymns for Infant Minds* (1809), as explored in Chapter 2. Though not directly naming children, pieces by Isaac Watts are represented: "Jesus shall reign where'er the sun" (31%) and "I sing the almighty power of God" (29%), the latter from his *Divine and Moral Songs for Children*. Bishop Ken's Morning Hymn ("Awake, my soul, and with the sun") and Evening Hymn ("Glory to Thee, my God, this night"), both written for the boys at Winchester College (1695) are unsurprisingly high (at 43 and 31%, respectively).

Despite these "obvious" inclusions in children's hymn books, one will quickly note that many other hymns were even more popular than the Taylors' hymns, hymns not written specifically for children, all in the top five: "Sun of my soul, Thou Saviour dear" (42%), "From Greenland's icy mountains" (41%), and "Hark! The herald angels sing" (40%), written by John Keble, Reginald Heber, and Charles Wesley, respectively, for the grand—and adult—hymn tradition. Even if these hymns' texts overtly appear to be within a child's "comprehension," to quote Mrs. Brock, being about bedtime, mission work, and Christmas, respectively, hymns further down on the list belie a child's "experience," such as the vivid portrayal of the Passion in "Rock of ages" (33%) or "Abide with me" (29%) which reflects upon the "eventide" of one's life. Thomas Hardy, in the chapter's epigraph from *Far from the Madding Crowd*, invokes another popular, adult-oriented hymn, John Henry Newman's "Lead, kindly light" as, in fact, quite commonplace for children to sing.

Adult hymns appear more frequently even when more child-oriented hymns on the topic existed. For instance, Augustus Toplady's "Rock of ages" most frequently teaches Christ's crucifixion to children despite being a fairly harsh Calvinist hymn on Christ's blood-letting couched in complex symbolism and syntax: "Let the water and the blood, / From Thy wounded side which flowed, / Be of sin the double cure, / Save from wrath and make me pure" (*Methodist Sunday-School Hymn and Tune-Book*, 1879, No. 166, v. 1).[2] Its popularity is more mystifying when we

---

[2]    The two hymn books with complete texts and music scores upon which I primarily rely in this chapter are the 1878 Anglican *The Children's Hymn Book for Use in Children's Services, Sunday Schools, and Families* (hereafter *Children's Hymn Book*), ed. Mrs. Carey Brock and "Published under the Revision of" Anglican clergy W. Walsham How, Ashton Oxenden, and John Ellerton, and the 1879 *The Methodist Sunday-School Hymn and Tune-Book* (hereafter *Methodist SS*) published by the Wesleyan Methodist Sunday School Union. I am grateful to a "used hymn book sale" of the Hymn Society of Great Britain and Ireland, July 2010, at which I was able to acquire first editions of these and other hymn books.

consider that the Taylors' *Hymns for Infant Minds* contained a hymn of similar Calvinist flavor, "Lo, at noon, 'tis sudden night," No. 25, catering specifically to children in its simple and straightforward explanation of the crucifixion:

> Lo, at noon 'tis sudden night!
>> Darkness covers all the sky!
> Rocks are rending at the sight!—
>> Children, can you tell me why?
> What can these wonders be?
>> —Jesus dies at Calvary! (v. 1, Hymn 25, *Hymns for Infant Minds*, 1809)

Vividly describing the Passion to a child's comprehension ("With a mig'ty groan he died! / Children, shall I tell you why / Jesus condescends to die?," v. 3), this hymn is yet only found in a handful of nineteenth-century hymn books in my calculations: six versus the 33 that carried Toplady's crucifixion hymn. Similarly, Reginald Heber's "Holy, holy, holy, Lord God Almighty" alone represents the topic of "the Trinity" in 33% of children's hymn books; Heber's hymn refers to the Trinity in poetic, if complex, rhetoric: "God in Three persons, blessed Trinity" (v. 1) … "Which wert, and art, and evermore shalt be" (v. 2, Hymn 3, *Methodist SS*). In contrast, C. F. Alexander succinctly and directly explains the Trinity in her *Hymns for Little Children* (1848), in Hymn 3 ("We are little Christian children … We believe in God Almighty, / Father, Son, and Holy Ghost"), yet this hymn was soundly neglected by most children's hymn-book editors of the century.

This cataloguing of hymns thus raises the question: why are so many "adult hymns" residing in such high numbers in *children's* hymn books? One could also invert the question, for many clear "children's hymns" were found in adult hymn books of the century: "I think when I read that sweet story," "There's a Friend for little children," and "All things bright and beautiful" are all found in at least one of five representative adult hymn books of the century, with the latter still found in twentieth-century adult hymn books, such as the 1964 American *United Methodist Hymnal*. Susan Drain, analyzing one of the most influential of these five adult hymn books, *Hymns Ancient and Modern*, specifically the selections included for children, concludes, "In the 1860 hymns, the viewpoint was decidedly adult; by 1875 [in the new edition] it has changed considerably"—but, she adds, "[t]he special needs of children have been fully recognized, though not necessarily met" (461).

Defining nineteenth-century "children's hymns" thus becomes an extremely complicated task. And yet this is what traditional scholarship on Victorian hymnody has often done: compartmentalize children's hymns in their own chapters, set apart from the larger discourse on (adult) hymnody.[3] Scholars effect

---

3   Ch. 14 ("Hymns of Childhood") in Gillman, *The Evolution of the English Hymn* (1927); ch. 18 ("Youth and Hymns") in Routley, *Hymns and Human Life* (1959); ch. 15 ("Hymns for Young People") in Allen, *Hymns and the Christian Faith* (1966); ch. 4 ("Hymns for Children") in Tamke, *Make a Joyful Noise* (1978); ch. 18 ("Different Traditions") in Watson, *The English Hymn* (1984); and part 2 ("Class- and Time-Conditioning of Children")

this pigeon-holing by defining a child-centered hymn much as I do. In addition to obvious intentionality and address—hymn writers writing for and naming children—which all scholars assume, there are three characteristics they also name: 1) language: "the simplest possible language" (Allen 155) and that which is not "beyond a child's reach" (Gillman 278); 2) content: topics and thoughts within a child's experience (Routley, *Hymns and Human Life* 250–51, 253); and 3) form: "repetition, with refrains," etc. (Watson, *English Hymn* 506). They then reference such writers as Watts, the Taylors, Alexander, and many of the other writers identified above, as "children's hymn writers." To the extent to which these definitions and examples help to verbalize what is a palpable difference between child-centered and adult-centered hymns, this makes logical sense.

However, we underrepresent the breadth of children's hymnody by failing to recognize what children were actually singing. Certainly hymn editors of the century saw the genre in much broader terms. We may speak of the "child-centered hymn," reflecting all the characteristics specified above, but the "child's hymn"—reflecting the variety actually found in children's hymn books—is a different matter. This phenomenon suggests a much more complicated situation of defining "the child" during the "age of the child," which reveals what Claudia Nelson calls a "fluidity of age" and merging of adult and children's characteristics and interests (*Precocious Children* 180), a realization that current children's literature scholarship is exploring.[4] It suggests nineteenth-century hymn editors' inability to resolve the Watts-Wesley controversy they inherited from the eighteenth century or their contentment in entertaining both approaches in their

---

in Adey, *Class and Idol* (1988). More recent scholarship in Victorian hymnody does not address children's hymns: consider *Music and the Wesleys*, ed. Nicholas Temperley and Stephen Banfield (2010), *Dissenting Praise: Religious Dissent and the Hymn in England and Wales*, ed. Rivers and Wykes (2011), and *Music and Theology in Nineteenth-Century Britain*, ed. Martin V. Clarke (2012).

[4]   Consider, for instance, a special issue on such "borderlands" in *The Horn Book* (May/June 2004): write the editors, "The borderline is drawn by adults to delineate books for children. Adults put it there; children wouldn't" (229). Lynne Rosenthal speaks of the "children's book for adults" while Claudia Nelson explores both children's books enjoyed by adults, and children's strategies used within adult books (see Nelson, "Adult Children's Literature in Victorian Britain," in Denisoff 137–49). Shavit explores the "ambivalent status" (65) of children's texts since they are read by adults, thus forcing the "children's writer to compromise between two addresses" (93). Nodelman's *The Hidden Adult* acknowledges the dual audience, and also that no compromise is needed if assuming children's intellectual capabilities for innuendo and veiled messages (209–10). Nelson's *Precocious Children and Childish Adults: Age Inversion in Victorian Literature* (2012) considers the crossover situations of old-fashioned children, arrested child-men, women as girls, girls as women, and boys as men. Unlike these scholars, the instability I examine is less affected by social factors or dual audiences than by an ideology of age distinction, or lack thereof, with adult hymn writers *not* identifying children as "children" in the assumed Victorian sense. Truly, as Nelson concludes, "Recognizing both the multivocality and the fluidity of age in Victorian and post-Victorian texts establishes the existence of complexities often overlooked" (180).

hymn books. Chapter 2 suggests a periodization of such approaches—put simply, a Watts-Wesley-Watts break-down of the century. This pattern certainly is true in basic approaches by hymn writers and their single-authored hymn books. As was suggested in the last chapter, though, hymn-book anthologies complicated this by intermingling theologies, approaches, authors, and eras. Thus, in hymn-book compilations, from which my data analysis mostly stems, child-centered and adult-centered hymns coexisted throughout the century.

Specifically, we must acknowledge the "crossover hymn,"[5] the hymn written for adults that yet crossed over to children's hymn books, and vice versa. The crossover hymn does not easily reside in either the "child's" or "adult's" hymn tradition—or resides, sometimes awkwardly, in both. The existence of such crossover hymns in many hymn books of the century challenges theoretical, historical, and even musicological constructs of "the child" in important ways. The task of this chapter will be to explore the fluidity of child-adult hymns in the nineteenth century, offering ideas and suggestions as to why so many "adult" hymns resided so frequently in hymn books purporting to be for children. Part I explores the ways adult practices and concerns—commercial, theological, even psychological—found their way into children's hymn books. Part II will then argue the importance of hymn tunes as a main factor in crossover favorites, placed in the context of nineteenth-century music history. The Coda, however, will interject a close explication of the most frequently appearing hymn, Jemima Thompson Luke's "I think when I read," to suggest various means of "adult" empowerment residing even in the most "child-centered hymn."

## Part I
## "I love to tell the story":
## Adult Legacy in Children's Hymn Books

In 1912, W. T. Stead's *Hymns That Have Helped, Being a Collection of Those Hymns, Whether Jewish, Christian or Pagan, Which Have Been Found Most Useful to the Children of Men* was published.[6] Though he had solicited input from readers for inclusion at the turn of the century, Stead also includes an Appendix listing the 100 favorite hymns by Victorian readers from an 1887 survey, presumably of an adult audience. Table 3.2 lists the top favorites, beginning with "Rock of ages, cleft for me," "Abide with me; fast falls the eventide," and "Jesus, lover of my soul."

---

[5]   I am grateful to an anonymous reader for the *Children's Literature Association Quarterly* who suggested this term to me in 2009.

[6]   Stead is less known for this work, but very well known for his journalism such as that exposing child prostitution. He was also an important peace activist, nominated for the Nobel Peace Prize numerous times. He died on the Titanic, ironically after having written a piece criticizing steamers for carrying too few lifeboats. Though Stead's "Introduction" was dated 1895, *Hymns That Have Helped* was published posthumously, carrying an epilogue about his fate on the Titanic.

Table 3.2    Turn-of-Century Reflections on Most Popular Victorian Hymns (adult selection)

| Stead's *Hymns That Have Helped* (1912): top favorites from an 1887 poll (of 3,500 people) | Cullen's *The 100 Best Hymns in the English Language* (c. 1900): selected, alphabetical | Bacon's *Hymns That Every Child Should Know* (1907): selected, alphabetical |
|---|---|---|
| 1. Rock of ages | Abide with me | Abide with me |
| 2. Abide with me | All hail the power | All hail the power |
| 3. Jesus, lover of my soul | Awake, my soul | Awake, my soul |
| 4. Just as I am | From Greenland's icy | From Greenland's icy |
| 5. How sweet the name | Hark the herald angels | Hark the herald angels |
| 6. My God and Father | Holy, holy, holy | Nearer, my God, to Thee |
| 7. Nearer, my God | Nearer, my God, to Thee | Rock of ages |
| 8. Sun of my soul | Rock of ages | Sun of my soul |
| 9. I heard the voice | Sun of my soul | When I survey |
| 10. Art thou weary | When I survey | While shepherds watched |

Six of the top 10 are found in the top 25 inclusions in children's hymn books as well, his subtitle referring to "the Children of Men" perhaps more aptly than even he intended. John Cullen (1836–1914) generated a similar list in his *The Hundred Best Hymns in the English Language* (n.d.) (see Table 3.2). My own study of five mainstream adult hymn books of the period, including Methodist, Anglican, Baptist, Gospel, and Irish Protestant (see Table 3.3) suggests the same list of top favorites consonant with children's favorites. Conversely, Dolores Bacon's 1907 *Hymns That Every Child Should Know* contains nearly the same list (see Table 3.2) and, surprisingly, omits "I think when I read that sweet story of old." Further, Bacon fails even to mention children in the foreword, instead stating her objective as compiling "the hymns that have endured longest and meant most in Christian religious history" (vi). What is best for the child, apparently, is simply that which has been most meaningful within an adult tradition.

From these surveys, compiled by those who were raised during the Victorian age and brought up on Victorian children's hymn books, the fluidity of children's and adult favorites is striking. In just a few cases could one argue that the list of favorites reflects those learned from children's classic hymn books: for, in fact, none from the Taylors' popular *Hymns for Infant Minds* is included in adult lists; only one hymn, "There is a green hill far away," comes from C. F. Alexander's popular 1848 *Hymns for Little Children*; and though Watts is represented six times, no hymn is from his *Divine and Moral Songs*. Rather, quite the opposite appears true: adult editors seemed to have included in children's hymn books those hymns that they themselves most enjoyed as adults.

One simple reason is economical. Children's hymn-book publication was clearly a commercial enterprise intended for adults as well as the occasional wealthy child consumer. Temperley points to the increased means of promotion

Table 3.3    Hymns Found in All of Five Prominent Adult Nineteenth-Century
Hymn Books: Anglican, Methodist, Baptist, Gospel, and Church of
Ireland (alphabetical).* (Those titles in bold are also found on the
list of top 25 children's hymns; those in italics, the top 50.)

| 1 | **Abide with me, fast falls the eventide** |
|---|---|
| 2 | **All hail the power of Jesus' name** |
| 3 | **All people that on earth do dwell** |
| 4 | **Awake, my soul, and with the sun** |
| 5 | For thee, O dear, dear country |
| 6 | **From Greenland's icy mountains** |
| 7 | God moves in a mysterious way |
| 8 | God of mercy, God of grace |
| 9 | *Hail to the Lord's anointed* |
| 10 | **Holy, holy, holy, Lord God Almighty** |
| 11 | *How sweet the name of Jesus sounds* |
| 12 | *Jerusalem the golden* |
| 13 | **Jesus shall reign where'er the sun** |
| 14 | **Nearer, my God, to thee** |
| 15 | Oft in danger, oft in woe |
| 16 | **Rock of ages, cleft for me** |
| 17 | **Sun of my soul! Thou Saviour dear** |
| 18 | **When I survey the wondrous cross** |

*    *Hymns Ancient and Modern* (1861), *A Collection of Hymns for the People Called Methodists* (1876 edition), *Psalms and Hymns* (1895), *Sankey's Sacred Songs and Solos with Standard Hymns* (c. 1896), and *Church Hymnal* (n.d.), respectively.

of hymn books in the nineteenth century, including advertisements in religious and musical journals, newspapers, and at diocesan festivals (*Music of the English Parish Church* I: 296–7). Hymn books were also marketing themselves. As far back as at least 1796, authors advertised their own books in the covers of their other books: Benjamin Rhodes's *Hymns and Divine Songs for Young Persons* ends with an advertisement for "A Concise English Grammar," also by Rhodes. By the mid- to late century, this was standard: *Golden Bells* advertises itself right on the back cover: note the appeal for large orders—"A large Discount off above prices for quantities." The success of such strategies spurred publishers to advertise their other books inside hymn books, some by the same author: see Woods's *Hymns for School Worship*, 1890, back cover. *Hymns and Rhymes for Children* (1871), for instance, has eight pages of advertising for adults in the back, including cooking books and Bible Dictionaries. This observation only underscores the obvious point that though hymn books were being sold for children, adults were the ones buying them.

By including adults' personal favorites, therefore, hymn editors expanded the commercial market for their hymn books, from Sunday school administrators needing to purchase books for their schools to parents or other adults simply wanting a versatile hymn book. This being the case, including adult favorites could become the single most successful way of selling hymn books. For instance, the major classical composers, best appreciated by adults, are often promoted: the 1855 *Sabbath School Tune-Book* highlights its use of "the works of Handel, Haydn, Mozart, Beethoven, Mendelssohn, and Croft" (v) while *The Domestic and Social Harp* (1848) features a picture of J. S. Bach on the inside cover. Promoting important hymn writers was also done, sometimes right in the title, as with *Hymns for the Church or Home Circle* (1861), subtitled *The Poetry Selected from Keble, Bishop, Heber, Milman, Mrs. Adams, Mrs. Steele, James Montgomery, Lyte, Grant, Alexander, Milton, etc*. Assured of classic composers and text-writers, adults could also be confident that "high-quality," classic compositions and texts important to a mature listening and reading public were included. One hymn book, *The Children's Hymnal with Accompanying Tunes* (1876), published by the Church of Scotland with assistance by William Henry Monk, guarantees its adult singers that "their" hymns would be included: "In issuing the Harmonized Edition of the 'Children's Hymnal,' the Committee desire to state that a considerable number of the hymns have been taken from the 'Scottish Hymnal'" (Prefatory Note). They continue, giving justification, "as it is important that children, while learning hymns suited to their youth, should also become familiar with words and music of those which will be most serviceable in after-life" (iii).

Indeed, their statement is key to understanding adult intentions, for hymn editors seem eager to implant in young minds the same staples of the faith that adults appreciated. That is, the child-adult distinction is also eradicated for theological reasons: Christian truths need to be disseminated to young and old alike. Many children's hymns bear the stamp of childhood only in poetry and approach; their topics would be found in the most common of adult hymns because of basic Christian ideals. Victorian hymn writers very much wanted children to know the vital beliefs of the Christian faith: human sin and Christ's Atonement for that sin; death and the Heavenly Reward; and our obligatory, earthly praise to the Creator.[7] Sometimes, it appears, hymn editors preferred well-known adult hymns to convey this theology. Considering these basic topics of Christian significance, we find child-centered and adult-centered hymns addressing them in high numbers throughout children's hymn books.

For one, the sins of humanity were a staple theme in early Protestant and Evangelical hymns still found frequently in Victorian children's hymn books. Both Anglican Bishop Thomas Ken's late seventeenth-century favorites "Awake, my soul, and with the sun" (in 43% of children's hymn books) and "Glory to Thee, my God, this night" (31%) focus on avoiding sinful deeds. This theme continues

[7]   See Adey's discussion of "Myth" consisting of the Trinity (Father, Son, and Holy Ghost), and the "Four Last Things": Death, Judgment, Hell, and Heaven (*Hymns and the Christian 'Myth'* 9).

through eighteenth- and early nineteenth-century Nonconformist theology like Congregationalist Jane and Ann Taylor's "God is in heaven, Can He hear?" (24%). Though not published in *Hymns for Infant Minds*, it is very much of that early Evangelical bent, exhorting the child reader to repent of sins. Sin is invoked, but sins of a child's ken: lying, doing small wrong deeds. In contrast, "adult" hymns tend to generalize about "Human Sin"; further, they more frequently link "sin" with Christ's atonement for that sin. One significant aspect is that, after these late eighteenth- and early nineteenth-century hymns belaboring the details for children, most nineteenth-century hymns recounting the Passion and Atonement of Christ are rarely addressed specifically to children but are adult hymns masquerading in children's hymn books. Children's and adult hymn books across the century contain various "adult" hymns that recount the blood of Christ and the awe of the crucifixion: Cowper's "There is a fountain filled with blood" (18%), Wesley's "Christ the Lord is risen today" (22%), and Watts's "When I survey the wondrous cross" (28%). This observation could explain why these and "Rock of ages, cleft for me," already discussed, were so frequently included, since fewer hymns of sin were being written specifically for children: as Chapter 2 suggests, late-century views of the middle-class child had shifted from "sinful" to "pure."

After the Christian's earthly life of sin and repentance comes the ultimate reward: the life in heaven. Thus, many hymns focus on this final trajectory. Classic hymns still find their way into children's hymn books, from the twelfth-century hymn "Jerusalem the golden!" by Bernard of Cluny, as translated by J. M. Neale in the nineteenth-century (22%), to Watts's "There is a land of pure delight" (also 22%). Others are new: Anne Shepherd's 1830s "Around the throne of God in heaven" (25%), Thomas Bilby's 1832 "Here we suffer grief and pain" (24%), and Andrew Young's 1843 "There is a happy land" (38%). All of these were popular inclusions in order to prepare and excite children about the afterlife, although only one (Shepherd's) addresses them specifically, to be discussed further in Chapter 6.

A final, frequent theme to appear in children's hymn books is that of praise to the Maker, the Christ, and/or the Trinity. Here we find classics such as John Milton's 1623 "Let us with a gladsome mind" (36%) or William Kethe's 1561 "All people that on earth do dwell" (25%). John Newton's 1779 "One there is above all others" (30%) and Edward Perronet's 1779 "All hail the power of Jesus' name" (31%) precede newer favorites such as Reginald Heber's 1826 "Holy, holy, holy" (33%) and Robert Grant's 1833 "O worship the King, all glorious above" (22%). Amongst the many hymns of praise only three—Watts's "I sing the almighty power of God" (29%) and "Jesus shall reign where'er the sun" (31%), from his *Divine and Moral Songs*, and C. F. Alexander's "All things bright and beautiful" (17%) from her *Hymns for Little Children*—are clearly written for children.

While a listing of titles in these categories suggests a similarity in theological approach, close comparisons obviously show denominational, personal, and age-appropriate distinctions. Among many examples illustrating differences between hymns for children and for adults, two of the above hymns of praise suggest a clarity and assertiveness in the child's hymn-text that are clearly missing from the adult version. Watts's "I sing the almighty power of God" is from his 1715 *Divine and Moral Songs for Children.* Set to many tunes (such as "Dublin," "Ellacombe," and "Washington") because of its common-meter structure, it is a lively hymn. The poetic techniques engage children on many levels: the "story" of creation with vivid natural imagery; personification ("sun to rule" and "stars obey"—v. 2); and anaphora ("I sing" beginning every verse). Other poetic elements—alliteration of "s" in "seas" and "skies" and "m" in "mountains" and "moon"—exaggerate simple sounds for youthful voices; further, simple concepts of God as king, His rule over flowers and clouds, His gentle qualities, are all calibrated to a child's understanding. Notably, the child remarks upon all of these by singing: "I sing the almighty power of God" (v. 1), "I sing the wisdom that ordained" (v. 2), and "I sing the goodness of the Lord" (v. 3). Through singing, the child praises the Maker:

> Lord, how Thy wonders are displayed
>> Where'er I turn mine eye;
> If I survey the ground I tread,
>> Or gaze upon the sky! (v. 4, Hymn 35, *Methodist SS*, 1879)

The empowered child singer is actively responding to the wonders of creation: surveying, treading, gazing.

When adults sing the wonders of the Divinity, the approach is somewhat different, as we might note by instancing the adult 1839 hymn "O worship the King" by Robert Grant, a lawyer and member of Parliament, who is recognized solely for this hymn. It is sung principally to the tune "Hanover" by William Croft (1708), which emphasizes the quick near-dactylic trimeter of the verse:

> O worship the King, All glorious above;
> O gratefully sing, His power and His love:
> Our Shield and Defender, The Ancient of days,
> Pavilioned in splendour, And girded with praise.
>> (v. 1, Hymn 26, *Methodist SS*, 1879)

Many powerful phrases define "the King": "Our Shield and Defender," "The Ancient of Days," "Our Maker, Defender / Redeemer, and Friend" (v. 5). The latter description of "Friend" and God's "tender mercies" (v. 5) suggest the gentler theology of mid-century, yet the "might" of God, evoked by the words "Almighty" and "power" and depicted as "chariots of wrath" (v. 2), repeatedly surfaces as well. As with Watts's hymn, God is seen as powerful over creation, His "bountiful care … streams from the hills [and] … descends to the plain" (v. 4). It is these "big words and images" which, Erik Routley presumes, "continue to attract children" (*Hymns and Human Life* 256). However, I would argue that Grant gives less agency to children. That is, the subject of the human response is never named, as all are in the imperative tense. Like Watts, Grant encourages his singers to "worship the King," "gratefully sing," and "tell of his might." Yet the command is given without an actor named outright. When humanity is mentioned, it is specifically as "Frail children of dust" and "humbler creation" (vv. 5, 6). Unlike Watts's exhortation of the child to "sing the almighty power of God," this adult singer is made to rhetorically deny his/her voice: "Thy bountiful care What tongue can recite?" and this disembodied "tongue" allows for only "lisping" by verse 6 ("lisp to Thy praise"). In short, I would argue, the child hymn is actually more empowering of the singer than is the adult version.[8] Though Watts's hymn was found in 29% of children's hymn books and Grant's "O worship the King" only in 22%, one still wonders why Grant's hymn appeared at all. In fact, in 16 of these hymn books, both hymns were chosen, while in six of them, Grant's hymn was chosen alone.

In essence, then, hymn editors included "crossover hymns" for sentimental reasons, their love of personal favorites; for commercial reasons, to appeal to their adult market; and for theological reasons, to convey religious convictions through a myriad of poetic imagery, complex or not. As the last example suggests, oftentimes the children's version could be more empowering, yet comparable adult hymns were still sought to complete children's hymn books. Therefore, another possible reason for the number of adult and child hymns co-mingling in children's hymn books is that the Victorians really did not create the split so readily acknowledged today between children's and adults' psychological needs: indeed, hymn writers quickly fall back onto the common tropes of childhood to address all Christians, child or adult. Consider the themes which so readily come to the fore in children's hymns, from fears to weakness, bedtime and story time. "Crossover hymns" suggest common traits in adult hymns as Victorians defined children and "children of God" in the same terms.

Of one such child-centered theme, we might consider hymns addressing fear—of the unknown, of darkness, and of the time before bed. Such hymns actually existed for both children *and* adults. Thomas Ken's classic 1695 "Glory to Thee, my God this night" (31%) joined a handful of contemporary adult hymns about nighttime, including James Edmeston's 1820 "Saviour, breathe an evening blessing" (24%) and Sabine Baring-Gould's 1865 "Now the day is over" (20%). "Sun of my soul, my Saviour dear," however, was by far the most popular "nighttime" hymn for children, found in 42% of hymnals, the third most popular hymn for children. It began as a personal poem of religious reflection by the Tractarian leader John Keble, who includes it as the second poem in his *The Christian Year* (1827). It was thus intended for adult contemplation and, indeed, became exceedingly popular in this market: 11 of the poems from the collection, including "Sun of my soul" were selected for *Hymns Ancient and Modern* (Bradley, *Abide* 21). Therefore, it is surprising to see it in so many children's hymn books of the period. For one, its heightened poetic language is far more complex then simpler bedtime hymns for children (such as Mary Lundie Duncan's "Jesus, tender Shepherd, hear me / Bless Thy little lamb to-night" of 1842). Instead, Keble invokes the symbolism of Christ the Sun: "Sun of my soul, Thou Saviour dear, / It is not night if Thou be near" (v. 1, *Hymns Ancient and Modern*,

---

[8]   Other pairs suggest this, too: the Taylors' "God is in heaven, Can He hear?" and Toplady's "Rock of ages, cleft for me"; and Luke's "I think when I read" and Horatius Bonar's 1846 hymn, "I heard the voice of Jesus say."

No. 11). Yet Keble contemplates nighttime as analogous with death: "Abide with me when night is nigh / For without Thee I dare not die" (v. 3). Such poetic and theological complexity, together with the fact that children are never invoked in the poem, makes it a surprising choice for hymn-book editors. Yet the hymn clearly suggests that all Christians are "children" in their need for God—"If some poor wandering child of thine / Have spurned to-day the voice divine" (v. 4)—equating the adult with the child in unmistakable terms.

Another "child" category surprisingly found in many adult hymn books is that of "story-hymns." It is no surprise that hymns for children reflect the world of storytelling, particularly for imparting theological lessons through biblical stories. Consider Luke's 1841 "I think when I read that sweet story of old" about Jesus embracing the children from Matthew 19 (46%); James D. Burns's 1857 "Hushed was the evening hymn" about the child Samuel (20%); and Jeannette Threlfall's 1873 "Hosanna, laud Hosanna, the little children sang" about the children on Jesus' arrival into Jerusalem (4%). Adults yet "tell stories" focused on Jesus' life,[9] as with W. O. Cushing's "O I love to think of Jesus / As He sat beside the sea" (1866, found in 2% of children's hymnals), or on Old Testament stories such as Sarah Flower Adams's very popular hymn "Nearer, my God, to Thee" (1841) based on the story of Jacob at Bethel (Genesis 28:10–22) (26%).

The adult was thus "lowered" to think like a child through stories, the act of storytelling "crossing over" into much of the adult hymn literature … and then back. "I love to tell the story" by Katherine Hankey (1866) was a popular adult hymn, found in two of the five adult hymn books I surveyed (both the 1895 Baptist hymnal, *Psalms and Hymns* and Sankey's 1896 *Sacred Songs and Solos*). It remained a common inclusion in adult hymn books into the twentieth century (*Hymnary.org* lists 1,001 American hymnals from 1866 to the present that still carry the hymn). Despite its late publication date and intended audience of adults, though, it was already found in 8% of children's hymn books by late century (including the 1878 *Songs of Love and Mercy for the Young*, the 1879 *Methodist Sunday-School Hymn-Book*, and the 1890 *Golden Bells*). Based on Hankey's long poem on the life of Jesus, titled *The Old, Old Story* (1867), the hymn reflects more generically on that story in order to emphasize the joy in the storytelling:

> I love to tell the story Of unseen things above,
> Of Jesus and His glory, Of Jesus and His love.
> > (v. 1, Hymn 405, *Methodist SS*, 1879)

---

[9]    An extremely large adult category, which was still not as large as it is today, is the Christmas carol. Those found in nineteenth-century hymn books include Tate and Brady's 1700 "While shepherds watched their flocks by night" (18%); Charles Wesley's 1739 "Hark! The herald angels sing" (40%); Reginald Heber's 1811 "Brightest and best of the songs of the morning" (22%); and James Montgomery's 1822 "Hail to the Lord's Anointed" (23%), all in the top 50 hymns for children.

Its simple rhetoric, internal rhyme (story-glory), and end-line couplets (above-love), combined with the engrossing tune ("Hankey") by William G. Fischer (1869), would appeal to children. Yet its pulse and vibrancy obviously appealed to adults as well. Thus it serves as an example of common objectives desired by both adult and children in a hymn: the joy of storytelling and hymn singing:

> I love to tell the story, Because I know it's true;
> It satisfies my longings, As nothing else could do. (v. 1)

An advocate of missions to South Africa (McCutchan 289), Hankey makes indirect note of "some [who] have never heard / The message of salvation / From God's own holy Word" (v. 3). By verse 4, the singer sings in Heaven where "in scenes of glory, / I sing the new, new song / 'Twill be the old, old story / That I have loved so long." A repetitive refrain added by Fischer—soaring to an E5 (high E above middle C)—creates a triumphant finish: "I love to tell the story / 'Twill be my theme in glory / To tell the old, old story / Of Jesus and His love." This adult hymn, delineating missionary work and even death, and never once addressing children, yet appeals to them with rhyme, repetition, and tune, attesting to a shared human interest in hymn singing.

The psychological similarity between the child and adult, rapt in stories of Jesus, becomes unconsciously manifest in one significant hymn, "Tell me the stories of Jesus," written by William Henry Parker and published in *The Sunday School Hymnary* in 1885 (set to the tune "Stories of Jesus" by Frederic Arthurs Challinor). Not nearly as popular in children's hymn books as those hymns discussed, probably because of its late composition date, it yet reflects Victorian themes of storytelling, childhood simplicity, and an unconscious eliding of child and adult. It begins as if from a child's perspective:

> Tell me the stories of Jesus, I love to hear
>> Things I would ask him to tell me If he were here:
> Scenes by the wayside, Tales of the sea,
>> Stories of Jesus, Tell them to me. (v. 1, *United Methodist Hymnal*)

Here, the singer-as-child is painted as rapt in attention to the stories Jesus tells. By the second verse, the singer imagines the scene full of other children: "First let me hear how the children / Stood round his knee," then positions himself within the scene, possibly as another child: "And I shall fancy his blessing / Resting on me" (v. 2). Interestingly, though, by the third verse, the singer has clearly differentiated himself from the children, "following" them into Jerusalem, as if now from an adult point of view:

> Into the city I'd follow The children's band,
>> Waving a branch of the palm tree High in my hand;
> One of his heralds, Yes, I would sing
>> Loudest hosannas, "Jesus is King!" (v. 3)

Now the singer-as-adult has joined the adulation and waves the palm branch during Jesus' triumphant march into Jerusalem, the hymn thus bridging the divided spaces between child and adult.

In short, these hymns reveal hymn writers much aligned in their definitions of children: their fears, their comfort in stories. What should also be clear, however, is that a great many "adult" hymns featured these themes as well, making them natural inclusions in children's hymn books. Ultimately, hymn writers—for children and adults—consciously or unconsciously reveal the psychological reality that adults and children share similar joys and fears, pleasures and trials. The editor of *The Domestic and Social Harp* (1848), O. P. Woodford, in fact addresses this point, stating in his preface that "parents will take pleasure in humbling themselves as little children to sing these hymns" (iii), while for children, these hymns "will remain in the mind in after life, and prove a safeguard against temptation and a support in trial" (iii). With child and adult defined in similar terms in their "humbleness," "pleasures," and times of "trial," it is no wonder that analogous hymns would appeal to both. Further, though the years of childhood might be distinct, the years of adulthood were ever fast approaching. Preparing the child for his future adult life seemed the task of the hymn editor. Both theologically and psychologically, adult hymns inspired Christian comforts, as the following testimony suggests: Stead writes that "I can remember my mother singing it [Newton's "Begone, Unbelief"] when I was a tiny boy, barely able to see over the book-ledge in the minister's pew; and to this day, whenever I am in doleful dumps … that one doggerel verse comes back as clear as a blackbird's note" (ix). Stead, remember, would go on to compile *Hymns That Have Helped*.

In conclusion, there are various reasons why adult hymns appear so frequently in children's hymn books, from the sentimental to the commercial, from the theological to the psychological. Adults bought hymn books for their youthful charges if books contained their own favorites as well. Sunday school teachers and parents would seek essential Christian truths and recognize innate commonalities, all being "children of God" with similar pleasures and fears. Hymns for children were therefore culled from children's hymn books, such as Watts's *Divine and Moral Songs for Children* and Taylors' *Hymns for Infant Minds*, and from adult hymn books such as the extremely influential adult hymn book, *Hymns Ancient and Modern* from which "Our blest Redeemer, ere he breathed," "Nearer, my God, to Thee," and "Abide with me" all derived. This overlap suggests that adult marketing disseminated not just ideologies but also actual song texts into the hands of children. Striking are the highly complex poetics used in many of these hymns such as Keble's "Sun of my soul," the third-highest represented hymn in children's hymn books. Conversely, very child-like hymns such as Hankey's "I love to tell the story" flowed back into adult hymn books. Thus, adult hymns and children's hymns mingled freely, expressing the same vital truths of the faith and of humanity. "Tell me the stories of Jesus" directly shows unconscious blurring of the child and adult viewpoint, suggesting the distinction between the two states to be less rigid than scholars of Victorian culture have traditionally suggested.

Yet none of these reasons fully explain why adult-focused hymns figure so prominently in hymn books, often eclipsing children's hymns in poetic and theological complexity and diminishing childhood agency, as the Watts-Grant comparison suggests. And so the question remains, if hymn books for children contained so many adult favorites, what appealed to children? What would enable hymn editors to claim their books had great "Popularity with Children," as the subtitle of an 1843 hymn book asserts? The explanation, I will argue, is the tunes, that great equalizer between adults and children, a medium that literate and illiterate, old and young could appreciate. The power of Fischer's tune to generate interest in Hankey's "I love to tell the story" in both adult and children's hymn books suggests the immense capacity to be found in that other aesthetic of hymns so rarely examined in this context: the music. The remaining section of this chapter attempts this examination.

## Part II
## "I sing the almighty power of God":
## The Power of Music in Delighting Children

The history of English hymn music is complex, and its distinctive use of meters and changing musical style would affect nineteenth-century children in powerful ways. Children's hymnody intersects with the general history of hymnody of the Victorian period in some important ways, three trends of which I will take up in this section, each with an exemplary hymn found frequently in children's hymn books. First to note is that congregational hymn singing reached a climax in the nineteenth century, and with this development came the desire to better train congregations and children to sing the often more challenging tunes, which consequently entered the child repertoire. Secondly, English hymnody had, throughout most of its history, used tunes and texts interchangeably, allowing children some degree of creativity, until the second half of the century when *Hymns Ancient and Modern* (1861) especially began intentionally pairing tunes and texts: often those hymns with the most recognizable tune achieved permanency whether the text was adult-centered or child-centered. Thirdly, though tunes of the past continued to be used in the nineteenth century, the century saw a flood of new tunes, by trained composers and amateurs alike, pour into churches and church hymnals. Indeed, tunes of the Victorian era bear a distinct emotional quality, to critics' dismay then and now, for, indeed, this music could often "carry away" its young singers. In all arenas, then, children's hymn singing overlapped with important features of Victorian hymnody, helping to explain why hymn music was, in many ways, the climax of a nineteenth-century child's singing experience. Ultimately, an examination of children's hymn-book music in the nineteenth century reveals how much children and adults alike loved to sing and explains why; such a plethora of tuneful child-centered *and* adult-centered hymns entered the hymn-book repertoire.

## I. Congregational Singing and Musical Education

Though congregations had sung in church settings since the Reformation, usually this practice was limited[10] and, instead, congregations repeated back metrical psalms "lined out" by a precentor. Or they would listen to a "west-gallery" choir and instrumentalists (later, a barrel organ) sing the psalms (in parish churches) or listen to a trained cathedral choir and organ (in cities, college towns) (see Bradley, *Abide*, ch. 1, and Temperley, *Music* I: chs. 8–9). Congregational singing was launched in an extremely powerful way with the eighteenth-century Methodist movement. As is well noted,[11] the Methodist movement was so successful and influential because of its passionate, engaging hymns and hymn singing where ordinary congregants could join in the music instead of mechanically singing back the words of the parish clerk or passively listening to a parish choir sing. Though favoring simple tunes, John Wesley nevertheless encouraged heartfelt, emotional singing ("the power of music" being its ability "to raise various passions in the human mind"[12]) and therefore turned to popular, if controversial sources for tunes to his brother's and other Methodist hymns, from operas to tavern tunes.[13] Using engaging tunes and unrestricted singing, often in the open air, the Methodists enticed many followers through music. Following their example, Dissenters of the turn of the century also composed "rousing and thrilling tunes" that greatly popularized hymn writers of the previous century: Watts, Wesley, Cowper, and Newton (Bradley, *Abide* 18). Routley points in particular to the evangelicals who "explosively increase[d] the vocabulary of their congregations. These people did not have to get along on six

---

[10]    Post-Reformation congregational music was mainly that of psalmody—metrical paraphrases of psalms set to simple tunes—as Calvinist leaders sought to limit music that could be distracting from biblical teachings. Thomas Sternhold and John Hopkins's "Old Version" of the psalms (1562) was later replaced by Nahum Tate and Nicholas Brady's "New Version" (1696). Especially as inaugurated by Watts, gradually non-biblical-text hymns were accepted in various Dissenting congregations.

[11]    For more about the success and controversy of the early Methodist hymn singing, see, among others, Benson, chs. 5–6; Gillman, ch. 12; Routley (*The Musical Wesleys*, chs. 2–3; *Hymns and Human Life*, ch. 7); Temperley (*Music of the English Parish Church*, ch. 7; "John Wesley, Music, and the People Called Methodists"); and Clapp-Itnyre, *Angelic Airs, Subversive Songs*, ch. 3.

[12]    From John Wesley's essay "The Power of Music," quoted in Routley, *The Musical Wesleys*, 15.

[13]    Though Charles and John Wesley used psalm tunes and German hymn melodies, they also revived the practice of the "parody hymn tune," that taken from another often secular source (Temperley, "John Wesley" 13). These might include bawdy, music-hall, or tavern tunes, Charles willing to "plunder the carnal lover" to rescue good, innocent tunes for evangelistic purposes. Methodists were frequently criticized for enlisting "profane Harmony," as charged a contemporary musician (both qtd. in Clapp-Itnyre, *Angelic Airs* 83).

metrical psalm tunes. The massive choirs ... led the singing and everybody joined in enthusiastically, carried along by the attractiveness of the music" (*Short* 50–51). Ultimately, leaders of the Church of England recognized this musical power:[14] Sir Robert Grant, member of the Anglican Church, wrote, "I am persuaded that the singing has been a great instrument in the Dissenters' hands of drawing away persons from the church, and why should not we take that instrument out of their hands?" (qtd. in Bradley, *Abide* 15). Competition for church singers thus propelled the High Church movement to write and promote hymns (Grant himself went on to author "O worship the King," discussed above). Through the High-Church Society for Promoting Church Music and its journal, *The Parish Choir*, for instance, Dr. Robert Druitt sought to encourage congregational singing. He sought hymns fitting congregations' abilities, encouraged unison singing, and found melodies within the comfortable range of the average human voice (Bradley, *Abide* 36; see also Temperley, *Music* I: 258). Ian Bradley writes that by the late 1860s, most churches in England and Wales had abandoned metrical psalms and lining out in favor of congregational hymn singing (*Abide* 36).[15] Congregational hymn singing, then, became a defining feature of Victorian music. As Nicholas Temperley writes, hymnody brought together "all parties in the Church and gave congregations a genuine and appropriate part to play in a joint performance with choir and organ" (*Music* I: 314).

Children had for several centuries formed a part of the choirs in parishes and cathedrals alike, and the "surpliced choirs" of boys and men are still to be found in the great Anglican cathedral services of today. Rev. Henry Croswell's records of his supervisory visits to 500 Anglican churches from 1872–1882, which include notations of the choirs, references this practice consistently in High and many Broad churches of that era. His records further suggest that Low churches relied on mixed-gender choirs (school or charity) or all-girl choirs (or girls and "young ladies"). Children thus undergirded choir-singing: of a random sample of 100 church choirs from his records, 90 included or were exclusively of children.[16]

---

[14]  Influenced by the success of the Dissenters, the Church of England ultimately accepted hymns into its worship after a judgment of the Consistory Court of York in 1820, opening up the floodgates to Anglican, specifically High Church and Tractarian, hymnody. This movement would culminate in the publication of *Hymns Ancient and Modern* (1861).

[15]  Thomas Hardy's fiction and poetry is filled with nostalgic references to the old psalm tunes as with Somerset in *A Laodicean* (1881, ch. 1). Poems honor them: "New Sabbath" and "Mount Ephraim" in "A Church Romance" and "Cambridge New" in "Afternoon Service at Mellstock (Circa 1850)." For more about music in Hardy's poetry, please see Clapp-Itnyre, "The Contentious 'Figure' of Music in the Poetry of Thomas Hardy."

[16]  From Henry Croswell's Diaries, November 1872–September 1886 (in two volumes; transcript only), located at the Bodleian Library, Oxford. The disparity of choirs between Low and High is quite significant, though perhaps not surprising: fewer than 10 High churches used anything but surpliced boys/men choirs, while the same were completely missing from Low churches who instead relied upon (in about equal numbers) male/female, children's, and girls/women choirs. This Anglican tradition is yet a rare moment of gendered children's hymn singing.

It is not surprising, then, that children were sought to lead the new emphasis on congregational hymn singing. Even during the days of psalmody, children—charity children, in particular—were used to improve unison church singing: children were taught metrical psalms, then scattered among the congregation to lead adults (Temperley, "John Wesley" 6). This trend was revived in the nineteenth century; by teaching children how to read and sing music, church musicians and hymn book-editors envisioned musical children greatly transforming the hymn singing during service. For instance, writes C. H. Bateman, editor of *Sacred Melodies for Children, Selected Chiefly on the Ground of their Popularity with Children* (1843):

> It is high time that Sabbath School Teachers should more attentively cultivate the musical powers of their scholars. It is the surest way of improving our congregational singing, and of giving to your labours an additional interest in the children's minds. It will robe their school in some of the sweetest and most pleasurable associations in their thoughts, and it will open to them a source of joy which in coming years may prove a real blessing to their souls. (8)

Croswell, in fact, refers to schoolboys aiding congregational singing at St. Luke's (March 1876) and girls' singing during a service at St. Paul, Whitechapel (September 4, 1881), which led to "fine congregational singing." Children contributed in other ways: Croswell comments on a young girl playing hymns for the congregation (St. Ann, Hoxton, September 12, 1875). If there was a disadvantage in relying so heavily on children, it was their inherent childishness: they were "beautiful singers but *badly* behaved," Crowell notes (St. Augustine, May 6, 1877; his emphasis).

It is much to children's credit that they could lead congregations in this way given that hymn music was becoming more ornate during the century. Printing four-part harmonies was becoming more common mid-century, as in *Hymns Ancient and Modern*, but also in those for children, such as *The Methodist Sunday-School Hymn and Tune-Book*, allowing choir directors to give children different parts to sing if desired (bass possibly excluded, depending on the boys' voice ranges). Indeed, new Victorian tunes were often written like part-songs of the period, with the lower voices given interesting melodic moments (Routley, *Christian Hymnody* 123; Temperley, *Music* I: 304). Older tunes were also harmonized and enthusiastically marketed, notably in children's hymn books: a hymn book of 1876 highlighted its "fresh and beautiful melodies harmonized in plain but careful manner" (*Silver Songs*, preface). Further, various hymn books now solicited prominent composers to "revise the harmonies" of hymns as Monk did for *The Children's Hymnal* (1876) and H. Elliot Button did for E. H. Mayo Gunn's *School Hymns: with Tunes* (1893). Given this complexity of parts, middle-class home singing accompanied by a piano seemed a perfect place to begin learning: "Our congregations are composed of families, and how can we hope to improve Congregational Singing better than by the constant practice of Part Singing in the domestic circle?" (Preface, *The Family Altar*, 1843). Rather than settling for simple monophonic singing, Victorians expected children to embrace and then lead homophonic part-singing first in their homes and then in their congregations.

But the musical education of children had moved well beyond the home by the 1840s, especially for working-class children. Led by W. E. Hickson, the "father of English school music" under Queen Victoria, the music-education movement exploded nation-wide in the 1840s and 1850s in hopes of ensuring that all classes, with or without musical options at home, would learn this most moral and generosity-inducing of art forms (as Hickson argued). Notably, much of musical education was done in the service of congregational singing. Those seeking to improve singing within the Anglican Church included John Turner (*A Manual of Instruction in Vocal Music*, 1833), Sarah Glover (*Scheme for Rendering Psalmody Congregational*, 1835), and John Hullah (*Wilhem's Method of Teaching Singing*, 1841). Hullah's mass singing lessons from 1839–1841 (and furthered by those whom he had taught) introduced singing to over 50,000 London working-class children (Bradley, *Abide* 33).

Most widespread, though, was the Tonic Sol-fa system, introduced by Glover but taken up and advanced by John Curwen, Congregationalist minister. His system of Tonic Sol-fa intended to make music-reading universal in its simplicity using a system of tones and pulses building off of a "movable doh."[17] Through his schools, journals, publications, and even children's stories, he advanced musical education for untold numbers of adults and children: "His early experience of teaching children, coupled with an understanding of factory assembly-line and business methods, enabled Tonic Sol-fa to expand at an exponential rate ... By 1870, Tonic Sol-fa had eclipsed its competitors and dominated the British sight-singing movement" (McGuire 20). Foremost his intent was to improve music-singing in church services and Sunday schools, and clearly children were central to this mission as his *The Child's Own Hymn Book* in 1841 and *Singing for Schools and Congregations* in 1843 attest, both of which went through many editions.[18] In the latter, Curwen writes of the power of music and poetry to inspire the young:

> They impress more deeply truths already taught; they give a language to the faith, and hope, and love, and joy, of youthful piety; they elevate the mind; and help to raise the heart to God. None but the heartless or the unwise can doubt the power for good or evil which poetry and music are constantly exerting on education, or fail to see the importance of earnest study and watchful care, that this power may be well applied. (xiii)

---

[17]  That is, the system used symbols for each of the notes of the scale (doh, ray, me, fah, soh, lah, te), then moved this scale to each key, always beginning the first note with the syllable "doh." This was in contrast to the "fixed doh" system which would begin its scale on the actual note/symbol ("ray" for D-major, for instance). See McGuire's "Brief History of Tonic Sol-fa" (8–13) and much more about the movement in his *Music and Victorian Philanthropy*. I use scientific pitch notation where middle C is written as C4, etc.

[18]  Some hymn books came out in two versions: "Old Notation" and "Tonic Sol-fa," such as *The Sunday Scholar's Hymn Book Consisting of Five Hundred Hymns, with Tunes for Use in Sunday Schools* (c. 1880).

Educating the young to partake in religious music was thus paramount.[19] Echoed Thomas Sturrock, a contemporary of Curwen's and also a children's hymn editor, in *The Sabbath School Tune-Book and Service of Praise for the Sanctuary* (1855): "It frequently occurs, however, that the best musical compositions are destroyed by bad singing. Singing must be studied as any other branch of education … To assist in obtaining this result the present work has been undertaken" (vii).

In summary, the congregation now had a central role in the music of the service, both in High and Low churches, and children were being sought to learn and then lead others in achieving musical aptitude. A later section will analyze the quality of the Victorian hymn tune more, but clearly as the century progressed, hymn tunes challenged children with their more complex harmonies, chromaticism, and modulations. When intricate harmony is introduced, children are doubly challenged to learn the music and sing it against another part. Clearly, then, Victorian children were trained, expected, and acknowledged to be strong musicians able to sing the musically challenging melodies and harmonies written for "adult" hymns, as with the soaring refrains to the tunes "Coronation" and "Diadem" (both used with "All hail the power of Jesus' name").

To end with a Wesley hymn, I hope to show just how difficult and invigorating these hymns and their tunes could be, and why music education was enabling children to bear a part in adult hymn singing as never before. Charles Wesley wrote "Christ the Lord is risen to-day" in 1739 and published it in the Wesleys' *Hymns and Sacred Poems*. It was not, notably, reprinted in his 1763 children's hymn book, *Hymns for Children, and Others of Riper Years*. Nonetheless, it was especially embraced by children's hymn-book editors, found in 22% of children's hymn books of the century,[20] beginning with Benson's 1806 Methodist *Hymns for Children and Young Persons* but included in other denominational books such as Anglican William Henry Monk's 1876 *Children's Hymnal with Accompanying Tunes*. Charles Wesley's text is majestic and appropriate for Easter morning (see Figure 3.1):

> Christ the Lord is risen today, Alleluia!
>     Sons of men and angels say! Alleluia!
> Raise your joys and triumphs high: Alleluia!
>     Sing, ye heavens: thou earth, reply. Alleluia!
>                     (v. 1, Hymn 171, *The Methodist SS*)

This majesty continues as the hymn reflects upon the resurrection of Christ ("once he died, our souls to save"), His triumph over death ("Where's thy victory,

---

[19]  For more about Victorian music education, see Clapp-Itnyre, *Angelic Airs, Subversive Songs*, ch. 1; and Bernarr Rainbow's *Land Without Music* (1967).

[20]  This number is skewed a bit in that a few of my hymn-book indices only gave the first four to five words of hymn titles and I could not always differentiate this from another popular title, "Christ the Lord is risen again! Christ hath broken every chain," a Bohemian Brethren hymn translated by Catherine Winkworth.

boasting grave?"), and the human response ("Raise your joys and triumphs high / Sing, ye heavens, and earth reply"). Wesleyan doctrine prevails, doctrine that, as described in Chapter 2, might be confusing, if not off-putting, to children: "Lo! The sun's eclipse is o'er / Lo! He sets in blood no more!" (v. 2), dark allusions to Good Friday and the crucifixion. Consider, especially, verse 3, the first two lines not often found in late twentieth-century hymnals:

> Vain the stone, the watch, the seal,
>> Christ hath burst the gates of hell
> Death in vain forbids His rise,
>> Christ hath opened paradise. (v. 3)

The opening lines again refer to details of the Good Friday sequence of events, from the stone that sealed Jesus' body in the tomb, to the plunge to Purgatory to redeem the fallen. By line 3, Death becomes a metaphorical, defeated figure ("Death in vain forbids His rise"), a haunting image.

The explanation for the popularity among children of this complex hymn probably lies in its tune, "Easter Hymn," equally exultant as the text, and popular enough to be found in 13 of 30 children's tune books of the century. Misattributed to J. W. Worgan, Henry Carey, and even Handel (McCutchan 191), the tune first appeared in *Lyra Davidica, or a Collection of Divine Songs and Hymns, partly New Composed, partly Translated from the High-German, and Latin Hymns; and set to easy and pleasant tunes, for more General Use* (1708).[21] Set there to the Anglican text "Jesus Christ is Risen today," it was altered by John Arnold (*Compleat Psalmodist*, 1741) which John Wesley then used (as "Salisbury Tune") in setting his brother's text "Christ the Lord is risen to-day" as published in his *Foundery Collection* of 1742 (C. Young 281). This is the tune found in nineteenth-century hymn books (and still used today): employing challenging melismas (a syllable set to multiple notes, typically five or more) in the triumphant "alleluias" after each verse, it is somewhat like a call and response (in fact, the *Companion* to the current American United Methodist hymnal suggests the congregation, choir, female, and male voices all take turns singing the alleluias [C. Young 281]).[22] Significantly, the well-known harmonization to this tune was given by Victorians, in *Hymns Ancient and Modern* (C. Young 281), where it was used with "Jesus Christ is risen to-day," Hymn 107, second tune.[23] The textures in the

---

[21] The tune book introduced lively airs to which, in Germany, peasants plow, servants labor, and children play (see Lightwood, 149–50), and this particular tune ("The Resurrection") is very danceable.

[22] Admittedly, John Wesley had argued against "vain repetition" and counterpoint, and anything else that would obscure the words. Yet Temperley points out that above all else, Wesley wanted emotional music to inspire followers. See his "John Wesley and Music."

[23] Many of Wesley's texts were given engaging, lasting tunes by nineteenth-century composers: "And can it be that I should gain" (Thomas Campbell, 1835), "O for a thousand tongues to sing" (Lowell Mason, 1839), "Love divine, all loves excelling" (John Zundel, 1870), and "Jesus, lover of my soul" (Joseph Parry, 1879) for example.

*THE LORD JESUS CHRIST.—RESURRECTION.*

Hymn **170** (Tune 78.)    **Holley.** L.M.

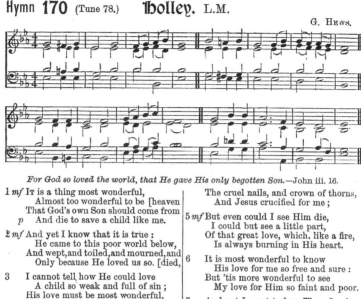

G. HEWS.

*For God so loved the world, that He gave His only begotten Son.—John iii. 16.*

1 *mf* IT is a thing most wonderful,
    Almost too wonderful to be [heaven
    That God's own Son should come from
  *p*   And die to save a child like me.

2 *mf* And yet I know that it is true :
    He came to this poor world below,
    And wept,and toiled,and mourned,and
    Only because He loved us so. [died,

3   I cannot tell how He could love
    A child so weak and full of sin ;
    His love must be most wonderful,
    If He could die my love to win.

4 *p* I sometimes think about the cross,
    And shut my eyes, and try to see

The cruel nails, and crown of thorns,
    And Jesus crucified for me ;

5 *mf* But even could I see Him die,
    I could but see a little part,
    Of that great love, which, like a fire,
    Is always burning in His heart.

6   It is most wonderful to know
    His love for me so free and sure :
    But 'tis more wonderful to see
    My love for Him so faint and poor.

7   And yet I want to love Thee, Lord :
    O, light the flame within my heart,
  *cr.* And I will love Thee more and more,
  *f*    Until I see Thee as Thou art.

Hymn **171** (Tune 312.)  **Easter Hymn.** 7.7.7.7.

*With Alleluia.*

H. CAREY.

156

Figure 3.1    "Christ the Lord is risen today." From *The Methodist Sunday-School Hymn & Tune-Book* (1879). From the author's collection and in the public domain.

**RESURRECTION.**

Raise your joys and tri-umphs high: Al - le - lu - ia!

Sing, ye heavens : thou earth, re - ply. Al - le - lu - ia!

2nd Tune. (Tune 314). **St. Chad's.** 7.7.7.7. *With Alleluia.*

W. H. MONK.

Christ, the Lord, is risen to-day, Al-le-lu - ia! Sons of men and an-gels say! Al-le-lu - ia!

Raise your joys and triumphs high! Al-le-lu - ia! Sing, ye heavens: Thou earth, re - ply. Al-le-lu - ia!

*He is not here: for He is risen, as He said.*—Matthew xxviii. 6.

1 *f* 'CHRIST, the Lord, is risen to-day,'
   Sons of men and angels say!
   Raise your joys and triumphs high :
   Sing, ye heavens : thou earth, reply.

2   Love's redeeming work is done ;
   Fought the fight, the battle won :
   Lo ! the sun's eclipse is o'er ;
   Lo ! he sets in blood no more !

3 *mf* Vain the stone, the watch, the seal,
   Christ hath burst the gates of hell ;
   Death in vain forbids His rise,
   Christ hath opened paradise.

4 *f* Lives again our glorious King !
   Where, O death, is now thy sting ?
 *mf* Once He died our souls to save ;
   *f* Where's thy victory, boasting grave

5 *f* Soar we now where Christ hath led,
   Following our exalted Head :
   Made like Him, like Him we rise,
 *mf* Ours the cross, the grave, the skies.

6 *f* King of glory ! Soul of bliss !
   Everlasting life is this,
   Thee to know, Thy power to prove,
   Thus to sing, and thus to love.

157

Figure 3.1    (continued)

verses are lush and homophonic,[24] and the parts almost become polyphonic in the alleluias as sopranos sing extended melismas, sometimes as many as six notes to a syllable, while alto, tenor, and bass move with their own distinct lines underneath. Children could sing these parts, it being found in four parts in most children's hymn-and-tune books, such as *The Methodist Sunday-School, Golden Bells*, and *The Sunday Scholar's Tonic Sol-fa Edition*. It was a further challenge in its key; nineteenth-century hymn books often used higher keys than is typical today, so that this tune was found in the 1879 *Methodist Sunday-School Hymn and Tune-Book* in the key of D major (as opposed to C major of current hymn books like the 1989 American *United Methodist Hymnal*) resulting in soprano lines which soar ultimately up to an F-sharp5. Furthermore, in the 1879 *Methodist Sunday-School Hymn and Tune-Book*, the editors label dynamics for each line, opening and ending verses sung at forte with middle verses sung at mezzo-forte, for example (a practice they use throughout the hymn book), exacting close attention and effort from the young singers. Its popularity in children's hymn books reminds us that children were assumed to be capable of this challenging musicality, even to the point of leading the congregation. Moreover, these musical details demonstrate the Victorians' delight in repetition and "show," all of which made for thrilling singing for the whole congregation. Wrote turn-of-the-twentieth-century author James T. Lightwood, "there is probably no tune in Christendom so universally sung on any festal day as is the Easter hymn, with its rolling 'Hallelujah,' on Easter morning" (qtd. in McCutchan 191). It is highly probable that many Victorian children eagerly anticipated singing this yet-popular Easter favorite.

## II. Stabilizing Text and Tune

English hymnody is complicated in that text and tune have been, and continue to be, separate aesthetics. This situation began with sixteenth-century psalmody in which only a few set tunes were composed to be sung to a variety of "metrical psalms" (as in Sternhold and Hopkins's "Old Version" of 1562).[25] In contrast, in the German hymn tradition, tunes were traditionally written for only one text, ever since the beginning of the Reformation when Martin Luther himself composed texts to specific tunes: "*Ein feste Burg ist unser Gott*" ("A Mighty Fortress is

---

[24]    Though the following terms can have a range of meanings within music scholarship, I will be using the definitions as given in the *Harvard Concise Dictionary of Music*, by Don Michael Randel. Polyphony, also known as counterpoint, is a melody against a different melody. Homophony and homorhythm are identical, in which one melodic line has support from other parts (chords) in the same rhythm. Monophony is simply one melodic line.

[25]    A late example of this cultural penchant to mix and match tunes with psalms can be seen in *The Scottish Psalter: Metrical Version and Scripture Paraphrases With Tunes* (London: Oxford UP, 1929) which cut the sheets of paper in half (sometimes called a "stable door") so that tunes on the top can be flipped to any number of text on the bottom (in this case, the Psalms), allowing the leader of the singing, or the singer himself, to mix and match different tunes with different texts.

our God"), set to the tune "Ein Feste Burg," is his most famous. Instead, English tunes were written separately and labeled with a name, traditionally a place associated with that tune (Scarborough, Leicester, Durham, etc.) or a person associated with the tune or text (Mainzer or Toplady, respectively). English psalms and hymns were then labeled by their metrical lines in order to identify what tunes would fit. "Common meter" (CM), written to indicate all syllables per line as 86.86, can be set to four lines of tetrameter-trimeter-tetrameter-trimeter poetry. Short meter (SM) is 66.86, and long meter (LM) is 88.88, while short meter double (SMD) is 66.86.66.86 and long meter double (LMD) is 88.88.88.88, etc. Thus, a hymn-text merely needed to be noted with these numbers or initials and the singer could recall a corresponding tune of that metrical pattern. Through the first half of the century in particular, most children's hymn books were text-only so the metrical label was imperative for finding a known tune of the appropriate meter, either by a Sunday school teacher or other adult, in a corresponding tune book. Children thus needed to know about a dozen tunes from memory to sing to a variety of texts. In many children's tune- and hymn books, then, tunes are indexed separately from hymn titles to enable teachers and singers alike to match hymns with tunes. *Morning and Evening Hymns* (George Cameron, 1857), for example, contains a Directory listing three to four tunes that could be used with each hymn.

Cataloguing the most frequently appearing tunes, as I did with titles, in 30 children's tune books of the century (again, tune books being less common than text-only hymn books), I give the results in Table 3.4. Interestingly, those listed are, almost without fail, all from the adult tune tradition; one cannot really single out any "child's tune" among the list (with only a few exceptions, most tunes on the list can be found in the adult *The Union Tune Book*, 1879, for instance). Secondly, these tune favorites do not always mesh with the most popularly appearing hymn-texts because of the instability of tune-text combinations. The intricate "Greek Air" which was most often linked with "I think when I read" is found in only four of these tune books, for instance, because it is not elastic enough to be used with other texts. Instead, tunes that have the flexibility to be sung to many common text meters are prioritized: common meter, short meter, long meter, and 7.7.7.7 alone represent the top 12 tunes. Hymn editors, in fact, appeared to enjoy setting new combinations of text and tunes for children. The popular German tune "Ellacombe" in 76.76D meter is assigned to "I ought to love my Saviour" in the 1893 *282 Hymns and Melodies*, to "Come, Sing with holy gladness" in the 1878 *Children's Hymn Book*, to "Hail to the Lord's Annointed" in the 1879 *Methodist Sunday-School Hymn and Tune-Book*, and to "There's a Friend for little children" in the 1877 *Presbyterian Hymnal*. Even in the twentieth century it can be found paired with various texts: "Hosanna, loud Hosanna" in the 1964 *United Methodist Hymnal* and Watts's "I sing the almighty power of God" in the 1992 *Hymnal: A Worship Book* for the Brethren and Mennonite churches. Likewise, the tune "Innocents" (77.77) is a flexible melody used for both "Jesus bless a pilgrim band" and "Gentle Jesus, meek and mild" in *282 Hymns and Melodies*; "Jesus, holy undefiled" and "Give Him, then, and ever give" in the *Methodist Sunday-School Hymn Book*; "Lord,

Table 3.4        The 25 Most Frequently Appearing Hymn Tunes in 30 Nineteenth-
Century Children's Hymn Books with a Separate Tune Index

|   | # in 30 | % | Tune Name | Composer* | Year* | Meter* |
|---|---|---|---|---|---|---|
| 1 | 19 | 63% | Old 100th | Louis Bourgeois | 1551 | LM |
| 2 | 15 | 50% | German Hymn | Ignaz Pleyel | 1790 | 7.7.7.7 |
| 3 | 14 | 47% | Bedford | Wm. Wheale | 1720 | CM |
| 4 | 14 | 47% | Vienna | J.H. Knecht | 1797 | 7.7.7.7 |
| 5 | 13 | 43% | Bethlehem (Doncaster) | Samuel Wesley | c. 1800 | SM |
| 6 | 13 | 43% | Easter Hymn | from *Lyra Davidica* | 1708 | 7.7.7.7 |
| 7 | 13 | 43% | Evening Hymn | Thomas Tallis | Mid-1500s | LM |
| 8 | 13 | 43% | Innocents | Anonymous | 13th C | 7.7.7.7 |
| 9 | 12 | 40% | Abridge | Isaac Smith | 1770 | CM |
| 10 | 12 | 40% | Melcombe | Samuel Webbe | 1792 | LM |
| 11 | 12 | 40% | St. Ann/St. Ann's | Wm. Croft | 1708 | CM |
| 12 | 11 | 37% | Glory | Gauntlett (also Anon. in *Methodist SS*) | 1842 | CM |
| 13 | 11 | 37% | Hanover | Wm. Croft | 1699 | 10.10.11.11 |
| 14 | 11 | 37% | Happy Land (Indian) | Indian air | 1849 | 10.10.13.10 |
| 15 | 11 | 37% | Harts | Benjamin Milgrove | 1769 | 7.7.7.7 |
| 16 | 11 | 37% | Hosanna | Henry John Gauntlett | Mid-1800s | 5.5.5.11 |
| 17 | 11 | 37% | Mainzer | Joseph Mainzer | 1841 | LM |
| 18 | 11 | 37% | Morning Hymn | Barthélemon | 1785 | LM |
| 19 | 11 | 37% | Rockingham | Edw. Miller | 1790 | LM |
| 20 | 11 | 37% | Westminster | James Turle | 1835 | CM |
| 21 | 10 | 33% | Dix | Conrad Kocher | 1838 | 7.7.7.7.7.7 |
| 22 | 10 | 33% | Farrant | Richard Farrant | Mid-1500s | CM |
| 23 | 10 | 33% | French (Dundee) | Tho. Ravenscroft | 1621 | CM |
| 24 | 10 | 33% | Martyrdom | Hugh Wilson | 1824 | CM |
| 25 | 10 | 33% | Stutgard | C. F. Witt | 1715 | 8.7.8.7 |

*        With supplemental information from www.hymnary.org.

to Thee glad songs of praise" and, again, "Gentle Jesus, meek and mild" in *The Children's Hymn Book*; and "Holy Bible, book divine" and "Christ is merciful and mild" in The *Sunday Scholar's Hymn Book* (c. 1880).

The fluidity of hymn tunes affected children in a number of ways: it forced children to be flexible, to learn a new tune with a familiar text or vice versa; it required them to recall many tunes from memory given only a name or a few bars; and it allowed them to mix and mingle tunes and texts themselves. Finding a familiar, favorite tune could enable them to forget the occasionally didactic, overly burdensome text and tolerate the hymn singing. Various editors seemed comfortable with and even encouraged children to make their own musical decisions: in his preface to *Lancashire Sunday-School Songs with Music* (1857), the Rev. J. Compston remarks that "for some of the Hymns of ordinary metres, no *special* tune is provided, reference being made to some tune of the same measure appropriated in the Music-Book to another Hymn; in which cases, the Singer has the option of selecting any other well-known tune which may be deemed suitable" (Preface; his italics). Compston, notably, does not distinguish a "teacher" but designates a "Singer" within his Lancashire Sunday School. Similarly, *The Children's Tune-Book* of the Wesleyan Church (1860) lists three different tunes for every hymn-text given and instructs the singer: "This index is designed to facilitate the finding of appropriate Tunes, and not to prevent the Hymn being sung to other suitable Tunes" (Index). Musical freedom is generously given and, through grammatical vagueness, opens up the possibility that not only may teachers benefit but also youthful singers who have access to the tune book. I would argue, in fact, that this world of tune selection and singing empowered children to distinguish their preferences and aesthetic taste.

As more hymn tunes were composed, more melodic variety was available for hymn-texts, although this often came at a cost. In fact, J. R. Watson has recognized that a hymn's permanence is often linked to the stability of its tune: of Watts's "God is the refuge of his saints," he writes: "There is no generally accepted tune for this hymn, and perhaps for that reason it is not as well known as it should be" (*Annotated* 141). Another phenomenon is that English and American audiences often split over popular tunes. First published in Rev. William J. Fox's Unitarian collection, *Hymns and Anthems* (1841), Sarah Flower Adams's "Nearer, my God, to Thee" was extremely popular on both sides of the Atlantic. A long list of adults cited this hymn as a favorite, including Queen Victoria, Theodore Roosevelt, and Edward VII (McCutchan 380); President McKinley was said to have quoted the refrain on his deathbed and it was used in his memorial services across the country (Nutter 170). It was also a popular inclusion in children's hymn books, being found in 26% of children's hymn books of my study. The hymn was thus popular among its various singers, English and American, adult and child. Yet they knew it to different tunes. In the first edition of *Hymns Ancient and Modern* (1861), Adams's text was set to J. B. Dykes's "Horbury." Though many others set it to music—including Arthur Sullivan, whose "Propior Deo" (1872) was favored by the children's hymn-book editors I consulted—it nevertheless became equated with "Horbury" for most English singers. But it was American composer Lowell Mason's "Bethany" (1859) which launched the hymn's popularity in America. This Atlantic split added to cultural confusion. The hymn has entered popular lore as being the last song to be played by the band led by Wallace Hartley when the Titanic sank on 15 April 1912. However, this legend cannot be confirmed with any certainty: since American and English citizens were both aboard the ship's lifeboats, and each had learned a different tune to the text, it seems unlikely they were all hearing the same song.[26]

Causing inspiration or chaos,[27] the tune-text fluidity would gradually dissipate, though certainly not disappear, in the later nineteenth century. *Hymns Ancient and Modern* (1861), edited by Monk, was such an influential hymn book in part because it began to solidify text and tune as had not been done before, first because it printed one tune on every page with the hymn (as opposed to separate books) and, second, because it commissioned many new exciting tunes which made the hymns extremely popular: "one of its strongest points was the provision of a proper tune for every hymn, and in many cases, a new tune which caught the musical fancy of its hearers" (Drain 238).[28] Some of the most influential pairings in *Hymns Ancient and Modern* included Monk's "Eventide" to accompany Lyte's "Abide with me" and Alexander Ewing's "Ewing" to Neale's "Jerusalem the Golden," making each very popular in adult and children's hymn books.

A comparison of two hymns mentioned earlier which both contemplate death puts this phenomenon in high relief and suggests how the permanent pairing of tune to text was a powerful quality in creating permanence for a hymn. Ann Gilbert (née Taylor) wrote "Death has been here, and borne away," first published in *Original Hymns for Sunday School* (1816). Gilbert puts the reality of death in direct, simple terms for children concerning the very common reality of the death of a sister, or "Christian sister" (often changed to "scholar"):

> Death has been here, and borne away
>     A sister from our side;
> Just in the morning of her day
>     As young as we she died. (v. 1)

Poignantly, the writer highlights the youth of the deceased, just "young as we." She then urges her young audience to consider death for themselves: "Perhaps our

---

[26]  See Yvonne Carroll, ch. 8, *A Hymn for Eternity: The Story of Wallace Hartley, Titanic Bandmaster* (2002). For a close analysis of both "Horbury" and "Bethany" to this text, see C. Michael Hawn and June Hadden Hobbs, 73–4, *Music and Theology*.

[27]  As another example of chaos caused by different hymn tunes, consider a scene in Hardy's *Mayor of Casterbridge* which shows an inebriated Michael Henchard bellowing out for his own combination "Psalm 109th" set to Wiltshire, with the band leader refusing that combination and offering another Psalm to his own tune (ch. 33).

[28]  For more about the history of *Hymns Ancient and Modern*, see Susan Drain; Temperley, *Music of the Parish Church*, 298–302; Bradley, *Abide with Me*, 60–76; Routley, *Humans and Human Life*, 79–81; and Benson, 506–14.

time may be as short, / Our days may fly as fast" (v. 2). Moralizing throughout, the writer urges preparedness and "willing feet / To meet our Saviour here" (v. 3), for "grace to teach us how to live / And make us fit to die" (v. 4). Very Evangelical and didactic, this early-century hymn addresses children directly in preparing for death in their lives and even for themselves. Set to various tunes—"Martyrdom" in the c. 1880 *Sunday Scholars Hymn Book with Tunes* or "St. Mary" in the 1879 *Methodist Sunday-School* (Hymn 430)—the words can take on a haunting effect (as with "St. Mary" set in D minor).

However, despite its appropriate text for children, this hymn is not among the most popular in children's hymn books, found in only 17% in my study. An adult hymn about death would greatly outpace Gilbert's, a hymn not in the least written for children yet found in a startling 28% of children's hymn books: "Abide with me; fast falls the eventide." It was written by Henry Francis Lyte and was premiered together with its memorable tune by William Henry Monk, the editor, in *Hymns Ancient and Modern* (1861) as Hymn 14 (see Figure 3.2). It was based on Luke 24:29, where the disciples ask the risen Christ to stay with them as the day ends: "Abide with us: for it is toward evening, and the day is far spent." Lyte uses the verse to reflect upon the death of a friend but makes the invocation personal and individually focused: "Abide with *me*."

> Abide with me; fast falls the even-tide;
>     The darkness deepens; Lord, with me abide;
> When other helpers fail, and comforts flee,
>     Help of the helpless, O, abide with me.
>                                   (v. 1, Hymn 14, *Hymns Ancient and Modern*, 1861)

Written shortly before Lyte's own death in 1847, the hymn, with its line about "the even-tide," quickly became associated with death. As Watson writes, "The long and beautiful lines allow the reader or singer to feel the movement of the hymn slowly and carefully, and to understand the unobtrusive connection between 'the eventide'" and the evening tide or "ebbing of our life" (*An Annotated* 274). In fact, it became a powerful inspiration to those on their deathbeds and for use at funerals in the late nineteenth and early twentieth centuries, bells tolling it at President William Howard Taft's funeral (McCutchan 502–3).

Its great appeal was thus to adults; this is reinforced by powerful but complex poetic devices, as exemplified in the second verse:

> Swift to its close ebbs out life's little day;
>     Earth's joys grow dim; its glories pass away;
> Change and decay in all around I see;
>     O Thou Who changest not, abide with me. (v. 2)

The repeated last lines (epistrophe) of "abide with me" are used as a chiasmus of "with me abide" (v. 1). Syntax is cleverly inverted to describe God's intervention in human relations: "help of the helpless" and "Change and decay in all around I see / O thou who changest not" (v. 2). All of these poetic devices imply a mature

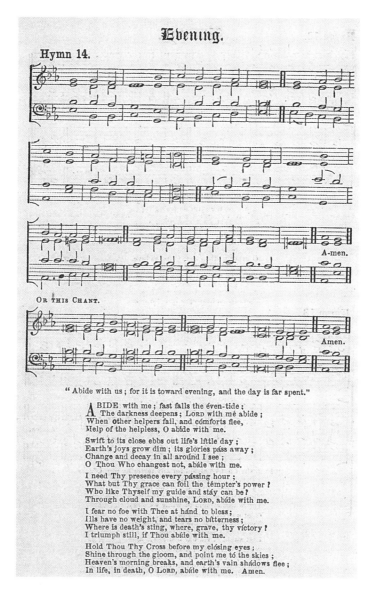

Figure 3.2     "Abide with me." From *Hymns Ancient and Modern* (1861). From
the author's collection and in the public domain.

poetry-reading audience. Not intended for children, it was yet selected by hymn book-editors as appropriate for children throughout the century. The beauty of the poetry possibly explains why and compliments the child's ability to understand these concepts, but, as has been discussed with Keble's "Sun of my soul," it could also confuse a child.

A more probable explanation, then, is the music, its tune greatly contributing to the hymn's popularity (Watson, *An Annotated* 275). "Eventide" was written by Monk specifically for Lyte's text as he wrestled himself with personal grief. Set in E-flat major, homophonic in structure, "Eventide" is haunting. For example, Monk creates tension with the use of non-chordal tones and minor chords at low points in the textual narrative ("fail and comforts flee" [v. 1]; "decay in all around I see" [v. 2]; "grave, thy victory?" [v. 4]; and "earth's vain shadows flee" [v. 5]). These are resolved—both musically and thematically—in the next, concluding lines of the verses with more "solid" tonic and dominant chords manifesting a determined confidence in the divine presence ("O abide with me"). Overall, its poignant beauty has lasted through two centuries, enjoyed by young and old alike.[29] And it is this distinction which probably accounts for its popularity over "Death has been here"—and likewise the various other pairings mentioned in this study in which more appropriate child's hymns without any consistent tune (such as the Taylors' "Lo, at noon, 'tis sudden night" and Duncan's "Jesus, tender Shepherd, hear me") are superseded by adult hymns (such as Toplady's "Rock of ages" and Keble's "Sun of my soul) with very consistent, popular tunes.[30]

In short, children were empowered with tune mixing and matching, but when tunes "stuck" to texts, they ensured the life of that hymn in adult and children's hymn books alike, even over more ostensibly children's hymns.

*III. Quality of Victorian Hymn Tunes*

Many early sources of liturgical music were mined for Victorian hymns. Tractarians brought back medieval Gregorian chants as part of the High Church "reform" to the Anglican church service (Temperley, *Music* I: 256). Tractarians also mined early, pre-Reformation sources for Latin texts which they translated, then set, often to new tunes. The title of the Tractarian-influenced *Hymns Ancient*

---

[29] As a contemporary example, I used "Abide with me" as a choral number sung during Matthew's funeral in a local children's theater adaptation of L. M. Montgomery's *Anne of Green Gables*. Of the many songs I also used for the production—many simple, sprightly ones like "Home, sweet home"—this hymn proved a favorite when I polled the 8-to-14-year-old singers.

[30] Keble's "Sun of my soul" was set to "Hursley" in 1855 ("Hursley" was Keble's parish) for *Hymns Ancient and Modern*: it matches this reflective tone through its wistful melody. "Redhead" (named for its composer) was most associated with "Rock of ages" (although in America it is better known to "Toplady" by American Thomas Hastings, *Spiritual Songs for Social Worship*, 1831), both memorable tunes. The stability of these tunes seems to have aided the permanency of these hymn titles.

*and Modern* thus had significance in representing the attempts of many to honor the past and present of church music.

Furthermore, Victorian hymnals inherited many inspiring tunes from earlier periods of psalmody and hymnody: for example, "Old Hundredth" from the 1551 *Genevan Psalter*, "Tallis's Canon" from a sixteenth-century tune by Thomas Tallis, German favorites such as Martin Luther's "Ein Feste Burg," seventeenth-century folk airs such as "Royal Oak," and tunes from seventeenth- and eighteenth-century composers such as Orlando Gibbons, Thomas Campion, William Croft, and Jeremiah Clarke (for example, William Croft's 1708 "St. Anne" was popularly set to Isaac Watts's "O God our help in ages past"). Again, referring to Table 3.4, one may note that many of the top tunes were those of the past: the most frequent was "Old Hundredth" (19%), written in 1551, followed by four from the eighteenth century: "German Hymn" (50%), "Bedford" (47%), "Vienna" (14%), and "Easter Hymn" (63%). Two following, at 43%, were from the sixteenth and thirteenth centuries, respectively: "Evening Hymn" by Thomas Tallis and the anonymous "Innocents." These were thus classic tunes, familiar to young and old hymn singers. Many of these popular tunes were expressly favored by hymn-book editors: O. P. Woodford, editor of *The Domestic and Social Harp; A Collection of Tunes and Hymns* (1848), encourages tunes such as "'Abridge,' 'St. Ann,' and 'the Old Hundredth' … rather than those whose chief claim to popularity seems to rest on the noisy declamation of their style" (iv). He goes on to say:

> In looking at the standard church tunes which have descended to us, we find that few have come from any one of the most eminent composers. It is only in moments of inspiration that even a man of true genius can originate a melody suited to their purpose. The great flood of new music…bears along doubtless many real gems, which will remain treasures; but probably the mass will speedily move on into the ocean of oblivion. No apology, therefore, can be offered for including in this collection so many old tunes…. (iv)

As the comments above imply, old tunes needed defending since recent, Victorian hymn compositions nearly glutted the market. Indeed, the nineteenth century is considered by many to be the zenith of hymn writing and hymn production. Temperley points to the "torrent of hymns and hymn tunes unequalled before or since," which peaked in the 1860s (*Music* I: 296). This torrent came about, first, because new tunes were being commissioned by hymn-book committees from composers for specific hymn-texts; in these cases, "the hymn tune became a highly crafted marriage of music to words, designed to enhance the spiritual and emotional impact of a particular text" (Bradley, *Abide* 140). Composers were given the words to which to set their tunes, thus writing what would carefully fit a text. Bradley suggests that "there is one overwhelming characteristic that nearly all [new] Victorian hymn tunes share and that is their careful matching to particular words" ("The Theology" 7), quite different from the frequent mix-and-matching of text and tune previously common in English hymnody.

Additionally, hymn writers culled from the work of major art-music composers of the era. Using the music of Ludwig van Beethoven, Henry Van Dyke wrote

"Joyful, joyful, we adore thee" (tune "Hymn to Joy");[31] while W. H. Cummings set music of Felix Mendelssohn to Charles Wesley's "Hark, the herald angels sing" (tune "Mendelssohn"). English art composers provided original tunes: Samuel Sebastian Wesley composed "Aurelia" set to Samuel John Stone's "The church's one foundation"; Arthur Sullivan composed "St. Gertrude" for Sabine Baring-Gould's "Onward, Christian soldiers"; and Ralph Vaughan Williams composed "Sine Nomine" for William Walsham How's "For all the saints." Williams also arranged many folk tunes into hymn tunes ("Forest Green," "Kingsfold," etc.). Likewise, composers flourished whose main medium was specifically that of hymn tunes: Monk, Henry Gauntlett, J. B. Dykes, Henry Smart, John Stainer, Robert Redhead, and Herbert Oakeley became some of the most prominent Victorian hymn composers of the era. Most notable of this list is John Bacchus Dykes,[32] Anglican clergyman, writer of over 300 hymn tunes such as those to "Lead, kindly light" and "Holy, holy, holy," considered by many scholars today as the quintessential Victorian tune writer: "No one better epitomizes the distinctive musical style of Victorian hymnody, with its lush chromatic harmonies, heavy use of repeated notes and stationary basses, close affinity to part song and parlour ballad and dramatic use of mood and melody to heighten the emotional and spiritual impact of the words" (Bradley, *Abide* 145).

As Bradley's description suggests, the Victorian hymn tune has a characteristic all its own, qualities that Dykes represented. One contemporary described its new quality thus:

> Their difference from the old style of hymn and psalm tune may be described roughly as consisting in a tendency to treat the short musical phrases of which the sections of tunes consist as connected sentences, rather than as made up of a succession of isolated chords. Hence the frequent occurrence of quasi-pedal phrases, and an indifference to passing dissonances so long as the musical passage brings itself well home at its close. (*Church Choirmaster* I, 1867; qtd. in Temperley, *Music* I: 305)

Not all contemporary musicians were complimentary of the burgeoning qualities they detected, however: wrote the great choral composer, S. S. Wesley, "the majority are contemptible and unworthy of being used in any service of public worship from their love-song affectation (and this even in tunes, by clergymen, to the most solemn words)" (qtd. in Bradley, "The Theology" 12). The English composer Charles Stanford wrote of their "slimy and sticky appeals to the senses"; that they are "flashy enough to seduce the untutored listener and to spoil his palate for wholesome and simple fare," while the early twentieth-century English

---

[31]   American Henry van Dyke wrote this text in 1907 although the tune had been adapted from Beethoven's Ode to Joy from his Ninth Symphony in 1864 by Edward Hodges.

[32]   Dykes was a child musical prodigy. With Tractarian sympathies, he entered the Anglican church ministry, eventually becoming precentor at Durham Cathedral, then vicar of St. Oswald's, Durham, where he wrote most of his many hymn tunes (Bradley, "The Theology").

composer Vaughan Williams referred to the "languishing and sentimental hymn tunes which so often disfigure our services" (both qtd. in Temperley, *Music* I: 303). Even today, the Victorian hymn has been castigated by some music scholars, whose criticisms Temperley ably refutes in *The Music of the English Parish Church*, vol. 1, pointing to many of their trends found also in popular and classical art music of the period (303–5). Put simply, Victorian tunes are seen as sentimental, emotional, and flamboyant, using melismas, passing dissonances, and standard harmonic progressions, among other distinctive qualities.

What is significant for us is that Victorians readily embraced these "new tunes" and used them extensively with children. Discussing such ornate hymn tunes, W. R. Braine argues, "If it be objected that they are too light, too melodious, and of a character not sufficiently severe and Church-like, it is submitted that, severity may be carried too far; it can hardly be right to deny sacred music a liberal share of the graces of harmony and melody, and thus render it dull, cold, and uninviting." In his hymn book, therefore,

> … one of his objects has been to produce a few Hymns of marked character, to contrast with and relieve the general body of what may, perhaps, be termed more orthodox church compositions, and especially such as should, from their flowing and melodious character, be *well adapted for use in the home circle*. (*Hymns for the Church or Home Circle*, 1861, Preface, my emphasis)

Braine particularly highlights the need for light, harmonious hymns in the home circle, implying that children could most benefit, *and* perhaps that children even preferred the newer, livelier tunes of the era.

Certainly the older "more orthodox" tunes contrasted with the "flowing and melodious" quality of nineteenth-century compositions: whereas early, sixteenth-century psalm tunes were "simple in structure" with "rugged and lasting qualities," the nineteenth-century tunes were "more florid in melody," using a variety of rhythms, and "softer harmonic chords" (Marks 258–60).

As one example of old tune qualities for children compared to newer, consider Thomas Tallis's "Evening Hymn" (alternately called "Tallis's Canon") of 1567, "the oldest English tune in common use" (Marks 258), which became uniquely associated with Ken's "Glory to Thee, my God, this night." In long meter, it is intended to be sung as a canon, one voice beginning the melody and the second voice singing the same tune a line later. Beyond this, it is a simple quarter-note homophonic melody which moves by predictable steps, almost chant-like, staying only within the octave (often the key of G, as in *The Methodist SS*, Hymn 485). If one compares this to another comparable tune of late century, one can see significant musical difference. "W. Jackson," a little-known and possibly amateur composer, wrote a new "Evening Hymn" for the 1896 *The Young People's Hymnal* (No. 10; see Figure 3.3). In 8.8.7.8.8.7 and the key of E-flat major, its three-quarter time signature creates a dance-like lilt. Its tune, in contrast to Tallis's, has unprepared dissonances, passing tones, and unpredicted tonal leaps, even jumping to E-flat5. Changes in melody reflect the poetic content: two interlocking sentences of three poetic lines each reinforced by the rhyme scheme (AABCCB). In short,

**10** **Evening Hymn.**—8.8.7. 8.8.7.

W. JACKSON.

*Let my prayer be set forth before Thee as incense; and the lifting up of my hands as the evening sacrifice.*

1 FATHER, in high heaven dwelling,
   May our evening song be telling
       Of Thy mercy large and free.
   Through the day Thy love has fed us,
   Through the day Thy care has led us,
       With divinest charity.

2 This day's sins, O pardon, Saviour,
   Evil thoughts, perverse behaviour,
       Envy, pride, and vanity ;
   From the world, the flesh, deliver,
   Save us now, and save us ever,
       O Thou Lamb of Calvary !

3 From enticements of the devil,
   From the might of spirits evil,
       Be our shield and panoply ;
   Let Thy power this night defend us,
   And a heavenly peace attend us,
       And angelic company.

4 Whilst the night-dews are distilling,
   Holy Ghost, each heart be filling
       From Thine own infinity ;
   Softly let the eyes be closing,
   Loving souls on Thee reposing,
       Ever-blessèd Trinity.

Figure 3.3 "Father, in high heaven dwelling." From *The Young People's Hymnal: Edition with Tunes* (1896), H. Elliot Button, ed. From the author's collection and in the public domain.

it is a more complex and less predictable melody and rhythm than "Tallis's Canon," quite emblematic of its age.

In fact, tune-book editors seem more aware of their child audience than their hymn-text editor counterparts, who rarely speak of choosing children's "favorite" hymn-texts. As one example, C. H. Bateman, in his *Sacred Melodies for Children* (1843), subtitles the book *Selected Chiefly on the Ground of their Popularity with Children* to establish the compilation within the aesthetic tastes of the young. Within the preface, he writes:

> I have always found, that to interest children in anything, we must condescend to their feelings and capabilities. They live in a world of their own, and all we do with them should take this into account. The melodies here are some of this nature, and have already, with one or two exceptions, acquired some popularity with children.... (7)

This desire to cater to what was "popular" among children shows great accommodation by editors.

Significantly, famous composers wrote with children in mind. Arthur Sullivan wrote tunes to Sarah Wilson's original texts for the illustrated *Hymns for Children* (1888), simple, quarter- and half-note rhythms yet in challenging four-part homophonic structure. Likewise, Dykes purported to have put children's tastes above even that of his musical peers when writing tunes to accompany *Hymns for Infant Children* (1862), as he states in the third person:

> He has made it his aim to provide music which—while, if possible, such as shall satisfy the taste of the musician—shall be pleasing and attractive to *children*.

> To ensure this latter most important result, he has taken the precaution of submitting all the little tunes to an august tribunal of very juvenile critics, anxious to admit none which did not seem to "take" with them, and meet their general approbations. And, in deference to their judgement, he has willingly altered or withdrawn tunes which, after a fair trial, did not appear to commend themselves. (Preface; his italics)

Ostensibly discarding the adult musical community, Dykes instead defers to the tastes of his "very juvenile critics." This results in some very tuneful and engaging melodies such as those written for "Oh, what a blessed child I am" and even "One day, dear children, you must die." The latter (No. 9) is a rather grim text ("Within the grave your limbs must lie / And cold and stiff your bodies grow"). However, Dykes's rich, homophonic textures and interesting melodic line ascending up to an E5 are engaging though not easy (see Figure 3.4), and certainly seem to offset the severe text.[33] Children, according to Dykes himself, apparently enjoyed this musical richness. Nowhere, though, does he insinuate that he is "writing down"

---

[33]  Note how the third line (which delineates the limbs in the grave) bears a melodic similarity to Robert B. and Richard M. Sherman's "The Perfect Nanny" from Walt Disney's *Mary Poppins* (1964); Dykes certainly seemed to have a sense for children's tunes!

Those trees so beautiful and gay,
That shade you from the summer's heat,
When Autumn comes their leaves decay,
And quickly fall beneath your feet.

Our GOD, Who reigns in Heaven above,
Has ruled that all on earth must die,
But they who His commandments love,
Will live again with Him on high.

Oh try to do His holy will
Be gentle, humble, meek, and mild,
Then the great GOD will bless you still,
And keep you ever His dear child.

Figure 3.4     "One day, dear children, you must die." From *Accompanying Tunes to the 'Hymns for Infant Children'* (1862), John B. Dykes, ed. Courtesy of Andover-Harvard Theological Library, Harvard Divinity School.

to children or simplifying his technique which, I would argue, remains similar to his approach to adult hymn compositions, both tuneful and richly harmonic. It is curious, then, that his children's tunes did not become better known, possibly because they were saddled with unappealing texts such as this latter.

Certainly engaging rhythms and melodies helped children learn these hymns. Elizabeth Gaskell suggests this in *North and South* (1855) when showing a working family's son reciting a Methodist hymn "far above his comprehension in language, but of which the swinging rhythm had caught his ear, and which he repeated with all the developed cadence of a member of Parliament" (347). However, as Gaskell also insinuates, the rhythms and tunes could also monopolize a child's attention. Some music teachers therefore showed undisguised concern at times that the singers would become carried away with the tune and miss the all-important Christian text, much as S. S. Wesley insinuated. In their Preface to *The Child's Own Tune Book* (1846, companion to *The Child's Own Hymn Book*), George Hogarth (arranger) and John Curwen (editor), desire to have "people so familiar with music, that it shall *not distract their attention from the words*, but heighten the expression of devout feeling, and spread the sweet sympathy of united praise" (my italics). Again, to focus his pupils' attention to the words, Curwen advises limiting the number of tunes learned: "Sing a few choice hymns and tunes well, and often. To children, too much variety is bewildering and unimpressive" (ii–iii). Music, then, should be a medium subservient to text, lest the beauty of the tune become an emotional distraction from the religious text.

Some hymn editors clearly showed concern for the newer tunes in their association with secular music of the age, either having been mined from popular sources or because Victorian tunes evidenced many qualities of part-songs and dance music: "Many tunes which some compilers have adapted as 'Children's Melodies,' we have rejected, although very popular, as they have been too much associated with the ball-room and convivial gathering" (vi), warned Thomas Sturrock in *The Sabbath School Tune-Book and Service of Praise for the Sanctuary* (1855). All of these comments reflect the societal concern for music's instability, one minute reflecting religious grandeur, the next associated with the secular and profane.[34]

Music, then, appeared to have had the power of devotion *or* distraction, and children were, quite unintentionally, endowed with that power when handed a hymn book with diverse tunes and texts. And anecdotal evidence suggests that children really could become enamored with a tune. "Jerusalem the golden," translated from a twelfth-century source by John Mason Neale for *Hymns Ancient and Modern*, could thus be considered an antiquated hymn in contrast to more recent "heaven" hymns more appropriate for children ("Heaven and earth" by Jane and Ann Taylor, for example). Yet it is found in 22% of children's hymn books. Neale himself suggested it was the tune (by Alexander Ewing, 1857) that is "with children the most popular," which is "no small proof in my estimation of the goodness of church music" (qtd. in McCutchan 513).

To sum up, I will end with that most "Victorian" of hymn composers: John Bacchus Dykes. He was commissioned by the committee of the 1861 *Hymns Ancient and Modern* to write tunes for it, many of which became famous. His "Lux Benigna" for John Henry Newman's "Lead, kindly light" appeared in the 1868 edition. It is incontrovertible that this tune made the hymn universally treasured, to dying soldiers and Holocaust prisoners (McCutchan 496). Newman himself confessed, "But you see it is not the Hymn, but the Tune that has gained the popularity!" (qtd. in McCutchan 497). This being Thomas Hardy's favorite hymn as well (Bradley, *Abide* 214), he imagines the effect the tune has on its young singers when describing Bathsheba, in *Far from the Madding Crowd*, overcome by hearing a choir of children sing the hymn, as quoted in the epigraph to this chapter, children who "were, unconcerned at the meaning of their words, because too innocent to feel the necessity for any such expression" (377). Hardy thus reflects on the hymn's effect upon children who are either too innocent or too caught up in the haunting music to give much thought to the somber lyrics: "Lead, kindly Light! Amid the encircling gloom / Lead Thou me on; / The night is dark, and I am far from home: Lead Thou me on."

---

[34]    I more thoroughly pursue the Victorian anxieties for unwholesome music in *Angelic Airs, Subversive Songs: Music as Social Discourse in the Victorian Novel*; see in particular discussions of religious music in chs. 1 and 3.

However, Dykes's "Lead, kindly light" was not nearly as popular in children's hymn books (at 15%) as his "Holy, holy, holy," set to Reginald Heber's 1826 text, a hymn found in 33% of children's hymn books and the eighth most popular hymn in my study. The tune, entitled "Nicaea" (Nicaea was the location of the Council that established the doctrine of the Trinity, A.D. 325 [McCutchan 18]) is sometimes thought to be Dykes's finest tune (Watson, *Annotated* 245). Set in the key of E major in *Hymns Ancient and Modern* (Hymn 135), the melody is set syllabically while the homophonic chordal system is intermixed with non-harmonic tones to create tension and resolution, often, though not exclusively, through the alto and tenor lines moving amongst the four parts. This movement, particularly on key words such as "holy," "golden," and "Persons," adds emphasis and elegance. Heber represents the Trinity with three repeated "holy's" which Dykes represents symbolically by moving upward through a broken triad for each "holy," creating movement and majesty (see Figure 3.5):

> Holy, Holy, Holy! Lord God Almighty! (v. 1, Hymn 144, *Children's Hymn Book*)

The meter is irregular—labeled 11.12.12.10 (note the apparent error in the meter given in this 1878 book)—which Dykes uses to create an ABAC musical scheme with an extended melody for the 12-syllable, second ("B") line:

> Early in the morning our song shall rise to Thee.

Because the third line partly repeats the first line (in verses 1 and 4), Dykes largely repeats the same melodic line as well, then emphasizes the final phrase by slowly descending an octave to the tonic chord with "… Blessed Trinity" to resolve the theme both musically and poetically:

> Holy, Holy, Holy, Merciful and Mighty;
>     God in Three Persons, Blessed Trinity!

The hymn's very luscious melody and intricate parts are both very Victorian characteristics. They create immense beauty and an emotional hymn to sing, for children as well as adults, resulting in one of the greatest hymns ever written about the Trinity (McCutchan 17).

What proves the power of the tune over the words, in fact, is to recognize the difficulty of the text. As earlier stated, Alexander had written a much clearer hymn about the Trinity in which she breaks apart and defines the Father-Son-Holy Ghost images. Heber does not define, he merely extols, repeating his refrain of the first and fourth stanzas: "God in Three Persons, Blessed Trinity!" The images themselves are poetic, if obscure:

> Holy, Holy, Holy! all the saints adore Thee,
>     Casting down their golden crowns around the glassy sea;
> Cherubim and Seraphim falling down before Thee,
>     Which wert, and art, and evermore shalt be. (v. 2)

Hymns to the Holy Trinity.

**143.**—ORILLIA.          7.7.7.7.          S. D. ROUTH.

*"Of Him, and through Him, and to Him, are all things: to Whom be glory for ever. Amen.*

GLORY to the FATHER give !
GOD in Whom we move and live ;
Children's prayers He deigns to hear ;
Children's songs delight His Ear.

Glory to The SON we bring,
CHRIST our Prophet, Priest, and King ;
Children raise your sweetest strain
To the Lamb, for He was slain.

Glory to The HOLY GHOST,
Who reclaims the sinner lost :
Children's minds may He inspire,
Touch their tongues with holy fire !

Glory in the highest be
To the Blessèd TRINITY,
For the gospel from above,
For the word that GOD is Love. Amen.

**144.**—NICÆA.          11.12.11.10.          REV. J. B. DYKES, Mus. Doc.

156

Figure 3.5     "Holy, holy, holy." From *The Children's Hymn Book* (1878),
[Mrs. Carey Brock, ed.]. From the author's collection and in the
public domain.

Hymns to the Holy Trinity.

*" They rest not day and night, saying, Holy, Holy, Holy, Lord God Almighty, Which was, and is, and is to come."*

HOLY, Holy, Holy! LORD GOD Almighty!
  Early in the morning our song shall rise to Thee ;
Holy, Holy, Holy! Merciful and Mighty!
  GOD in THREE PERSONS, Blessed TRINITY !

Holy, Holy, Holy! all the saints adore Thee,
  Casting down their golden crowns around the glassy sea ;
Cherubim and seraphim falling down before Thee,
  Which wert, and art, and evermore shalt be.

Holy, Holy, Holy! though the darkness hide Thee,
  Though the eye of sinful man Thy glory may not see,
Only Thou art holy ; there is none beside Thee
  Perfect in power, in love, and purity.

Holy, Holy, Holy! LORD GOD Almighty!
  All Thy works shall praise Thy Name, in earth, and sky, and sea ;
Holy, Holy, Holy! Merciful and Mighty !
  GOD in THREE PERSONS, Blessed TRINITY. Amen.

157

Figure 3.5    (continued)

The biblical reference to "glassy sea" (Rev. 15:2) is mystifying to children, as would be "Cherubim and Seraphim [angels] falling down before Thee" in this context. And Heber's use of antiquated verbs ("Which wert, and art, and evermore shalt be," v. 2) and inverted syntax ("Though the eye of sinful man Thy glory may not see," v. 3) are also hard to decipher, in fact obscuring the sterner theology ("the eye of sinful man"). Yet the majesty of the tune sweeps a singer along so that the obscure and stern references are quickly forgotten. In short, the most Victorian of composers, Dykes, was able to promote a complicated hymn-text through its emotional appeal and musical vigor, for adults and children alike.[35]

As the three discussions show, music was paramount in disseminating hymns to children, and this music was coming from the adult tradition. Rare was the tune written for children and when it was (as with Dykes for *Hymns for Children*), it did not enter the common repertoire. Hymn-book editors could and did include universally favorite tunes with little regard for difficulty, unapologetically mining adult hymn books without hesitation: "All the tunes from the 'Church of Scotland Psalm and Hymn Tune Book' are reprinted as they stand there" (*The Children's Hymnal*, 1876); and "The Editor has endeavoured to provide … many of the hymns … in use in the Services of the Churches, and which can be sung with equal fitness by old and young" (*School Hymns: with Tunes*, 1893). The *Juvenile Harmonist* (1843) may have been a separate hymn book for the young published by the Sunday School Union, but 30 of the 60 hymns correspond to identical hymns in the adult *Union Hymn Book*, while their *Union Tune Book* (1837, 1842, 1854, and 1879) supplied tunes for generations of adults *and* children, being "suitable for use in Congregations and Sunday Schools" as its subtitle attests. C. H. Bateman, editor of *Sacred Melodies for Children* (1843) makes it very clear, in fact, that he chose tunes because of their popularity to adults: "And now, dear children … You will, I think, like all the tunes in this book very much when you know them. They are most of them great favourites wherever they are known, and have been selected for you simply on this ground" (5). Clarifies a late-century hymn-book editor, J. R. Griffiths, for his *Bible Christian Sunday-School Hymnal with Tunes* (1898): "In the case of hymns which are in common use in the Sunday-School and Congregation alike, it has been his object to provide tunes likely to be used in the latter, so that they may be familiar upon scholars passing thither from school" (v). Hymn editors very intentionally shared the most popular adult hymn tunes of the day with their children, for their future edification and also simply because they were "great favourites."

Writing reflections on their Victorian childhood, authors will often comment on hymn singing. An occasional person, such as the art critic Forrest Reid, recalls his antipathy to conservative religion and therefore "I hated these hymn-tunes …

---

[35]    As one example in the present: when recording many hymns for a conference presentation for me, my then 9-year-old daughter and her 11-year-old friend picked "Holy, holy, holy" as their favorite and asked to sing it repeatedly.

and the instruments associated with them—organs and harmoniums" (130–31). More often than not, however, memoirists recall "those hymn-tunes caught from an open church door [which still] have the power to knock at the heart and compel an answer of smiling recognition" (Burke 50–51); their "early susceptib[ility] to the magic and melody" of hymns (Palmer 55); "even my dull mind felt their beauty and power" (MacDonald 35), while one recalls fleeing the Anglican service to "the more rousing hymns at a neighboring Methodist chapel" (Okey 11).

In fact, Lucy Larcom attributes her love of hymns to exactly what I have argued, the music and sense of story: the "melodious echo, or a sonorous ring … the hint of a picture or a story, or by some sacred suggestion that attracted me" (59). When discussing hymns, it is important for her to note the tune: "How the meeting-house rafters used to ring to ['Rise, my soul, and stretch thy wings'] sung to the tune of 'Amsterdam'!" (68). Furthermore, she shared this love of hymns with her mother and took the lead in teaching her mother, "reading or repeating them to her, while she was busy with her baking or ironing … and it pleased her to know that so small a child as I really cared for the hymns she loved" (58).

In short, the Victorian era represented an apex of congregational hymn singing, and children were directly involved, being called upon to lead others with their musically trained expertise. Empowered in this way, they were also sanctioned to select text/tune combinations, to (ostensibly) direct famous composers such as Dykes in their composition style, and to participate in the thrust for newer, livelier tunes. Perhaps the greatest allowance that Victorians gave children was bequeathing adult hymns to them, complete with their infectious melodies. Use of adult-centered texts was most pronounced in Tractarian/Anglican and Methodist circles, as described in Chapter 2, yet many of their most popular hymns evidenced infectious tunes which would appeal to children, including Neale's "Jerusalem the golden," Monk's "Abide with me," and Heber/Dyke's "Holy, holy, holy" of the former, and Wesley's "Christ the Lord is risen today" of the latter. There were risks: children were relied upon to lead choral and congregational singing, yet squirmed in their seats. Swept along by rousing Victorian tunes, children might not comprehend the text at all. Ultimately, it could be claimed that there never really existed a "child's tune" during the era because favorite tunes moved fluidly between adult and children's hymn books. Musical enjoyment, the joy of singing, was a shared human experience between adults and children, the most psychologically analogous trait of all.[36]

---

[36]    From June 22–26, 2015, a music colleague and I taught a children's choir about 20 Victorian hymns, both "child-centered" and "adult-centered" ones, for a professional recording. Polling them at the end of the week about their favorite hymns, I was amazed that, even today, "adult" hymns led the list: "All hail the power" and "Holy, holy, holy." Hearing their comments and watching them sing, I knew it was the infectious melodies. And I can confirm that age matters not since I loved both hymns myself as a child, and love them still as an adult.

**Coda**
**"I think when I read":**
**Empowering Children through their Hymnody**

The various hymns discussed in this chapter are among the top 25 hymns found in children's hymn books. Their musicality, theology, and poetics at once challenged the child singer and confirmed a merging of child-adult aesthetic sensibilities in what Victorians believed could be sung, comprehended, even enjoyed by old and young alike. They suggest the Wesleyan view of children, that of raising a child's intellect through hymnody: "But when they do understand them [hymns], they will be children no longer, only in years and in stature," as John Wesley famously decreed (Preface to *Hymns for Children* 1790). I end with a discussion of the most frequently appearing hymn in children's hymn books, "I think when I read that sweet story," as a final reminder that Victorians did not completely disavow the child-ness of their children, that the Wattsian view of children needing simpler concepts, robust tunes, and a focus on them as *children* was never completely forgotten by hymn-book editors. Found in 46% of all the hymn books of my study, "I think when I read" was *the* children's hymn. Nutter and Tillett would later (1911) identify it as "the most popular of all modern hymns for children" and Erik Routley includes it as one of 24 significant children's hymns of all times (*A Panorama* 126). The only hymn written by Jemima Thompson Luke to become popular, it has an interesting origin. Luke (then Thompson) was helping at the Normal Infant School on Gray's Inn Road, London, where she heard the children singing a Greek marching tune. It so caught her ear that a few days later during a coach ride, she was inspired to write down the words to the first two verses on the back on an envelope for the village school she was shortly to visit. Her father later heard the children singing it, asked her for a copy and sent it, without her knowledge, to the *Sunday School Teacher's Magazine* which printed it the next month, in 1841. The gender implications are notable (her father printing it anonymously without her permission), especially since this could be considered one of the few hymn tunes edited, if not written, by a woman. Indeed, it has not escaped my notice that the many focal hymns just analyzed in Part II were all written and composed by men. It is a regrettable but true fact that almost all Victorian hymn composers were men, and many of the favorite adult hymn writers were also male (Adams excepted). Women seemed to excel at children's hymn writing, complicated by the fact that they were socially defined as "children" as well, a phenomenon I take up in a related study. Fewer women's hymns were paired permanently with memorable tunes (Alexander's "All things bright and beautiful" and "Once in royal David's city," and Hankey's "I love to tell the story" are exceptions); Drain discusses the absence of women's hymns, and subsequently tune-pairing, in *Hymns Ancient and Modern*. It therefore seems appropriate to give the last nod to a woman who clearly had the craft of child-centered hymn writing in full command when penning this most favorite of children's hymns. To the extent that she adapted a folk tune and made it world-famous, she might also be credited as a tune editor, too.

Salamis, or "Greek Air" as it is usually labeled, is a cheerful tune often in G or A major, with high leaps into the upper register, making it appropriate for children's young voices.[37] The original tune, smoothed out to 11.8.11.8 meter, provided longer phrases allowing for more words per line. Luke uses an anapestic tetrameter-trimeter, which further emphasizes the marching. The first two verses were entitled "The Child's Desire," and with first-person diction, are an intimate outpouring of exactly what a (Godly) child might be desiring as he/she recalls the story of Jesus calling the little children to Him:

> I think, when I read that sweet story of old,
>> When Jesus was here among men,
> How He called little children, as lambs to His fold,
>> I should   like to have been with them then.
> I wish that His hands had been placed on my head,
>> That His arms had been thrown around me.
> And that I might have seen His kind look when He said,
>> "Let the little ones come unto Me." (v. 1, Hymn 147, *The Methodist SS*)

The first verse reflects wistfully on that moment with many physical images of Jesus' touch while the second verse reminds the child that she will "see Him and hear Him above."

> Yet still to His footstool in prayer I may go
>> And ask for a share of His love;
> And if I now earnestly seek Him below,
>> I shall see Him and hear Him above.
> In that beautiful place He is gone to prepare
>> For all that are washed and forgiven:
> And many dear children are gathering there,
>> For of such is the kingdom of heaven. (v. 2)

Action verbs inspire this hymn and, ultimately, empower the child who is the main actor. The first verse contrasts the child's passivity ("think," "read," "like," "wish," "might have seen") with the various actions of Jesus: calling, placing his hands, throwing his arms "around me." The actions of Jesus, though in past tense, inspire the child in the second verse to action: "go," "ask," "seek," "shall see ... and hear." The third verse, added later "to make it a missionary hymn" (Luke, qtd. in McCutchan 440) makes clear who may be left out of this heaven,

---

[37] American hymnals of the mid-twentieth century altered the tune to be less high-ranging (in the key of E-flat versus the key of G such that the highest note is an E-flat5 versus a G5) and repeated melodic phrases ("How He called little children" repeats with "as lambs to his fold"). Both tactics simplify the tune a bit for youthful voices. See Hymn 74 in *Hymns of Childhood for Primary and Junior Grades*, ed. I. H. Meredith, Arthur Grantley, and Edith Sandford Tillotson (1939), and Hymn 179 in *Praise and Service Songs for Sunday Schools*, ed. Gordon D. Shorney and G. Herbert Shorney (1927), for example.

the unbelievers of other lands: "But thousands and thousands who wander and fall / Never heard of that heavenly home." If some children in the third verse are crippled by unhealthy action, "wandering" and "falling," one child—namely the first-person singer—is given healthy agency to help:

> But thousands and thousands, who wander and fall,
>     Never heard of that heavenly home;
> I should like them to know there is room for them all,
>     And that Jesus has bid them to come.
> I long for the joy of that glorious time.
>     The sweetest, the brightest, the best,
> When the dear little children of every clime
>     Shall crowd to His arms and be blest. (v. 3)

Only indirectly is the call for action expressed: "I should like them to know" and "I long" but if action is needed it is clearly placed in the realm of the child. The ultimate agency means action for all children—"of every clime"—who "Shall crowd to his arms and be blest." The mission message of verse 3, then, contributes further incentive to a hymn that is truly empowering of the child. And the tune mirrors that agency in its pulse and vitality.

In this last, child-centered hymn, then, poetics and theology may have been "simplified," Wattsian-fashion, for the sake of children's comprehension. But the lively tune reinforces a true agency further reinvigorated by active verbs and calls for action. Combine this child-centered hymn with the musical, theological, and poetical intellect needed to navigate through adult-centered hymns, Wesleyan-fashion, and children truly were "thinking" when they were reading the *many* "sweet stories of old" passed down to them.

## Conclusion

The Victorian period is heralded as the first society to truly distinguish and treasure the child. This chapter should begin to dismantle the former view; though hymn books fell into periods where either Watts's or the Wesleys' views of children held sway, clearly hymn-book compilations throughout the century continued to feature individual hymns of both persuasions, both adult-centered and child-centered hymns. In this respect, hymn-book editors never seemed able to resolve the Watts-Wesley controversy, never deciding for sure whether children needed hymns written simply and plainly ("child-centered") or more metaphorical and poetical ("adult-centered"). For this reason, crossover hymns abounded in these hymnals.

But the other statement about Victorians and children is substantiated by this study: Victorians truly treasured their children, bestowing upon them the richness of their own "adult" hymn tradition, both the complexity of texts and the beauty of tunes. Their favorites could and did become a child's; catalogues of most popular hymns for both adults and children bear this out as does anecdotal evidence of children's favorites. To treasure their children was, in more cases than not, to lift the child up to the adult in theology, music, and poetics. But hymns written expressly for children still abound, the "top" hymn being that which reminds both adults and children of Christ honoring children with His attention and love. Rather than compartmentalizing children's hymns in separate categories, contemporary hymn scholarship needs to examine all of the century's hymns together for, indeed, Victorians defined their hymns less in terms of age than the requisite praise best displayed by the genre. Furthermore, children's hymn singing is an integral part of the dynamic Victorian hymn tradition and deserves a central place in the scholarship.

# Chapter 4
# Staging the Child:
# Agency and Stasis for Children in Art and Hymn-Book Illustrations

'Twas on a Holy Thursday, their innocent faces clean,
The children walking two and two, in red and blue and green,
Grey-headed beadles walk'd before, with wands as white as snow,
Till into the high dome of Paul's they like Thames' waters flow.

O what a multitude they seem'd, these flowers of London town!
Seated in companies they sit with radiance all their own.
The hum of multitudes was there, but multitudes of lambs,
Thousands of little boys and girls raising their innocent hands.

Now like a mighty wind they raise to heaven the voice of song,
Or like harmonious thunderings the seats of heaven among.
Beneath them sit the aged men, wise guardians of the poor;
Then cherish pity, lest you drive an angel from your door.
    —Blake, "Holy Thursday," from *Songs of Innocence* (1789)

William Blake's sympathetic focus on children is often considered the beginnings of the "cult of the child" which would lead to the century's romantic idealization of childhood. Here, in *Songs of Innocence*, he accentuates children as "innocent" and "clean," likened to "flowers" and "lambs" with a "radiance all their own." Of course in *Songs of Experience*, Blake will acknowledge the bitter truth: these young children in the rich nation of England are yet starving and impoverished. But, to construe the *ideal* portrait of children, Blake notably turns to a scene of religious song and performance. Here, on "Holy Thursday" (Ascension Day, the 40th day after Easter), charity school children walk to St. Paul's to sing for those in attendance, with hymns an important part of the liturgical concert.[1]

There are several aspects of Blake's scene relevant to the content of this chapter. First is the "staged" nature of this Ascension Walk. Here, the poverty of

---

[1]   See Temperley (*Music* 104–5), Gillman (279), and my Chapter 1, for more about these important annual fundraising events for charity schools: "[A]nnual singing services were held in St. Paul's, where the sight of the four or five thousand children in their quaint uniforms and the sound of their young voices served to impress the minds of the Church-people the educational value of hymnody" (Gilman 279). Further, "The excitement of the occasion undoubtedly stimulated the children's musical efforts, and raised large sums of money in their support" (Temperley, *Music* I: 105).

these paupers and orphans has been masked, their dirty hands scrubbed "clean" and their everyday poverty eschewed for cathedral grandeur, a "show" for the "aged men" and others. Secondly is that this poem, like others in the collection, has been beautifully illustrated by Blake, with images interwoven with words. In the case of "Holy Thursday," pictures of indistinct pairs of children trudging behind the beadles, above and below the text, dim the joyous mood of the poem. Similarly, children's hymn books, especially by the second half of the century, would use images to interpret the meaning of their texts. Less obvious but just as potent is the non-visual element: the music of their hymn singing, their voices becoming "like a mighty wind" or "harmonious thunderings." There is power and might to the children's music which contrasts with their social marginalization and their coerced visual march to St. Paul's.

Given that hymns were mainly sung in the privacy of home or Sunday school, or collectively during worship, it may seem surprising to think of hymn singing also as a performative act. Chapter 5 will demonstrate ways in which children performed hymns during temperance rallies. Perhaps the most visual contexts for hymn singing, though, were the charity services, Sunday school anniversaries, and Whit-Walks. Sunday school anniversaries were a highlight of every year for those attending Sunday schools: a chance to dress in their finest, join in a parade through town, and recite or sing specially prepared pieces for their parents (Laqueur 177). Likewise, Whitsuntide, a week of holiday following Whitsun ("White Sunday" or Pentecost), was another occasion for a Sunday school parade, or Whit-Walk, usually held on Whit-Friday, or the Friday after Pentecost. Girls wore white dresses, boys, their best clothes, and a band often accompanied them through town. Children sang as they walked, ending up at an outdoor bandstand or inside a church. Hymns were also used during the anniversary service, and often the children of the Sunday school were given special verses or parts to sing apart from adults.[2] Hymns that the children sang were then sometimes sold, "the profits applied to the support of the School."[3] Other times, collections were taken during or after the hymn singing, another way to raise funds to support the Sunday school. Recalls one participant:

> The Sunday School anniversary was something to look forward to and the services were taken by a special preacher … We left the chapel at 9 a.m. in the morning and took provisions with us and sang our songs as we passed through the villages and I used to play an accordion to help them … of course *there were collections for chapel funds along the way*. (qtd. in K. Young, *Chapel* 44; my italics. See other reminiscences of Anniversary and Whit-Sundays, 40–48.)

---

[2]    See Haworth Church Sunday School bulletin for Sunday, July 21, 1844. Another hymn sheet for the Wesleyan Sunday School, Priory-Place, Doncaster, prints seven hymn-texts as "to be Sung by the Children" on Sunday, April 30, 1848.

[3]    As requested in the preface to an 1813 hymn sheet: "Hymns to be sung by the Children of the Sunday School, at the Methodist Chapel, Frome, on Sunday, May 30th … and a Collection Made for the Benefit of the School."

If children were being co-opted to raise money for the schools, however, they did not seem to mind.

Further co-optation occurred in the sheer performance, the girls "dressed in white with their hair in curls" (K. Young 46). Charles Shaw, recalling "Charity Sundays" of his youth, acknowledged the artifice, that "[i]f you had seen some of those boys and girls coming home from their work on the Saturday afternoon, with the smudge of clay on their clothes and faces, some too in patches and rags, you would not have known them again … on Charity Sunday"; that truly the children were "on the stage" this day (Shaw, *When I was a Child* 209). Furthermore, the cost for clothes and other finery fell on working-class parents and thus this was "an anxious time for parents. New clothes had to be found …" (Shaw 209; see also Winifred Foley [60]). Yet the opportunity to see their children admired by all the town seemed worth it: "On that day the poorest parents were proud as their children passed their door in the procession of scholars. There was a throb that brought smiles and tears to their faces, if only for a few moments" (Shaw 210). Despite the obvious artifice and petitions for money during these parades and hymn-sings, still, if Shaw and others are any indication, these were true highlights of the year, singing being a vital part: "A trumpet gives the keynote, and then follows a burst of song from hearts elated and inspired by all the expectations and hopes of the day … If the day happened to be a sunny one, no lovelier sight could be seen in all England … Hundreds of children with shining 'morning faces' and throbbing 'morning hearts'" (Shaw 211–12). During Charity-Services, Anniversary-Sunday, and Whit-Walks, then, children's agency came about in the expansive energy they could bring to the parading and the singing, the genuine joy emoted with song, unfettered in the outdoor festivities.

I use the vitality and visuality of these hymn-singing walks as a useful trope to discuss the visual component of hymns throughout the century, namely the illustrations found in hymn books to accompany the written word, much as Catherine J. Golden suggests that we "see dance and theater as forms of visualization along with book illustrations" (*Book Illustrated* 8). Jonathan Bate writes that "[a]n illustration of a dramatic text is a peculiar thing. It makes meaning by freezing a single moment, whereas the unstoppable motion of time, the piling of action upon action upon reaction, is the very essence of drama" ("Pictorial Shakespeare," in Golden 33). So it was true of children plucked from the vibrancy of walking and singing, and the dramas of their own lives, and positioned as subject of illustrations stagnant on the page. Though "staged" on these walks, their very bodies became staged on the page, culminating most tellingly in the magic lantern slideshows for hymn-sings of late century which frequently relied upon staged and sexualized photographs of young girls.[4]

---

[4]  Staged children and child performance as representing both child co-optation and vital experience are examined by Martin Danahay in "Sexuality and the Working-Class Child's Body in Music Hall," Monica Flegel in *Conceptualizing Cruelty to Children in Nineteenth-Century England*, ch. 3, and Marah Gubar in *Artful Dodgers*, chs. 5–6.

Indeed, seventeenth-century society viewed pictures as symbolic of the material body, while verse represented the incorporeal soul (Kooistra 66), and it may have been the inheritance of this ideology, a resistance to all things non-spiritual, that prevented hymn-book editors from employing many pictures. Illustrations—images to accompany and elucidate a text—are infrequently found in children's hymn books; in my study of over 200 hymn books, only around 30 boast any kind of illustrative image, beginning around 1800 but increasing significantly mid-century due to technical advances. Focused on verbal didacticism, and also a desire to keep printing costs low for Sunday school usage, most hymn-book editors seemed to ignore Comenius's sanction that "pictures are the most intelligible form of learning that children can look upon" (qtd. in Feaver 7). Pictures are therefore the exception, not the rule, in children's hymn books.

When illustrations do appear, they emerge from two specific artistic movements which both peaked in the nineteenth century: first, the Illustration movement whose "Golden Age" came in the 1860s, and, secondly, the children's illustrated "picture book" which came into its own with the work of Randolph Caldecott, Kate Greenaway, and Walter Crane in the 1870s. Placing images within a text, these movements engaged art and literature as "Sister Arts." I will position my analyses within the growing field of illustration studies, whose "theory frequently aims to delve deep into the psychology and the paratexts which illustrations, by their complex nature, almost invariably present" as Paul Goldman writes ("Defining Illustration Studies: Towards a New Academic Discipline" 15). By acknowledging illustrations as an important paratext to hymn books, and by considering the various contexts of hymn illustrations—commercial, cultural, artistic, historical, and theological—I hope to show that despite their simplicity—and even scarcity—within children's hymn books, illustrations, when they appeared, were complicated aesthetic products that paralleled strides being made in illustrations directed at the young.

Notably, while the child was not always object of the hymn-book illustration, he was always a viewing subject within the intended audience. In contrast, a third movement which I will explore made the child the object, only, of art while appealing to an adult audience: high art, as represented by the work of the Impressionists and then photographers, both of whom took as one of their feature foci that of The Child. This focus demonstrated late-century co-optation of the child—in particular, the little girl—for the aesthetic pleasure of adults or for their religious conversion as in the late-century magic lantern hymn slideshow photographs which gendered children in problematic ways. Yet I will argue that hymn books may have avoided these "static notions of the Beautiful Child," to use Rebecca Knuth's phrase (95) by relying mainly on illustrations of biblical, domestic, and adult images of the engraving tradition, and also by their eventual inspiration from the children's picture-book field, of immersing the child in innocuous, vibrant images of herself.

Art historians are increasingly turning to children's studies, a subfield which seeks "to enlist the methodologies and accumulated cultural capital of art history in ways that are not just *on* or *about* children but are also *for* them" (George Dimock in Brown 189). This exploration is imperative for, indeed, images were a leading way of defining childhood in the nineteenth century. Endemic to these pictorial presentations were the age, class, and gender assumptions made more manifest in the visual even than the textual. Specifically within hymnody, a hymn's textual meaning might avoid some of these biases, as argued in Chapter 1, by using a first-person, individualized approach to audience: anyone, from children on Whit-Walks to those in Anglican churches, may feel included in the hymn-texts they sing. In contrast, illustrations must portray what was ambiguous in the original: show the ages, the class, and the gender of the subjects. Pictures in children's hymn books, for instance, would often elide the child with the adult in curious ways. The introduction of lavishly colored pictures moved hymn books into an upper-class context with the illustrations reflecting this intended audience. And speaking to a broader, adult audience, magic lantern hymn shows co-opted images of the little girl in uncomfortably sexualized ways.

The next three sections will pursue each of these trends: 1) the Illustration movement and its influence on hymn-book illustrations, but also the age-confusion to come from this adult aesthetic; 2) the children's picture-book movement with its notable awareness of its youthful audience, but also an increasingly privileged audience; and 3) the high-art obsession with the child as object, especially little girls as object. Not unlike Whit-Walks, children were being staged visually in all three contexts, but I will also assess the opportunities for physicality, play, and singing which, like the Walks, were offered to children, metaphorically, as they enjoyed these illustrations away from any expectation to perform themselves. Then, by examining Isaac Watts's *Divine and Moral Songs for Children* as republished with illustrations throughout the nineteenth century, I will pull together many of these trends, showing how illustrations could convey much about the changing ideologies of age, class, and gender in their religious portrayals for and of children. Ultimately, I will suggest that the power of the music seemed to hold an energy that allowed children to burst from their pictorial confines with the agency of song.

**Part I**
**Technique and the Problematics of Age:**
**Hymn Books in the Golden Age of Illustration**

Acknowledging that the biblically based images in many children's hymn books were certainly indebted to the rich Christian art tradition of medieval and Renaissance artists—of Giotto and Raphael—I would argue that children's hymn-book illustrations are more direct inheritors of the modest tradition of book illustration which reached a peak in what art historians refer to as "England's Golden Age of Illustration," beginning around 1850 and peaking in the 1860s, as wood and steel etchings and engravings accompanied texts in everything from books to periodicals to advertisements. As Lorraine Janzen Kooistra explains: "With the rise of wood engraving, the improvement of paper quality coupled with a decrease in cost, the advent of the steam press, and increasingly sophisticated distribution networks made possible by the railway, illustrated periodicals, newspapers, and books of all kinds proliferated" (2). Furthermore, the type of illustrative material was immense; the label "illustration," as Julia Thomas suggests, "encompass[ed] a variety of publications, all with different pictorial conventions (magazines, journals, newspapers, fictional and nonfictional books, posters), as well as different mechanisms of reproduction (wood, copper and steel engraving, etching, aquatint, mezzotint, lithography, photography), not to mention the different styles adopted by individual artists" (*Pictorial Victorians* 4). As contemporary J. Whitaker, speaking in 1853, boasted, "[we are] an age of illustration, and with much apparent truth; for we have pictorial books of art and science. We use art everywhere; in the temple, the schoolhouse, the dwelling" (qtd. in Curtis 7). Pre-Raphaelites, known for their paintings, yet embraced the aesthetic of the art book (such as the famous wood engravings created by Dante Gabriel Rossetti for his sister's various poems; see Kooistra, ch. 2), while the Victorian novel itself often became synonymous with the illustrations accompanying the text, as with George Cruikshank's famous pictures to Dickens's *Oliver Twist* and John Tenniel's defining illustrations of Lewis Carroll's *Alice in Wonderland*. Created by accomplished artists in new mediums, then mass produced to enhance the texts of middle-class publications, 1860s illustrations were a distinct phenomenon. In fact, various scholars within illustration studies have recognized the often intense competition between text and picture during this time. By the 1870s, pictures lost, at least in adult fiction (Golden 7): "the artist was now battling the author," art becoming "literature's hieroglyphic handmaid" (Curtis 41, 104). By the end of the century, engraving was replaced by photography, and line art became secondary to the literary pen (Curtis 37).[5]

But at their best, "images worked together with texts and, at times, at cross purposes with texts, creating complexities and tensions" (Golden 8). This is even true of religious texts; Frances Knight argues the importance of visual images to convey Christian piety of the era, pointing to various standard Bible editions—even "the most humble"—which featured illustrations (e.g., John Cassell's *Illustrated Family Bible* [1859]; see 37–9). Illustrations would especially appeal to children, "crucial as a way in which a first exploration of faith could be made" (37). This was also true of religious-tract illustrations which, though small stock images, yet gave impoverished children a delightful and rare "glimpse of pictorial decoration," as Helen Rogers shows (67).

Pictures, it is safe to say, were always secondary to the religious text and musical scores of hymn books, however, and only became more pronounced due to the increase in publishing technology mid-century. J. S. Bratton points to the "revolution in printing" which allowed for improved binding and casing of books;

---

[5]    See also Julia Thomas's discussion of "linguistic imperialism" (6–9). For more about Victorian illustration, see Catherine J. Golden, ed., *Book Illustrated: Text, Image, and Culture, 1770–1930* (2000); Gerard Curtis, *Visual Words: Art and the Material Book in Victorian England* (2002); Lorraine Janzen Kooistra, *Christina Rossetti and Illustration: A Publishing History* (2002); Julia Thomas, *Pictorial Victorians: The Inscription of Values in Word and Image* (2004); and Paul Goldman and Simon Cooke, eds., *Reading Victorian Illustration, 1855–1875: Spoils of the Lumber Room* (2012).

that "The juvenile publishers were amongst the first to use these new methods of production, and the cheap but gorgeous Sunday school prize book was in some measure the direct result of technological advance" (20). Nowhere can one better see the increased printing capabilities than looking at children's hymn books, of various economic markets, throughout the century. Hymn books were, in early century, very small, sometimes only 3 × 4.5 inches, so as to fit in pockets, either by the man of the family for taking to church, or for children who had the good fortune to own books to be able to carry in trousers or dress pockets to school— "pocket wear" as one editor refers to them (Betts, *Children's Hosannah*, Preface). The small hymn books of the late eighteenth century and early nineteenth century used stylized font as the only ornamental component of the cover or cover page. An occasional illustration appears on cover pages of mid-century hymn books: children singing in *The Sunday School Union Hymn-Book*, 20th ed. (1835; see Figure 1.2), and Jesus holding "the little children" in *The Children's Hymn Book* (1854). Influenced by the mainstream Illustration movement, decorative frontispieces adorn such hymn books as *Songs of Gladness* (1871) and *Sacred Songs* (1900), while actual illustrations embellish such hymn books as *Hymns for Children* (1871) and *Short and Simple Prayers* (1882; see Figure 1.1). By late century lavish type and color illustrations occasionally appear in children's hymn books no doubt meant as the Sunday school gift books for good work to which Bratton (above) alludes. Indeed, Kooistra argues that the Society for the Promotion of Christian Knowledge (SPCK), with its wide circulation, "ensured that even the poorest homes would have access to visual imagery and printed texts" (4). Furthermore, compulsory elementary education for all children after 1870 increased demand for books of all kinds, particularly those that appealed to children visually (Kooistra 91). Hymn books also entered the new market of upper/middle-class, illustrated gift and holiday books (Kooistra 2; Lundin 26–8).[6] Thus, children's illustrated hymn books fell into at least three markets: upper-class gift books, middle-class/working-class school textbooks and prize books, and working-class Sunday school books.

Hymn books followed the tradition of illustrated religious books. One was the emblem book, small, illustrated books of moral or religious intent most popular in sixteenth- and seventeenth-century Europe which featured a woodcut or copper-engraved picture enhancing a prose or poetic text for a "striking presentation of a message" (English Emblem Book Project, Pennsylvania State University).[7]

---

[6]    A sampling of other middle- to upper-class moral-religious publications boasting an illustration or more include: *Pretty Poems for My Children*, ed. Emma C. Somers (London, 1849); *Here a Little and There a Little, or Daily Manna for the Lambs of Christ's Fold ... by a Mother* (London, 1851); *Soft Showers on the Opening Bud; or, Easy Scripture Lessons for Young Children* (Halifax, 1859); *Music for the Nursery*, rev. Philip Bass (London, 1874); and *Songs for the Little Ones in Twilight Hours*, words by A. D., music by Mrs. Arthur Goodeve, illus. F. L. F. N. (Bristol, 1880).

[7]    Emblem books of theological focus include *Emblems, divine and moral together with Hieroglyphicks* [sic] *of the life of man* (London, 1736) and *The School of the heart,*

Britain had its own emblem-book tradition from Elizabethan times to a Victorian revival (see chs. I and IV in Höltgen). As in the style of some emblem books (such as Peacham's *Minerva Britanna* [1612] in Höltgen 80), many early nineteenth-century hymn books, chapbooks, and miniatures used a single woodcut or engraving framed over the hymn-text for further elucidation, as in editions of Isaac Watts's *Divine and Moral Songs*. More importantly, emblem books prioritized a religious-didactic message to the reader, many encouraging readers to see the Divine in the ordinary. Children's hymn books and chapbooks regularly feature religious messages couched in a daily scene (a family gathered to read the Bible, for example). If intensely didactic, though, most illustrations in these hymn books and chapbook woodcuts were much simpler images, less symbolic and intricate, which F. J. Harvey Darton describes as "direct solid images" where only "the core of [the illustrator's] particular subject" is given (283–4; see Figure 4.5 for an example).

Later, these woodcuts and copper engravings would be replaced by wood engravings, a process of printing invented by Thomas Bewick in the late eighteenth century which allowed for sharper detail and shading,[8] and this became the standard technique for book illustrations of the nineteenth century. The Brothers Dalziel became some of the most famous engravers mid-century, including that of religious illustration. Constructing the engravings based on famous artists' work, their religious publications included *The Parables of Our Lord and Saviour Jesus Christ* with illustrations by John Everett Millais (1864) and *The Bible Gallery* (1880–1881) using the artistic work of Ford Madox Brown, William Holman Hunt, Frederick Sandys, Simeon Solomon, and Edward Burne-Jones.[9] Characteristic of

---

*or, The heart (of itself gone away from God) brought back again to Him, and instructed by Him* (London, 1778) (see Emblematica Online, University of Illinois, Urbana-Champaign). I am also grateful for emblem-book guidance from Heather McAlpine, University of the Fraser Valley.

    [8]    Line engraving on copper had become standard during the eighteenth century; it was not until the end of the century that Englishman Thomas Bewick revived interest in wood art by inventing the process of wood engraving on the end of the log. Both woodcuts and wood engravings are done in relief ("letterpress") with the wood carved out around the image which was then inked and printed. The difference is the part of the wood being carved: woodcut, the older technique, uses the grain side of the wood, cut into planks with a knife. Wood engraving, however, uses the harder wood at the end of the log carved with a burin for a more intricate design; wood here doesn't splinter with the thinner cuts. Also, artists lowered parts of the block "to print faintly and to create delicate designs" (Lundin 32). To the naked eye, however, it is often hard to tell the difference in technique. Because wood engraving had become the standard technique by the 1840s and after for mass publication, especially periodicals, I will refer to the wood art in hymn books as wood engravings unless otherwise known. See Helen Gentry's article in Mahony, specifically 161–4; William Vaughan, "Facsimile Versus White Line: An Anglo-German Disparity" in Goldman and Cooke, 33–52, especially 33–5; Anne Lundin, 32–3; and also Norman Kent, "The Woodcut Versus the Wood Engraving" (1945), available online at www.woodblock.com.

    [9]    See Laura MacCulloch, "'Fleshing out' Time: Ford Madox Brown and the *Dalziels' Bible Gallery*" in Goldman and Cooke.

this Golden Age of illustration, these illustrations of biblical scenes showcased realism and attention to detail; Laura MacCulloch points to Brown's illustrations for the *Bible Gallery* which showed biblical people "as real people from a specific time period" (116). Landscapes and setting details flourished as artists "toiled … at filling the whole picture" (Darton 284).

Children's illustrated hymn books never boasted an illustrator of the caliber of Millais or Brown; in fact rarely is the illustrator identified. An exception is the 1848 edition of Watts's *Divine and Moral Songs for the Use of Children* (London: John Van Voorst) which is identified on the cover as including "Thirty Illustrations Drawn on the Wood by C. W. Cope, A. R. A, and Engraved by John Thompson," the former a Victorian painter with several frescoes in the House of Lords and the latter a well-renowned Victorian engraver of science books and bank notes (note a Cope/Thompson illustration, without discussion, from this book included in Overton 30). In this book, finely detailed illustrations attempt to replicate the time period of the 1840s and also of the biblical, Roman era. Mary leads the young Jesus to the temple with the Pharisees, Sapphira and Ananias lie dead in the marketplace, both settings mirroring the Roman era in their details. Indeed, this text appears to be a part of the trend, 1840–1870, during which, according to MacCulloch, artists "embraced this new research [of historians and archaeologists] and incorporated it into their work … [becoming] part of the new, more visual representation of history" (135). Other engravings depict domestic, outdoor, and church scenes, all with vivid detail and "shading" through hatching[10] (see Figure 4.6 for one such example).

*Texts and Hymns Selected for Children* by H. J. Sturge (London, 1857) also reveals the strides being made in book illustration, this time to accentuate especially a scene of children. In an impressive engraving opposite its frontispiece, significantly bearing the artist's name in the lower left corner, "H. Anelay" portrays Christ gathering the children to Him (see Figure 4.1). Here, six children of varying ages look adoringly at Jesus, hands crossed or heads bowed in reverence. Near-center is the Christ, small ringlets for a beard, eyes lovingly welcoming all children while a hand clasps one child on his lap. Classical pillars and marble steps create a more elaborate setting than the countryside chronicled in Matthew 19:14. Anelay's scene is circular as he creates an ornate frame of scrolls and lattice to border it. Every detail has been carefully engraved. These books in many ways exemplify features of the age of illustration: mass produced illustrations, typically wood-engravings, more and more created by accomplished artists; scenes of domesticity, medievalism, romance, and landscapes, with "deep feeling" still rooted in the real world. Thus, "the illustration produced during this time represented a radical change in the aesthetics of the printed page, marking a significant development from the graphic art of the earlier Victorian period" (Goldman and Cooke 1; see also 2–3).

---

[10]   Hatching originated in medieval art but peaked in the fifteenth and sixteenth centuries with the work of Albrecht Durer whereby small, close lines are cut, etched, or engraved within the image to appear as lighter, "shaded" tones.

Figure 4.1     Frontispiece by H. Anelay to *Texts and Hymns Selected for
               Children* (1857), H. J. Sturge, ed. From Internet Archive.

Given the time and cost of producing these illustrations, though, it is no
surprise that publishers would recycle "stock" images not necessarily drawn to
specific texts.[11] Common in book illustrations, it was certainly true for hymn-book
publishing and worked against strides of the Illustration Movement where images
and text were so closely wedded. Stock images of biblical scenes, idyllic scenery,
and happy families adorn these books even though they do not exactly represent

---

[11]   Discussions in Julia Thomas (28), Kooistra (13), and Larson (11) reveal how
common the practice of using stock images was in Victorian publishing.

the accompanying hymn. For example, the engravings in *Hymns and Poems for Very Little Children* (1875) invoke an idyllic countryside with pastoral images of cattle, sheep, and deer scattered throughout the book. However, no hymns address animals or even the countryside. Hymns of the seasons likewise show contented communities. The hymn for "Autumn" (Hymn No. 26), for instance, shows families contentedly picking apples despite lyrics which describe the "[strong] waves when they toss to the sky" (and make no mention of apple-picking). One can see the influence of the emblem book in which the didactic message often overrides the connection to text.

This tendency is also true of *Hymns and Rhymes for Children by the Daughter of a Clergyman* (1871): many simple wood engravings of cherubic children reading books (presumably the Bible) or bowing in prayer. Such pictures are used even when they do not directly apply to the text: "God is love" (280) or "Thou shalt not steal" (124), respectively. Likewise, *Hymns for Children*, written by Sarah Wilson, illustrated by Jane M. Dealy and Fred Marriott (1888), boasts vivid illustrations, framed by small, inlayed flowers and branches, with idyllic images of English estates (No. 8) and praying girls (No. 9). The images do not always match the hymns, however: an estate adorns No. 6 about Good Friday, and a lamb embellishes the evening prayer, Hymn No. 10. All these choices reflect mid- to late-century tendencies of sentimentalizing and lightening theology: how much better to emphasize an image of reverence than of theft, of happy homes rather than of the bloody Passion.

Another result of this recycling, however, is that stock images take the place of children's vibrant action. In *Hymns and Rhymes for Children by the Daughter of a Clergyman*, for example, with the exception of a joyous crowd of children dancing to "Hurrah! Hurrah for England" (opposite page 46), most images show static children standing, reading or sitting, sometimes reflecting the docility so suggested in the hymn, yet many times not meeting the agency given in the text. Ken's "Awake, my soul" which encourages children to "shake off dull sloth" and "direct … all my powers, with all their might" yet shows an image of two girls passively reading (40); Julia Carney's "Little drops of water" which espouses great actions from young people ("Little seeds of mercy, / Sown by youthful hands, / Grow to bless the nations, / Far in heathen lands") is illustrated merely with a young girl walking to fill her water pitcher (131). Recognizing as I will in Chapter 5 that animal-child analogies suggested an integrated world view, it is yet perplexing that animal images replace those of the child for hymns in which animals are not even mentioned. For example, in *Hymns and Poems for Very Little Children*, the poems suggest healthy action for children, yet unrelated animals are pictured: "try always to be good" (Hymn XV) is illustrated with goats on a hillside, while Jesus bidding the children come to Him (Hymns XIX) ends with a picture of a hen and her chicks. Thus, static images replace the textual images of children working, playing, and singing found throughout the hymns, while animal imagery replaces the image—and action—of the child altogether.

Stock images may be the explanation for the last trend I wish to examine, but they do not completely elucidate it: that is, the many images of adults used with children's hymns. For example, "God entrusts to all / Talents, few or many / None so young and small / That they have not any," a popular hymn by James Edmeston, is, in *Hymns and Rhymes*, accompanied by an illustration of a young man cutting down a tree to suggest the abilities of even a young woodchopper, yet it is not clearly of a child at all, thus belying a message of a *child's* might (112). Even more obviously problematic is the book's image to accompany "The Shepherd Boy," for clearly it is an old man, white beard and large frame, pictured amidst his flock. This was a stock image (it is used, more fittingly, for "Behold the shepherd," Hymn III, in an 1820 edition of Barbauld's *Hymns in Prose for Children*, for instance). However, given the number of images available of children, it is a surprising choice for "The Shepherd *Boy*." Likewise, *Infant Altar; or, Hymns and Prayers for Children* (1889) utilizes many images of biblical (adult) figures (for Bible verses 1 Samuel 17 and 1 Samuel 1, of David and Goliath, and Samuel and Hannah, respectively) and fails to provide images for the corresponding *child's* lesson: "Listen to me while I ask Thee to make me a good child" (25) and "O Lord, forgive me for sinning" (43). Stock images enforce the biblical story even when the child's hymn book itself focuses on the child.

*Hymns for Little Children* (1867) shows this trend most acutely. Published during the Golden Age of Illustration, it boasts impressive artwork. However, as one of the few illustrated editions I found of C. F. Alexander's famous hymn book, itself very much focused on the little child, only 11 of its 40 wood engravings even depict children, and these include Jesus as a baby and young boy. Alexander's Hymn 15, "I believe in the Holy Ghost" (from the Apostle's Creed), describes a "sickly child" who listens to a bird out of his window just as "There is a Holy Dove that sings / To every Christian child." Alexander attempts to explain the Holy Ghost using the metaphor of a singing dove to a child, but the editors instead choose for the accompanying illustration a stock image of the Holy Spirit on Whit-Sunday (Pentecost, the appearance of the Holy Spirit to the disciples as described in Acts 2); gone is the image of the "sickly child." Likewise, for Alexander's "Hush! little Christian child / Speak not that Holy Name" the editors include the scene from John 8 of the woman caught in adultery surrounded by Pharisees and guards, a very difficult crime to explain to young children and very different from the crime of verbal profanity described by the text.

In short, hymn books of the Golden Age of Illustration moved away from the simple woodcuts and copper engravings of earlier emblem books and religious texts to embrace the realism and detail of imagery offered by mid-century illustration practices. Some images, as that of Christ with the children, create splendid likenesses of children. In other cases, however, hymn-book editors failed to meet another quality of the Illustration movement: intently matching picture with text. In such cases, one could definitely say, to use Catherine Golden's words, that image was working "at cross purposes with texts, creating complexities and tensions" (Golden 8). Often the vibrant child was replaced with stasis … or replaced altogether by the adult image. The child herself was effaced from the pages of her own self-labeled "children's hymn book," suggesting a failure of image to adequately display the age and agency of children at play and in song, or to adequately display the child at all.

## Part II
## Audience and the Problematics of Class:
## Hymn Books in the Golden Age of Children's Picture Books

This deficiency was remedied by an art movement which followed closely behind this age of illustration, and which was certainly influenced by it: what could be termed the Golden Age of Children's Illustration, particularly of the 1870s and 1880s when, of course, the Golden Age of Children's Literature and the cult of the child had both reached their peak. With a desire to bring detail, color, and imagination to bear on illustrations which appear in balanced proportion to texts of children's poetry, fairy tales, and stories, artists such as Walter Crane, Kate Greenaway, and Randolph Caldecott created the modern "children's picture book." Truly, too, their books all highlighted the vivacious child, exuded a child-like energy, and displayed a deliberate awareness of their youthful audience. The expense of such books, however, created class issues which need exploring.

Though illustrations for children could be said to have begun with William Caxton's printing press and such books as his *Book of Courtesy* (Eaton 6),[12] the "first" children's picture book is generally acknowledged to be Comenius's *Orbis Pictus* ("The Visible World in Pictures," c. 1657). Tiny woodcuts found in seventeenth- and eighteenth-century chapbooks and John Newbery's *A Little Pretty Pocket-Book* (1744) and *Little Goody Two-Shoes* (1766) ushered in the era of children's "picture books." Nevertheless, their more artistic influence did not take immediate hold: many "toy books" for children of the first half of the nineteenth century used "crude lines and harsh colors, devoid of beauty," simply splashing on color for effect to the detriment of the text (Lundin 30).

During the first half of the nineteenth century, children's books evolved from such cheap "toy books" to true objects of art which attracted a large, middle-class market (Lundin 29–31). William Blake had the vision of creating "picture books as aesthetic objects" (Lundin 1), not necessarily for children but certainly featuring them, as discussed with the chapter's epigraph. Single-handedly beginning the process of illuminated printing[13] to which he added vibrant watercolor, as for

---

[12]    Useful histories of children's book illustrations include: Bertha E. Mahony, et al., eds., *Illustrators of Children's Books, 1744–1945* (1965); Edward Ernest, *The Kate Greenaway Treasury* (1967); William Feaver, *When We Were Young: Two Centuries of Children's Book Illustration* (1977); Anne Lundin, *Victorian Horizons: The Reception of the Picture Books of Walter Crane, Randolph Caldecott, and Kate Greenaway* (2001); and Jacquelyn Spratlin Rogers, "Picturing the Child in Nineteenth-Century Literature" (2008).

[13]    Also known as relief etching, this involved drawing a design with an acid-resistant medium onto copper, then using acid to remove the copper around the picture to reveal it in relief; once inked, it could be stamped onto the paper. This is the opposite of standard etching in which the design is pushed into the plate, the ink fills these lines, and the design then is a raised one on the paper (intaglio technique).

*Songs of Innocence and Experience* (1789), Blake created poetry and pictures "that should never be divided. In drawings and text alike we are conscious of the sense of upspringing life, of freshness of vision; of spiritual energy which, for all its force, is perfectly controlled … [a] never-to-be-forgotten experience" for children (Eaton 21).

Three artists would take this art into a realm specifically for children. Walter Crane brought detail and color to enliven alphabet books (*Railroad Alphabet*, 1865), nursery rhymes (e.g., *Sing a Song of Sixpence*, 1867) and fairy tales (e.g., *The Frog Prince*, 1874). Kate Greenaway's images made their first appearance in the magazine *Little Folks* in 1873. Her *Birthday Book for Children* (1880) and *The Pied Piper of Hamelin* (1888) established her as one of the first women illustrators for and *of* children (Overton 77, 79). Randolph Caldecott, working in color engravings, published *Hey-Diddle-Diddle, and Baby Bunting* (1882) and *A Frog He Would A-Wooing Go* (1883), also making a name for himself through the pages of *Harper's Monthly Magazine* (Overton 68). Crane, Greenaway, and Caldecott all benefitted from the new procedures of engraving, gravure, and lithography to print illustrations (Gentry 166).[14] All three published with Edmund Evans (1826–1905), therefore often called "the triumvirate of Evans" (Lundin 2), who was considered one of the most important Victorian printers of colored children's illustration. In successive line from Thomas Bewick (Lundin 8), Evans, in addition to using these new techniques, developed the process of chromoxylography, an intricate color woodblock printing process.[15] Such techniques allowed for fine detailing (consider the exquisite details in Crane's *The Frog Prince*), scenic perspective (as seen in Caldecott's *A Frog He Would A-Wooing*), and vibrant colorings (Crane especially). Color was an especially important element of these artistic pictures for children: the "skillful use of color—'the last and most sacred element of beauty'—was considered essential" to them (Lundin 31). Furthermore, these techniques and the artistic vision of such illustrators produced energetic animals living and dressing as humans, fantasy creatures such as spoons and forks coming to life, and very life-like and *lively* images of children intended for their youthful audience. This latter quality is perfectly portrayed in Kate Greenaway's dancing, frolicking children in her illustrations to Browning's *Pied Piper of Hamelin* (1888). In *Words about Pictures*, Nodelman notes the "pure sensual pleasure offered by brightly colored pictures" as corresponding to the "delight in the innocent joys of childhood" of the late nineteenth century (3). What is also significant, though, is that such vibrant illustrations came at a cost, literally, in the expense of printing such detail and color (Ernest 17), and thus not every child was enjoying these strides.

---

[14]   For full information about "Graphic Processes in Children's Books," see Gentry 157–72.

[15]   Thomas Bolton developed the technique of transferring an image through photography onto wood in the mid-1860s; George Baxter developed aquatinting for printing images in color. Evans built upon these, originating processes by which color was applied to wood blocks such that specific pigments and tints could be transferred onto the page. Each color used a different block so that up to nine blocks could be used for a single illustration (Lundin 33, 8).

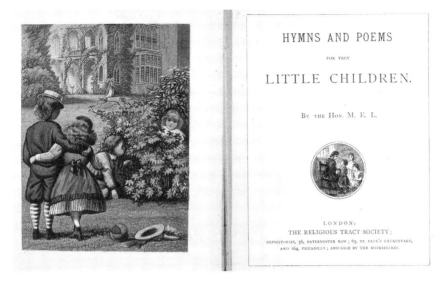

Figure 4.2      Frontispiece to *Hymns and Poems for Very Little Children* by Hon.
               M. E. L. [Margaret Elizabeth Leigh Child-Villiers, Countess of
               Jersey, 1849–1945] (1875). Courtesy of The Lilly Library, Indiana
               University, Bloomington, Indiana.

Some hymn books gradually absorbed this animation and color, especially
by the 1870s and 1880s, as seen in a handful of hymn books. Certainly not
"picture books," in that text dominates over pictures, hymn books yet show some
of the color and vibrancy influenced by these important children's illustrators.
The colored illustrations for *Hymns and Poems for Very Little Children* by Hon.
M. E. L. [Margaret Elizabeth Leigh Child-Villiers, Countess of Jersey, 1849–1945]
(London: Religious Tract Society, 1875) reflect this influence in small ways. Most
images are black-and-white engravings, many already discussed. Two of the
four colored images depict more adults in Bible scenes (Joseph being sold into
slavery [Hymn No. 14]; shepherds for the Christmas hymn [Hymn No. 20]), but
two others emphasize idyllic nineteenth-century childhood. The last color plate is
presumably to illustrate the previous hymn XXXV, "Look to Jesus," and the line
"My hands are very feeble … Yet … give them … Some work to do for Thee." The
illustration takes this unassuming line and greatly enhances the active agency of a
child. Here, the picture depicts a child giving food to a stranger: detailed images of
snow and ice around the house and vivid colors of the family's dress underscore a
vibrant scene with a young girl, centered, with a wistful look and generous action.
Even more eye-catching is the title illustration showing a game of play outside
a rich estate: everything, from the children's elegant clothes to the ball and hats
lying on the ground, evokes a life of ease (see Figure 4.2). If betraying the class
for whom this book was published, these details also reveal the child audience for

whom the book is intended: indeed, the two adults of the picture are cast far in the background as the four children take center stage, playing with joy and vigor.

A late 1880s hymn book also suggests hymn-book editors' debt to the burgeoning children's picture book field, if also revealing a much higher-class context for such books. *Hymns for Children* (1888) not only boasts music by the famed Arthur Sullivan, but illustrations by Jane M. Dealy and Fred Marriott who depict cherubic childhood throughout: a boy looking over a pier to the ocean (for "Another sun shines bright," No. 2) and a child—gender unspecified—who kneels in prayer, Jane Dealy drawing the drooping hat almost as angel's wings ("His Temple is not made with hands," No. 4). In fact, the reverse of the above phenomenon (adult images replacing children's) can also be found: for the Christmas hymn, "Oh, Christmas night, full round and bright," Dealy replaces biblical shepherds with two contemporary children in matching blue-and-white-striped sailor suits, arms placed lovingly about each other (No. 7 and cover). Children's wonderment now replaces even biblical records of adult worship. *Songs for the Little Ones at Home* (1868) flaunts its being "Illustrated with Sixteen Coloured and Sixteen Tinted Pictures, from Designs by Eminent Artists" (not named) which include exquisite landscape engravings. Children amongst nature, exploring, playing, are featured in the colored plates, including an image for one of the few hymns per se ("The Star Child"; see its pair, "All Things Speak of God") where a life-like boy lies in bed while a human-looking angel hovers; blues and browns accent this absorbing scene. Again, the scenes are engrossing, if laden with class-specific details from the fine clothes to the plush bed.

A final example of a very direct influence of children's picture-book publishing on children's hymn books is a republished version of Watts's *Divine and Moral Songs for Children* (London: Elkin Matthews, 1896) as "Pictured in Colours by Mrs. Arthur Gaskin" (Georgie Evelyn Cave Gaskin, 1866–1934; her illustrations use the initials GECG). A jeweler, she turned to the visual arts of her husband, Arthur Gaskin, influenced at first by his linear decorative style. *The Oxford Dictionary of National Biography* notes that she later changed to "a more distinctive style that suited the Kate Greenaway world of her imagination, with doll-like children in smocks and bonnets, drawn in fine outline and often in colour" (qtd. in "Mrs. Arthur Gaskin" Exeter Exhibition 2012 website). Her illustrations for *Divine and Moral Songs* also evidence the influence of Japanese art, introduced to Britain in 1862 with the International Exhibition, and characterized by abstract flatness, open white spaces, dull coloring, intricate patterns and decoration.[16] Pastels—greens, blues, oranges—accentuate children's clothes and domestic items, while dresses, stuffed chairs, and bed curtains are further adorned with floral print. Certainly these domestic, class comforts betray the privileged life of these children, lounging in bed and enjoying expensive toys. The children themselves display round faces, pink cheeks, and tulip-shaped lips featured in every picture—truly the Romantic child of affluence and leisure. With captions of the critical verse placed

---

[16]   Lundin 6; Effeny 28, 92; consider Mary Cassatt's well-known, Japanese-inspired *The Letter*, 1890–1891.

Figure 4.3     Hymn No. 1, "A General Song of Praise to God." From *Divine and Moral Songs for Children by the Reverend Isaac Watts DD*, Pictured in Colours by Mrs. Arthur Gaskin (1896). Courtesy of The Lilly Library, Indiana University, Bloomington, Indiana.

underneath each picture, the illustrations faithfully complement the text. And those verses highlighted also depict healthy agency of the children: "Th'eternal God will not disdain to hear an infant sing" is affixed to a young girl singing in her bed (see Figure 4.3); "Whene'er I take my walks abroad how many poor I see" shows a young, warmly dressed girl looking with concern upon ragged children in the snow. Whereas a book like *Hymns and Rhymes* might show a contented family to demonstrate the line, "But children you should never let such angry passions rise," Gaskin depicts angry-faced children fighting over a doll. Children are very much alive and even culpable in these illustrations. The life-like quality of her illustrations is further demonstrated in that Gaskin sometimes dressed her two daughters in the dress and design of her book illustrations ("Mrs. Gaskin" Exhibition website), as real life imitated the life-like creatures of her books, much as Greenaway's illustrations influenced children's fashions (Ernest 13).

All examples, though few, demonstrate the debt to children's picture books of hymn-book publishing which created a small market for high-end, illustrated hymn books for children. An implied upper-class child audience is revealed within the illustrations and assumed by the cost of publishing such colorful and intricate illustrations, which explains the limited impact of such books. Children play on their large estates, sing leisurely in their beds, dress warmly in the winter, and wear expensive clothes in all seasons. Yet within eye-catching, scenic illustrations, one can appreciate a new focus on the lively child, acting and playing with enthusiasm. "The power of the illustrator," writes Jacqueline Spratlin Rogers, "helped define this new concept of 'childhood' through clothing, body language, and actions" as indicative of the strides being made in society at large (45). Hymn books participated in this visual re-definition of active, if class-based, childhood.

## Part III
### The Problematics of Art-Objectification:
### Staging and Sexualizing the Child in High Art and Photography

The "fine arts" or "high art" of the academy also imbided this fascination with the child subject in the late century, across all of Europe, painters working in oil and watercolor mediums and intricate realism far beyond the art movements just described.[17] Yet here the context is significantly different in that the child image was on display before adults, not children—unless they happened to be brought to an art exhibit or gallery with an adult. Childhood was actually a new subject matter for "high art" as art historian Anne Higonnet points out: "the subject of childhood did

---

[17]    For histories of children in art, see Anita Schorsch, *Images of Childhood: An Illustrated Social History* (1985); Sarah Holdworth, *Innocence and Experience: Images of Children in British Art from 1600 to the Present* (1992); Marilyn R. Brown, ed., *Picturing Children: Constructions of Childhood Between Rousseau and Freud* (2002); and Greg M. Thomas, *Impressionist Children: Childhood, Family, and Modern Identity in French Art* (2010).

not always seem suitable to intellectually ambitious art" (in M. Brown 201). Greg
M. Thomas identifies the limited contexts of child imagery in Renaissance through
eighteenth-century artwork, beginning with the Christ child, cherubs, then moving
into child portraiture and genre painting (see his *Impressionist Children*, ch. 1). In
this context, children were used symbolically in four distinct contexts: "religious,
amorous, dynastic, and didactic" (G. Thomas 12). Two traditions of the nineteenth
century that both began in reaction to mainstream art—English Pre-Raphaelites
and French Impressionists—would "[shift] emphasis from generalizations about
childhood to specific descriptions of individual children, [thus] freeing their
child subjects from traditional styles and motifs ... [and] inviting the viewer
to find meaning in children's detached isolation as independent individuals"
(G. Thomas 12). Consider how, in melancholy tones of browns and blues, Briton
Rivière's *Sympathy* (1877) depicts the inner emotions of a little girl sitting
forlornly on the carpeted stairs while her pet dog droops his head sympathetically
over her shoulder.

But the intense focus on living, emoting children perhaps came at a cost,
especially for little girls: "art began blurring the formerly clear boundaries
distinguishing adults from children, such that innocence occasionally pivoted into
themes of sexual knowledge" (G. Thomas 23).[18] Pre-Raphaelites were particularly
inclined to sexualize their subjects, including young girls. John Everett Millais, a
member of the Pre-Raphaelite Brotherhood early in his career, can be considered
in this context. His late-career *Cherry Ripe* (1879) depicts a demure little girl in
Regency attire sitting by a plate of cherries in a "potentially provocative pose"
(G. Thomas 24). Leslie Williams suggests that the little girl's "black-gloved hands
between her thighs is indeed unambiguously sexual, as is the title" (150). Printed in
the *Graphic*'s Christmas Annual of 1880, it sold over 500,000 copies to delighted
consumers (L. Bradley 179). Together with his various other popular paintings of
little girls (e.g., "For the Squire"), Millais demonstrated "the Victorian art market's
willingness to perceive girlhood as a commodity at once to be admired and to be
devoured" (Williams 127).[19]

In France, this phenomenon was also true: paintings featuring young girls which
had instant, and international, appeal, such as William Adophe Bouguereau's *The
Nut Gatherers* (1882); Pierre-Auguste Renoir's *Two Sisters (On the Terrace)* (1881)

---

[18]    James Kincaid's influential *Child-Loving: The Erotic Child and Victorian Culture*
(1992) has exposed the widespread Victorian predilection of seeing the child as a sexual,
erotic being. In the sense that this is a demeaning, incredibly harmful way of seeing children,
I will always cast this as a problematic posture in this chapter.

[19]    For more about this painting and Millais's late-career focus on little girls, see Greg
M. Thomas (23–4); Laura Bradley, "From Eden to Empire"; Leslie Williams, "The Look of
Little Girls"; and Caroline Arscott, "Childhood in Victorian Art." Arscott tends to excuse
Millais since his own children, nieces, nephews, and grandchildren were his models (100);
she also reminds us of other Victorian painters—Thomas Webster, Frederick Daniel Hardy,
and Arthur Boyd Houghton—who often showed the "chaotic, amusing activities of children
at play" (101). Sadly, their works are still less known than the work by the Pre-Raphaelites
and Impressionists whom I examine here.

and *A Girl with a Watering Can* (1876); Edgar Degas's many ballerina girls (which were initially seen as too sexual); and American Mary Cassatt's signature focus on young children, from *Children Playing on the Beach* (1884) to *The Bath* (1892). Greg M. Thomas argues that many of these images were influenced by the current fetish in girls' dolls; he is particularly critical of Renoir for commodifying young girls along with their dolls (*Children's Afternoon at Wargemont*, 1884); objectifying little girls themselves *as* dolls (*Girl with a Watering Can*, 1876), and, most dangerously, sexualizing young girls by placing them next to eroticized adult women (*Promenade*, 1876; *Two Sisters*, 1881): "In *Promenade* [Renoir's] warm tones, rich texturing, and emphasis on points of sensual attraction such as lips, hair, and eyes all focus attention … under the slightly lascivious gaze of Renoir and other men envisioning them as future beauties" (49).[20]

Of course, much of the unease with such artwork stems from its realism. Photography would be another step in co-opting the living body of a girl "on stage" for an infinite audience of limitless reproductions. Indeed, due to the technology of photography, a child had to literally freeze for the camera so that active children could never be shown without blurring. Lewis Carroll's well-known photographs of the child Alice Liddell have received the most criticism for their sexual, static qualities. Photographs such as *Alice Liddell as 'The Beggar Maid'* (c. 1859) reveal the "staged" nature of the photograph, and her torn clothes and bare shoulders lend themselves to modern allegations of Carroll's "pedophiliac projections of adult male sexual desire onto the innocent bodies of Victorian children" (G. Thomas 24). Diane Waggoner tempers this by arguing that "Dodgson made one of the first attempts to visualize difference between children and adults in the new medium of photography, a medium that claimed to provide a greater fidelity to its subject than earlier modes of representation" (158).[21]

Due either to prudishness or cheapness, or both, hymn-book editors never utilized artwork of the caliber of a Millais or Renoir, nor any photographs, in their hymn books of my study. Within the hymn-singing world, though, another practice co-opted eroticized images of little girls for supposed religious transformation:

---

[20]     Manet and Cassatt turn the gaze back upon the audience, Thomas argues, whose child-subjects "flout[] the rules of feminine decorum" (as with Cassatt's *Little Girl in a Blue Armchair*, 1878; Thomas 58). Despite Cassatt's many unrestrained child-portraits, Alison Effeny yet reminds us of their gendering: boys are "generally the focus of adoration" (as with *Mother and Boy [The Oval Mirror]*, 1901) while little girls take on traditional activities of sewing and grooming (126).

[21]     I am clearly taking a more conservative stance on the issue of Carroll's girl-photographs. Waggoner, for instance, further argues that Dodgson was able to gain the girls' trust through play and thus they willingly corroborated in this "play" for the camera. Carol Mavor's "Dream-Rushes: Lewis Carroll's Photographs of the Little Girl" examines various nude and posed photographs that Carroll took of little girls. Addressing the "obvious sexuality that Carroll captured on the photographic plates," she disavows not only his "innocent" intentions, but the innocence of the models as well (157). Marah Gubar's most recent contribution to this debate is to argue that Carroll "*declines* to establish a firm line of division, representing child and adult as genuine collaborators. At the same time, he hints that the smaller party might not be an entirely willing partner" (110).

the magic lantern shows of late century which utilized photographs of little girls during the shows.

The magic lantern (or stereopticon) was invented in the 1650s and lasted through, even competed with, the era of silent film.[22] It has been called the "single most important popular visual entertainment and means of instruction in Western culture for two and a half centuries."[23] It reached its peak in the late nineteenth century when almost every public institution had a lantern and nearly every middle-class household had at least a "toy" lantern. Joss Marsh suggests that from the 1860s to 1890s, as many as 1,200 lantern lecturers might have been traveling around England (333). Magic lantern shows thrilled large crowds in public concerts; they could also entertain families in the privacy of their homes where even children could present shows with toy lanterns. Artists like American Joseph Boggs Beale specialized in painting slides; with the advent of photography, landscapes and "live model illustrative slides" began to dominate. The topics of such shows were extremely diverse, from politics to scientific discoveries, from retellings of classic stories to temperance propaganda. Live music was used, a narrator might lead the audience through the stories, or a soloist could sing songs written to accompany the slides, often encouraging "sing-alongs" from the audience at key points. Children enjoyed these; Thomas Burke recalls a music-enhanced magic lantern show in the 1890s of "Hansel and Gretel" which was "greeted by the unusual approval of a long-drawn OO-oo-ooo ... We sat back and wallowed in colour, and above our heads the lantern sent through the dark a silver spear made of dancing dust" (67).

Thrilling to children, magic lanterns were used for Sunday school and Bands of Hope (temperance) meetings. Magic lantern shows could also serve as religious didacticism for adults, part of traveling religious revivals and temperance meetings. Here the focus might include hymn singing, either by the audience or a soloist, with slides displaying the hymn-texts or a relevant visual.[24] Children's hymns were a part of this tradition, and I have found slides to the children's hymns "Gentle Jesus, meek and mild," "I think when I read that sweet story," and "Jesus

---

[22] The lantern itself consisted of at least one lens, with the "bi-unial" and "tri-unial" lantern, mid-nineteenth-century inventions, sporting two and three, respectively. Pictures were painted on strips or individual glass slides, about 4 inches on each side. The glass slides were inserted into the lantern in front of a light (candle, kerosene, limelight or, later, electric light) so as to project images onto a large white screen. See Joss Marsh's "Dickensian 'Dissolving Views'" and Sally B. Palmer's "Projecting the Gaze," which places the stereopticon in the context of Foucault's theories of spectacle (25–7).

[23] "David Francis Collection of the Screen Experience: The Magic Lantern and Victorian Culture at the Lilly Library, 8th–29th May 2010," program notes.

[24] Religious hymn-sing slides are less commonly shown and auctioned by magic lantern recreators and collectors today. I have found almost forty hymn titles thanks to the help of Professor Joss Marsh and David Francis, who, as members of the Magic Lantern Society of the United States and Canada, have been collecting magic lantern memorabilia and slides, and hosting magic lantern shows, for many years. The five children's hymn slides I will discuss come from their collection.

bids us shine." Slides to these hymns utilize photographs of cherubic little girls positioned as in prayer or religious reflection. The idealization of children is very much in keeping with late-century Romanticism of childhood. Further, positioning them as angels invokes the purity of children needed to spiritually reform those in the viewing audience. Yet the artificiality and sexuality of these staged portraits aligns these photographs with the high-art fetish with children just described. It also elides the actual energy and agency of children as might be seen in their authentic singing and certainly as chronicled in the hymn-texts themselves.

For instance, the hymn "Gentle Jesus, meek and mild" is an early children's hymn written by Charles Wesley and published in *Hymns and Sacred Poems* (1742), then later republished in *Hymns for Children* (1763). It is the only children's hymn by Wesley ever to become popular, possibly because, unlike most of his hymns, it uses the voice of the child; too, it uncharacteristically avoids all mention of sin, death, and repentance. Instead, this hymn is entirely focused on the worth of the child:

> Gentle Jesus, meek and mild,
>    Look upon a little child,
> Pity my simplicity,
>    Suffer me to come to Thee. (v. 1)

This sentiment was especially in keeping with Victorian ideology of the second half of the century; it is no surprise that I found it most commonly in hymn books after 1849, often set to very charming tunes. At first glance, the hymn seems demeaning of the child: "Pity my simplicity," etc. However, its textual focus on the child reminds the child singing it and the adults listening that in God's Kingdom even "a little child [has] a place" (v. 2). Further, it reminds the audience that Jesus Himself was "gentle, meek, and mild," and He was "once a little child" (v. 3). While a child might be pitied for his simplicity, so too was Jesus "pitiful and kind," pity being a Christian virtue, not derogation.

The meekness and simplicity of a child is captured in this 1890s magic lantern slide issued by the Band of Hope Union (children's temperance organization) of the UK. This slide was no doubt used to accompany a soloist since it does not give the hymn lyrics for audience participation. Instead, the audience is asked to contemplate the figure of a golden-haired child, pink-cheeked and cherubic, bending piously in prayer. Her white nightgown not only suggests her purity, however, it compromises her private dress for all to see. A "live-illustrated slide," this is a photograph of a real child, posing in dutiful submissiveness, clearly with additional paint touch-ups to enhance her blond (Anglocentric) hair. Despite the openness of the textual words, speaking to all children, this slide synthesizes what had become the ideal Victorian child: blond, pure, and solemn. Nor is she active and singing, in contrast to the tune "Innocents" often used with the hymn which not only suggests "innocence" but a sheer active energy. [25]

---

[25]    This hymn has been associated with many tunes, Martin Shaw writing one especially for it in 1915 ("Gentle Jesus"). The tune "Innocents," from an old litany, is set to the hymn

"I think when I read that sweet story of old" has already been addressed as the most frequently appearing hymn in nineteenth-century children's hymn books so it is no surprise to see it appear in magic lantern slideshows. As argued in Chapter 3, despite its simple language for children, this hymn commands action from its youthful singers, both in their own lives and around the world, as expressed in the various action verbs found in verse 2:

> Yet still to his footstool in prayer *I may go*
> > *And ask* for a share of His love
> And if I earnestly *seek Him* below
> > I shall *see Him* and *hear Him* above. (my italics)

Action is clearly placed in the realm of the child. Again, though, the 1890s magic lantern slide renders staged, not active, children. Two slides that are extant for this hymn give the words and a child's image for these two parts of verse 2. Consider the first image given for the verse, "Yet still to His footstool in prayer I may go," to which sits a little girl, probably as young as 3, chubby cheeks, blue eyes, hands in prayer. The verse's text positions the child as subject ("I may go"), yet in the slide she has become object of the audience's gaze. The second slide may be showing an angel in white missing only her wings to help listeners visualize this "heavenly place" (see Figure 4.4); still, the drooping sleeve suggests something more earthy and sexual. As with other photographs and staged pictures of children of the period, significant are the attempts to render childhood innocence, the gendering of that innocence as feminine and fair; yet, at the same time, the obvious *construction* of that innocence—from the painted cheeks to the nightgown falling from the little girl's shoulders—is disturbingly sexual, not unlike Carroll's famous photographs. In Figure 4.4, the colorings to augment a black-and-white photograph also create the idealized blond-haired and blue-eyed little girl. Most importantly, the girl is staged and stagnant, a far cry from active children actually "seeking Him" and singing this energetic tune, the singable "Greek Air." What these slides further impair then, are the supposed synthesis of picture, text, and tune.

The third hymn referenced by the Band of Hope Union in a magic lantern show is "Jesus bids us shine," attributed to the American hymn writer Emily Huntingdon Miller as in *282 Hymns and Melodies* (1893).[26] It is a sweet hymn invoking Matthew 5:16 about "let[ting] your light shine before men," and John 1:5 ("The light shines in the darkness, and the darkness has not overcome it"). Here, Jesus urges children to shine:

---

in *282 Hymns and Melodies for School and Family Use* (1893). This tune especially exudes "innocence," being in a major key, with simple three-note scale progressions both up and down the scale. It even reaches up to an E5 (two above middle C), this high note suggesting an angelic purity.

[26] "Jesus bids us shine" was first published in Barrett's *Book of Praise of Children* (1881) and was actually by Susan Warner, author of *Wide, Wide World*.

In that beautiful place He has gone to prepare
  For all who are washed and forgiven;
And many dear children are gathering there,
  For "of such is the kingdom of heaven."

Figure 4.4     Magic lantern slide to verse 2 of "I think when I read that sweet
               story of old." Courtesy of the Kent Museum of the Moving Image.

Jesus bids us shine With a pure clear light,
Like a little candle Burning in the night;
In this world of darkness, So we must shine,
You in your small corner, And I in mine.
                        (v. 1, No. 103, *282 Hymns and Melodies*)

The child's location in a "small corner" at first connotes tight spaces where children
might be trapped; however, the analogy of a candle in a corner suggests the greater
reflection of that light outward when held against a wall, clearly an important
lesson for marginalized, disempowered children. Furthermore, Jesus bids them
shine in "many kinds of darkness": "sin, and want and sorrow" (v. 3), noting from
heaven when "their light grows dim" (v. 2). It is an interesting mixture of warning
and welcome for the luminosity of the child. Its tune, "Little Soldiers," as used
in this 1893 hymn collection, is borrowed from the previous hymn, "We are little
soldiers / fighting for the Lord" (No. 102), which helps to explain and highlight
the emphatic beats. The tune exudes buoyancy and an action-inducing tempo. The
magic lantern slide to accompany the hymn is, once again, in stark contrast. A
young girl holds a candle but very little light radiates out from it, thus limiting the
power of the literary metaphor. Further, the girl is *doing* nothing as the text might
encourage, but merely looks serenely up to heaven. Once again it is a very young

girl, static and staged in a white nightgown, which she holds up to show her bare feet in an artificial, unchild-like way. As this is a real live girl, her body and clothes arranged clearly for the viewers' pleasure, it is a troubling image.[27]

These three children's hymns for the most part allowed for childhood empowerment—through text and tune—and encouraged childhood activity, whether it be saving souls on a Whit-Walk or imbibing tuneful doctrine in the Sunday school. Children attending a magic lantern show would have this activity, though, only through the singing of the hymns, if part of a Sunday school, while their static other-selves were flashed onto the screen. As Sally B. Palmer argues of magic lantern spectacles, "[t]he stereopticon, with its masterful and innovative technological aspects [gave] intense and immediate stimulation, delivered excitement" and, in the process, "disseminated a reassuring image of the benevolent nature of current social structures" (26–7). Angelic, erotic, stagnant images of little girls would not be questioned in this "normalizing" context.

Hymn books, due to conservative, mainstream approaches, never entered such sexist, sexualized territory. Illustrations of little girls in hymn books might be faulted for passive portrayals of young girls, but even in this realm, late-century images could show much agency from both genders. A final illustration to conclude this discussion is from Blanche McManus's illustrated edition to Watts's *Divine and Moral Songs* entitled *Childhood's Songs of Long Ago* (1897), used as the image on this book's cover. Here McManus envisions a child, a young girl of 4 or 5, clutching her hymn book and gazing up in wonder as she sings. Her affluence is evidenced by her ruffled coat, feathered hat, and the fact that she has her own cushioned pew at church. But her independence of worship and in the singing is also significant, and highlighted by McManus blocking off all but the tops of the heads of the adult parishioners behind the wall of her pew. Eyes averted away from us, fully clothed in her Sunday finery, she is much in contrast to sexualized images of young girls. While not shown in active play, she is clearly in active worship. Her open mouth and eyes looking intently heavenward all display active engagement with the hymn singing, suggesting a young girl in full control of her actions. It is certainly an image that a child could enjoy of herself.

In conclusion, children's hymn books took inspiration from the various art movements peaking during the mid to late nineteenth century: more realistic Bible illustrations, more vivid images of themselves as active children. Their failure was in utilizing stock images indiscriminately such that the child was often

---

[27] Admittedly, the slide for the second verse is more curious. Here is a young girl, quite a bit older than the infants previously shown, and though she is still staged, she is photographed out of doors, not the tight quarters of a "corner" by any means. Neither is she cherubic and clean; rather she is in working-class garments, basket on one hip, hand on the other, almost with an air of defiance about her. It is a rare moment of a "real" child pictured in these slides, one who is unkempt and even a bit "saucy." The slide thus offers more empowerment to the working-class child than perhaps even the text admits, appreciating (or perhaps justifying) her arduous work in the field. It could also be another example of a stock image being used with no connection to the text.

elided in favor of the adult. And vibrantly illustrated families and scenes featured children of leisure much more often than working class children who might be using, if not purchasing, these decorative hymn books. What hymn books avoided, though, was the problematic sexualizing of young girls, as seen publically and prominently through Pre-Raphaelite, Impressionist, and magic lantern exhibitions and reproductions. Indeed, the hymn book's retroactive return to adult images could, in fact, neutralize this situation and work, not to differentiate the child and adult bodies, as Waggoner says of Carroll's agenda, but to posit both within a non-corporeal, all-encompassing spiritual world. Part of a conservative, book-reading culture, hymn books would eventually embrace the active agency of their child readers, but never as eroticized "others."

In the last section, I will once again engage these various issues of adult imagery, class elitism, and gendering by tracing one famous hymn-text—Isaac Watts's *Divine and Moral Songs for Children*—throughout 100 years of nineteenth-century hymn-book illustrations which paralleled the Emblem-Book Revival, the Golden Age of Illustration, and the Golden Age of Children's Picture Books. It is a rare opportunity to freeze the text so as to be able to focus on the changing illustrations and how they portray a century's worth of ideological re-interpretation of this classic hymn book.

## Part IV
## Divine and Moral Songs for Victorian Children

Isaac Watts's *Divine and Moral Songs for Children* (originally entitled *Divine Songs Attempted in an Easy Language for the Use of Children*, 1715) effectively began the genre of hymn books written for children, as shown in Chapter 2. These hymns were child-centered, Watts writing that they were to "give the minds of children a relish for virtue and religion" (Preface) as he speaks about them directly ("The eternal God will not disdain / To hear an infant sing" Song I), in their language ("O may I then with joy appear," Song III), about sins of a child's ken (quarreling, lying, and mischief). Steeped in eighteenth-century Calvinist theologies (Original Sin, Hell, etc.), this text yet continued to be an effective tool for Victorians in teaching children Christian virtues, social productivity, and familial duties. The influence of this book was tremendous: it had gone through 25 editions by 1761 (Rogal, "Library Gazette" 167); more than a thousand editions were printed between 1750 and 1850 (according to Wilbur Macey Stone, qtd. in J. Shaw 135); and, "[w]hen the nineteenth century began, Watts's *Divine and Moral Songs* was a standard textbook in every school in Britain and America" (J. Shaw 135). Its influence certainly did not die away during the nineteenth century either: "I sing the almighty power of God" (Song II) was found in 29% of hymn books throughout the century. The book had become common enough in mid-nineteenth-century life that authors frequently refer to it. Song XX was especially popular, reading: "How doth the little busy bee/ Improve each shining hour / And gather honey all the day / From every opening flower!" For instance, in Dickens's *David Copperfield* (1849–1850) Doctor Strong quips, "'What does Doctor Watts say,' he added, looking at me, and moving his head to the time of his quotation, 'Satan finds some mischief still, for idle hands to do'" (ch. 16). Alice attempts to recall this well-learned verse, although it invariably comes out wrong in Wonderland: "How doth the little crocodile / Improve his shining tail ..." (ch. 2).

In my research, I found over 20 editions of *Divine and Moral Songs*, mostly British but a few American, published between 1800 and 1897. Without exception they all contained pictures, perhaps the rationale for printing yet another, "new" version.[28] In the tradition of the emblem book, the illustrations were meant to be viewed as an equal partner to the text. After the advent of wood engraving, which allowed for pictures and words to be printed together on the same page, images were typically printed above each hymn, much like emblem books, although unlike a common approach at mid-century to place pictures after the words (J. Thomas, *Pictorial Victorians* 9). By late century, images would weave in and around the text; in this respect such anonymous illustrators worked much like Christina and Dante Gabriel Rossetti who "sought a dynamic, interactive relationship akin to that found in the emblem books they both admired. Image and text should mutually explicate each other, and the details of the picture should be 'read' for their symbolic meaning" (Kooistra 67).

In terms of technique, these hymn books show great disparity and growth. Early versions occurred from 1802 through 1841: often these are small chapbooks (3 × 4 inches), some are even smaller miniatures (2 × 3 inches), and many contain woodcuts, two being attributed to Thomas Bewick (1812, 1814 editions). Some are clearly stock images of pastoral and domestic scenes not directly depicting the hymn's meaning (some of the 1812 images are the same found in another 1831 hymn book, for instance). By and large, however, more detailed and artistic illustrations begin to appear after 1850 commensurate with the Golden Age of Illustration (an 1848 hymn book by Cope and Thompson, already discussed, being an earlier example). Woodcuts were replaced by wood engraving as developed by Thomas Bewick, and printing advancements allowed for smaller lines, crisper images, and more foreground and background details. Due to cheaper printing costs, the number of illustrations to be included in a single book increased from an occasional illustration to one for almost all of the 28 hymns. The Golden Age of

---

[28] I am grateful to Cambridge University Library (UK), the Newberry Library (Chicago), the Lilly Library (Bloomington, IN), and the University of Illinois Library for sharing the numerous nineteenth-century editions of Watts's hymn books discussed in this chapter and listed in the Works Cited. Here they will be identified by their year of publication, except, due to duplications, the following distinctions: *Divine Songs* (New York: Clark, Austen, 1851) is notated as "1851b" and *Divine and Moral Songs for Children By the Rev. Isaac Watts, D.D.* (London: T. Nelson and Sons, 1857) is notated as "1857b." The 188- edition is not dated, and so I use the date as approximated by the University of Illinois Library. The newest edition is titled *Childhood's Songs of Long Ago, Being Some of the Divine and Moral Songs Writ by Rev. Isaac Watts, D.D.* Picturings by Blanche McManus (New York: E. R. Herrick, 1897).

Illustration peaks in these Watts editions of the 1860s and later, with ornate details and dramatic flourish. Take, for example, the black-and-white wood engravings of the 188- edition of Watts's poems. Floral borders, pastoral landscapes, and frolicking children all reinforce the spiritual tranquillity of the collection (see one example as Figure 4.7). Childhood and domestic serenity seep through the illustrations as families gather to read and sing, but violence breaks out in frames from other times and places: a Roman soldier impales an arrow through another soldier, while an African king wields a menacing knife over a sacrificial victim.

Besides advancements in artwork, the illustrations become a microcosm of changing social and religious ideologies. This is because all 20 collections of illustrations are for the same text; only the decisions to highlight certain hymns with pictures and to interpret the same hymn distinctly change over this 100-year span. "Illustration highlights textual plurality," writes Julia Thomas (*Pictorial Victorians* 14); further, illustrations are "social *processes*, involving a complex network of relationships in historically specific situations that change over time" (Kooistra 7). These are pivotal concepts in approaching the undulating illustrative content of Isaac Watts's most famous children's hymn book reissued throughout every decade of the nineteenth century. For instance, Watts writes most hymns in the first person so the gender is open to interpretation. Illustrators were bound to gender specifications when illustrating children and betray gender stereotypes when tying specific actions to certain genders. Additionally, illustrators revealed religious and cultural biases when selecting which hymns, verses, and actions to illustrate.

Admittedly, some hymns found interest from illustrators throughout this time span with little variation in interpretation: Watts's "The Sluggard," Moral Song I ("'Tis the voice of the sluggard; I heard him complain, / 'You have waked me too soon, I must slumber again'") is a standard inclusion (also parodied by Lewis Carroll as "'Tis the voice of the Lobster," *Alice*, ch. 10). In hymn books it is typically illustrated with a young boy (the song identifies the sluggard as male) lounging in bed while the sun shines in the window (the 1848 hymn book actually identifies the time on the clock as 10 o'clock). Divine Song XX, the famous "How doth the little busy bee," another inducement to work, is found in almost every one of these hymn books with a beehive featured, sometimes being admired by children. But many other illustrations show remarkable variety in theological principles, social and gender ideologies, and adult-child difference, three concepts explored already in general artwork and hymn books of the century which come into high relief through these evolving images.

Not surprisingly, biblical images appear frequently within hymn books, referenced as they are by Watts himself. For example, Watts uses the story of Ananias, struck down dead in a lie (Acts 5:3–5) in Song XV, as a warning "Against Lying," and this proved an ever-popular image for illustrators (1818, 1840, 1848, c. 1850, 1851b, 188-). However, the 1810 and 1848 editions (latter by Cope) highlight instead the death of Ananias' wife, Sapphira (verse 4, "So did his wife Sapphira die … [when she] confirm[ed] that wicked lie"). By and large, however, more biblical pictures feature in earlier hymn books; by late century, illustrators use contemporary life to teach moral principles. An 1802 edition depicts the story of the Good Samaritan to accompany the Morning Hymn, Song XXV ("So, like the sun, would I fulfill / The business of the day"), whereas later editions will depict a child praying or a sun rising (both used in the 188- edition). Like other Watts books of early to mid-century, many of the beautiful wood engravings of the 1848 version depict Jesus as a child ("Examples of Early Piety," Song XIV), inspiring a young girl ("Against Pride in Clothes," Song XXII), and at the Cross ("Praise to God for our Redemptions," Song III). Likewise, the story "Love Between Brothers and Sisters" (Song XVII) features that of Cain and Abel's dispute (from verse 4; also highlighted in the 1810 edition illustration), all for hymns that would, later, regularly depict contemporary children pouring over a book, sporting new clothes, or quarreling with a sibling, examples of the modern instance as illustrators attempted to make Watts's induction more relevant to contemporary children. The 1848 edition marks this transition metaphorically: the "Cradle Hymn" (Moral Song VIII) opens with a detailed engraving of Mary worshipping before the baby Jesus as cattle feed in troughs behind; the closing illustration features a nineteenth-century baby in middle-class comfort: curtained bed, lit candle, and bowlful of food at the bedside. Hereafter, the "Cradle Hymn," will become prominently illustrated with contemporary children, families, and pets which replace the Holy Family and stable animals (see 1857, 1869, and 188-).

Likewise, angels and divine images feature early on in hymn books (c. 1800, 1810, 1812): angels also frequent various illustrations in the 1841 edition, assisting humans, hovering close. Thomas Bewick's woodcuts in the 1814 hymn book show angels singing above the sky in "How glorious is our heav'nly King" (Song I) and the actual "eye" hovering over young boys for "The All-Seeing God" (Song IX, "Almighty God thy piercing eye"). Except for decorative angels, divine figures disappear by late century.

Furthermore, the sternness of religion has relaxed by late century. In many hymn books of the first half of the century, Watts's Calvinist doctrine of sin and retribution is visually highlighted. Moral Song IV, "The Thief" ("Why should I deprive my neighbor / Of his goods against his will?") is accompanied by a woodcut of a hanging (verse 4 reads that "a young beginner" might on "the gallows end[] his days") in many early hymn books (c. 1800, 1810, 1812, 1818, and 1841), whereas the 1869 hymn book shows a boy slinking down the street; in 188-, a young girl hides an apple from her scolding mother; and in 1897, two boys steal fruit off a farmer's tree. Focus turns to the immorality of stealing within a child's experience, not the dire consequences. Likewise, the didactic hymn "Against Scoffing and Calling Names" (Song XVIII) narrates the biblical story of children calling Elisha "bald-head" and then being killed by wild bears (2 Kings 2:23–5). Earlier hymn books show Elisha and the children (1812, 1848) and sometimes the actual bear attack (1810, 1840, 1851b), whereas later hymn books (1869, 1897) illustrate two young boys scoffing at a fellow boy in the street: the deed made relevant to contemporary children emphasized over the biblical story and gruesome punishment.

Likewise, images of death and divine punishment haunt early hymn books: Song X ("Solemn Thoughts of God and Death") is repeatedly illustrated (1803, 1810, 1857) with mourners at a gravesite (similarly, see Figure 4.6); the 1810 illustration depicts children at a child's interment. In the 1810 and 1812 hymn books, Hymn XXIII, "Obedience to Parents," has illustrations actually depicting the terrifying lines, "To him that breaks his father's law … What heavy guilt upon him lies / How cursed is his name! / The ravens shall pick out his eyes / And eagles eat the same" where giant birds chase down a boy in the 1810 version. Song XIII ("Why should I say, 'Tis too soon / To seek for heav'n, or think of death?") is shown, in an 1841 hymn book, with the figure of a young boy struck down to illustrate the line, "One stroke of his almighty rod / Shall send young sinners quick to hell" (verse 5). Later hymn books mute the horrific image; the 188- hymn book instead highlights the line, "A flower may fade before 'tis noon" with an image of a drooping peony plant. Heaven and hell are vividly depicted by Bewick in the 1812 edition, for Watts's Song XI "Heaven and Hell" ("A heaven of joy and love … a dreadful hell / And everlasting pains"), with winged angels contrasted with naked pleaders. By 1848, only the last verse ("Then will I read and pray") is highlighted with the image of a young girl praying at the knees of her mother.

Later hymn books allay or avoid these dark textual moments, choosing to illustrate more joyful moments instead. Songs XXVII and XXVIII, "For the Lord's Day Morning" and "For the Lord's Day Evening," are especial later-century favorites (1848, 1857, 1869, and 188-), Cope and Thompson depicting adults and children eagerly climbing the stairs to the church in knickers and bonnets ("To-day, with pleasure, Christians meet," v. 3, Song XXVII) in the 1848 edition (see their Song XXVIII as Figure 4.6). Despite a lightening of hymn-texts, however, the portrayal of non-Christians, as will be argued in Chapter 5, does not lighten in these hymn books' illustrations: the Africans shown killing one another and committing human sacrifice in the 188- hymn book is even more debasing than an 1802 image entitled "The European giving instruction to the African" (see Figure 5.1 in the next chapter).

A close look at one hymn offers reflection upon changing theology seen through illustration. "I sing th' almighty pow'r of God" ("Praise for Creation and Providence," Song II), Watts's most popular hymn in all children's hymn books across the century, discussed in Chapter 3, offers ample imagery to inspire future illustrators:

> I sing the almighty power of God,
>    That made the mountains rise;
> That spread the flowing seas abroad,
>    And built the lofty skies. (v. 1)

Many biblical principles are referenced throughout this hymn and thus illustrators of different ideological perspectives could highlight what was most appealing to them. For instance, early Evangelical perspectives influenced an 1803 edition such that the wood engraving depicts Adam and Eve and original creation for this hymn, the illustrator focusing on verse 3, "He formed the creatures with His word, / And then pronounced them good"—with humanity clearly being the most important of that creation to highlight. In another early depiction (c. 1800), a woman holds center stage between a tree and a stream, with her Bible held prominently in her hand to show that the Bible dictates this admiration for nature. The 1814 Bewick woodcut shows an adult man with two cows grazing before the rising sun, domesticated animals keeping this reverence within the human realm of creation. An angel hovers over a prayerful child's footsteps in the 1848 edition, thereby highlighting verse 8, "His hand is my perpetual guard. / He keeps me with His eye."

In the 1869 edition, the same hymn features boys learning to sing with their tutor, highlighting the various pronouncements to "sing" opening verses 1–3 and thus the importance of a child's intentional praise. By the 1880s hymn book, the illustrator intersperses various nature scenes—a picturesque scene at the ocean side, a man observing the sunrise, a moon setting above a marsh, and a woman admiring her flowers—taking visual liberties with elements of the creation only alluded to in verse 5:

> There's not a plant or flower below
> > But makes Thy glories known;
> And clouds arise, and tempests blow,
> > By order from Thy throne. (v. 5)

The seventh and eighth verses which contain images of hell and mild admonishments ("In heaven He shines with beams of love, / With wrath in hell beneath ...Why should I then forget the Lord...?") are yet integrated within a natural idyllic scene, of deer drinking at a stream, birds flying above and squirrels perched in the trees. Now a present-day idyllic creation, moved out of the Garden of Eden, and wild animals, not human's beasts of burden, are promoted for praise and gratitude even against the more unsettling aspects of the text.

As a second point to consider, these various hymn-book illustrations also demonstrate a century's worth of social change. This begins with changes in human interaction with the animal world, socio-theological concerns which would lead up to the Bands of Mercy (animal welfare organizations) of the 1870s and 1880s. "Praise for Creation and Providence," as just noted, changes from that of Adam and Eve's creation to the natural creation, vivid sunsets, mountain grandeur, and vast oceans displayed with detailed wood engravings in the 188- hymn book. Scenes in early books are typically domestic or town scenes; they move outdoors mid-century, with children reading books and playing in nature. The animal world is, early in the century, solely represented by beasts of burden (cows in the 1814 hymn book), orderly insects (human-created beehives are very popular images), and aggressive dogs or bears. The latter images originate in Watts's poetry: "Let dogs delight to bark and bite" in Song XVI (see Thomas Bewick's engraving of angry dogs in the 1814 version) and God sending "two raging bears" in Song XVIII. Later editions tend to replace the analogous animal for the literal child who quarrels and calls names. Or, at other times, the animal used in the analogy becomes the literal object of interest, as in Moral Song V, "The Ant, or Emmet" in which an ant's work ethic is praised: later illustrations show the actual ants in fine detail (188-, 1897) as children, like scientists, watch in admiration (1897). The change from an agrarian to urban lifestyle is shown through animals: Moral Song II, "Innocent Play," describes "Abroad in the meadows to see the young lambs," a scene so commonplace in early century that it is rarely illustrated, but by mid-to-late century, 1850 and 1869 hymn books portray the scene with nostalgia for a way of life being lost, in pastoral serenity. Notably, too, middle-class children observe the sheep at a distance, not working alongside them. Furthermore, pets become very common, slipped into scenes as the cat is in an 1869 image of a girl reading her Bible, or made part of the story as dogs accompany their begging masters (1850, 188-). The animal world has changed from threatening bears to friendly pets, from that to be contained, to something to be admired, or at least exploited differently (a phenomenon to be thoroughly discussed in the next chapter).

Given the exploitation of little girls in high art and photography, gender is a relevant issue to examine in these editions of Watts's hymns. As has been true of other hymn-book illustrations, these books' engravings mainly present collective humanity and rarely individualized subjects such that sexuality and eroticism are rarely delineated, let alone co-opted, at the expense of the child. Yet gendering still takes place in the domestic scenes thus shown. Notably, Watts's hymns are almost entirely rendered in the first person; thus, either gender may be assumed by his various future audiences. Illustrations are more socially bound and thus these images display Victorian ideologies of gender roles. Boys play (1803, 1810, 1841, c. 1850, 1897), girls pray (c. 1800, c. 1820, 1848, 1857, 188-, 1897), mothers teach and comfort (c. 1800, 1802, 1803, 1810, 1814, 1848, 1857, 1869, 188-, 1897), and male tutors teach boys (c. 1800, 1803, c. 1820, c. 1850, 1857, 1869) throughout the century. For instance, "The advantages of early religion" ("Happy the child, whose youngest years") very often shows a mother instructing her young charges within the comfort of the home (1841, c. 1850, 1869, 1896). Most images for "Against Quarrelling and Fighting," "Against Evil Company" (Song XXI), and others about naughty behavior show boys (1803, 1814, c. 1820, 1841, c. 1850, 1851b, 1869; 188-); the antithesis, "let love through all your actions run" is exemplified by two girls in a fond embrace (c. 1850). Typically Song XXII, "Against Pride in Clothes" portrays women and girls flaunting clothes for others or in front of mirrors (1803, c. 1805, c. 1820, 1841, 1851, 188-, 1896).

Variations occur as illustrators and ideologies change. The 1802 illustrations show both genders fighting (Song XVI, "Against Quarrelling and Fighting") and also playing hoops and badminton (Song XXIV, "Why should I love my sport so well?"), a very early example of what will come to predominate in later editions (1851, etc.) where, for these respective hymns, an 1851b hymn book depicts girls fighting, and in the 188- hymn book, a single girl plays with her badminton racket as late-century girls were more encouraged to engage in outdoor activities. The 1857 illustration of "The Advantage of Early Religion" (Song XII) shows both boys and girls studying the globe, a book, and a map of Europe; its image for

"Against Quarrelling and Fighting" is of a small girl and boy huddled lovingly over a book (see also 1818, 1851, 1896). Both the 1869 and 188- hymn books feature domestic fathers, rare before now, leading their families over their evening devotionals (for Song VII, "The Excellency of the Bible" and Song XII, "The Advantages of Early Religion). Likewise, the 1869 version of "Pride Against Clothes" depicts a young boy showing off his clothes for others, and the 1897 hymn book implicates both a boy and girl. Many gender stereotypes remain a constant facet of hymn-book illustrations, but small strides can be seen in gender equity and opportunity.

As previous examples suggest, these books invoke a middle-class readership for whom conventional scenes of comfort and learning prevail: food-laden tables, canopied beds, roaring fires in the grate. Thus, Song IV, "Praise for Mercies, Spiritual, and Temporal," which begins "Whene'er I take my walks abroad, / How many poor I see! / What shall I render to my God / For all his gifts to me?" takes on greater significance for the middle-class readers/singers as they are confronted with social disparity: "Not more than others I deserve, / Yet God hath given me more" (v. 2, from the 188- edition). It is a notable hymn upon which to reflect briefly.

Indeed, the hymn tackles grave issues of poverty, inequality of wealth, spiritual gratitude, and predestination. The child speaker/singer is endowed with power through the many active verbs: "I see," "I render," "I behold," and "let me love." Admittedly, the power of this child is achieved by contrasting him/her with the many faceless poor: clauses like "I have food while others starve" (v. 2), "How many children in the street / Half naked I behold! / While I am clothed from head to feet / And covered from the cold" (v. 3); "While some poor creatures scarce can tell / Where they may lay their head / I have a home ..." (v. 4) and "let me love Thee more than they" (v. 6) all pit the rich child against the unfortunate "other" who is rhetorically separated in the "other" half of each clause. Swearing, cursing, lying, and stealing seem to be in the domain only of the materially oppressed (v. 5), though readers of the rest of the book realize that these sins tempt the middle-class child just as readily. Its concluding point is put in the form of a question—"Are these Thy favours day by day, / To me above the rest?"—as the child questions the undeserved, predestined fortune given to some over others. The skepticism is noteworthy, but brief, as the child is ultimately to learn gratitude and loyal service.

Eventually Watts does answer the question, in his Moral Songs (social outreach apparently not being a divine topic in 1715). Moral Song VI, "Good Resolutions," urges the middle-class child towards generosity; amongst other good resolutions, the child resolves:

> Should I e'er be rich or great
>    Others shall partake my goodness;
> I'll supply the poor with meat,
>    Never showing scorn or rudeness. (v. 2)

Next delineating kindness to the blind, lame, deaf, and dumb, this child narrator is able to make the connections with "the other"—"I deserve to feel the same, /

If I mock or hurt, or cheat them" (v. 3; 188- version). "The Beggar's Petition," occasionally appended to *Divine and Moral Songs*, helps the child understand why a man might beg, due to misfortunes and loved ones' deaths.

These two former poems were popular fodder for illustrators of Watts's hymns throughout the century, but illustrators also struggled in depicting both the middle-class privilege and calls for social outreach encouraged by Watts. One of the earliest hymn books, of 1803, shows only the comfort to be appreciated in Song IV: a woman sits in front of her fire reading while a servant sweeps behind her. Bewick's 1814 illustration of the same hymn depicts two men walking through the town with a shadowy figure of a woman in front of a house; prostitution may be subtly implied, taking verse 5 (about lying and stealing) in a completely different direction. Another early hymn book (c. 1800) focuses again on "the walk"—of a family of finely dressed parents and children through town. Here, the illustrator is depicting verse 3 and the speaker's gratitude for clothes while others are "half naked" on the street. The 1807 hymn book portrays "the poor," too, in the form of a lame man with a crutch into whose hat the parents of a family drop a coin. Cope and Thompson's 1848 illustration finally depicts a child within this context: a young girl, finely dressed with bow and hat, stands with her mother contemplating a shame-faced woman crouched on some steps. The scene blends biblical details (stone edifices, women's head shawls) with nineteenth-century ones (the little girl's dress and the English countryside), and this partly obscures whether the woman, with her open robe and free-flowing hair, is a prostitute or not. Regardless, the rich merely look on.

Three later illustrations greatly depart from the above trend, showing children reaching out to those in need. Lossing's beautiful woodcut for the c. 1850 hymn book details two young children reaching out to place coins in a blind man's hat while his faithful dog looks on. In the 1869 illustration, the poor have come to the rich in the form of a beggar who hold outs his old hat for a girl leaning out her window to drop in a coin. Two 1890s hymn books (1896, 1897) detail exquisite images of young people—both the paupers and the rich—met in icy winter and, in the 1897 version, the warmly dressed girl of affluence has taken her hand out of her warm muff to give the other children coins, while a fellow child philanthropist, in the engraving for "Good Resolutions," brings out a full tray of food for the beggars at her door. The 188- illustration is especially revealing in depicting social outreach of this period. Note that the middle-class children, rather than "seeing" and "beholding" at a distance, as suggested by the poem, are clearly interacting with one of the poor on their walk through town, appearing to be handing her money in exchange for a flower. More importantly, the middle-class girl—placed more prominently than her male counterpart in the foreground—is leaning in towards the shoeless girl in rags, in what appears to be a kindly gesture. Further, she is not simply giving charity but, rather, buying some flowers which the girl, with a basket on her arm, appears to be selling. "Good Resolutions" (Moral Song VI) further describes exactly this gesture to the poor: "Where I see the blind or lame, / Deaf or dumb, I'll kindly treat them"; this first-person child narrator even takes on the perspective of the poor: "If I should be poor and sick, / I shall meet, I hope, with pity."[29] This illustration shows sentimentality but also true sympathy as a young girl stops her play (she is holding a hoop) to place some coins in the hat of a blind violin player. Ignoring the delightful dog who holds the hat and draws readers' attention, the girl looks up empathetically to the man. After decades of visually avoiding, or reproachfully depicting, the poor, later illustrations suggest authentic empathy placed in the prevue of actual children. Rather than simply "seeing," these children are helping their less fortunate counterparts in admittedly small ways, but this active agency may become substantial social change as they mature.

These last observations point to ways in which the presentation of children and child agency also evolve, a third area to interrogate by means of these illustrations. Because of the flexibility of first-person perspective, Watts's moralizing dictated in the early eighteenth century yet becomes expansive enough to include all people—male and female, adult and child—in his admonitions and advice. Bearing out the fact that late eighteenth- and early nineteenth-century society was still dressing children in similar fashion as adults (Schorsch 43), many of these early illustrations show adults or adult-looking figures modeling the desired behavior referenced in the hymn (e.g., c. 1800, 1807, and 1812). This is true of the 1803 hymn book in which adults and children are only distinguishable by size, as with Song V, "Praise for Birth and Education in a Christian Land," showing a tutor handing a book to a smaller person also in vest and cravat. The use of adults is especially interesting in the engravings for poems as "Against Idleness and Mischief" (Song XX), featuring a *woman* holding a book; or "Obedience to Parents" (Song XXIII) which depicts an aged, stooped woman stepping into another woman's house—even though these two poems are clearly addressing *children's* mischief and disobedience, respectively. Again, re-using stock images can partially explain this lapse but it is awkward at times, as in Moral Song II, "Innocent Play," which shows what appears to be an adult couple out at night under the moon; such love-making is clearly not meant by the text urging childish play to be "harmless" and "sweet." Thomas Bewick's woodcuts of 1814 reveal a similarly odd focus on adults, for songs of child-like wonderment such as "I sing the almighty power of God" (Song II) and "Great God, with wonder and with praise / On all Thy works I look" (Song VII). Notably, Watts's open first person allows for varying interpretations of age, and thus "Divine and Moral Songs *for Children*" of course may express lessons of praise and gratitude to adults, too.

Mid-century illustrations (in the 1840, 1841, 1848 hymn books) are significant in showing children more distinctly but also usually accompanied by an adult who appears to be teaching the child the lesson of the hymn, pointing to the beehive (1841) or the destitute woman on the street (1848). Many illustrations still feature

---

[29]    I point out an early version of such sensitive philanthropy, in the 1802 edition of "Good Resolutions," where two illustrations depict a young girl serving a ragged boy and man a plate of beef, and a girl and boy lean over to pick up the walking cane of a blind man. These focused illustrations of the poor are yet rare in early-century hymn books that I have observed.

adults exclusively, as worshippers (see Figure 4.6), members of society, even angels. As I have observed in Chapter 2, mid-century hymn books still focused heavily on the adult, or the child-as-adult, and with these hymn books the focus on adults appears to be a direct carry-over from earlier imagery.

However, in hymn books of the second half of the century the contemporary, Romantic child begins to take precedent. Adults may still accompany children in pictorial scenes but now the child is clearly the focus, groups of children learning and playing. Children are singularly culpable for their misdeeds, being shown quarreling and idly playing. But they are also featured as those who engage in learning and in social outreach. The latest Watts hymn books—of 1857, 1869, 188-, 1896, and 1897—aided by advancements in illustration and influence from Greenaway, et al., reveal a more realistic child, rounder, softer (see Figure 4.3), but also a child empowered by the lyrics of these songs to behave responsibly and maturely.

The 1857 hymn book illustratively announces this new child-centered view in its frontispiece engraving (the artist identified as S. Egevans). A wizened scholar teaches children in a wooded garden but they monopolize the picture, six children surrounding him, peering up at him, sitting on his lap, with eagerness and longing to learn. The decorative frontispiece, its artist (George Meason) also identified, is embellished with trellis and roses, and entwines a picture of a young girl engaged in reading (no doubt the Bible) but also looking out the window at the rising sun, thus denoting the outward-reaching work prescribed for her in the book's hymns. The first hymn, "A General Song of Praise to God," is headed by an arresting engraving of an infant clapping his or her hands, as if already enjoying the song, "How glorious is our heavenly King." Of the remaining 14 illustrations, all include children (with the exception of sheep for "Innocent Play").

Four beautifully illustrated, colored plates in the 1869 edition of *Divine and Moral Songs for Children*[30] show children engaged in the greater world around them: a boy and girl, stylishly dressed, pointing to the sunset before them ("Praise for Creation and Providence"), a boy peering intently over the book of his mother or older sister ("Advantages of Early Religion"), a girl and boy observing a swarm of bees from beehives in the garden, their own sturdy boots, sunbonnet, and garden tools nearby suggesting their own participation in garden work ("Idleness and Mischief"); and a boy pointing to a lamb running beside its mother amongst a flock of sheep while his sister gently places her arm around him as they together study nature around them ("Innocent Play"). If sentimental, these illustrations employ the precision and allure of detail and color to the fullest, much as a Caldecott or Greenaway picture, privileging the world of children and their own acute engagement with it.

---

[30]    Classmark Waddleton.d.9.722. There are four color plates, covering an entire page each, in this hymn book: 1) Frontispiece: "Praise for Creation and Providence." 2) Opposite page 24: "Advantages of Early Religion." 3) Opposite page 38: "Idleness and Mischief." 4) Opposite page 54: "Innocent Play." The rest of the illustrations within the text are black and white. My thanks to Clare Welford, Cambridge University Library, for help, in person and by email, with questions on this book.

The 188- edition fulfills many of these themes, the illustrator's late-Victorian viewpoint obvious throughout the images. For instance, Song XXII, "Against Pride in Clothes," cautions the reader, "How proud we are, how fond to show / Our clothes, and call them rich and new" while the accompanying drawing shows a little girl preening herself in the latest fashion (full dress, bows, puffed sleeves and feathered hat) before a mirror, picking up on the allusion to Eve in line 4. Drawings of children enforce typical gender roles (girls sewing, boys prancing outside) but many times these roles are reversed: girls sport while boys sing. Mothers are most visible, as with the cover illustration showing a mother reading the Bible to her children, but a very Victorian-looking father in long side-burns teaches a young girl how to read in the picture accompanying Song XII, "The Advantages of Early Religion." Portraits of young girls and boys could so easily become stereotyped visually, but this illustrator, taking his cue from the ambiguity of Watts's text, makes the prominently displayed praying child on the Contents page to be nearly androgynous. Angels embellish a frame illustration to Song I, sublime nature becomes the focus for Song II, a family of robins demonstrates familial love for Song XVII, and scenes from the Bible enforce themes "Against Scoffing" (Song XVIII) and "Obedience to Parents" (Song XXIII). But throughout its pages, children play, study, preen, steal, embrace, and plainly hold center stage. These are truly "Divine and Moral Songs *for Children*."

By late century, this child-like approach has become heightened, as in the 1897 *Childhood's Songs of Long Ago, Being Some of the Divine and Moral Songs Writ by Rev. Isaac Watts, D.D.*, whose engravings by Blanche McManus place us entirely into the world of the child: praying before bedtime ("Evening Song"), playing hoops ("Innocent Play"), and singing in church ("General Song of Praise"; see cover image). The children's round faces and handsome attire could be called doll-like, and fall into the commodification of children described by Greg Thomas, particularly true of the child with chubby face and bare shoulders in the illustration for "The Rose." However, her cheeky grin and direct glance at the viewer, along with the engraving's one-step remove from a real child body, negate such concerns. She is simply arranging roses with her friends in free and authentic elation. Instead of merely representing staged beauties, these children are accomplishing small feats: feeding the poor ("Good Resolutions"), saving ants ("The Ant or Emmet"), and helping mothers ("Obedience to Parents"). Perhaps more importantly, they are acting like children with all of their flaws: thieving apples ("The Thief"), oversleeping ("The Sluggard"), and fighting ("Against Quarrelling and Fighting"). It is significant, too, that McManus has avoided not only illustrating theologically conservative, harsh hymns, but avoided including them altogether, selecting only those that "lend themselves most readily to the method of treatment expressed and the understanding of children at present day" ("Introduction").

One illuminating hymn and its corresponding images (see Figures 4.5–4.7) will demonstrate this increasing reverence for and empowerment of the child. Song XXVIII, "For the Lord's Day Evening," reflects on the act of worship from the child's perspective:

S O N G   XXVIII.

Figure 4.5        Isaac Watts's Song No. 28, "Lord, how delightful 'tis to see."
                  From *Divine Songs Attempted in an Easy Language* (London,
                  c. 1800). Courtesy of The Lilly Library, Indiana University,
                  Bloomington, Indiana.

> Lord, how delightful 'tis to see
>     A whole assembly worship Thee!
> At once they sing, at once they pray;
>     They hear of heaven, and learn the way. (v. 1)

Watts's Calvinist images of temptation (nothing "Shall tempt me to forget this day"), law-breaking ("That I may break Thy laws no more"), and absolution ("hoping pardon through His blood") are evident in the text. Yet they are mingled with the happy images of church havens, assemblies of worshippers, and Sunday joy ("'Tis like a little heaven below"). This is a less common hymn to illustrate (possibly because it is a later Song, XXVIII, and not all small chapbooks even included it) but I will focus on three hymn books' images which reveal the change of attitude towards the child.

    In the earliest image, from the c. 1800 hymn book, the Song XXVIII ("For the Lord's Day Evening"; also repeated as the Frontispiece) is illustrated with the picture of an adult woman (the presence of breasts and hips corroborate this on what is otherwise a sketchy image) who points backwards towards a church building (see Figure 4.5). Indeed, we see an assemblage of six people as described

Figure 4.6    Isaac Watts's Song No. 28, "Lord, how delightful 'tis to see." From
*Divine and Moral Songs*, illustrated by C. W. Cope, engraved by
John Thompson (London, 1848). From Internet Archive.

in the verse; however, they are standing before tombstones in the cemetery of the
churchyard, apparently at a funeral. The doleful expression of the woman belies
the joy of the day. Both features thus turn our attention to the last verse, which
reminds readers that, "hoping Pardon thro' His Blood, / I may lie down, and wake
with God" (66) the presumed meaning to this visual scene of mourning, almost
like an emblem image in its pointed symbolism.

An alternative image to accompany this hymn comes in the Cope and
Thompson hymn book (1848) already explored (see Figure 4.6). Here, Cope
creates a much more intimate gathering of worshippers, placing the scene within
the church interior, showing the various heartfelt emotions of solemnity, of shame,
of enlightenment shown by parishioners' faces and body postures while listening
to the pastor high above in his ornamental pulpit. Thus, Cope has picked up on
Watts's lines about "singing," "praying," "the texts and doctrines of thy Word"
(books are open to represent hymn books and Bibles). He presents both the
"delight" of the day (exemplified by one eager man on the left) and the regret
of "breaking thy laws" (two men on the right of the picture hold their faces in
their hands) and those who are clearly thinking "of Christ, and things divine."
It is a striking image clearly executed during the era of illustration's supremacy.

Figure 4.7     Isaac Watts's Song No. 28, "Lord, how delightful 'tis to see." From
               *Divine and Moral Songs* (London, 188-). Courtesy of University
               Library, University of Illinois at Urbana-Champaign.

These two images, then, reflect Evangelical thoughts of death changing to High Church focus on worship. Yet neither depicts a child in their hymn books *for* children.

The latest book of the three, the 188- hymn book, however, puts the child once again at center stage (see Figure 4.7). Like other images in the book, its picture is superfluously framed by holly vines. Like Cope, this anonymous illustrator features a scene of worship to represent Song XXVIII, complete with paneled pews and a stained-glass window peeking through the upper left corner. Rather than remorse and repentance, though, this illustrator focuses on Watts's opening lines about delight and song: "Lord, how delightful 'tis to see / A whole assembly worship Thee! / At once they sing, at once they pray...." People stand holding hymn books with pleasant expressions on their faces. But the artist's perspective is from the back right row; thus, due to dimension, the minister is diminished in size to a small figure in the upper right corner, and rows of adults and families are also scaled down. This is all in order to feature three children standing with hymn books in their hands, looking the most attentive of all. Both boys arch their faces upward, while the girl, adorned in a bonnet and petticoat, stares wistfully ahead. Unlike the man in the row ahead of them, who must look down at his book, all three children appear to know the words already and have no need to look at the hymn books they hold. It is a Romantic view of the child, singing happily, engaged and actively a part of worship, the most important part of the "whole assembly." It is an image very indicative of its era. And it is an image that children would enjoy of themselves.

## Conclusion

Hymn-book illustrations, then, help to deepen our understanding of the Golden Age of Illustration, the peak of the nineteenth-century British children's picture book, and the high-art fetishization of the child. Affected by both the technical advancements (engraving, color) and production realities (stock images, cost of illustration), and often limited by their own conservative concern for visual distraction and desire to keep costs cheaper for the Sunday school market, hymn-book editors yet gradually privilege the picture in order to honor the Divine and, by late century, the child. Taken chronologically, children in these hymn books began as little adults, were often replaced with scenes of adulthood, and then become Romanticized—almost idealized—for their flawless and faulty nature. As the century concluded with visual idolization of the child, magic lantern shows froze the image of the child in place, stagnant and staged, and very visible to entire crowds of viewers. If less noticeable, hymn-book illustrations suggest another dimension to "child viewing," a much more nuanced view of children as they interacted with adults, other children, and the world around them. Illustrations in children's hymn books solidified but at times also diversified the endemic ideologies of age, class, and gender defining the Victorian child, a reminder to art historians not to neglect hymn-book illustrations when examining artworks as cultural texts.

Illustrations to Watts's *Divine and Moral Songs* allow us to see the changes theologically and socially, as the child ultimately comes into her own. In fact, the three hymns I highlighted in this last section furnish the child this agency from the verb-choice given in the texts themselves, as she "*sings* the almighty power of God," "*walks* abroad," and "*sees*" and "*learns*" amongst "a whole assembly." Despite the many hymns "against" doing immoral acts, Watts's songs also allow children a great deal of action, the greatest action being the act of song. Early-century illustrators do not always invest in this imagery, preferring to show children learning from adults or adults themselves modeling the behavior. Yet late-century depictions put the heart of worship, reform, and song squarely within the child's purview. Ultimately, it could be conceded that hymn-book editors cared less about the illustrated child than the singing child; that aural power was always more central to their theology than the visual. The empowered child singer was thus able to overcome the "*static* notions of the Beautiful Child" (Knuth 95; my italics). Accordingly, the Anniversary and Whit-Walks taking place throughout the century very well symbolized this yoking of singing and action, literally, as the active children claimed centrality before the adults in their community, their voluminous songs of praise dwarfing their visual presence on the streets. No doubt many of these hymns were those of Isaac Watts, whose child-centered hymns had proclaimed this active engagement for over 100 years, whose most popular hymn for Victorians was about *singing* the power of God.

# Chapter 5
# Reforming Society:
# Missionary, Bands of Hope, and
# Bands of Mercy Hymns

> Go out, children, from the mine and from the city,
>> Sing out, children, as the little thrushes do …
> When we sob aloud, the human creatures near us
>> Pass by, hearing not, or answer not a word.
> And *we* hear not (for the wheels in their resounding)
>> Strangers speaking at the door;
> Is it likely God, with angels singing round Him,
>> Hears our weeping any more?
>> —Elizabeth Barrett Browning, "The Cry of the Children" (1843)

The Industrial Revolution created factory jobs for tens of thousands of people, including children, but its overuse of working-class child labor in manufacturing, mining, and cottage industries incurred public outcry, Elizabeth Barrett Browning and Charles Dickens being some of the more prominent literary voices. Adults sought to rescue both the child and childhood itself, reformers emerging from such disparate groups as literary professionals, socially concerned churchgoers, middle-class philanthropic reformers, working-class agitators, and some visible upper-class politicians such as the Earl of Shaftesbury,[1] all to address child overwork and suffering. At stake, truly, were the very lives of children, who could die from unsafe conditions and sheer exhaustion. Thus, the reformation of children's lives "was the product of philanthropic or compassionate motives, together with the concern for social control, at a time of unprecedented social change" (Hopkins 6); it was accomplished specifically through factory reform, church schools, government reform and enforcement, and a national education system, much of which has already been discussed.[2] Consequently, Laura

---

[1]  Anthony Ashley Cooper, Seventh Earl of Shaftesbury, is known for authoring the Ten Hours Act of 1833, the Miners and Colliers Act of 1842, etc., but Eileen Wallace also points to the less-known though equally important work of George Smith, whose fight to reform child labor in the brickfields led to the Factories and Workshops Amendment Act of 1871 (124–5).

[2]  For more about child-focused reform, see Hopkins, *Childhood Reformed: Working-Class Children in Nineteenth-Century England*; Sommerville, *The Rise and Fall of Childhood*, ch. 15; Horn, *Children's Work and Welfare, 1780–1880s*; Duckworth, *Fagin's Children*, chs. 8–10; Cunningham, *Children and Childhood*, especially ch. 6, and *The Children of the Poor*, ch. 4; and Cunningham and Innes, eds., *Charity, Philanthropy and Reform, from the 1690s to 1850*.

C. Berry suggests that "[r]epresenting childhood as endangered is instrumental to nineteenth-century debates" (4), and thus a phenomenon vitally important to childhood studies.[3]

What might be questioned in this scenario, however, is how much children were victimized subjects only and how much agency children might have had in child-labor and other reform movements that effected this "unprecedented social change."[4] Indeed, one might note how often reform exploited children further, in showing their susceptible, separate condition. In "The Cry of the Children," Barrett Browning evokes both aspects: children's right to be free from work as well as their extreme sympathy and vulnerability. She uses music as a metaphor in that children's natural desire is to sing freely "as the little thrushes do." Yet she undermines this independent status by a sentimental portrait of abused children who can only sob so unsuccessfully that no one, perhaps not even God, hears. Their attempt at self-help fails. Dickens's approach to child-victimization is akin to Barrett Browning's: as Marah Gubar suggests, "Dickens's strong sense of the child's vulnerability to adult exploitation led him to align himself with those authors and activists [such reformers as Mary Carpenter and Ellen Barlee] who were committed to erecting a barrier between adult and child" (8). Catering to a child's vulnerability, adult reformers thus diminished a child's ability to resist and respond.

In short, nineteenth-century children were the objects of attempted political, labor, and human-rights improvement throughout the century. Much as Gubar has traced ways in which Golden Age children's literature sought to chronicle and encourage the middle-class child reader's resistance to adult domination, in this chapter I argue that children actually did establish their own voice and personhood through their singing *and* became a vital force of social transformation themselves. This was achieved in part through their dissemination of three types of hymns: missionary, temperance, and animal welfare. Bands of Hope and Bands of Mercy were children's organizations used in the temperance and animal welfare movements, respectively. They continued the practice of missionary institutions of using children and their hymns to reform the adult world. These movements challenged the idea that philanthropy was one-directional: adults rescuing children. Rather, children were sanctioned to help those older than themselves, in a form of "reverse reform." Admittedly, one might see this trend as yet another way to exploit children, to mouth the words of adult reformers.[5] However, running through many

---

[3]   Berry considers debates imbedded in literary and social writings in *The Child, the State, and the Victorian Novel*, as does Monica Flegel in *Conceptualizing Cruelty to Children in Nineteenth-Century England*, ch. 4.

[4]   Elizabeth Massa Hoiem is pursuing ways in which children were involved in Chartist rallies against child labor. Organized by adults, these movements yet co-opted children's rhymes, even occasionally hymns, to become rallying songs for the children: using the tune to "Here we suffer grief" to "We will have it!" for example. These were infrequently published, however, which is why I have found fewer hymn books devoted to social welfare, other than the factory hymns explored in Chapter 1.

[5]   An argument proposed by Troy Boone, *Youth of Darkest England*, of middle-class imperialists "incorporating working-class youth into the imperial enterprise" (16).

of the songs and hymns is rhetoric expressing the child's own worth and power, to think and act for good. Indeed, the political song has been a means of achieving self-respect and reform for centuries. Michael Scrivener points, for instance, to the role of song texts in the Reform Movement of 1792–1824, as sung at political gatherings and demonstrations to heighten emotion and collectivity (26).[6] So it is no surprise that reformists should turn to songs and hymns, then, the medium of reform *and* children.

In what follows, I will examine three eras of philanthropic children's hymnody: mission hymns of the Evangelical, early decades of the century, especially of the 1840s; Bands of Hope temperance hymns of mid-century (1860s and 1870s); and Bands of Mercy hymns of late-century (1890s) liberalism. These three different eras correspond in many ways with those eras delineated in Chapter 2, but they also reflect changing world assumptions being conveyed to the young. Jeroen J. H. Dekker has described European philanthropy of the late eighteenth and early nineteenth centuries as falling into two categories: Christian philanthropy which offered humane help to "marginals" while "maintaining differences in standards of living" ("Transforming the Nation and the Child" 131). Modern philanthropy, developing out of capitalism and utilitarianism, sought to eliminate difference by "elevating them from marginality" primarily through education of children (131). The three movements I explore fall into these historical categories: Christian missions and missionary hymns especially of the early era built upon Anglo-centric views of "other" non-Western peoples; Evangelicals wrote hymns to emphasize "difference" from colonial peoples who were said to lack education, religion, even morality, much as Esme Cleall writes of missionary thinking generally being "orientated around the concept of difference" (3). In this context, the child was encouraged to prize her superiority and asked to evangelize until the world should become one: a Christian conformity, with social hierarchies still intact. Indebted to the missionary movement, the temperance movement could yet be called a more modern philanthropic movement which used education, especially among children, to ameliorate difference among classes and single-handedly improve the lot of the poor. Difference could thus be overcome, according to temperance propaganda, and the movement recognized personal shortcomings, even that children themselves could be victims of drink. The child was needed to fight immoderation, either of his own or others' doing. Finally, as a late-century philanthropic movement modeled after Bands of Hope and taken up by the Royal Society for the Prevention of Cruelty to Animals (RSPCA), Bands of Mercy advocated a new world view that attempted to remove difference even on the species level, encouraging tolerance and understanding of all of God's creatures. Though these hymns often acknowledged children to be among the perpetrators of animal cruelty, children were clearly to act as vital facilitators in bringing inter-species harmony to the world.

---

[6] For more about working-class song and literature as propaganda, see also Martha Vicinus, *The Industrial Muse: A Study of Nineteenth Century British Working-Class Literature* (1974).

Reviewing the limited existence of children's letters and diaries of the period (see Chapter 6), I can affirm that these three issues—missions, temperance, and animal welfare—were of considerable concern to children. In 1883, 7-year-old Mary Chard wrote to her parent-missionaries about the "funny black" and "funny Chinese" in the photographs they sent, but shows interest that "Father [will] go out every day to teach the heathen about GOD" (March 30, 1883 entry) and desires to help: "send me some patterns of the poor people's clothes you are working for" (October 5, 1885 entry). Emily Shore, 12-year-old daughter of a minister, showed concern in her 1832 diary for a woman "quite starved" by a drunken husband, and noted that her Mama was helping her (*Journal of Emily Shore* 22). Finally, 13-year-old Adela Capel wrote a one-page diatribe in her 1841 diary against the cruelties of hunting and the adults who "kill animals for the mere pleasure of killing" that it "is very wicked to take the life which God has given when it is [in] our power to restore it" (26).

To press reform on these issues to the wider, adult audience in public ways such as singing, not just in private dialogue in diaries, must have been extremely satisfying to children. Ultimately, hymns challenged children in these various ideologies but also empowered them to create a better world of their own making: more religious, more self-disciplined, more merciful—no small feat for smaller persons.

## Part I
## Spreading the Gospel through Missionary Hymns

Though dissemination of Christianity began during the Roman era, mission work in its modern sense stemmed from "a much broader missionary awareness" of late eighteenth-century English Evangelicals whose religious revivals sparked a desire to spread the Christian message and lifestyle not just among Protestant nations but around the globe (Stanley 55).[7] Stephen Neill estimates that four-fifths of Protestant missionaries over the last 250 years have hailed from English-speaking nations (222). Writings such as the *Plan of the Society for the Establishment of Missions among the Heathen* (1783) by Wesleyan follower Thomas Coke inspired not only Methodist missionaries to the West Indies, but conversion zeal among other denominations as well (Thorne 24; Stanley 65). Long-established mission organizations, the Society for the Promotion of Christian Knowledge (SPCK; est. 1698/9) and the Society for the Propagation of the Gospel (SPG; est. 1701), both

---

[7]    For background on Christian missions in the nineteenth century, see Brian Stanley, *The Bible and the Flag* (1990); Stephen Neill, *A History of Christian Missions* (1964), Part Two; David Spurr, *The Rhetoric of Empire* (1993); Susan Thorne, *Congregational Missions and the Making of an Imperial Culture in Nineteenth-Century England* (1999); Catherine Hall, *Civilising Subjects* (2002); Julie Melnyk, *Victorian Religion: Faith and Life in Britain* (2008); Esme Cleall, *Missionary Discourses of Difference* (2012); and various essays in *Christian Missions and the Enlightenment* (2001), ed. Brian Stanley. I am grateful to Winter Jade Werner for introducing me to the work of Brian Stanley in particular.

Anglican, were joined by newer, late eighteenth-century voluntary societies: the English Baptists (1792), the London Missionary Society (LMS, 1795, mainly Congregational), the Anglican Evangelical's Church Missionary Society (1799), the British and Foreign Bible Society (1804) and, later still, the Universities' Mission to Central Africa (UMCA, est. 1859). Christian missions began most predominantly in India and China in the first half of the century, then moved into Africa (such as the Cape of Good Hope, Bechuanaland [now Botswana], Nyasaland [Malawi], and Uganda) and the South Pacific (Fiji). Missionary and imperial proliferation added over 4 million people to the British Empire during the century (1815–1914).[8] The foreign missionary movement saw increased acceptance and support throughout the first decades of the nineteenth century, concurrent with colonial expansion itself, the 1830s and 1840s becoming the "high point of the missionary movement's popularity" (Thorne 66).

During this era, then, the typical churchgoer would encounter news from the mission field on a weekly basis, from sermons to prayer meetings, religious periodicals to full-length missionary accounts; consequently, the "home ministry was quick to pay homage to the foreign mission cause, insisting that it came first in their faith" (Thorne 6). Some British citizens left to be missionaries while many more people supported these efforts from England, raising money, entertaining mission speakers, subscribing to missionary periodicals, and in other ways "feeling themselves part of an important international movement" (Melnyk 103). As Julie Melnyk reminds us, "Most Victorians did not see religion as a matter merely of individual salvation and private worship. For many, religious faith was a dynamic force that found its outlet in efforts to reshape the world" (103). Mission work was predicated upon this principle of global reformation.

Children were very much a part of these efforts. They would listen to the missionary sermons and attend lectures given by missionaries touring England. A missionary service at the Booth Congregational Chapel, near Halifax, in the early 1820s, reportedly led to a "remarkable revival of religion … chiefly among the young persons" while the missionary Robert Moffat's visit to Edinburgh gave "Our little children" inspiration they "never can forget" (both qtd. in Thorne 66). Missionary support and leadership came mainly from the middle- and upper-middle classes, so their children were naturally drawn into this missionary zeal and also its obligatory fundraising. The image of Mrs. Pardiggle's large brood

---

[8]    The imperialist nature of missions has been the prevailing argument for the past 50 years, that missionaries came with "the Bible in one hand and the gun in the other" (qtd. in Stanley, *The Bible and the Flag* 11), but recent scholars such as Brian Stanley have worked to reframe the discussion within missionaries' original moral and theological intentions (59). Likewise, Andrew Porter argues that missionaries oftentimes saw themselves as "anti-imperialist" (13). Susan Thorne acknowledges the sincere commitment of missionaries, their protests against slavery in the West Indies, fight against land appropriation in Africa, and the high death rates of missionaries themselves. Nevertheless, "missionaries were never able to sever altogether their connection to British imperial[ism]," and mission work was ultimately the best means to obtain imperial control (*Congregational Missions* 8–9).

of boys (from Dickens's *Bleak House* ) "voluntarily" donating money and gifts to missions abroad is perhaps the most famous satiric reference to this fact. The allusion is relevant, though, in suggesting the frequent coercion of children for missionary purposes.

For example, Sunday school children of the working classes were constantly tapped for missionary funds. This practice struck some observers as problematic on many levels: teachers complained that the children were reduced to begging for mission money, while the Sunday schools themselves often gave up half of their yearly earnings to missions that cut into their own operating expenses (see Thorne 131–5). Most egregious was that working-class families who could often barely pay for Sunday school fees, food, and clothing for their own children were being asked to sacrifice funds for people and children they would never see. Wrote one critic: "It is a sin and a crime to send money, even £10,000, out abroad to convert the heathen, who know nothing of Christianity as yet, when thousands of poor civilised Christians are destitute and starving at home" (qtd. in Thorne 136).

Children participated more actively and energetically when freed from mere money-collecting,[9] as when involved in mission dramas and musical entertainment for home rallies.[10] Clearly, hymns were featured in such fundraising concerts and missionary meetings, too. Hymns schooled the singers, teaching them the value of and need for mission work to "save" the unbelieving throughout the world. Missionary hymn books of my study included: *The Juvenile Missionary Manual* (1843), *Hymns for Schools, Missions, and Bible Classes* (1866), *Hymns and Songs for Mission Services & Conventions with Tunes* (1887), and *The Young People's Mission Hymn Book for use in Sunday Schools, Bible Classes, Mission Services, and Temperance Societies* (Baptist, 1911). Especially later in the century, general children's hymn books carried a small section on missions.[11]

The missionary hymn tradition for children, as with other hymn traditions, could once again be said to have begun with Isaac Watts's *Divine and Moral*

---

[9]    Karen A. Kelly writes of a specific example in America when the Episcopalian Church, shortly after the Civil War, launched the Domestic Missionary Army of the Young Soldiers of Christ to enlist children in evangelism and missions. Yet the "enlistment" of young soldiers fell off in 1872 when the emphasis changed to money-collecting only (231). See "Let the children have their part," 200–237.

[10]    Thorne writes of turn-of-the-century missionary dramas publically performed by children in native dress and blackface (see footnote 8, 204). Of music-making, see an American book, *Missionary Concerts for the Sunday-School: A Collection of Declamations, Select Readings, and Dialogues* (comp. Rev. W. T. Smith, Cincinnati, 1881), which includes songs for the school.

[11]    For example, *Songs of Gladness: A Hymn Book for the Young* (1871) highlights its mission hymns under "Christian Missions: Their Necessity and Success." The *Children's Hymn Book for Use in Children's Services, Sunday Schools and Families* (1878) and the *Methodist Sunday-School Hymn-Book* (1879) both contain about 10 in their "Missions" sections, many being adult-centered mission hymns. By 1893, *282 Hymns and Melodies for School and Family Use*, edited by E. W. and J. Gall Inglis, contains 25 hymns in its Missionary section and many of these specifically address children.

*Songs* (1715). Song 5 is the first of several examples to enter the nineteenth-century repertoire. In unminced words, Watts clearly assumes the superiority of the English to the non-Christian "other":

> 'Tis to Thy sovereign grace I owe
> > That I was born on British ground;
> Where streams of heavenly mercy flow,
> > And words of sweet salvation sound. ...
> How do I pity those that dwell
> > Where ignorance and darkness reigns!
> They know no heaven, they fear no hell,
> > Those endless joys, those endless pains. (Song 5)

Song 6 reflects missionaries' deep concern for the idolatry of the nonbelievers,[12] thanking God for His grace "That I was born of Christian race, / And not a heathen or a Jew ... How glad the heathen would have been, / That worshipped idols, wood and stone, / If they the book of God had seen, / Or Jesus and His gospel known" (Song 6). It also begins a trope used in many other mission hymns, of "heathen" worshipping "wood and stone," which is biblical (Deuteronomy 4:28) and not a documented practice of nineteenth-century indigenous peoples.

Following on their mentor's heels, Ann and Jane Taylor open their *Hymns for Infant Minds* (1810) with a mission hymn, "I thank the goodness and the grace / Which on my birth have smil'd / And made me, in these Christian days, / A happy English child" (Hymn 1). The verses continue, pointing, in negation, to the various advantages the "happy English child" enjoys over his pagan-born counterpart: "I was not born, as thousands are, / Where God was never known" and continues the biblical allusion to pagan worship of wood and stone: "And taught to pray a useless pray'r, / To blocks of wood and stone" (v. 2). The life of the native "other" is severely defined:

> I was not born a little slave,
> > To labour in the sun,
> And wish I were but in the grave,
> > And all my labour done! (v. 3)
> I was not born without a home,
> > Or in some broken shed;
> A gipsy baby; taught to roam,
> > And steal my daily bread. (v. 4)

Ultimately, the English child thanks God, "who hast plann'd / A better lot for me, / And plac'd me in this happy land, / Where I may hear of thee" (themes found also in the Taylors' Hymn No. 50, "God made the world—in ev'ry land"). Both songs by

---

[12] Idolatry was perceived by many nineteenth-century English as visible proof of humanity's open defiance of God, an attitude denounced throughout the Old Testament. Stanley points out the missionary's authentic alarm for all nonbelievers biblically condemned to eternal perdition (see *The Bible and the Flag* 63–7).

Watts and the Taylors were very popular throughout nineteenth-century children's hymn books (the Taylors' appears in 23% of children's hymn books). They reflected the "colonial complex" generally undergirding missionary ideology: that "Only Western man was wise and good, and members of races, in so far as they became westernized, might share in this wisdom and goodness" (Neill 220).

Hymns were, of course, following much of missionary literature for children that polarized other cultures and religions as sadistic and almost non-human. Consider missionary catechisms that children were made to learn, as from *A Missionary Catechism for the Use of Children; Containing a Brief View of the Moral Condition of the World and the Progress of Missionary Efforts Among the Heathen* (1821). The children's rote answer to the question "What is the present state of the Jews?" is "They are generally ignorant, degraded, and persecuted" (8), and to the question "What is the character of this [Mahometanism] religion?" they respond, "It is an absurd compound of Paganism, Judaism and Christian heresies" (9–10). Further stories are told of Indians hanging their children in baskets to be devoured by birds of prey, and Africans leaving sick relatives in the fields to be eaten by wolves (40–41). Isolated cases and specific customs confirmed the depravity of all non-Christian peoples in the evangelical mind-set, and the desperate need for Christian conversion.[13]

Perhaps the most famous missionary hymn, for children and adults alike, was Reginald Heber's "From Greenland's icy mountains" (1823), "endlessly caroled by multiple generations from Birmingham to Bombay, from Kingston to Cairo" (Hall 301). The second Anglican Bishop to serve in India, 1823–1826, Heber wrote the hymn in 1819 for a meeting of the Society for the Propagation of the Gospel of Foreign Parts. Twentieth-century commentators continued to praise the hymn: Nutter and Tillett (1911) commented that "There are many missionary hymns, but this is universally known as *the* missionary hymn" (343), and McCutchan (1937) wished that other hymn writers "had been similarly inspired" (468). Clearly, nineteenth-century children's hymn-book editors privileged it as well, including it in 41% of children's hymn books of my study. Further, it was used to open both children's hymn books (e.g., *Juvenile Harmonist*) and Missionary sections (*Children's Hymn Book*; *Methodist Sunday-School Hymn Book*).

---

[13] Consider *Girls and Girls: A Missionary Book* (London: Church Missionary Society, 1896) which attempts to distinguish between the healthy, happy girls of England and "the down-trodden girls of Africa, or the despised and ill-treated girls of India, or the girls in China whose very birth is looked upon as a calamity" (4). A story told in *Divine and Moral Songs by Isaac Watts, D.D. Illustrated by Anecdotes and Reflections* (Philadelphia, c. 1850) describes the many ways children are offered up as sacrifice in India—drowning, starving, and murder—often by their own parents. As Stanley acknowledges, "In many islands cannibalism, infanticide, human sacrifice, and homosexual practice were endemic. The prevalent evangelical belief that God had given up non-Christian, idolatrous peoples to the consequences of their own depravity seemed amply confirmed" (*The Bible and the Flag* 158). All practices were thought to be obliterated upon conversion, resulting in natives' "childlike innocence" (Hall 186).

In 7.6.7.6.D meter, iambic poetic meter, and rhyme scheme of ABABCDCD, the hymn is poetically intricate and rhythmically engaging,[14] although occasionally clarity is sacrificed (Africa must become "Afric"). Its imagery depicts the beauty of other lands now named, from Greenland to India:[15]

> From Greenland's icy mountains
>> From India's coral strand,
> Where Afric's sunny fountains
>> Roll down their golden sand.
>> (v. 1 *Methodist Sunday-School Hymn- and Tune-Book*, No. 546)

As the hymn continues, however, we are told the problems with these lands, despite their luscious climate:

> What though the spicy breezes
>> Blow soft o'er Ceylon's isle,
> Though every prospect pleases,
>> And only man is vile! (v. 2)

The hymn lays the sin of vanity and ignorance at the feet of the native peoples, picking up Watts's biblical descriptions of stone-worshipping practices:

> In vain with lavish kindness
>> The gifts of God are strewn;
> The heathen, in his blindness,
>> Bows down to wood and stone. (v. 2)

The singers are clearly favored by God, if self-serving in their priorities:

> Can we, whose souls are lighted
>> With wisdom from on high,
> Can we to men benighted
>> The lamp of life deny? (v. 3)

---

[14]  It was set to a variety of tunes: Heber wrote his own tune, "Heber," as used by the 1879 *The Methodist Sunday-School Hymn and Tune-Book*, but they also suggested "Missionary," written by Lowell Mason. "Albion Chapel" by Haydn is a jaunty tune in the *Juvenile Harmonist* (1843), while How, Walsham, and Ellerton set it to the stately Lancashire by Henry Smart in *The Children's Hymn Book* (1878).

[15]  Greenland was actually served by missionaries first from Copenhagen (Hans Egede, 1722–1736), and then from Moravia, beginning in 1733 (see Neill, 200–203). This not being a site of English missionary work, Greenland probably appealed to hymn writers to suggest a northern-most site, representing the entire globe needing conversion. Hall writes that India was "exciting and exotic in the imagination of the English missionary public, but it was extremely difficult to convert 'the heathens'" there and thus the success rate of conversion was "miniscule" (307). Both the thrill and the need may be reasons why India played so heavily in hymn writers' imaginations.

The hymn ends with appeals to the listeners to share their God-given gifts to "each remotest nation," completing the nature motifs of the opening stanza, as Christianity becomes the tidal wave to inundate the rest of humanity:

> Waft, waft, ye winds, His story,
>    And you, ye waters, roll,
> Till, like a sea of glory,
>    It spreads from pole to pole ... (v. 4)

The lines smack of imperialist ardor, yet the fact that the reformation is ambiguously given to "we"—both adults *and* children—speaks to a growing trend of allocating rigorous work to children, in this case, of inciting a revolution from "Greenland's icy mountains" to "India's coral strand."

A woodcut (in an 1802 edition of Watts's *Divine and Moral Songs* with other hymns) is an early, visual example of what would become important ideals to Victorians as the era commenced (see Figure 5.1). An image to "The Golden Rule" (Hymn No. 10), it takes the message of loving thy neighbor to Africa where a "European [is] giving instruction to an African," literally, by handing him a book, no doubt a Bible. Stereotypes proliferate, from the handsomely clothed, confident European male to the more bewildered looking, sparsely clothed African. What is notably in contrast to Watts's and the Taylors' texts, is that reformative *action* is shown, and action by children, for clearly these are children's figures matching those in the rest of the book. The important task of instructing others has become a child's task.

The ability to convert is given exclusively to children in the most popular children's hymn of the century, "I think when I read that sweet story of old" (1841), which ends with a "missionary verse" added later by its author Jemima Thompson Luke:

> But thousands and thousands, who wander and fall,
>    Never heard of that heavenly home;
> I should like them to know there is room for them all,
>    And that Jesus has bid them to come. (v. 3)

The thousands who "wander and fall" are contrasted with the singer's more enlightened position. Yet Luke's desire to evangelize ("I should like them to know") differs from Watts's and the Taylors' hymns which merely register gratitude for the cultural difference.

One missionary hymn book of the 1840s exemplifies many of these issues of difference, homogeneity, and conversion, especially as targeted to children. *The Juvenile Missionary Manual; Containing Hymns and Prayers, Designed for the Use of Children Either in Private or at the Meetings of Juvenile Missionary Associations*, edited by a Mrs. Sharwood (London, 1843),[16] contains reflections

---

[16]   I am grateful to the librarians at the Cambridge University Library, particularly Claire Welford, Helen Hills, and Stella Clarke who, in August of 2010, helped me procure and photocopy the missionary and especially temperance books used in this chapter.

*The European giving instruction to an African.*

## 10. *The Golden Rule.*

BE you to others kind and true,
  As you'd have others be to you,
And neither do nor say to men,
  What e'er you would not take again.

Figure 5.1    Hymn No. 10, "The Golden Rule." From Watts's *Divine Songs for Children* (London, 1802). Courtesy of The Lilly Library, Indiana University, Bloomington, Indiana.

in nine chapters, with hymns and prayers. The text fully delineates "The duty of sending the Gospel to the heathen" (ch. 1), "The ignorance, vice, and misery of heathen children" (ch. 3), and the "Conversion of the Jews" (ch. 9). Hymns which follow the chapters are more nuanced in reflecting each of these topics. One message they convey to children, following themes of Watts, is due appreciation for God's apparent privilege to "British ground" where "streams of heav'nly mercy flow, / And words of sweet salvation sound" (Hymn 30, v. 2). Whereas other nations claim monetary wealth, Britain claims a "nobler prize":

> I would not change my native land
>> For rich Peru with all her gold;
> A nobler prize lies in my hand
>> Than East or Western Indies hold. (v. 3)

The child is taught sympathy—"How do I pity those that dwell / Where ignorance or darkness reigns!" But he is moreso taught gratitude in his own situation as the hymn concludes: "Thy praise shall still employ my breath / Since thou has marked my way to heav'n …" (v. 6). Another, Hymn 39, reiterates this message more forcefully, marking the difference between the Christian and non-Christian children with stereotypes:

> 'Tis sweet to be a christian child,
>> And read God's holy word
> But thousand little negroes wild
>> Of God have never heard. (v. 1)

As the hymn concludes, the child learns to sing her gratitude: "We'll all unite our feeble pow'rs / To show our thankfulness" (v. 4). In these hymns, where God has privileged one race over another, humanity becomes polarized, into "The happy child of England" and "The dusky child of India" (Hymn 71). Too, religions are dichotomized and while both may share similar attributes, their difference is highlighted (Hymn 69):

> See them torture their own bodies,
>> Peace and pardon to obtain!
> Show them how the blood of Jesus
>> Cleanseth souls from every stain … (v. 2)

While the hymn acknowledges the violence to be found in both religions, tortured or bleeding bodies part of the culture of both, it exonerates that of the Christian religion and does not acknowledge the violence to be found in Western culture or perpetrated on non-Western peoples.[17]

Another hymn, No. 21, sung to the popular "Abridge" tune, abruptly opens with the question: "How wretched must the heathen be, / Who do not know the Lord; / In whose abodes of cruelty; / Base idols are ador'd" (v. 1). Verse 2, following the mission literature just described, goes so far as to depict all non-Christian parents as infant-murderers:

> Their helpless babes no pity find,
>> No friendly arm to save,

---

[17]   See Cleall, chs. 5–6, for an in-depth analysis of European violence perpetrated on natives.

When by their parents' hands consign'd
    To an untimely grave. (v. 2)

Again, humanity is polarized, specific cases become generalities, and difference is exaggerated. "Heathen people are typically represented in this period more as sinners than as sufferers," notes Thorne (75). The resulting message in the above hymns is simply that of pity and gratitude, but occasionally hymns will encourage more missionary intervention: "Go where Christ was never *named*, / Publish freedom to the slave" (Hymn 19; her italics), while others encourage the Christian virtue of self-denial:

No! you need not cross the waters,
    Nor of friends a farewell take;
*Only self-denying prove*
    To exhibit christian love [sic]. (Hymn 56, v. 3; her italics)

Some mission literature acknowledged sameness—"the same feelings of nature as ourselves, the same moral wants, the same faculties of improvement, the same dread of misery, the same desire of happiness, and the same capacity of enjoyment"—but the next step was to close the loop and create homogenous religious believers as well, "partakers of the precious faith with us, and sharers of the same common salvation" (Rev. John Johnston, 1818, qtd. in Thorne 75). It was of course an impossible task, certainly not to be achieved simply by children's good intentions.

Nevertheless missionary hymns highlight the power of children to change the world, even if, by modern-day standards, this change may not have been desirable. Hymn 56 just quoted, in fact, opens by appealing to children:

Children of this favoured nation!
    Go! Your little mite prepare,
High and low, of every station
    Seek to send the Gospel where
Old and young to idols bend;
Come to them, salvation send. (v. 1)

Another hymn in this vein is Hymn 51, an important hymn in anticipating trends of late-century children's hymns. Set to the tune Portsmouth New, in iambic trimeter with ABABCC rhymes, it is a catchy verse taking a simple, Wattsian point of view for the child. It opens by acknowledging the child's weakness:

Can I a little child,
    Do anything for those
Who are by sin defil'd,
    To lessen their sad woes?
I do not see a reason why
I should not, if I do but try.

But then real actions of real children are delineated. A child may pray ("First, then, I would implore / The Lord to change their heart") and a child can offer his "little store" of money for missionary work ("That some kind teacher may be giv'n, / To point out Christ the way to heav'n," v. 2). A child's smallness ("feeble mite" as a clever homonym for money) is then negated in the final lines:

> … And who would then refuse,
>     To give their feeble mite?
> That all the heathen world may know,
> What blessings Jesus can bestow. (v. 3)

That this "little store" of money could be all the child has to live on is, of course, not addressed. But the small child *is* acknowledged, rhetorically speaking, to be part of an epic cause, both financially and emotionally.

Another mid-century missionary hymn takes the child's role a step farther in becoming the voice of the converted. James Edmeston, author of the very popular "Saviour, breathe an evening blessing" (1820), also wrote a fairly popular missionary hymn, "Little travelers Zionward" (1846). It was found in 15% of children's hymn books of my study and uses much the same rhetoric as Heber, centering once again on India and Africa, well-known sites of British expansion, along with the common trope of "Greenland." However, Edmeston imagines young converts of these nations now entering "the portal of the sky" and identifying themselves in a heavenly roster to God:

> "I from Greenland's frozen land,"
> "I from India's sultry plain,"
> "I from Afric's barren sand," …

Now the rhetoric is less unflattering of the local people, instead emphasizing the union with children "from islands of the main" who will come together in a Christian cluster to their Maker. Because sung in first person, the middle-class English children take on the identity of their far-off counterparts.

These Evangelistic missionary hymns of mid-century, then, tended to emphasize the objects of conversion and the enormity of the task for Christians. Missionary hymns did not disappear later in the century but they did refocus along the lines of other later-century hymns, such as temperance and Bands of Mercy shortly to be discussed, to more clearly give power to child singers. Consider a number of missionary hymns in an 1893 hymn book, *282 Hymns and Melodies for School and Family Use*, edited by E. W. and J. Gall Inglis. Their Missionary section begins with acknowledging the shortcomings of little children, highlighting their "littleness" ("We are little friends of Jesus" No. 109), their potential dumbness ("If for Jesus you can speak … though your tones are low and weak" No. 110), and doubts ("What can I give to Jesus?" No. 111; "I am not skilled to understand" No. 116). Other hymns then affirm how much children can do, beyond mere money-collecting: "join and pray" and, when older, go to "the far-off lands … Should'st Thou call us by and by" (No. 179). Indeed, even the Chinese and Indian citizens cry, "Come and help us!" (v. 4) and child singers recognize that through themselves, "the lost may hear and live" (v. 3).

Unlike earlier hymns in which children are benumbed by pity, then, these hymns denounce passivity and urge action, an outward agenda for the child to pursue: "The world to Christ *we bring*" (No. 185), "*Go*, bear the joyful tidings" (No. 186), "*Go forth* and work for Jesus" (No. 188, my italics). By late century, this empowerment of children outweighs the condescension to the "other," as hymns refer less to problematic "heathen" actions then to the reformative solutions achieved by children, less to human difference or religious hegemony than youthful unity.

Finally, these hymns acknowledge the philanthropic needs right in Britain, which is no longer presented as a model society. "Hark! The Voice of Jesus Crying" (No. 189) conveys this message directly:

> If you cannot cross the ocean,
> And the heathen lands explore,
> You can find the heathen nearer,
> You can help them at your door ... (v. 2)

Written in the second person to speak to the individual child, this hymn affirms the answer to all children hindered by doubt and diffidence: "Here I am; send me, send me!" Children can be asked to do no more.

Stories in missionary literature increasingly hailed the work of child-missionaries: Mary who converts her entire family to Christianity through missionary tracts (from the LMS archives, Thorne 118–20); a 3-year-old girl living in India with her missionary parents who converts servant "Sammy" to Christianity (*Divine and Moral Songs ... Anecdotes and Reflections*, c. 1850, 27). Even more stories, though, continued to tote the financial contributions, the "little mite," that a child could contribute. Told *of* children, these stories inspired; sung *by* children, hymns became a buoyant rallying cry of action.

In short, missionary hymns especially through the 1840s espoused Evangelical principles of personal righteousness and the outward duty of conversion; they did this by identifying an "otherness" of the subjects to be converted. Children were taught their own British superiority, and that race was hierarchical, but that cultural and religious difference could and should be eliminated. By late century, cultural and religious variation was more tolerated though a racial hierarchy still existed.[18] Clearly children's hymnody was much a part of the colonization by nineteenth-century Britain of indigenous places such as "Afric" and China.[19] Yet if these

---

[18]  Stanley demonstrates that though stringent ideas of eternal punishment for non-Christians, of England as a model society, and of Christianity as the attainment of human progress all lightened due to end-of-century liberalism, missionary beliefs of racial inferiority and the existence of satanically influenced cultures remained fairly constant even through late century (ch. 7, *The Bible and the Flag*).

[19]  I have focused on hymn singing conducted at home in Britain but, obviously, music and hymn singing were vital to the mission field where "evangelical mission schools

hymns did not empower other nationalities, they did empower the British child, revealing a growing appreciation for the child as an agent of global change.

## Part II
## Reforming an Intoxicated Nation through Temperance Hymns

Developing at the same time as the mission movement, from the same middle-class Dissenting sects (McGuire 122), the temperance movement propelled the English population towards a more inward-directed reformation. Hymns were once again essential to disseminating this education, and entire hymn and songbooks were devoted to temperance.[20] If missionary hymns postulated difference, temperance hymns worked under the modern-philanthropic model that those marginalized could, through education, be raised to the desired moral and social "sameness." Identifying the drinking problems of those in this marginalized group, temperance hymns also acknowledged the problems of the singers themselves, narrowing the moral disparity between sinner and reformer. Finally, temperance hymns almost from the beginning of the movement promoted children's agency to reform the social world around them.

The temperance movement was an immense catalyst for reform in the nineteenth century. All classes, Protestant denominations, ages, and genders were actively involved at some point. To many, intemperance was an epidemic of appalling proportions. One temperance leader in 1861 cited that every 10 minutes a "drunkard dies in our land" and 50,000 die every year; further, "thousands of criminals, paupers, and lunatics are made, filling the country with destruction, desolation and woe" (Ludbrook, *The Temperance Meeting Melodist*, back cover). Yet there was economic pressure to keep alcohol available, from English drink taxes, agricultural production of alcoholic components, to the sense that beer-drinking was simply patriotic (Harrison, *Drink* 62). Lilian Lewis Shiman, author of *Crusade against Drink in Victorian England* (1988), breaks the century's temperance movement into four unique phases.[21] The first was that of moderate

---

often incorporated a healthy dose of hymn singing" (McGuire 128). See his discussion of music and the Tonic Sol-fa system used by foreign missions in *Music and Victorian Philanthropy*, ch. 4.

[20]　I examined almost 20 British Bands of Hope hymn and songbooks, as listed in the Works Cited. American Bands of Hope hymn books examined but not discussed in this chapter but which showed similar trends include *Ripples of Song* (New York: National Temperance Society, 1863); *Temperance Chimes* (New York: NTS, 1884); *Band of Hope Songster*, compiled by J. N. Stearns (New York: NTS, 1885); *Rallying Songs for Young Teetotalers*, compiled by Miss L. Penney (New York: NTS, 1886), and *Capper's Temperance Melodist*, American Edition (n.d.).

[21]　Shiman's two works from which I draw are her *Crusade against Drink in Victorian England* (1988) and an earlier *Victorian Studies* article (1973), "The Band of Hope Movement: Respectable Recreation for Working-Class Children," which informed a chapter in the book but which focuses more on class issues. See also Brian Harrison's

temperance in the 1830s, led by middle- and upper-class agitators. The next, teetotaling phase of the 1840s was led now by working-class converts, but due to the polarizing effect of absolute teetotalism, many church sects, such as the Wesleyan Methodists, took official positions against temperance. The 1850s and 60s were focused on ultimately failed temperance legislation, as led by the United Kingdom Alliance. The third phase (mid-1870s to 1890s), though, was dominated by Gospel temperance, a hugely successful era for temperance in which the Church joined temperance (as with the Church of England Temperance Society). Agitators, especially from America (Francis Murphy, Richard T. Booth), brought ideas to convert to temperance crowds of people who signed pledge cards by the thousands.[22] Enthusiasm even led to an official temperance political party, the Liberal Party (1891). However, with the defeat of the "Newcastle Program" at the polls (1895) the movement waned in the last years of the century. The fourth phase (the 1890s to WWI) was little more than local, isolated movements.

Children were a part of the temperance movement in two distinct ways: one, because they were the social group to first learn intemperance from parents or other adults, they were the first needing to be taught the importance of abstinence; and, two, because they carried weight with the adults in their lives, the principles of temperance taught to them might trickle out into the larger adult community, reverse reform in action. In the 1830s, temperance leaders educated children, and in 1847 the first society was established to cater specifically to children: the Band of Hope as founded by the Leeds Temperance Society under the leadership of Rev. Jabez Tunnicliff and Mrs. Anne Jane Carlile. The idea spread, first in industrial areas, later in village towns. Eventually many populations and religious sects had their own "Bands of Hope," including the Church of England, the Wesleyans, the Baptists, the Society of Friends, and even, though to a lesser degree, the Roman Catholic Church (called the Children's Guild) and a Jewish Band of Hope of London (Shiman, *Crusade* 135). Clearly it behooved both Sunday schools and Bands of Hope to be in close connection, each drawing members and teachers from the other; in this respect, it appears that the churches worked with Bands of Hope more enthusiastically and earlier than with the larger temperance movement. Gospel temperance, though, solidified ties between churches and Bands of Hope: the Wesleyan clergy themselves established a successful Band of Hope organization in the 1870s, for example (Shiman, *Crusade* 138). By the end of the century, the Band of Hope organizations could boast 3 million members (Fahey 790).

---

very thorough history, *Drink and the Victorians: The Temperance Question in England 1815–1872* (Pittsburgh: U of Pittsburgh P, 1971); his "Religion and Recreation in Nineteenth-Century England" in *Peaceable Kingdom: Stability and Change in Modern Britain* (1982); and Rob Breton, "Diverting the Drunkard's Path: Chartist Temperance Narratives," *Victorian Literature and Culture* 41 (2013): 139–52.

[22]  The temperance movement really began in America, first coming to English awareness in the 1820s. In 1830, the *Evangelical Magazine* urged its countrymen to follow the American lead (Harrison, *Drink* 101). As Harrison reminds us, "Temperance, peace, anti-slavery, penal reform and Christian missions were all Anglo-American campaigns" with immense exchanges of inspiration and ideas (101).

Clearly class politics were imbedded in the Band of Hope movement. While organizers and leaders usually came from the middle classes, the majority of young members and most of its teachers were of the upper working classes; to many of the latter, the organization offered "a new cultural identity … [in] respectable society" (Shiman, "The Band" 66, 49).[23] Both boys and girls, ages 5 to 16, came for the entertainment, dynamic speakers, and enthusiasm of the teachers. Working-class parents enjoyed the rare recreation offered by such meetings and therefore usually granted the requisite permission for their child to join (Shiman, *Crusade* 148). The children's pledge was straightforward, beginning with personal resolve, then moving to social reform: "I voluntarily promise to abstain from Porter, Ale, Wines, ardent Spirits, and all intoxicating liquors as a beverage, and from tobacco, and I will try to induce others by example and advice to do the same" (from Esterbrooke, *Bands of Hope: Their Importance* [1850] 7). Given that the child-members were of the working class and had been, in most cases, working themselves all day, the weekly meeting was kept short (usually one hour) and was very lively. Literature was published by a variety of groups—the National Temperance Publication Depot, the Church of England Temperance Society, the Wesleyan Methodist Sunday School Union—to provide teachers with a quantity of activities for their meetings: stories, songs, speeches, recitations, and dialogues. Children gave recitations, took examinations, and participated in competitions, teachers awarding prizes for success. In many cases, the programs were delivered by the children; as one example, *Try Your Best; or, Proof Against Failure: a Complete Entertainment for Bands of Hope and Juvenile Temples* (by W. Wightman, 1878) states that the "idea of the Author is, that the whole programme should be sustained by children" (3). Indeed, even the Chairman who begins the meeting is a child, and names of the children who speak are to be modified with the names of the actual children present (3). If "admitted to the meeting" at all, adults are to sit apart and "behind all the children" (Esterbrooke 9). The frontispiece illustration in *Recitations and Concerted Pieces for Bands of Hope and Sunday Schools* (1892), in fact, shows children reciting with adults shown well in the back. One member of a Band of Hope recalled years later a perhaps "grittier" portrait of their meetings:

> Most Methodist churches had a Band of Hope. This was a riotous assembly. As in the case of the Sunday School, most of those who came had no connection whatever with the church and, furthermore, being held on a week night it always seemed to me that further unruly license was claimed. Still, they were interesting meetings. The great achievement was to recite. I well remember my first effort in this direction. … The hymns at these meetings were of a real rousing type. We would raise the roof…. (qtd. in K. Young 118)

---

[23]    Breton explores the class nature of temperance, that the working classes often suspected that their beerhouses—a main place of meeting and recreation for the working class—were being targeted more for political reasons than temperance. See "Diverting the Drunkard's Path." Harrison demonstrates that the working class could be more militant teetotalers even than the middle class (Harrison, *Drink* 135–6).

Clearly the Bands of Hope meetings catered to an active child, reciting, singing, even carousing.

A quick look at stories in the temperance literature will shed light on how differently literature and music approached the issue of children and temperance. Firstly, temperance stories were very didactic: a clock falls on a drunkard and knocks some sense into him to curtail his drinking habit (*Try Your Best* 7), for example. *First Steps to Temperance*, published by the National Temperance Publication Depot (1883), uses straightforward lessons, pointing out how animals and native peoples drink water, not alcohol (in Lesson 11, "Natural-Water Drinkers"), for example. These are followed by questions, most rhetorical in nature ("What does *all* drink lead to?"). As Shiman points out, "creative thinking was not encouraged. Instead, drink was simply the devil, to be shunned and rejected automatically by all children" (*Crusade* 139).

Secondly, much of the Bands of Hope literature suggests the depraved influence of adults upon young children. Children's souls are "so pure and white" and are tempted by "Crime" and "Drink" in the allegorical poem "Who Bids for the Children?" (Pacis, *Arrows for Temperance Bows* 1–3). A young child in a high chair is tempted by his father's beer-filled mug, shouting in response, "I mean to grow up as fast as I can, / And I'll *always* drink beer when I'm a man!" ("A Little Child Shall Lead Them" in *Recitations and Concerted Pieces* 22). In *Bands of Hope: Their Vast Importance, and How to Form and Sustain Them* (1850), London Band of Hope founder John H. Esterbrooke writes that in the capital, boys of 9 or 10 are already frequenting beer shops as they try to "ape the man," having seen nothing but "scenes of dissipation and vice" at home (3). He asks the parents: "what security can you give them against this awful consequence [becoming loathsome slaves of intemperance], if you teach them, either by precept or example, to value intoxicating drinks, and assist in forming that very appetite which has proved to thousands the source of their temporal and eternal ruin?" (5). His hyperbolic rhetoric makes clear that the evil begins with parents who cannot divorce themselves from drink. Even other adults are not exempt from immoral influence: "Mistaken kindness presents the errand-boy with ale, or the little relative with wine, when on a visit. Holiday pleasures and birth-day fetes are made the means of inspiring the young mind with erroneous opinions as to the value and properties of alcoholic drinks, presented with much parade and praise" (3). In short, in the temperance literature, much is made of the corrupting, if well-meaning, influence of adults upon their children, while children seem not to have any influence for good or bad upon the adult world. Instead, adults need to learn reform for their children's sake: "first to abstain from all intoxicating drinks, and to teach your children to follow your example" (Esterbrooke 5).

Music was an integral part of the temperance movement, enjoyed by the Band of Hope member just quoted. Charles McGuire makes this clear when analyzing the Tonic Sol-fa sight-singing system used by John and Spencer Curwen which undergirded much of the temperance movement (69).[24] Needless to say, music also played a fundamental part in the success of the Bands of Hope: "The influence for good of the cultivation of such music among the children could not be overrated" wrote a Band of Hope teacher (qtd. in Shiman, *Crusade* 141). Orchestras were organized with free instrumental lessons given to the children. Even more prominent were the Bands of Hope choirs, competing and performing throughout the country. In 1862, a combined, thousand-member choir of the Bands of Hope began giving annual concerts in London to packed crowds, culminating in one at the Crystal Palace in 1886 (Shiman, *Crusade* 141). Throughout the country, choirs competed, and children marched in parades and performed in other public events. Such events gave children an alternative to drinking-related frivolities, but they also disseminated temperance ideologies in a very public way (Shiman, "The Band" 57, 60). L. E. Jones (c. 1892) recalls walking with the Band of Hope "through the streets of Fakenham at the head of a procession of teetotal children," a day of "public commitment" (ruined within a few weeks when his father gave him port-wine; *A Victorian Boyhood* 11).

On the local level, music was crucial to the success of the weekly meetings, one of the highlights of the night's recreation. Esterbrooke instructs his teachers to "Open the Meeting with lively singing [of] … a Temperance melody" (6, 8). John R. Newman reiterates in his *Hints on Working Senior and Junior Bands of Hope*, published by the Church of England Temperance Society in 1897, "Always begin and close with singing and prayer" (10). And his Number One way to interest children in attending is to "Have a good hymn-book" (he specifically recommends the *Young Crusader* hymn book through the CETS) and "Use the most lively tunes and the most stirring words" (13); he refers elsewhere to "action songs" and "marching tunes" to elicit energy and enthusiasm (12, 14). One temperance song opens, "Welcome to our festive meeting / Welcome to our happy throng; / To beguile the moments fleeting, / Let us raise the cheerful song" ("Festive Song," No. 8, *The Temperance Meeting Melodist*). One participant, Robert Roberts, recalled that the Band of Hope meeting in Salford was the "cultural highlight of the week" with "capering on the stage in song and uproarious sketch" (qtd. in Horn, *Schoolchild* 154). Clearly music was crucial to entertain and inspire.

One challenge to temperance reformers in using music was the reality that drunken people sang, too; that "uproarious" music had been, for centuries, associated with drunken bar-room revelry. One temperance song describes the scene "when, 'mid mirth and music, / 'Mid the song and jest, and laughter, / Goes round the wine enchanted …" (qtd. in Burnett 58). Even more discouraging was the drunkard, having learned favorite Sunday school hymns in his past, using

---

[24]  In chapter 2 of *Music and Victorian Philanthropy*, McGuire suggests three ways in which Tonic Sol-fa singing aided the temperance movement: as a moral influence, as a distraction from alcohol, and for the attraction to the temperance movement itself. Yet temperance movements did not embrace Tonic Sol-fa with as much fervor as Tonic Sol-fa embraced temperance, and when it fell with the failure of the 1895 Reform Bill, Tonic Sol-fa fell, too. Ironically, the Curwens could not have picked a worse reform to sponsor.

those same hymns while on a drunken spree, as John Burnett, Wesleyan minister and author of *Bands of Hope in Town and Village; How to Start and Work Them* (1877), lamented:

> We once saw a band of young men, who having been trained in such a [Sunday] school, leave a public house ... all much the worse for drink ... They walked a little way, filling the air with their laughter and noise, and then linked arms and sang—"There is a fountain filled with blood ... I do believe, I will believe, that Jesus died for me." (11)

The irony of misused hymn singing was painful for Burnett to acknowledge and his urgent appeal is for Sunday schools to take up temperance more ardently in their teachings.

If used by the inebriated, still, hymns and songs were a pivotal vehicle for reform by Bands of Hope leaders. First of note is that temperance music often passed unreservedly between adults and children, not surprising given my argument of Chapter 3. In a survey of 15 Band of Hope song and hymn books, many are adult favorites, not distinguishable as adult or child songs (see Table 5.1).[25] One of the most popular songs found in Band of Hope hymn books was W. B. Bradbury's "Dare to do right" (five of 15), yet it was enjoyed by adults, too, featured in an 1898 Church of England Temperance Society Exeter Hall Meeting:[26]

> Dare to do right! Dare to be true!
> You have a work that no other can do;
> Do it so bravely, so kindly, so well
> Angels will hasten the story to tell.
> (v. 1, "Exeter Hall Meeting Programme—Music Edition")

This program lists songs as hymns, and thus begs the question of the genre of Band of Hope hymns. Many inclusions in Band of Hope hymn books are unmistakably hymns: popular hymns of the period are found, such as Thomas Ken's "Glory to Thee, my God, this night" or Frances R. Havergal's "Take my life." Many hymns directly mention God (or angels, as above), but many others

---

[25]   In my survey of Bands of Hope songbooks, I found much less consistency than in regular hymn books. The most popular hymn was not found in even half of the books (five of 12), and other frequently occurring songs included only two at the four-of-12 level. Many more titles were found only in their respective books. I conclude that song writers were often working independently of each other to write and market their songs. I am grateful to my Victorian literature student, Patricia Findley, who calibrated some of these hymn titles for an Honors project in Spring 2012.

[26]   This meeting of April 26, 1898, a program for which is now housed in the British Library, was held in the Sanctuary of Westminster, featured addresses by the Archbishop of Canterbury and the Lord Bishop of Chichester, and was liberally sprinkled with temperance hymns, sung both by choir and congregation. Exeter Hall, London, was an important site for temperance meetings, including the conference of November 8, 1883, which united many temperance societies into the National Temperance Federation (*Crusade* 190).

Table 5.1    Most Frequently Appearing Songs or Hymns in 12 British Band of Hope Songbooks, 1860–1899

| Title | # of books |
|---|---|
| Give me a draught from the crystal spring | 5 |
| God bless our youthful band | 4 |
| Yield not to temptation | 4 |
| Dare to do right | 3 |
| Drops of crystal water,—oh, the summer showers | 3 |
| In the ways of true Temperance | 3 |
| Just in the dawn of youth we stand | 3 |
| Just one more song before we part | 3 |
| Kind words can never die | 3 |
| Little drops of water | 3 |
| O come, come away, ye youths of Britain, hasten | 3 |
| Sampson, the strongest man | 3 |
| Speak softly! Speak softly | 3 |
| Sun of my soul, Thou Saviour dear | 3 |
| Sweet Saviour, bless us ere we go | 3 |
| There is a happy land | 3 |
| Touch not the cup; it is death to thy soul | 3 |
| Try again | 3 |
| Wine is a mocker, strong drink is raging | 3 |

are more secular in nature, moral though not specifically religious, and editors invoke terms such as "Hymns and Songs" (Ludbrook), "Melodies and Hymns" (Murphy), or "melodies … [and] airs" (Winskill) to title their collections. Much of the ambiguity possibly stemmed from the division between temperance and religious groups until united during the Gospel temperance era. It is therefore useful to consider each genre separately initially.

Of songs more secularly didactic, we see great variety. Some directly address young people's misuse of alcoholic drink. Some use sentimental rhetoric to show the sad deaths of children due to their inebriated parents, in hopes of reforming adults in these children's lives. But others, through parodies of popular melodies, energetic tunes, and military terms, clearly were encouraging children to "fight" the world of drink, a venue where one sees real agency of empowered child singers marching as if into battle to reform the intoxicated world about them.

Consider the first type of song, that cautioning children against alcoholic drink and encouraging clear water. Songs extolling the purity of water were especially popular, even if the reality of clean water was decades away. In fact, three of the

19 most frequently appearing temperance songs from 12 common Bands of Hope songbooks were focused on water: "Give me a draught from the crystal spring," "Drops of crystal water," and "Little drops of water" (Table 5.1).

"Give me a draught from the crystal spring," for instance, places water in its natural setting:

> Give me a draught from the crystal spring,
> > When the burning sun is high;
> When the rocks and the woods their shadows fling,
> > Where the pearls and pebbles lie.

Enticing and pastoral, this water is contrasted with alcohol, which singers flatly refuse:

> … But if aught from the worm of the still you bring,
> > I will pour every drop away.
> > > (No. 27 in *The Temperance Meeting Melodist*, 1861)

Other didactic songs are specifically for the youth themselves and, in contrast to much temperance literature, focus on youth who make wise or poor decisions without adult interference. Inspired by the ballad tradition, these songs chronicle stories of young people hovering on the brink of adulthood who are facing critical decisions about drink. This one is a sentimental example of repentance made too late:

> Kiss me, Mother, ere I die;
> > Gladly would my soul have tarried,
> For 'tis hard so soon to die,
> > And my life so much miscarried.
> Oh! The wine-cup made me stray,
> > Reckless of thy tender pleading;
> And I wandered far away,
> > Ne'er thy kindly warning heeding.
> > > (v. 3, No. 7, *Winskill's Band of Hope Melodist*, 1870)

If this youth has ignored his mother's solicitous advice, others extol the youth who reforms, as with "Teetotal Charlie":

> I spent my youth in folly, and it filled my heart with pain;
> Those youthful days are over, oh, they'll never come again!
> But now in early manhood, by Temp'rance I will try.
> To do my duty to the world, and from temptation fly.
> > (v. 1, No. 23, *Winskill's Band of Hope Melodist*)

Other songs address young women, both in the way they are tempted to drink and tempted to marry men of drink. "The Pride of the Village" imagines a "lovely maiden" who was "lov'd and admired where'er she did roam" who yet was "[l]ured by the wine-cup, sadly did she fall" which has catastrophic effects on the village itself ("Bringing grief and woe to all"). As with the dying lad above, Mary dies, too, and the song ends with a warning to all young women:

> Oh, ye lovely maidens, of strong drink beware;
> Thousands it has ruined—Oh, take care!
>
> (v. 3, No. 24, Winskill's Band of Hope Melodist)

In other songs, young women are warned of "settling" for a drunken man who will pull them down. As Maggie concludes, in "Maggie's Trials":

> For I tell you that no man shall ever wed me,
>     Unless, unless from drink he is free.
>
> (v. 1, No. 18, Winskill's Band of Hope Melodist)

The fact that both genders are addressed is significant. Alcoholism is not simply a problem of men, and girls and boys are both appealed to in order to rectify the problem, on a personal and national level. Further, children could themselves be the "fallen," the "other"—unlike missionary eliteness.

While children need to save themselves, the second message in Bands of Hope songs is that children may positively influence the adults in their lives, a message that seems to come across more frequently even in the songs than the prose recitations just discussed. Often this message is conveyed through sentimental songs. One notable example is called "Who will go for Father now?," found in Winskill's *Band of Hope Melodist* (Song No. 4). First a story is narrated about "Little Mary" whose job it was to bring her father home from the "Sickle and Sheaf" each night. One night a flying glass hits her and kills her; her last words to her father are "there'll be nobody to go for you, father." From this poignant story is built the song whose chorus concludes:

> Soon with angels I'll be marching,
>     With a crown upon my brow;
> Ere I go, O! can you tell me?—
>     Who will go for father now?

Such sacrifice of children to save their wanton parents joins similar themes of child suffering because of irresponsible parents. Children envision "that happy day" when "No drunkards' children cry for bread" but "poor men's fam'lies [are] amply fed" (v. 4, No. 10, *Temperance Meeting Melodist*). Yet children are not always the passive victims, but are often shown to fight back. Children appeal to God ("The Children's Prayer," No. 25, *Winskill's Band of Hope*). Children also appeal directly to the drunkard to swear restraint:

> … See the wife you once loved so true and sincere—
>     Say, can you rejoice in her pain?
> Your children so sunken, though once loved so dear—
>     Sign the pledge, and you'll raise them again.
>
> (v. 2, No. 39, Popular Melodies and Hymns, 1871)

Indeed, temperance leaders keenly felt the impact of children's singing directly upon the reprobates they might encounter: "We have known regular tipplers attracted from the public-house by a Band of Hope meeting. It was the singing and reciting of the children which allured them" (Burnett 68).

Not surprisingly, what appealed to addicted adults also ameliorated the heavy didacticism for children: the vitality of the tunes. As both Esterbrooke and Newman advised, Band of Hope songs and hymns should be "lively" and "stirring"—and most were. "Onward Christian soldiers, Marching as to war" is only the most familiar of a large handful of "marching" songs in the temperance repertoire: "March along," "Marching onward," and "March, my little children," etc. Energy was also given by the use of rounds: the United Kingdom Band of Hope Union prioritizes rounds in their *Hymns and Songs for Bands of Hope* (1894), children coming in at staggered times, singing texts like "All united, firm and true, the Temperance path we will pursue" or "Now with voices clear and strong, Sing a merry Temperance song." Different fonts are used to designate various dynamics, softer or louder, to ensure animated singing. The result is entertaining music-making to appeal to children and assure their continued attendance at the Band of Hope meetings. Tunes also enforced the message: "Temperance hymns used highly-charged emotional language and catchy Sankey-style tunes to hammer home their message of the evils of the demon drink" (Bradley, *Abide with Me* 187).

Singers were also energized by parodies of familiar, rousing tunes now with new temperance words. It should be pointed out that Band of Hope hymn and songbook writers were just that: writers of texts, not composers, and almost all songbooks of my study give words only, utilizing well-known tunes, usually referred to with a hymn tune name ("Abridge") or song title ("Tramp, tramp, tramp"), to designate the corresponding music.[27] This enabled songbook editors to produce their books as small, inexpensive, pocket-size chapbooks. Many are parodies of popular songs: the rousing chorus to "Weel may the Keel row," a popular sailor's tune, becomes "But there is comfort springing / Where sober bands are singing / For they are pledged to bringing / Sound help to all who flee" (*Try Your Best* 16–17), for example. Using the tune to "Auld lang syne," children sing "Shall e'er cold water be forgot," and to "Home, sweet home" they now sing "'Mid the sparkling of glasses or goblets of wine" (both in Newman Hall's *Harmonised Hymns and Songs for Bands of Hope*, 1862). Using the popular American tune to "Jesus loves me," G. M. Murphy adapts it to "I love water pure and bright" (No. 22) and to the popular hymn "Kind words can never die" his singers now mouth "Our cause can never die" (No. 33 in *Popular Melodies and Hymns*, 1871). Writers would also parody some of the most popular hymns of the period. Winskill quotes "Amazing Grace" to emphasize a spiritual reformation:

---

[27] Two exceptions in my study, which were larger books able to accommodate musical scores to their songs, even if they were well-known tunes, are: *Harmonised Hymns and Songs for Bands of Hope*, compiled by Rev. Newman Hall and harmonized by Rev. C. G. Rowe (1862), and *Hymns and Songs for Bands of Hope* (1894) by the Committee of the United Kingdom Band of Hope Union.

"Once he was blind, but now he sees" (No. 6, v. 2). "There is a happy land, far, far away / Where saints in glory stand, bright, bright as day" is co-opted to become "There is a happy time, not far away / When temp'rance truth shall shine, bright, bright as day" in Walter Ludbrook's *The Temperance Meeting Melodist* (No. 32, 1861). To the most popular children's hymn of all, "I think when I read that sweet story of old / When Jesus was here among men," Ludbrook sets the cleverly altered words "I think when I read the sad stories of woe / Which drunkenness brings upon men" (No. 17). That hymn's tune ("Child's Desire") was also utilized with the words "There is a sweet land where the weary shall rest / and the wicked shall trouble no more" (No. 49) in *Popular Melodies and Hymns*. Using hymns known and enjoyed by singers, these temperance song writers promoted temperance messages to children and adults alike.

Sometimes, though, this practice became awkward. "Teetotal Charlie," mentioned above, was actually set to the drinking tune "Champagne Charlie." This practice was not uncommon and the Salvation Army, for instance, was not averse to using drinking songs to set their Christian messages, and used "Here's to good old whisky" to become "Storm the forts of darkness" to inspire. Nevertheless, this approach was much criticized, as the *Church Times* remarked of the Salvation Army: "Can anyone suppose that St. Paul would have thought of adapting Christian hymns to the melodies used by the votaries of Dionysus or Aphrodite?" (qtd. in Bradley, *Abide* 186). This was a risk that temperance leaders were willing to take, however, if they could capitalize upon familiar and engrossing tunes, then lead singers to more wholesome lyrics.

Their choice of tunes is significant, in fact, as many song writers used tunes stemming from America's recent Civil War with their militant and patriotic fervor. P. T. Winskill (in *Band of Hope Melodist*, 1870) uses the stirring melody "Old John Brown" ("Battle Hymn of the Republic") to fight the war against intemperance:

> Lift up the Temperance standard,
>     And the flag of freedom wave;
> Come and help to save the drunkard,
>     Ere he sinks into the grave.

The rhetoric of war is interspersed throughout, as is the rhetoric of slavery:

> Tho' the foe is great and mighty,
>     And doth noble minds enslave,
> Yet to victory we'll march on. (v. 1, No. 5)

Another uses the Civil War tune "When Johnny comes marching home" to reflect on a reformed father:

> Oh! What a glorious change has come,
>     Hurrah! hurrah!
> Father now comes sober home,
>     Hurrah! hurrah!

No more he to the ale-house goes
But buys good food and decent clothes,
    And makes us all feel
    Joy and peace at home. (v. 1, No. 6)

The change is reflected through the motif of music: "No more he sings the drunkard's song" (v. 2).

The use of actual military tunes underscores a major theme of these temperance songs: even as hymn writers were utilizing more militant language in the latter decades of the nineteenth century (Drain 70), so, too, did temperance writers, equating their own cause as a "war" against intemperance and evil. They took up the *language* of war as well: the "nation's direst foe— / The demon—Alcohol" (Ludbrook, No. 21). Consider one song in Ludbrook's *The Temperance Meeting Melodist* (1861), published just as the Civil War commenced:

To arms! against our nation's foe;
    The cause of wretchedness and woe …
Say, shall the foe destroy our land?
    Or shall we join the temp'rance band? (vv. 1–2, No. 6)

Almost recklessly, writers engage children in the harsh concepts of war co-opted for Christian glory. Bands of Hope are referred to as "our noble army" which is "Marching 'gainst the foe" and children are asked to help "lay the monster low" (No. 19). Children are encouraged to join the attack, and assured of success, as in "We shall do it" (Winskell's, No. 15):

Yes, we shall do it—yes, we shall do it;
Yes, we shall do it; shall chase him [the foe] from our land. (chorus, No. 15)

What is momentous in these militaristic temperance songs is the empowerment of children to build the army, to lead the charge, to fight the demon drink. Shiman suggests that the tone of Band of Hope songs became more militant by the 1890s (*Crusade* 152), but I would place this militancy much earlier, in the 1860s, if not earlier, as the above examples suggest. Shiman also writes that Band of Hope children were needed as "active agents of change who could be controlled and manipulated by the organizers of the movement" (*Crusade* 151). Not denying ways in which children were manipulated for political ends, I suggest that it is nevertheless significant that children were seen to be political "agents" at all, and for most of the last half of the century. Indeed, many Band of Hope leaders enforced this message: "make children feel that they have influence, and an important part to perform in sustaining their movement" (Esterbrooke 8). "The aim of the Band of Hope is to save the children from intemperance," writes Burnett (1877), "[b]ut it seeks not only to save the children themselves from drunkenness and its attendant evils, but also to make them a blessing to all around them" (68).

Perhaps the genre which most consistently highlighted children's agency in achieving social sobriety was the hymn, since it focused on children's God-given rights and power. Temperance hymns are found scattered throughout the above-mentioned temperance songbooks (most published in the 1860s and 1870s), and are also featured in such books as *Our National Temperance Hymn and Song Book* (1865), compiled by the Rev. Henry A. Hammond, and *Hymns for Children with Opening and Closing Services and Songs and Hymns for Bands of Mercy and of Hope* (1894), edited by Charlotte Farrington and published by the Sunday School Association. These latter reflect Shiman's so-defined third phase, Gospel temperance, of the 1870s–1890s, when many church sects joined the movement. For many temperance workers of this period, temperance is a Christian call to action, such that the "Temperance Hymn" invokes divine help for the cause: "Our fathers' God, our keeper! / Be thou our strength divine!" (*Hymns for Children*, No. 334).

Notably, such hymns greatly empowered children. The very popular hymn for children (found in 17% of hymn books), "God entrusts to all" by James Edmeston, found as No. 17 in *Our National Temperance*, takes the Parable of the Talents and applies it to what every child can do:

> Every little mite,
>      Every little measure,
> Helps to spread the light,
>      Helps to swell the treasure
> God entrusts to all,
>      Talents few or many;
> None so young or small,
>      That they have not any. (v. 3)

This agency was particularly salient in the temperance cause. Furthermore, boys and girls each have specific duties, as the "Band of Hope hymn" (No. 340, *Hymns for Children*) demonstrates:

> *Boys*: Give to the boys true courage,
>      That as men they grow
>      When drinking comrades tempt them
>      They'll firmly answer "No!"
> *Girls*: And keep the girls all steadfast,
>      And may they help to win,
>      By love and good example,
>      Weak souls from paths of sin. (No. 340)

These are different, stereotypical roles, which assume boys to be the victims of drink while girls are the potential saviors, unlike earlier songs which recognized girls' fallibility, too. But both are agents of social reform, placed into the hands of the even the youngest "boys" and "girls."

Temperance hymns acknowledge the sacred talents which children specifically bring, their courage and their steadfastness, to "swell the treasure"—this time not focused on the monetary "talent" as the biblical parable and the many missionary hymns for children assume. Further, God entrusts them, and hands them an exclusive responsibility to minister in small ways to the redemption of others. The genre of "hymn" may become obscured in these songbooks, as I have just described: ballads and military songs run fluidly with hymns of faith. Interestingly, it seems that the ballad genre tended to sentimentalize the child caught up in death and misery, "melting the hearts" of adults; military songs inspired children to "fight the foe" of sin and intemperance, with words and musical fervor; while the hymn genre evoked the might of God to empower even the smallest of children for change and for good.

Shiman recognizes the deficiencies of the Band of Hope movement, its members often turning to drink when they reached adulthood and many adults remaining unmoved by children's influence; still, "there is no doubt that it should be listed among those forces that contributed to the transformation of attitudes towards the role of children in the community" ("The Band" 51). Specifically, temperance children were handed a great deal of power especially through their hymns and songs. Further, unlike missionary hymns, temperance hymns reminded children that they, too, could harbor such vice, humbleness being an empowering virtue as well. The "other" was very oftentimes oneself. Such temperance songs and hymns are in contrast to Bands of Hope literature which continued to place the reformative power upon adults. In focusing on the fallenness of the adults, and the redemptive power of children, the Bands of Hope songs and hymns are startling reminders of Victorian adult-child power relations quite in reverse of what is often considered "Victorian social reformation"—adults aiding children. Instead, "Many, very many, such cases may be given, in which the parents have been reclaimed purely through the efforts of the little ones" (Burnett 69–70). And the efforts, specifically, are that of song, as one Band of Hope worker described: "Was it not likely that a little girl singing a verse of some sweet melody in the hearing of her poor drunken father would melt his heart. And that the hymns that taught the worship of the Blessed God would sink into the little one's minds … their singing would be like the great shout of Jericho before the walls of intemperance" (qtd. in Shiman, *Crusade* 141). It was the quality of music to reach far and wide, to break down age barriers, to appeal to head and heart, to bring down "the walls of intemperance," all as sung by empowered child singers.

## Part III
## Singing Hymns of Mercy for God's Creatures

If missionary hymns peaked in the 1840s and temperance hymn- and songbooks in the 1870s, a reform movement climaxing late century and very much modeled after the success of the Bands of Hope were the Bands of Mercy, designed to bring animal welfare to national awareness through the voices of children; once again reverse reform empowering children to bring about transformation to the nation. By late century, as I have suggested, even missionary and temperance hymns were evoking more tolerance for the "other" while persistently appealing to the abilities of children. The Bands of Mercy would perfectly model this new world view in many ways. By embracing the marginalized state of animals, the movement expanded what even constituted a member of society, and by acknowledging the worth of the small and helpless, this ideology clinched the increasing attention to children and their own rights as citizens. Another aspect of this movement was its expanded borders as English and American work dove-tailed, briefly seen earlier with the Bands of Hope. If not uniting Western and non-Western people, it yet set the tone for a non-Euro-centric focus and encouraged unity of work, not homogeny of creed as had been seen with missionary hymns.

Throughout history, animals have been exploited for food, transportation, companion, and sport, with abuse—undernourishment, neglect, whippings, cruelty, and death—a part of their existence. Sport, in particular, expanded during the late seventeenth and eighteenth centuries; to the centuries-old spectator sports of bull-baiting and cockfighting were added fox hunting and horse racing of the upper classes (Turner 3). Much animal cruelty went hand-in-hand with drinking. In beerhouses, cockfighting, dog-fighting, and badger-baiting (dogs set on badgers) lingered through the nineteenth century, and ratting was a common sport (sewer rats turned loose into pits to be killed by dogs) (Horn, *Pleasures and Pastimes* 65–6).

Animal welfare grew out of many eighteenth-century movements: the Industrial Revolution, revolutionary spirit, and Evangelical revivals all contributed to increased concern for animal wellbeing across Anglo-American society.[28] Individuals championed animal welfare, such as Jeremy Bentham, a vocal critic of animal suffering. Many children's books of the period focused on children's compassionate treatment of animals, from *Goody Two-Shoes* (1765; John Newbery, publisher) to Sarah Kirby Trimmer's *Fabulous Histories* (1786).[29] However, as

---

[28]   As people moved to towns as part of the Industrial Revolution, and thus were further removed from the harsh, day-to-day realities of agrarian life, their sympathy for animals increased: indeed, the first animals to be defended were cattle, sheep, pigs, and horses (Turner 33). Thomas Paine's Revolutionary rhetoric inspired animal-rights treatises by such writers as John Oswald (*Cry of Nature*, 1791) and John Lawrence ("Rights of Beasts," 1796). Concern for "God's creatures" also came from religious revival. Bull-baiting (pitting dogs against angry bulls), for instance, was condemned by many Evangelical sects for its complicity with gambling and rowdiness as well as its cruelty to bulls and dogs (Turner 21).

[29]   Goody Two-Shoes rescues a raven and pigeon from cruel treatment by boys; Trimmer's human protagonists protect a family of robins in their orchard. Turner writes about "Storybooks preaching kindness to animals—which English children could avoid only by illiteracy" (19). If not quite that common, I have found a number of books about animals beyond the now-common classics: "Lubin and His Dog Tray" and "The Mouse's Petition" from *Mrs. Charlton's Pathetic Poetry for Youth; Calculated to Awaken the Pathetic Affections* (London, 1811); *The Squirrels and Other Animals* (London, 1840); *The Trial of an Ox for Killing a Man*, Pennybook (Banbury, n.d.); *Our Pets and Playfellows in Air, Earth, and Water*, by Gertrude Patmore (London, 1880); *The Book of Saints and Friendly Beasts* by Abbie Farwell Brown (Boston, 1900); *Another Peep at the Birds* (Philadelphia:

James Turner suggests, animal welfare during this era was often focused on what cruelty and compassion revealed about humans (14). For instance, Isaac Watts invoked animals to teach morality in *Divine and Moral Songs* (1715), as in "The Ant, or Emmet" (Moral Song V):

> These emmets, how little they are in our eyes!
> We tread them to dust, and a troop of them dies,
>     Without regard or concern:
> Yet as wise as we are ... [there are]
> Some lessons of wisdom [we] might learn. (v. 1)

Noting this instance of human cruelty only to show human obliviousness, Watts then refocuses our attention on the ants' industriousness and preparation for the future, how "they manage their work in such regular forms" as motivation to his young readers not to "trifle away all [our] prime" (verse 2).

Christopher Smart singularly departs from this tendency in his *Hymns for the Amusement of Children* (1770) by advocating mercy for its own sake, then anthropomorphizing animals in the struggle for Christ's kingdom ("Yet they are serious in the fight / Of Christ, the King of kings," v. 7, Hymn 27). This extreme sense of beastly spirituality reflects the radicalism in his "My Cat Jeoffry" (from his *Jubilate Agno*, 1759–1763), in which he extols the divinity in his cat. These ideas of animals' religious intentionality set the stage for the Romantics who imbued animals with "pristine innocence, a spontaneous joy ... [even] moral virtues" (Perkins 3) quite in contrast to Watts's portrayals. Further, writers such as Rousseau argued children's "inherent connection with animals" (Flegel 45). Thus, having been earlier portrayed (by Watts and others) as "the animal's natural and sadistic predator, the child, within Romantic poetry, instead [began to] share with the animal a quality of transcendent, yet fragile innocence" (Flegel 47). This alliance of the child with the animal continued into the next era.

The nineteenth century has been described as a watershed for animal rights, "the emergence of a new, distinctly modern sensibility" (Turner xi). The upsurge of science during the era accounted for an increased understanding of the animal kingdom in all its many forms. Indeed, Darwin's mid-century theories catapulted science in a new direction by making "the human more animal and the animal more human, destabilizing boundaries in both directions" (Morse and Danahay 2). Harriet Ritvo argues in *The Animal Estate* of a "fundamental shift" of the Victorian era in which "the advent of self-consciously enlightened humanitarianism" actually worked against animal welfare: "people systematically appropriated power they had previously attributed to animals, and animals became significant primarily as the objects of human manipulation" (2). Victorians turned their attention to many of these "animal objects," from domestic companions, to beasts of burden, to wild

---

American Sunday-School Union (n.d.); and *One Hundred New Animal Stories*, by Alfred E. Lomax (London: SSU, c. 1900). For more about the animal story in the nineteenth century, see Demers, *A Garland*, ch. 9; and Jackson, 143–4, 166–8.

game in imperial territories.[30] Brian Harrison (in *Peaceable Kingdom*) breaks up the nineteenth century into five distinct periods of animal welfare, beginning with the establishment of the Royal Society for the Prevention of Cruelty to Animals (RSPCA) in 1824, and its early concern for horses and cattle which culminated in (Richard) Martin's Act of 1835 to enact fines to cattle abuse, bull-baiting, and dog-cropping (carts). The next phase led to a number of Acts through the 1840s to 1870s which extended protection to many other animals of recreation and transportation. In its third phase, the RSPCA turned to defense of wild birds. While meeting with success here, the RSPCA, in its fourth phase, in the 1870s, tackled a completely different arena—vivisection—which meant for the first time contesting the work of the educated classes even as scientists were making headway in scientific experimentation (the diphtheria antitoxin was among the first to come about due to animal experimentation; Turner 115). In the wake of such advancements, the best the RSPCA was able to do was to impose inspections on laboratories. In its fifth phase, the Society took on aristocratic pleasure sports, again with mixed results, only able to restrain "deliberately cruel acts" (Harrison 90). After these failures, Turner suggests, the RSPCA gave up their divisive political agenda, including vivisection and field sports, instead turning by late century to innocuous work such as "teaching children to be kind to pets and birds and caring for stray dogs" (122).

Actually, this form of animal education was of long standing in children's literary and hymn contexts of the nineteenth century where urging kindness to animals—usually household pets—rarely became political. Nevertheless, hymn writers insisted on Christian mercy to all of God's creatures, often in very pointed terms. An early hymn book, the *Harrington-School Hymns* (1818), includes awareness of the animals who "must be slain": "Spare them, while they yield their breath, / Double not the pains of death / Strike them not at such a time / God accounts the stroke a crime" (Hymn 193, "Cruelty to brutes," v. 2). In the *Christian Mother's Hymn Book* (1855), the author turns her young audience's attention to the most lowly of animals and one most vulnerable to young feet by preaching: "Turn, turn thy hasty foot aside, / Nor crush that helpless worm; / The frame thy wayward looks deride / Required a God to form" (Hymn 28, v. 1).

Authors also make use of animal imagery to cater to the young and teach a religion of good works, not bodily might. For instance, the author of *Hymns and Rhymes for Children, by the Daughter of a Clergyman* (1871), "Daughter," focuses repeatedly on animals in her rhymes, the modest anonymity of this female editor

---

[30]     Many of these are considered in *Victorian Animal Dreams: Representations of Animals in Literature and Culture* (2007), edited by Deborah Denenholz Morse and Martin A. Danahay. Of the burgeoning field of animal studies in Victorian culture, see Turner, *Reckoning with the Beast* (1980); Harrison, ch. 2: "Animals and the State in Nineteenth-Century England" in *Peaceable Kingdom* (1982); Ritvo, *The Animal Estate* (1987); Baker, *Picturing the Beast* (1993); Kete, *The Beast in the Boudoir* (1994); Kean, *Animal Rights* (1998); Rothfels, *Representing Animals* (2002); Beers, *For the Prevention of Cruelty* (2006); and Perkins, *Romanticism and Animal Rights* (2003). See Morse and Danahay's "Introduction" for a useful overview of Victorian animal studies in the last 30 years.

possibly carrying over into her personal attention to other "invisible" creatures around her. Woodcuts show various animals—sheep, dogs, birds—to parallel the innocence of children described in the hymns. Her attention to animals is often a simple reminder of God's Creation, the God who "made the pretty bird to fly" and "the cow to give nice milk." At other times, humans may learn from the loyalty and duty of animals, one hymn even suggesting a parallel with a loyal dog and our loyal *God*: "The dog will stand and watch the sheep, / Or guard the house while men do sleep; / And so should we both watch and pray / That God would keep us night and day" (28). Also found in this hymn book are poems which are more didactic, offering lessons of kind treatment to those more vulnerable: "I'll never hurt my little dog, / But stroke and pat his head ... Poor fellow! I will give him food, / And he'll love me again" (21) or "I love little pussy, her coat is so warm; / And if I don't hurt her she'll do me no harm" (29). Children learn to appreciate that birds belong in the wild: in "The Child and the Bird" (by Lydia Maria Child) both the "child" and "bird" are given a "singing" voice with which the bird thanks the child "for all thy care" yet remonstrates that "my snug little nest" is "better than [a] golden cage" (64). This hymn book also demonstrates parallels between abused animals and suffering children (such as "Blind Johnny": "Be kind to little Johnny Bell ... He cannot play at ball or top" 47). Children have much in common with animals in their vulnerability and need for protection. This depiction reflects other mid-Victorian portrayals by Dickens and Collins who, as Monica Flegel argues, aligned "the child with the animal as a victim in shared suffering—and shared cruelty" (*Conceptualizing Cruelty* 50). This prevailed even in the face of the opposite imagery, that of the "savage child," animal-like in its violence (51; note the child's propensity to "harm" her dog and her pussy, above). These images also contrast with the more political, empowering hymns of the Bands of Mercy movement shortly upon the horizon.

Little scholarship has been written about the Bands of Mercy movement.[31] Modeled after Bands of Hope, Bands of Mercy were established by Catherine Smithies in 1875 in Britain to educate children about animal welfare. As Diane L. Beers writes, "the solution seemed deceptively simple and enticing: teach the children, and the children would rise to heal the world" (87). In 1882, the Band came under the auspices of the RSPCA. By 1892, there were 800 chapters throughout the country (Harrison 129). In 1882, George T. Angell and Rev. Thomas Timmins founded the American Band of Mercy organization where it grew to 27,000 Bands by the early twentieth century. This success in America paralleled the rapid expansion of animal welfare in general, which English advocates often enviously noted. "[O]ur cause," wrote the RSPCA's *Animal World*, "has made

---

[31]   No mention is made of Bands of Mercy in Turner, Ritvo, Morse and Danahay, or Baker, with only passing references in Harrison, Flegel, and Beers. As a result, I am relying on *Band of Mercy Advocate*, volumes 1–5, and an American website, "Be Kind: A Visual History of Humane Education, 1880–1945," through the National Museum of Animals and Society (a California-based organization), found at http://bekindexhibit.org/exhibition/bands-of-mercy/, accessed July 2013.

more progress in the United States during fifteen years, than in England during fifty years" (qtd. in Turner 52). Turner reminds us that on both sides of the Atlantic, within the animal movement the "wealthy and influential supplied its leaders, the solidly middle-class its followers" (52). This sets it apart from Bands of Hope which catered largely to the working classes.

Given the success of Bands of Hope and the already close connections between temperance and animal activism,[32] it is no surprise that Bands of Mercy, despite differences in the class of children, intentionally followed the approach of Bands of Hope to appeal to its youthful audience. Like the latter, Bands of Mercy leaders held weekly, evening meetings; unlike Bands of Hope, they were also able to operate in schools after the Education Act of 1870.[33] Children recited stories, read poems, learned lessons, viewed magic lantern slides, and sang songs on the humane treatment of animals. Their Declaration, like the Band of Hope pledge, focused first on personal commitment, then on social change: "We agree to do all in our power to protect animals from cruel usage, and to promote as far as we can their humane treatment" (*Advocate* 3: 95). Children could also purchase membership cards (*Advocate* 1: 37) and pins, eight-cornered stars featuring barnyard animals with the Band of Mercy label or with the lion and the unicorn image and the slogan "Be Merciful After Thy Power," designs unveiled in 1883 (*Advocate* 5: 35).

*The Band of Mercy Advocate* itself, which ran from 1879 to c. 1889, engaged children visually and thoughtfully. It featured beautiful, professional engravings of animals in wild or domestic settings throughout its pages. Each issue contained stories about children helping animals or retracting harmful behavior, news items about the movement, a fully scored song per issue, and often a tribute to a prominent animal rights leader (Catherine Smithies, the Baroness Burdett-Coutts, the Earl of Harrowby, and the Princess Beatrice). The *Advocate* also highlighted writings from children themselves, such as a poem, "The Frog," by an 11-year-old girl (2: 34) followed by a poem-writing contest (2: 38) encouraging additional contributions from children whose winning poems were then printed in a later issue (86–8). Two observations here will contrast with remarks I make later about Bands of Mercy hymns: the coverage of animal species of concern is immense (guinea pigs, toads, bees, monkeys, elephants, spiders, camels, grasshoppers, sea lions, and mountain goats), and the editors do not shrink from discussing controversial issues such as vivisection (2: 71). Secondly, many stories single out

---

[32]    Convergence between temperance and animal-welfare agitation occurred throughout the century, seen in the abstinence and vegetarian principles of the Bible Christian Church, for example. Also, the American Women's Christian Temperance Union joined forces with antivivisection groups in the 1880s to fight experimental physiology (Turner 93). Sarah Eddy's Bands of Mercy hymn book includes "Dare to do right" (No. 41), popular among Bands of Hope, and an actual temperance song, "The Water-Drinkers" (No. 40).

[33]    Thus, Bands of Mercy met in schools as well as homes or meeting places. Some states in the United States mandated Bands of Mercy education in the schools: by 1897, Maine and Washington had laws requiring "systematic teaching of kindness" to animals (at least 10 minutes each week) (Eddy 160).

boys as needing specific counsel in their interactions with animals: "Bobby and the Birds" (1: 13–15), "Peter's Pets" (1: 21–3), "Pincher's Friend" (1: 27–8), even a direct "Appeal to Boys" (1: 29), for example. Hymn coverage is less species-inclusive but more gender-inclusive.

As with Bands of Hope meetings, songs and hymns formed the staple of Bands of Mercy meetings. Bands marketed their meetings as being song-filled (as examples, see reports of the Crossgar and Southwark meetings, *Advocate* 3: 70–71). Yet in contrast to dozens of temperance song and hymn books, I have found only two music books for Bands of Mercy, the book *Songs of Happy Life* by Sarah Eddy (1897) and a collection within *Hymns for Children with Opening and Closing Services and Songs and Hymns for Bands of Mercy and of Hope* (London, 1894). The *Advocate* also featured one song per issue, such as "The Bird's Petition" (vol. 1, issue 3) and "The Song of the Bee" (vol. 1, issue 6), the same or similar songs to be found in Eddy's songbook shortly to be discussed.

*Hymns for Children*, edited by Charlotte Farrington and published by the Sunday School Association, suggests late-century secularism in many of its hymn choices and even the first pages where the epigraph is a line of poetry, not scripture. In her preface, Farrington immediately invokes her youthful audience: "Singing is the part of worship which children find most easy, natural and delightful" (iii). She also acknowledges how this book will differ from its predecessors, with evangelical Sunday school and missionary hymns quite possibly meant as her reference: "We need from time to time to re-adjust our hymns to the changes which are passing over our religious feelings themselves, to their altered relations, emphasis, temper. And we also want to appropriate more and more of those new songs which Trust and Hope are always singing, and in which our own time is so rich" (iii). Conspicuously, then, many of the "songs" are secular, although their frequently used refrain of "God's creatures" and other invocations of God keep the religious message alive (and justify their inclusion in my discussion of reformist hymns). The last section, some 100 pages, entitled "Songs and Hymns for Bands of Mercy, and of Hope" is filled with songs of this new temper, hymns which exalt peace (No. 286), in which men *and women* forerunners are honored (No. 287), and in which "it matters little if [we are] dark or fair" since all are "Beautiful faces" (No. 288). A hymn by the American co-founder of Bands of Mercy, Thomas Timmins, likewise urges children, "Of every land and race, / To join before thy face" (Hymn No. 318). This open approach to gender and race is in marked contrast to the limited scope of early-century missionary hymns.

Much like temperance and missionary hymns, though, these hymns espouse the abilities of children, despite their small size and political naiveté:

> Frail and youthful as we are,
> We would be like yonder star:
> Shining always pure and bright,
> Evermore a source of light. (v. 1, No. 283)

Despite bodily limitations, children exude a purity that can set an example for the adult population. Many of the hymns in this section provide confidence to their young singers: "If anything seems hard to do, / We should not fret or cry" (No. 284) for "There is work on earth for me, / There are sins to fight and wrongs to right" (No. 296). As Hymn No. 356, by Thomas Hincks, concludes:

> Scorn not the slightest word or deed,
>     Nor deem it void of power … (v. 1)
> A whispered word may touch the heart
>     And call it back to life…. (v. 2)

For those who work in Bands of Mercy and of Hope, the hymn reminds them

> No act falls fruitless; none can tell
>     How vast its powers may be … (v. 3)
> … God is with all that serve the right,
>     The holy, true, and free. (v. 4)

Late Victorians clearly had great faith in their small children.

Much of the "work" and "words" required of Band of Mercy members related to giving voice themselves—through song—to these "voiceless creatures" ("Band of Mercy," No. 311) and "Filling souls with pity / For the dumb and weak, / Telling all the voiceless / We for them will speak" ("Bells of Mercy," No. 309). This seemed a crucial void which singing could fill: to bring language—and aesthetically pleasing language at that—to a population of animals unable to speak in their own defense.

Furthermore, this late-century world view amends the Old-Testament mind-set as human hearts replace animal sacrifices as gifts before God:

> Lord, what offering shall we bring,
>     At thine altars when we bow?—
> Hearts, the pure, unsullied spring
>     Whence the kind affections flow. (v. 1, No. 306, by John Bowring)

Admittedly, many of these Mercy hymns directly mention only the more appealing animals—birds (No. 308) and pets (No. 302)—quite in contrast to the *Advocate*'s coverage of even insects and elephants. One moment of species diversity is in Hymn 317, "Doth God for oxen care?" to which is answered: Yes, since "His hand hath formed" it. Beasts of burden should neither be sacrificed on altars nor abused by owners. Very few hymns take up this cause for beasts of burden or divisive topics like vivisection, although quite a few indirectly allude to these larger "Cruel acts and dire oppression" (No. 311).

Unlike many of the Bands of Hope temperance hymns which suggest a militancy necessary to win converts, the Bands of Mercy hymns encourage children instead to be "tender, and trusty, and true. / Brave to the battle of life we will go" (No. 292), the very attributes needed by society in its acts towards animals. In her "Band of Mercy Anniversary" hymn (No. 313), a Mrs. Nash reiterates doing "battle for the right" and "counsel[ing] mercy kind / To all whom we may find ... man, or beast, or bird" (v. 2). Thus, "Mercy, Love, and Right" replace the battle cry (No. 313). In fact, this compassion extends beyond animals to human empathy, to "lead the blind" and "feed the poor" (No. 306), to help "all the weak and helpless" (No. 294). Post-Darwinian, these hymns allow the slippage from species to species in a non-hierarchical, expansive gesture. If Western thought has traditionally created animals and humans as binary opposites (Baker 78), Mercy hymn writers appeared comfortable in the easy break-down of such oppositions. American Bands co-founder George Angell wrote, "When the rights of dumb animals shall be protected, the rights of human beings will be safe" (qtd. in Turner 55). This acknowledgement of species' similarities would help children themselves, animal activism expanding at exactly the time that legislation to ameliorate child suffering from poverty, overwork, and illiteracy became most pronounced. Indeed, "animal protection embodied the [humanitarian] temper of the age ... [T]he compassion once lavished mainly on animals helped to found settlement houses, to abolish child labor, to enact old-age insurance, to endow medical research" (Turner 35, 139).

Given the success of Bands of Mercy in the United States, it is not surprising that the most important book for Bands of Mercy meetings was by American Sarah J. Eddy, *Songs of Happy Life for Schools, Homes, and Bands of Mercy*, published simultaneously in the United States (Providence, Rhode Island: Art and Nature Study Publishing) and England (London: George Bell and Sons) in 1897, containing a mixture of songs, poetry, and prose. The transatlantic quality of the book can be felt on every page: when recommending further publications on the subject, Eddy acknowledges books by Americans (Angell), an English collection (*Humane Educator and Reciter*, out of London), and a Canadian publication (*Aims and Objects of the Toronto Humane Society*) (165). Furthermore, poetry and hymns are by a mix of British and American writers, from Horatius Bonar and S. T. Coleridge to W. C. Bryant and James Russell Lowell; from C. F. Alexander to Lydia Maria Child and Emily Huntington Miller. Clearly it would take an international commitment to protect the world's animals.

Notably, too, many of these writers are secular poets; the title of Eddy's book reveals end-of-century secularism informing Bands of Mercy (*Songs of Happy Life*) even though "songs" naming God are very prevalent and could count as hymns. Another quality of note, which reflects changing educational practices of the late century, is a list of composition topics ("The Rights of Cats," "Examples of Animal Intelligence," 164) which, rather than being lines to memorize, or catechisms to rotely answer as often found in missionary and temperance literature, become opportunities for creativity and critical thinking.

This book is also in marked contrast to the missionary hymn books quoted earlier. For one, it moves beyond conversion and conformity to issues of acceptance, protection, and the right simply to live: "The object of Bands of Mercy is to encourage in every possible way brave, generous, noble, and merciful deeds; to protect not only the dependent races, but also every suffering human being that needs and deserves protection" (158). The rhetorical slippage is again notable: "dependent races" apparently refers to animal creatures, though "race" is technically an expression for humans. Now the marginalized could be any living creature: "A Band of Mercy would so teach children ... kindness to the fellow creature, whether it be an erring man, a suffering child, a dumb animal, or any living creature" (158). In contrast to earlier notions of "barbarianism" as a lack of (Christian) religion, the American educator Horace Mann redefines "barbarian" as an attitude of unloving superiority to which any person could succumb: "However loftily the intellect of man may have been gifted, however skillfully it may have been trained, if it be not guided by a sense of justice, a love of mankind, and a devotion to duty, its possessor is only a more splendid, as he is a more dangerous barbarian" (qtd. in Eddy 158). In fact, the Bands of Mercy make continual use of the argument that cruelty to animals begets cruelty to humans, and vice versa; Eddy, quoting Angell, reminds readers that only 12 of 2,000 criminals in American prisons at the time had ever had a pet when a child (162), that, indeed, "the roots of wars, riots, anarchy, and every form of cruelty" could be wiped out by "humane education of children" (qtd. in Eddy 162). These are complex social theories with which to engage children.

Consequently, children should be at the center of anti-cruelty reform: "all such reforms must begin with the children, because their hearts are tender, because they are impressionable, and because they indirectly educate their parents" (anonymous quote, Eddy 159). These reasons are reminiscent of Bands of Hope, and the optimism that children will positively influence the adults in their lives. Furthermore, and often in contrast to temperance ideologies, is the idea that children's innate sympathy will inspire them, not any inducement from others: "Touch a child's heart, make it to vibrate with the sufferings of another, make it to have sympathy, sympathy in its truest sense, a like suffering for every object of distress, and the child willingly goes to the rescue" (same anonymous quote 159). The quality that sets children apart, their sympathy, becomes not a mark of vulnerability but a catalyst for social reform.

Another distinguishing feature is that such songbooks had the smallest of children in mind; if Bands of Hope purported to teach children as young as five, their songs did not necessarily cater to them in style, but Eddy's book includes many simple songs extolling "The Chipmunk" (No. 31), "A Little Mouse" (No. 33), "The Grey Kitten" (68), and "The Lady-Bird" (74), with references to sharing food and shelter with such small creatures. Many are included simply for a liveliness appealing to young children: No. 30, the popular "Over in the Meadow" (lived a mother fish and her little fishes two), is subtitled "Kindergarten Play for Eleven Children," and each child is given an animal about which to sing. Also like temperance songbooks, known melodies are used with new words to provide rousing choruses: "Auld Lang Syne" now supports the lyrics "Look out o'er all the land, / Look forward, forward, never back, / And gladly lend a hand" (No. 28). The literal *action* required of these songs, marching and acting, leant inspiration to the political action that would be later required of adult advocates.

Of course, children are not blameless. The songs themselves often demonstrate children's own ability for cruelty. One hymn, "Little Hands" (No. 25), speaks directly to children in simple language and rhyme (ABCB), contrasting the charm of the little child with the harm he can do:

> Little hands and dimpled fingers
>> Are not made to pinch and tear,
> But to move in deeds of kindness,
>> And to fold in thoughts of prayer. (v. 1)

Another song, "Don't Kill the Birds" (No. 60), with its engaging tune, urges humility and responsibility, reminding its singers of the worth of these little lives which can never be replaced:

> The little birds, how sweet they sing;
>> Oh, let them joyous live,
> And never seek to take the life
>> Which you can never give. (v. 1)

In contrast to human moralizing in earlier hymns such as Watts's, many of these songs target children's malicious play as specifically causing harm or even death to animals:

> Don't rob the birds of their eggs, boys
>> 'Tis cruel and heartless and wrong;
> And remember, by breaking an egg, boys,
>> We may lose a bird with a song.
>> ("Don't Rob the Birds, Boys," No. 68, v. 1)

This hymn, notably, references boys directly, but it (and "Voice of the Helpless," to be discussed) are rare moments that gender the crimes of young children. In most cases, first-person language keeps culpability genderless, unlike many stories to be found in the *Advocate*. If anything, these middle-class hymns distance themselves from some of the class issues of temperance: that egg-hunting might be done for economic need, as Monica Flegel reminds us ("How Does Your Collar Suit Me?" 260).[34] Mercy hymns rarely acknowledge this dimension.

Flegel also points to the separation of the child from the animal by the 1890s as the National Society for the Prevention of Cruelty to Children (est. 1884) worked to distance itself from the RSPCA: "[a]lthough animals and children began the century as companions, they ended it as adversaries … to the detriment of

---

[34] For example, the RSPCA was often criticized for attacking bull-baiting and ratting, working-class sports, more vehemently than the upper-class sport of fox hunting (Harrison, *Peaceable Kingdom* 148), or of being discriminatory towards Irish Catholics when fighting their custom of maiming cattle (103).

both" (*Conceptualizing Cruelty* 72).[35] Children, it seemed, could never compete with the innocence and vulnerability of animals in the public mind-set (69). Bands of Mercy songs took quite the opposite approach, humanizing animals to create sympathy. Indeed, in contrast to earlier mission hymns which used difference to effect change, Band of Mercy songs relied on the technique of anthropomorphizing animals to prove to children that animals were not very different from themselves. In *Songs of Happy Life*, birds "play among the trees" (No. 60), are "clothed" by God (No. 50), "cry" when wounded (No. 55), and when they sing, they are really saying "I love you" (No. 66). "The Little Bird's Nest" (No. 80) reminds children that to take a bird's life robs a family of a member just as with humans:

> … I must not in play steal the birds away,
> To grieve their mother's breast.
> My mother, I know, would sorrow so,
> Should I be stolen away … (v. 1)

"Lullaby" (No. 86) makes the analogy clear by applying the lullaby motif not only to humans (v. 2) but also to the bird mother herself (v. 1):

> In your tiny nest now lying,
>     Birdie darling, go to sleep …
> Sleep now, birdie, Sleep and dream, my birdie now.
> Sleep now, my birdie, Nestle 'neath thy loving mother's wings … (v. 1)

Depicting a typical bedtime scene and personifying animals in relationships that children enjoy, these songs urge understanding, tolerance, and a desire to find common life experiences.

Though mammals such as mice and horses are addressed, most of the songs within *Songs of Happy Life* are focused on bird welfare, one entire section on Birds, in fact, so as to provide music "suitable for Bird Day" (7). This reflects late-century activism which, led by the RSPCA, the Association for the Protection of British Birds, and others, resulted in several Wild Birds Protection Acts (of 1872, 1876). By the nineties, advocates turned their attention to the slaughter of birds for women's hat fashions. One song in *Songs of Happy Life* reflects this politically sensitive issue: "The Voice of the Helpless" (No. 65) by Carlotta Perry contemplates the various birds of the air who are killed for sport and vanity (see Figure 5.2). Set to a poignant tune by L. B. Marshall in F major, this maudlin piece is much in keeping with contemporary, sentimental drawing-room ballads such as Thomas Moore's "Eveleen's Bower" (1808) or Arthur Sullivan's "The Lost Chord" (1877), both musically and emotionally. However, now the song extols "a woodland tragedy":

> 'Tis the cry of the orphan nestlings, 'Tis the wail of a bird that sings
> His song of grace in the archer's face, 'Tis the flutter of broken wings … (v. 2)

---

[35]   See her discussion of child-animal ideologies during the century and the work of the RSPCA as precursor and then competitor to the NSPCC in *Conceptualizing Cruelty* (ch. 2).

Figure 5.2    "The Voice of the Helpless," Song No. 65. From *Songs of Happy Life: For Schools, Homes, and Bands of Mercy*, compiled by Sarah J. Eddy (London, 1st edition, 1897). From Internet Archive.

If the archer, presumably adult, is the guilty party from afar, the third verse brings culpability to the very young girls who may sing this song:

> Oh! lovely, unthinking maiden, The wing that adorns your hat,
> Has the radiance rare, that God placed there, But I see in place of that,
> A mockery pitiful, deep, and sad … (v. 3)

Deepening the guilt, the fourth verse personifies this tragedy as a human one, the song now addressing a human mother who, it suggests, is not unlike an animal mother:

> Oh! Mother you clasp your darling, Close to your loving breast;
> Think of that other, that tender mother, Brooding upon her nest …
> Does no sound touch your motherhood? (v. 4)

Functional co-opting of nature for human vanity is described—"that little dead bird on your bonnet" and "the hummingbird on your velvet dress" (v. 5)—and compared to a human tragedy; the child asks her Mother to "think of that other mother brooding upon her nest" as all singers and listeners are urged to see connectedness with, not objectification of, the "other."

Children are thus forced to admit their personal culpability in a larger, societal problem: that their choice of fashion can have far-reaching moral implications. Daughters in turn school their mothers to think of those other "mothers" as children attempt the reform of adults. Notably, the second American edition (1898) has replaced "The Voice of the Helpless" with a much more innocuous song about a girl enjoying the daisies ("Marjorie") for its No. 65, one of only a few changes made between editions. I suspect the intense, guilt-laden, politically charged "The Voice of the Helpless" was too sensitive an issue for American audiences whose lucrative egret-plume trade was driving the Everglades egret nearly to extinction—until the Lacey Bird and Game Act of 1900 made such killings illegal.[36] In *Reckoning the Beast*, James Turner suggests that animal-welfare advocates turned to bird protection because it was less divisive (122) but this example proves otherwise; he furthermore argues that because birds had an important role in limiting insects, their preservation was only important for human comfort, thus suggesting anthropocentric motives (125). One could also argue a diminished anthropocentrism with these many "bird hymns." The hymns urged children to think beyond their own sport and fashion, using concern for birds as a powerful metaphor of the delicate balance of human-animal existence. Indeed, by the early twentieth century, whole species of birds had become extinct due to the unchecked hunting by humans, including the dodo (extinct by the eighteenth century), the great auk (extinct by mid-nineteenth century), and the passenger pigeon (extinct by 1913). An awareness of species preservation, then, was not at

---

[36] See PBS: Ken Burns's *National Parks: America's Best Idea*, 2010, http://www.pbs.org/nationalparks/parks/everglades/, accessed July 2013.

all an unimportant lesson to take into adulthood when facing the larger battles of animal exploitation and eradication.

Perhaps the ultimate quality shared by both animals and humans as highlighted in these songs and hymns is the innate desire for freedom. The hymn by Lydia Maria Child, "The Little Maiden and the Little Bird," discussed earlier in which a child wants to cage a bird, concludes "No, little maiden! God guides me / Over the hills and over the sea; / I will be free as the rushing air, / And sing of sunshine ev'rywhere" (No. 64). "A Cry for Liberty" (No. 56) also anthropomorphizes this as a loss of liberty in the first-person perspective of the bird:

> O Liberty! sweet Liberty! I pine and faint for thee!
> 　Fain would I burst my prison bars,
> And soar among the free! (v. 1)

The chorus becomes an apostrophe to Liberty:

> O Liberty! sweet Liberty! When wilt thou come to set me free?

Unlike temperance hymns, militarism is used more sparingly with Mercy hymns, but songs on animal liberation do call up passionate fervor for the singers with often heartrending music and lyrics. At other times, familiar, rousing tunes associated with liberty and patriotism seem appropriate: the tune to "The Star-Spangled Banner" is used for "The Watchword" (No. 107); likewise, "Glory! Hallelujah" ("Battle Hymn of the Republic") is co-opted for "Lift aloft our banner" (No. 20):

> To protect the weak and helpless, to act kindly unto all,
> Whether human or dumb creatures, high or low, or great or small,
> For right, gentleness, and justice, for each one we loudly call,
> God's Cause is marching on … (v. 2)

Despite the militarism connoted by the tunes, however, the rhetoric itself is not martial, and for the child who may take out his powerlessness upon powerless animals (Flegel, "How does" 260), Bands of Mercy urge that children march for "right, gentleness, and justice," not as to war. Consider No. 7, "We are marching from the mountains … To undo the heavy burdens" (v. 1) with "our peaceful banners" and the "pledge of Love and Mercy" (v. 3). This hymn, also found in the *Jubilee Entertainment of the New Brunswick Bands of Mercy* published for the Queen's Golden Jubilee (1887), describes the pledge resounding in greeting from the "stately homes of England" to the "wide plains of Columbia" in universal peace.

The universality of freedom is highlighted in various other hymns. The English educator W. E. Hickson's words are adapted to the tune "America"/"God Save the Queen" for No. 105, "God bless our native land" to convey powerful lyrics about inter-species' peaceful existence on earth, as in verse 3:

> And not this land alone, But be thy mercies known from shore to shore;
> Lord, make the nations see, That men should brothers be,
> And form one family, The wide world o'er.

This song does what many Reform Movement songs would do: by "appropriating the almost sacred national anthem, the song boldly rewrites the meaning of nation, and what the sacred entails in relation to the state" (Scrivener 27); that the sacred duty of Britain should be "just and righteous laws … [to] uphold the public cause" (v. 2). That is, children sing praise for what Britain will become, not what it currently is. Children are encouraged to think of freedom and peace on the larger, social scale, that "men should brothers be" (v. 3). This is made explicit by the inclusion of a poem by James Russell Lowell made into the song "True Freedom" (No. 104), which evokes the question of slavery: "If there breathe on earth a slave, Are ye truly free and brave?" (v. 1). Thus, children singing these hymns are invited to consider demanding questions of liberty, for the animal and all humanity.

Children are a major part of this reformed society. If children should ever doubt themselves—as cowslips might wonder "I'm such a tiny flower, I'd better not grow up"—Hymn No. 6 reminds children by the last verse:

> How many deeds of kindness
> A little child may do …
> How much a feeble one may do
> For others by her love. (v. 4)

And unlike early missionary hymns, one hymn asks that "God Bless the Little Children"—"Wherever they may be!" (No. 17). Reverse anthropocentricism equates children now with nature: "Flow'rs in crowded city [sic], Like birds in forest free, God bless the little children, Wherever they may be!" (v. 1). Though never naming Africa or China, children around the world are no doubt alluded to in this hymn, the natural metaphors suggesting that all living elements are "bless[ed] … Wherever they may be!" It is a commanding late-century response to early colonialist rhetoric, once again embedded in the hymn genre.

An empowered child singer emerges from this Band of Mercy ideology as exemplified in their songs and hymns. Children were also exhorted to curtail their own misguided treatment of animals and seek a more tolerant world accepting of difference, of animals but also of other people and of children themselves. Bands of Mercy hymns need to be considered within the scholarship of Victorian animal studies. Literally speaking, the songs are simple and sentimental, but metaphorically they expose the entire dilemma of one species co-opting others for its own pleasure. It is true that they fail to specifically address the many politically charged areas (and admittedly gruesome topics for song) of animal co-optation such as bull-baiting and vivisection, etc. Campaigns in prose such as those appearing in the *Advocate* are better able to discuss these topics. Yet hymns acknowledge the ability to suffer, the desire for freedom, and the right to live of all living creatures. Personifying relationships, addressing vulnerability and powerlessness, then *singing* these messages are all tactics to align children with the many animals around them. Indeed, hymns may not reflect the variety of animal species acknowledged in the *Advocate*, but hymns notably illuminate birds to become a powerful metaphor of the agency of *song* achieved by birds and children themselves, a model even for Barrett Browning's "little thrushes."

By extension, children were speaking against their own co-optation, not unlike children's own political songs.[37] When the National Society for the Prevention of Cruelty to Children was established in 1884, they would write that rather than "nobodies to the State," children deserved "secure reasonable treatment … for the extension and the enforcement of liberty" (qtd. in Horn 208).[38] By promoting welfare of other small, voiceless creatures, children may ultimately have saved themselves, for within 14 years of the first Bands of Mercy in England, the Prevention of Cruelty to, and Protection of, Children Act of 1889 was finally passed to protect children themselves from what they had been urging for the animals: "secure reasonable treatment" and "enforcement of liberty."

## Conclusion

Certainly reform was in the air in the nineteenth century, including movements to convert the world to Christianity, to curtail the nation's drinking, to amend cruel treatment of animals, and to end child abuse. These philanthropic movements were certainly well within the child's sponsorship. Even when children could not cross the ocean, their work was needed to support missions with their singing and their charity. Children approaching adulthood could correct their own desire for drink and seemed to have a positive effect on exhorting abstinence in the adults around them as well. And charity towards animals could certainly begin at home, in a child's own world as he then urged fair treatment of animals in the larger world around him, embracing relationship despite difference. As these three movements progressed, children were humbled, realizing their own fallibilities, not British superiority, even as they sought to create a world of tolerance and peace. Particularly as I have shown in contrast to fictional and prose propaganda, songs and hymns created empowered child singers to reform the adult world around them. Importantly, by supporting these causes, children indirectly emancipated themselves, too.

---

[37]  I have not found many hymns which actually addressed children's own suffering and need for child labor reform, except for those about factory children discussed in Chapter 1. The NSPCC's Children's League of Pity, formed in 1891 after the Bands of Mercy to help underprivileged children and still active today, yet did not, to my knowledge, disseminate hymns to promote its cause.

[38]  Flegel acknowledges the incredulous fact that the NSPCC (1884) was not established until 60 years after the RSPCA (1824), although she shows that abuse against children was certainly condemned by society and the law as early as the late 1780s (39–40).

# Chapter 6
# Resurrecting the Child:
# The Cult of the Deathbed, Hymns of Faith,
# and Children of Life

> That night, as Libbie lay awake, revolving the incidents of the day, she caught
> Franky's [child] voice through the open windows. Instead of the frequent moan of
> pain, he was trying to recall the burden of one of the children's hymns:—
>
> > "Here we suffer grief and pain,
> > Here we meet to part again,
> > In Heaven we part no more.
> >          Oh! That will be joyful," etc.
>
> … [T]he young child's craving for some definite idea of the land to which his inner
> wisdom told him he was hastening, had nothing in it wrong or even sorrowful for—
>
> > "In Heaven we part no more."
> >          —Elizabeth Gaskell, "Libbie Marsh's Three Eras" (1847)

The general impression of nineteenth-century children's hymnody is that of
morbid death hymns, where "death is described vividly and dramatically,"
often with "dark and pessimistic warnings" (Tamke 84, 87). I want to confront
this impression directly in this chapter, acknowledging its veracity but also its
incompleteness. Undeniably, children died in horribly high numbers throughout
the nineteenth century, and at one end of the century, preachers morosely prepared
all children for their potential fate while on the other end of the century, writers
waxed sentimental over fictional children's death-scenes. Children were caught
up in what has been called the "cult of the death-bed" (Knight 50) and "the age
of the beautiful death" (Ariès, *The Hour of Our Death* 409), as both mourner
and as object of mourning. However, I will not end this book with eschatological
debate only but with life-affirming energy. Indeed, children showed an intense
zest for life through their hymn singing, as I have shown in previous chapters.
Though fiction writers and hymn writers were inclined to paint sentimental
portraits of children on their deathbeds—Franky, above, joins Little Nell in *Old
Curiosity Shop* and Helen in *Jane Eyre* and many other "holy deaths" of children
in nineteenth-century literature—these are yet in contrast to the living vitality of
children of the era, shown in children's approach to hymn singing. Some of that
vitality resides in the hymns themselves, offering comfort and joy amidst harsh
doctrine, denominational difference, even death itself.

   We see some of these conditions in this excerpt from Gaskell's short story
"Libbie Marsh's Three Eras" (39). Here, little Franky, who is crippled from birth,

lies awake singing "Here we suffer grief and pain." The scene is complex in many ways. It is essentially Franky's deathbed scene in that the section following opens with his funeral a few months later. His neighbor-friend, Libbie, hears his plaintive singing and recalls their conversation earlier in the day while enjoying an afternoon at Dunham woods:

> "Libbie, is Dunham like Heaven? The people here are as kind as angels; and I don't want Heaven to be more beautiful than this place. If you and mother would but die with me, I should like to die, and live always there." She had checked him, for she feared he was impious; but now the young child's craving for some definite idea of the land to which his inner wisdom told him he was hastening, had nothing in it wrong or even sorrowful, for

> "In Heaven we part no more." (39)

The scene is sentimentalized in the young child's innate awareness of his own demise, and religious in its obvious acceptance of the heaven to which he will go. Yet Gaskell's liberal, Unitarian beliefs are evident in that hell is not mentioned and Jesus does not preside over heaven. Other Unitarian hallmarks include the focus on earthly suffering to achieve heavenly peace.[1] Instead, this heaven can only be grasped in the worldly terms of a child. Franky's own earthly suffering, both in health and poverty, takes on greater meaning with the hymn lyrics, "here we suffer grief and pain." Reference to "the burden" of the hymn also takes on a dual meaning, for "burden" could refer to the chorus as well as the burden Franky is carrying, a term which Gaskell uses in reference to Franky's impoverished mother earlier (32). Too, its verse about the pain of parting is especially poignant as he makes clear his yearning to take Libbie and his mother to heaven with him. That is, his human relationships tie him to earth more earnestly than desire for eternal wholeness and bliss.

The intertextual reference to this hymn also complicates the picture. "Here we suffer grief and pain" was an extremely popular hymn throughout the century, included in 24% of children's hymn books. (Recall that it was also referenced by Thomas Hardy as the Sunday school song sung by the Durbeyfield children, a scene used in my Chapter 1 epigraph). Written by Thomas Bilby, the hymn was published in 1832 in his *Infant School Teachers' Assistant* publication. Its lyrics simply and repetitively underscore the grief of this world in contrast to the joys of the next: "Here we suffer grief and pain … In heaven we part no more."

---

[1]    Unitarian eschatological beliefs included the belief in a future life, of a corporeal body in that life, of a paradise (not of heaven but of a re-paradised earth) of human bliss or of a corrective suffering ("hell") for the wicked who may ultimately achieve bliss. Many denied Christ's divinity, as did Gaskell (she wrote that Jesus Christ, "however divine a being he was he was *not* God," qtd. in Webb, "The Gaskells" 156). See Geoffrey Rowell, *Hell and the Victorians*; Timothy Larson, *A People of One Book*; and R. K. Webb's "Quakers and Unitarians" and "The Gaskells as Unitarians" for more about Unitarian doctrine and other religious doctrine I will utilize in this chapter.

Bilby's version of heaven, though, is more overtly Christian than Gaskell's, invoking Jesus directly in verse 2:

> All who love the Lord below,
> When they die to heaven will go,
>     And sing with saints above. (v. 2, Hymn 238, *282 Hymns and Melodies*)

The "Saviour we shall see / Exalted on His throne," Bilby points out too (v. 4), a conviction lacking in the lines quoted by Gaskell. As Infant School teacher himself, Bilby spells out what Gaskell seemed to imply about the special place for children in heaven, that "Little children will be there, Who have sought the Lord by prayer" (v. 3). By the last verses, Bilby's hymn exudes the joy of heaven which Franky seeks: "O! how happy we shall be!" (v. 4) and "There we all shall sing with joy / And eternity employ / In praising Christ the Lord" (v. 5).

The action of singing, which replaces Franky's "frequent moan of pain," is confirmed as that which he may do forever in heaven. And, indeed, the tune of the hymn would allow him the opportunity to dance there, too, unfettered by bodily handicaps. The anonymous tune belies the severity of a grieving world, being surprisingly "joyful" (the tune name, as it came to be called) in order to emphasize the joy of heaven. Often in E major, its 6/8 time gives it a lilt that is infectious and, no doubt, accounts in part for the hymn's popularity. Opening with a simple two-bar melody continuing one step up in the third measure, the sequence breaks in the fifth measure—"In heaven we part no more"—where emphasis is now given by a new melodic line. This verse ends on the dominant chord, but is immediately resolved by the tonic chord opening the chorus, symbolically affirming the joy to be found in heaven. The chorus, longer in fact than the verse itself, focuses on the glory of heaven, with downbeats emphasizing every "joyful" in the lines:

> O, that will be joyful!
> Joyful, joyful, joyful!
> O that will be joyful!
> When we meet to part no more.

Spritely and simple, the hymn appeals to children though it addresses "all" and "we" in its appealing verses. As John Julian wrote in 1907, "Although suited in sentiment more to the aged than the young, yet mainly through the tune to which it is set and the refrain, it has become a very popular hymn with children, and is in extensive use in Sunday-schools" (513). Strikingly, Gaskell cuts off right as Franky begins what was the true "burden" ("chorus") of the hymn. Yet she places it after possibly the most joyous day in Franky's life as he and his friends enjoy the Whitsuntide sun in Dunham woods, the joy coming from earthly events. But, too, this hymn seemed to appeal to children in their earthly play and learning.

It is exactly these tensions between suffering and joy, death and life, passivity and agency which I would like to explore in this chapter. Laurence Lerner's *Angels and Absences: Child Deaths in the Nineteenth Century* (1997) thoroughly examines the social and literary portrayals of child-deaths across the century. For these he borrows from Structuralist theory the terms "semiotic" and "semantic" to define the power of the text to create emotions (semiotic) and the emotions generated by knowing the referent is genuine (semantic): in other words, sentimental rhetoric in contrast to "real suffering" (20–22). Elizabeth Gaskell creates the semiotics of death through her portrait of Franky, the semantics paralleling this portrait being the reality of her only son's death in infancy in 1845, two years prior to the story's publication. Hymns particularly find themselves in an intermediate place in that they are manifested textually as a fictional, semiotic narrative (or within another narrative) but become semantic expressions sung by very real mourners like Gaskell. An awareness of both the semiotics and the semantics—the outward and inward meaning of death, if you will—of the cult of the deathbed will inform this study.

The cult of the deathbed stretched across the century. This will be shown in Part I where I consider early-century written portraits of children's "holy deaths" and then the later-century, sentimental cult of postmortem portraits, visual images of the deathbed, and literary portraits by Charles Dickens and others used to produce immense sympathy for the pure child.

If nineteenth-century society had become enraptured with child deathbed tableaux, as found in literature and culture, then hymn books are both complicit and more complicated, as I explore in Part II. Surely these hymns insisted upon children's sins, taught them to shun joys of this world, and prepared them for death, often in very humorless and maudlin terms. Yet this paper takes a revisionist look at these hymns, suggesting ways in which nineteenth-century hymns, especially of late century, are joyful, even exuberant in their focus. A close look at the children's hymn tradition will show hymns of death to be more nuanced, exuding conflicting emotions of severity, fear, comfort, and joy. Hymn ideologies were never constant, revealing once again an undulating century of theological upheaval, as hymns on hell revert to those focused on the earthly loss, the century closing with hymns of heaven. Partly this follows the century's theological shift from focus on the Atonement to that of the Incarnation, Jesus' death to His life (as Boyd Hilton argues in *The Age of Atonement*); certainly it follows the gradual lightening of religion by the end of the century.

Yet, children themselves were *not* ready to die, despite portrayals by adults. They were not always ready to imbibe adults' didactic theologies, either. It is this central conflict that I wish to resurrect and deconstruct in Part III of this chapter: in spite of adults often depicting children as "dead" and thus more controllable, children exert a powerful agency. Lacking the in-depth child commentary, interviews, and videos we could conjure up as proof in this century, I must rely instead on other proof: the delightful parodies of hymns that children wrote, their jottings and marginalia found within hymn books themselves, and, when available, the commentary on hymns, on life and death, that children wrote in their journals. Hymns are thus a conduit between the reality of death they sentimentally or doctrinally addressed and the very lively children who sang them.

## Part I
## Dying Holy, Dying Still:
## Child-Death in Life and Culture

There is no doubt that the nineteenth century was a deadly era for children. Unaided by modern medicine, exacerbated by urban crowdedness, epidemic diseases ravaged: measles, whooping cough, diphtheria, scarlet fever, smallpox, and especially tuberculosis. Pamela Horn cites contemporary reports that between 1860 and 1879, half of deaths from diphtheria were children under 5, while whooping cough caused two-fifths of all deaths under age 5 (*Victorian and Edwardian Schoolchild* 69).[2] Due to polluted, unsanitary, and crowded conditions in cities, many urban children died: half of all deaths in the industrialized counties of Cheshire, Durham, and Lancashire in the 1890s were children under 5 (Horn 70). High casualties existed in London for the same reasons: 160 out of every 1,000 born would die before age 1 in the 1890s (Davin 17). Lerner reminds us, too, of the many child-deaths in factories and mines, both from accidents and overwork (12–13). Yet death affected all classes: even the young Princess Charlotte (granddaughter to George III and only child to the Prince Regent) died shortly after giving birth to a stillborn son (see Lerner's extended commentary 1–11). It is equally astounding to realize how many authors and well-known Victorian persons experienced the death of a child throughout the century: Josephine Butler, Margaret Oliphant, Rudyard Kipling, S.T. Coleridge, Percy Bysshe Shelley, Alfred Lord Tennyson, George Henry Lewes, George McDonald, Mrs. Henry Wood, and, of course, Elizabeth Gaskell. Many, many more nameless parents grieved over the loss of a child. Some scholars suggest that mourning a child was peculiar to the nineteenth century; that parents of earlier centuries were so immune to early death as to become indifferent or resigned (Philippe Ariès, Lawrence Stone). Though this seems hard to fathom, both Zelizer and Lerner nevertheless claim a "dramatic revolution in mourning children" in the nineteenth century (Zelizer 25), both in America and England. Yet Lerner points out that statistics were no higher, percentage-wise, than in previous centuries and were clearly declining overall late in the century with medical advancements such as the smallpox vaccination and the Vaccination Act of 1853 (159–61). Zelizer argues that child-deaths led to social pressure for more medical research, sanitary improvement, and better parenting, to likewise lessen mortality (27–8).

If the death rate of children was waning, then, it does beg the question why the mantle of mourning was escalating. Certainly the late-century Romantic cult of the child was responsible in large part for the sentimentalized portraits that emerged

---

[2]   For facts and commentary on real and fictional child-deaths, see Pamela Horn, ch. 3: "Health and Welfare," *The Victorian and Edwardian Schoolchild* (1989); Anna Davin, *Growing Up Poor: Home, School and Street in London 1870–1914* (1996); Jacqueline Banerjee, "Dying Young: A Social Problem and Its Repercussions in the Victorian Novel" (1992); and Laurence Lerner, *Angels and Absences: Child Deaths in the Nineteenth Century* (1997).

in literature and culture: virtue is inherent in youthfulness so that youth must die to preserve that virtue (Grylls 136). So was the general attraction of the deathbed in the nineteenth century which became "an opportunity to witness a spectacle that is both comforting and exalting … [yet] this death is no longer death, it is an illusion of art," writes Ariès (*The Hour of Our Death* 473). The "deathbed topos" as Lerner refers to it (129) became extremely prolific by mid-century. One characteristic was that of "sentimentality," "a sadness that has lost all unpleasantness and [has] become a warm glow" (Lerner 183); "[f]or the reader of a novel, there is no substratum of actual grief that is being rendered more gentle and delightful: his response is equal to his reading of the text" (188). Though sentimentality is purported to encourage sensitivity to others, it is, importantly, "no longer death" nor "actual grief."

"Holy dying" stories find themselves an intermediary in that they fictionalize what, in most cases, were true stories of a child's death. Joyful Death portraits stemmed from the tradition inaugurated by James Janeway's *A Token for Children: Being an Exact Account of the Conversion, Holy and Exemplary Lives, and Joyful Deaths of Several Young Children* (1672). With poignant and powerful stories before them of even the youngest of children embracing their Saviour before their deaths, Janeway and his imitators hoped to convert many lost souls who might read these testimonies. The tradition continued well into the nineteenth century. Consider stories of holy deaths from *Brief Memoirs of Remarkable Children, Whose Learning or Whose Piety is Worthy the Imitation of those Little Boys and Girls Who Desire to Improve their Minds, to Increase in Wisdom, and to Grow in Favour with God and Man*, Collected by a Clergyman of the Church of England (London, 1822). Almost all are portraits of young children, both boys and girls, who were prodigies in their godly behavior and religious wisdom … and all die early. For instance, Little Nanette died on July 9, 1819 at the age of 5 years and 5 months. Her final year is recorded by her mother in order to "have in my possession a review of my dear little girl's life" (67). As she writes:

> I had told her, either that day or the one previous, that she now would soon be in heaven, when she exclaimed with animation, "Oh I am glad of it! there is no more pain or sorrow there." She slept more than usual that night … About six, I suddenly awoke, and looking at her, found her eyes open, but a great change was visible in her countenance; I asked her some question, when, with the greatest of difficulty, she slowly articulated—No!—Now the long dreadful moment was arrived! I could only lean on God for support to go through the agonizing scene that followed: she fixed her eyes on me while she had any remaining sense; but severe were her last struggles … I was constrained to cry out, "Lord, then let her suffer as long as thou wilt"; when immediately a great calm came over my mind; I sat down at the foot of the bed to wait his will, and in a few minutes she breathed her last! The solemn stillness of the presence of the Lord was around us, and I felt as if we were surrounded by ministering angels, come to bear her gentle, happy spirit, to that Redeemer whom she had so constantly and so ardently longed to behold in his glory! (101–2)

The scene is charged with pathos as the mother watches her daughter breathe her last, but she is sure to give edifying moments of divine presence, complete with "ministering angels" and assurances that Nanette's spirit is being taken upward to her Redeemer. One may point to these semiotic gestures of religiosity and sentiment, but the scene must remain a semantic one: a mother is witness to the real death of her child.

Nanette's mother positions her tale within the tradition of memorials to the dead, whether of words or stone; to make the life lost both tangible and public. With the widespread use of daguerreotype photography by the 1850s at the same time that the cult of the deathbed was waxing (Linkman 8), honoring the dead child became both public and visual. Parents who had lost a child desperately attempted to claim an image before interment, hiring daguerreotypists and later photographers to take postmortem portraits. In her reading of this practice in American nineteenth-century culture, Karen Sánchez-Eppler recognizes the staged and static nature of these tableaus. Given the slow exposure time of cameras in this era, it was nearly impossible to capture a sharp portrait of a live, wiggling child, such that, ironically, usually the clearest photographs of children were of them completely immobile in death: "photography not only imitates death, but requires a deathlike stillness" (116). Ultimately, a dead child is more easily controlled, by camera and by the adult world. This is painfully obvious in a photograph in Audrey Linkman's *Photography and Death*, titled *Two Children Standing to Attention beside a Dead Sibling Laid out in a Parlour*, c. 1910 (56); the crispest image of the three is the deceased sister's while we can hardly make out the blurred features of the squirming living brother.

We have these photographs, in fact, because of the entire commercial postmortem photography industry that rested upon, even changed the outward expressions of, grief and mourning for the child. Sánchez-Eppler concludes: "its ways of wielding the trauma of children's deaths, [was] a means of mediating between the private mourner and a commercial world … capable of circulating emotion" (148). Given that holy death tales also circulated sentiment, this is perhaps not unique to postmortem portraits, but suggests the acceptance and propagation of sentiment thrust outward into the larger society for commercial gain of a child's final, and most intimate, moment.

Though deathbed stories, postmortem portraits, mourning clothing, tombstones, wreaths of hair, and other ritualized emblems of mourning operated for adults as well, the unique position of the dead child in cultural acts of bereavement cannot be denied, especially in visual images. Consider a magic lantern slide to accompany the famed Victorian hymn, "Abide with me" (see Figure 6.1). As discussed in Chapter 3, this was a widely popular hymn only metaphorically about death ("fast falls the eventide") and not at all descriptive of a child's death specifically, being written in first person ("Lord with me abide"). Its Christian comfort at death is, however, clear: "Hold Thou Thy Cross before my closing Eyes; / Shine through the gloom, and point me to the skies" (v. 5; for the score, see Figure 3.4 in Chapter 3). It was used at many public (adult) funerals throughout the century, including that for Baptist leader Adoniriam J. Gordon and William Howard Taft (McCutchan 502–3). Yet, one will note that in the magic lantern slide of the hymn with "life models," the "deceased" is a young girl, perhaps 5

Figure 6.1    "Abide with me" magic lantern slide. Courtesy of the Kent
Museum of the Moving Image.

or 6 years of age, in a colored recreation of the deathbed. The scene exemplifies
the cult of the deathbed, excessive in the flowers and greenery strewn about the
bed and chairs. Clearly the room is a middle-class parlor with its rich drapery,
wallpaper, ornately framed pictures, and vase visible in the left corner. Obviously
a black-and-white photograph has been colored—even the girl's hair is tinted,
much as a dead child's features would have been "fixed" for a postmortem portrait.
But the "ghost" of her black-and-white self is still evident, and it is ironic that
the parents' black clothes are some of the few items not colored to be in keeping
with the requisite black mourning clothes. The further staged-ness of the scene
is evident in that the mother bends unnaturally towards the husband, with a right
arm resting in an uncomfortable position. As Julia Thomas notes of the generic
child-death image, "Such scenes are all too familiar in Victorian literary and visual
culture. It could even be said that they were done to death" ("Happy Endings" 79).
Examining various images from periodicals and books, she further demonstrates
how *many* deathbed images of the period, though purporting to address the divine,
yet become caught up in details of the earthly domestic (93). This magic lantern
image thus follows a very common trend where no religious icons (cross, angel

icons) are to be found: here, only the words of the song will presumably register the Christian message.

Literary writers enter into this public cult of the deathbed, fueling it throughout the century: various children die in Mary Sherwood's *The History of the Fairchild Family* (1818), Barry Lyndon's 9-year-old son is killed in a horse-riding accident in William Makepeace Thackeray's *Barry Lyndon* (1844), the pious Helen Burns dies in Charlotte Brontë's *Jane Eyre* (1847), Linton Heathcliff dies an early death in *Wuthering Heights* (1847), various working-class children succumb to their impoverished circumstances in Elizabeth Gaskell's *Mary Barton* (1848), and Flora's baby dies in Charlotte Yonge's *The Daisy Chain* (1856). Gradually the sentimentality and sensation intensified, as in Mrs. Henry Wood's *East Lynne* (1861) where Isabel must watch her son Willie die without his knowing her identity as his mother. Late in the century, ironic child-deaths pervade the fiction of Thomas Hardy: the illegitimate baby Sorrow of Tess, dying for her mother's sin (*Tess of the d'Urbervilles*, 1891), and the suicide-murder of Father Time and sibling, "Done because we are too menny" in *Jude the Obscure* (1895).[3] What Karen Sánchez-Eppler concludes about American culture could be said of the British as well: "Dying is what children do most and do best in the literary and cultural imagination of [the] nineteenth century" (101). Ultimately, children must die in order to retain their child-like purity. Or, as James Kincaid notes, "The good child is patient, quiet, submissive; the best child is eternally so: that overstates the case—only slightly" (234).

Within a religious context, the story of Abraham's willingness to sacrifice his son Isaac as the paschal lamb looms large (Genesis 22:5–8), but the Father's supreme sacrifice of the Son at the Passion set a formidable model for Christians henceforth. In the nineteenth century, the cult of the child first raised up the child, then sacrificed it for the sins of the century. Clearly, many literary children die for a "sin": the sin of the child's own doing, such as Augusta Noble who plays with fire despite parental warnings and is burned to death, teaching strict Evangelical discipline, in *The Fairchild Family*. For the older child like Maggie Tulliver, it is the sin of leaving innocent childhood and growing up into a sexualized being; her death literally returns her to a de-sexualized union with her brother Tom as they drown together in each other's arms. Other times the child dies for the sins of others, such as Little Eva who dies as sacrifice to the horrors of slavery in *Uncle Tom's Cabin*. As Sommerville describes, "If the attraction of their innate innocence is not sufficient to work a change in adults, then the children may sicken and die as a punishment on them" (173).

Dickens, however, is legendary for such scenes of sentiment and sacrifice: Paul Dombey in *Dombey and Son*, Little Nell in *The Old Curiosity Shop*, Jo in *Bleak*

---

[3]  See Lerner's chs. 3–4 for thorough contemplations on "methods by which pathos is aroused and the reasons for its popularity, and with the religious and political significance of the topos" in Victorian fiction (129). See also Jacqueline Banerjee, "Dying Young: A Social Problem and its Repercussions in the Victorian Novel," who explores "the literary skills, sympathetic imagination and challenging spirit with which a number of the Victorian novelists approached this disturbing subject" (37).

*House*, even lesser-remembered death's like Lucie Manette's son in *A Tale of Two Cities*. Undoubtedly Dickens is making social commentary about the poverty of children, and also the co-optation of them—such as Oliver Twist used as staged mourner at funerals—but the pathos and frequency with which Dickens presents child-deaths, even of the middle classes, suggests "some deep-seated association, in Dickens's fiction, perhaps the Victorian mind, between children and death" (Lerner 118). Further, this anxiety for a child's vulnerability seems precisely because Dickens divides adults from children "whose purity is either destroyed by contact with adult culture or helps to regenerate it" though often it kills the child (Gubar 8).[4]

Most prominent of the sacrificial children is Little Nell who, it could be argued, dies for the sins of her grandfather and society at large. Dickens's *The Old Curiosity Shop* (1840–1841) contains the quintessential deathbed tableau, whose anticipated death of Little Nell brought swarms of Americans to the New York wharf where the boat bearing the next installment of the series was docking, all to see if Little Nell had really died. In this novel, the child bears the brunt of a weakened, demented grandfather who cannot protect her childhood from the strains of poverty, social stigma, and persecution from the evil Quilp, then further drains their resources with his gambling addiction. Her death is thus both a relief from her earthly trials, and the hardest trial yet for the grandfather, and possibly all readers, as shown in this extended excerpt:

> For she was dead. There, upon her little bed, she lay at rest. The solemn stillness was no marvel now.
>
> She was dead. No sleep so beautiful and calm, so free from trace of pain, so fair to look upon. She seemed a creature fresh from the hand of God, and waiting for the breath of life; not one who had lived and suffered death. …
>
> She was dead. Dear, gentle, patient, noble Nell, was dead. Her little bird—a poor slight thing the pressure of a finger would have crushed—was stirring nimbly in its cage; and the strong heart of its child-mistress was mute and motionless for ever….
>
> The old man held one languid arm in his, and had the small hand tight folded to his breast, for warmth. It was the hand she had stretched out to him with her last smile—the hand that had led him on through all their wanderings. Ever and anon he pressed it to his lips; then hugged it to his breast again, murmuring that it was warmer now; and as he said it, he looked, in agony, to those who stood around, as if imploring them to help her.
>
> She was dead, and past all help, or need of it. The ancient rooms she had seemed to fill with life, even while her own was waning fast—the garden she had tended—the eyes she had gladdened—the noiseless haunts of many a thoughtful

---

4    Other authors who discuss this child-death fetish of Dickens include Grylls 135–7; Sommerville 170–73; and Banerjee 26–8.

hour—the paths she had trodden as it were but yesterday—could know her no more.

> "It is not," said the schoolmaster, as he bent down to kiss her on the cheek, and gave his tears free vent, "it is not on earth that Heaven's justice ends. Think what it is compared with the World to which her young spirit has winged its early flight, and say, if one deliberate wish expressed in solemn terms above this bed could call her back to life, which of us would utter it!" (652)

Four times the narrator must repeat the anguished phrase "She is dead." Other topoi of sentiment proliferate: her grandfather's desperate hope that her hand will still be warm, reminders of the places she will never haunt again, amazed recognition that her own bird still lives while she is dead, recollections of the kindness she gave to others in life. Her death is given as the final sacrifice for her grandfather, and she prepares a path for him with "the hand that had led him on, through all their wanderings." Though the narrator refers to Nell's departure from "the hand of God," he makes no mention of her return to God; instead the last—and only—Christian words come from the mouth of the schoolmaster who reminds all hearers (including the readers) of a Heaven whose joys are so great that no living person "could call her back." Purporting a Christian message rejoicing in the final, heavenly destination, most of the scene is yet a sentiment to the life left behind, forfeited for others. As a result, the narrative ends for Nell. Moreover, Nell's purity separates her from the adults, shown most notably by the fact that in the original illustration of her death (by George Cattermole) Nell lies alone as per Dickens's request (J. Thomas, "Happy Endings" 91). As Ginsburg suggests of Little Nell, "when the child is defined by an innocence that shields and separates it from the adult social world, it cannot grow up" (91).[5] Or, most disturbingly, her sexual interest to other men must be arrested by death, "the blooming child out of pornography, caught by death just as that bloom is at its height and preserved like freeze-dried corn" writes Kincaid (239), death both protecting and preserving her sexuality from the voyeurism of men at her deathbed and all readers.

Three distinct features of the cult of the child-deathbed emerge from the above analyses. One is that literary deathbed scenes, despite being conceived as part of a narrative, rarely engage in the "next chapter" so suffused are they with earthly sentiment. Visual images of the deathbed are similarly saturated with sentimental domestic details at the expense of overt Christian messages. Secondly, is that the deathbed itself becomes a powerful metaphor to subdue and separate children who can only be captured by the photographic process by their stasis, must always exist apart because of their purity—and become staged props for both reasons.

---

[5]    For other studies which resonate and amplify some of these themes, see: Wilfred P. Dvorak about Nell's sacrifice for the avarice of her grandfather (65–6); Sarah Winter who contrasts OCS, and Nell's death, specifically, with earlier didactic literature (45–6); Catherine Robson about Nell's centrality yet vulnerability as a representative "ideal girl" (197ff.); Michal Peled Ginsburg who analyzes the child-adult binary (90–94); and Tyson Stolte who addresses Dickens's unconvincing nods to a spiritual heaven at Nell's death (201–2).

Images become *of* the dead child, not *for* them. Finally is the very real fact that many children died or witnessed death during the Victorian era.

Hymns, as part of the cultural fabric, reflect some of these trends. However, they, by their very definition, avoid many others. For one, as reflecting Christian eschatology, they consistently offer to children a narratological next chapter, though that might include, especially reflecting early-century, Evangelical-based theology, a fiery hell. This judgment was nevertheless reserved for all, adults as well as children, with no sacrificial requisite, no children staged or set apart. Nonetheless, hymn writers reveal their humanity and, despite a reputation for writing morbid, chilling or sentimental jingles, frequently reflect on their earthly losses even as heaven calls, a trend I note especially of mid-century hymns. Finally, hymns could assure children of a heaven which, by late century, seemed almost guaranteed to them. Despite saccharine portrayals of heaven, it was also a place that resonated with the voices and activity of singing children—not their stasis, or staged-ness. Simply speaking, the hymn literature changed from hell- to earth- to heaven-focused, with noteworthy nuances within all hymns. In a world in which death was omnipresent, children wrestled with questions and apprehensions, as their writings demonstrate. Yet almost as frequently the record suggests hymns' ability to console and even energize. After all, the child would be actively singing them.

## Part II
## Fearing the Fire, Grieving the Life, Rejoicing in Heaven:
## Child-Death in Children's Hymn Books

Given the reality of death during the century, it is understandable that children themselves shared confusion and sadness about the losses around them. Their journals show this. Lady Adela Capel of Cassiobury, writing a diary at ages 13 and 14 (1841–1842), clearly lived a life of leisure and thus amused herself with the rabbits and deer on the estate. But when one of her fawns, named Fairy, died, Adela's entry for that date (Wednesday, November 17, 1841), betrays her utter despair: "In the afternoon went to the Farm—Fatal!—News!—Poor Fairy was—Dead! It [was] a sort of Distemper that she has died of. Alas! Alas!" Again on Friday the 19th, she writes, "Oh Fairy, thou love of my heart, why have you left me," sentiments further dwelt upon in a self-composed seven-stanza poem in which she writes as "Her now sad and disconsolate Mistress" (*A Victorian Teenager's Diary* 45). Similarly, Leah Manning, writing in her autobiography, *A Life for Education*, remembers her 1890s childhood and her great confusion over death and the afterlife, as during funerals:

> I was not emotionally involved with the mourners, shedding their tears into black-bordered handkerchiefs. It was the dead, being lowered into the black earth, about whom I had an overwhelming curiosity. I had been taught that on the Judgment Day they would rise uncorrupted, either to enter into the glory of the Lord, or to be cast into hell fire to burn everlastingly. I had once experimented with a pet kitten which had died and been buried with full rites under our walnut tree. A week later I dug it up. It certainly wasn't uncorrupted.... (22)

Both Adela and Leah struggle with the deaths of beloved animals but also the concept of death and teachings of the church. An American girl, Caroline Richards, records in her 1850s diary the tragic accident of a beloved Sunday school teacher, which prompts a deep reflection on the transience of life:

> August 30, 1858—Rev. Mr. Tousley was hurt to-day by the falling of his barn which was being moved, and they think his back is broken and if he lives he can never sit up again. Only last Sunday he was in Sunday School and had us sing in memory of Allie Antes:
>
> > "A mourning class, a vacant seat,
> > Tell us that one we loved to meet
> > Will join our youthful throng no more,
> > 'Till all these changing scenes are o'er."
>
> And now he will never meet with us again and the children will never have another minister all their own.... (103)

That he who commemorated one death can be so quickly fallen himself puzzles Caroline. Significantly, it is the singing of a hymn (which she can quote verbatim) which ties the two tragedies together... and perhaps brings some comfort.

What these three vignettes suggest, then, is that children, surrounded by death themselves, struggled with the meaning of life and death. It was therefore not morbid to present hymns to them which tackled these weighty issues head-on. Undoubtedly what hymns offered to children were consolation and clarity of a Christian kind. They offered children Christian answers to "the next chapter": eschatological principles in the traditional Four Last Things—heaven, hell, death, and judgment.[6] Recognizing that hymns were a central way to convey this theology, preachers, parents, and Sunday school teachers disseminated hymns liberally, as we have seen. Although the Christian doctrines of death, judgment, heaven, and hell will appear in various guises throughout these hymns, I will suggest three basic trends evinced in these hymn books, with shifting emphasis. Firstly, carrying over from eighteenth-century Calvinism, early-century hymns convey a fearful portrait of everlasting Hell still used to scare the child into a dutiful submission. By mid-century, hell's fires diminish as hymns now focus on the moment of Death, with the allure of the earthly life the child is leaving creeping into these verses. By late century, hymn books have now turned to focus almost solely on the

---

[6] "Indeed there were few issues which figured more prominently in the nineteenth-century theological debate," argues Geoffrey Rowell in *Hell and the Victorians* (1), who considers denominational distinctions (Unitarians, Tractarians, etc.) throughout his study. Michael Wheeler, in his eschatological study, *Death and the Future Life in Victorian Literature and Theology*, explores the variety of struggles that theologians, writers, and other voices of the era brought to bear on these concepts, doing less with denominational difference or historical trends. See also Frances Knight's *The Nineteenth-Century Church and English Society*.

perfection of Heaven, bright songs and catchy choruses not only inviting children to sing for joy but suggesting that heaven is inhabited almost exclusively by such singing children.

One can look simply at the sections of hymn books labeled in their Contents to begin to see this shift: early hymn books contain such sections as "Of Departure out of this Life; of the last Judgment; and of the Glory of the saved" (*Hymns for Children*, 1797); "Death and Judgment" (*Children's Hymn Book*, 1811; *Sunday School Union Hymn Book*, 1835); and "Death, Resurrection and Ascension" (Gadsby's *Selection of Hymns for Sunday Schools*, 1835). Depending on denomination, this focus would continue into the 1870s and beyond: "The Fall of Man," "Sin," and "Death and Judgment" in the *United Methodist Free Churches* (1870) and "Death and Burial" in the Anglican *Children's Hymn Book* (1878). Most mid-century books, however, looked both to hell and heaven: "Death and the Grave" and "Heaven" (*A Book of Praise for Home and School*, 1869), "The Life to Come" in the *Methodist Sunday School Hymn Book* (1879), while many late-century hymn books dispensed with a section on death and hell altogether in favor of "Heaven" only, as was true of *Golden Bells* (1890), *282 Hymns and Melodies* (1893), and *Hymns and Bible Songs for Sunday School* (1895). Frances Knight, in *The Nineteenth-Century Church and English Society*, concurs: "Hell as a literal reality had a greater prominence in the period roughly between 1800 and 1850 than it had earlier or later, and a greater attention was given to heaven from the 1860s" (48).

A close look at the hymns themselves will bear out these general trends. As discussed in Chapter 2, eighteenth-century Calvinist theology, which endorsed a hell-or-heaven destination for disembodied souls, undergirded much of Isaac Watts's theology as found in *Divine and Moral Songs* [1715]) even as he rejected Predestination.[7] Indeed, Watts polarizes a heaven and hell very much in order to counsel morality to his youthful readers. He describes a heaven "beyond the sky ... of joy and love" where "holy children when they die" go. In contrast, hell is vividly painted:

> There is a dreadful hell,
>     And everlasting pains;
> There sinners must with devils dwell
>     In darkness, fire, and chains. (v. 2, Song XI, "Heaven and Hell")

Clear demarcations are made, associating good behavior with heaven, and sinful actions with hell. Significantly, he does not differentiate between adult and child sin; all will meet their just fate. But Watts uses his hymns to prepare children for their own very possible death, in his Song X: "There is an hour when I must die, /

---

[7]    Watts was the son of a Puritan deacon and later joined a Congregationalist church, a denomination which emerged from Puritanism. Both employed Calvinist doctrine. John Calvin (1509–1564) had prioritized the doctrine of Predestination, in which only certain Elect were destined to enter heaven, although their moral living was still vital. Watts rejected this doctrine, however.

Nor do I know how soon 'twill come; / A thousand children, young as I, / Are call'd by death to hear their doom" (v. 4). Similarly, the Methodist doctrine of late eighteenth-century adhered to a theology of grace and punishment, of heaven and hell, from which the child was not exempt, as in this description of hell found in Charles Wesley's *Hymns for Children, and Others of Riper Years* (1763): "We shall with many stripes be beat / The sorest judgment feel / And of all wicked children meet / The hottest place in hell" (Hymn 48, v. 8). Wesley's incredibly popular "Jesus, lover of my soul" (in 14% of children's hymn books), though full of Methodist sentiments of sin ("False and full of sin I am," v. 3) and necessary grace ("Plenteous grace with Thee is found," v. 4), reminds all singers, children and adults alike, however, that Jesus, like a lover, provides full comfort:

Jesu, Lover of my soul,
    Let me to Thy bosom fly,
While the nearest waters roll,
    While the tempest still is high:
Hide me, O my Saviour, hide,
    Till the storm of life be past!
Safe into the haven guide,
    O receive my soul at last!
        (*Methodist Sunday-School Hymn and Tune-Book*, 1879, Hymn 302, v. 1)

Children might not comprehend the imagery of a lover, but they could certainly appreciate the metaphor of storms and safe haven. It would mean a great deal to suffering children, as we shall see.

In the nineteenth century, the heirs to Calvinist/Puritan theology were the Baptists and Congregationalists who, along with Methodists, made up the main Nonconformist sects comprising the Evangelical Movement; common to all (though with increasing debate as the century wore on) were belief in Original Sin, the Day of Judgment, Heaven and Hell, Christ's Atonement, Justification from that Atonement, and Eternal Life. Such beliefs inform Congregationalists Jane and Ann Taylor's *Hymns for Infant Minds* (1809). For instance, sin and guilt plague those who lose a loved one, as they candidly flesh out in their Hymn XXXI, "A Child's Lamentation for the Death of a Dear Mother" where the child must

… recollect with pain
    The many times I griev'd her sore;
Oh! if she would but come again,
    I think I'd vex her so no more. (v. 3)

This posture is highlighted, in the early editions of their *Hymns for Infant Minds*, with an engraving (by their brother Isaac, an accomplished engraver himself) of a young girl weeping on the mother's grave with this verse given below it (see Figure 2.1 in Chapter 2).[8]

---

[8]   The copy of this hymn book which I use was owned by James Montgomery, famous hymn writer himself, who noted in the margins which sister had written many of the hymns,

Here, too, the Taylors didactically but honestly depict a dialogue between Child and Mamma (Hymn XXI) to teach about the body and the soul, opening in a rather macabre manner, but also depicting honest questions from a frightened child:

Tell me, Mamma, if I must die
One day, as little baby died;
And look so very pale, and lie
Down in the pit-hole, by its side? (v. 1)

The mother distinguishes between the body and soul—"while their bodies moulder [sic] here, / Their souls with God himself shall dwell" and does not spare the horrors of hell "where wicked people go," where "the good God shall never smile … For since they chose to be so vile, / He leaves them to the way they took" (Hymn XXI). Nevertheless, Mamma also imparts comfort:

Those who have lov'd him here below,
And pray'd to have their sins forgiv'n,
And done his holy will, shall go,
Like happy angels, up to heav'n. (v. 6)

Hymn books of early decades continue the Evangelical focus on death, judgment, and guilt, sometimes invoking a Miltonic Satan. In Hymn 174 of Robert May's *The Children's Hymn Book* (1811), the child singer imagines approaching "God's tribunal" to hear God say, "Depart, ye cursed, far away; / With Satan, in the lowest hell, / Thou art for ever doom'd to dwell" (v. 4). With alliterative d's to punctuate the damnation, this hymn would be a troubling hymn to sing. Likewise, Gadsby's *A Selection of Hymns from Various Authors for the Use of Sunday Schools* (1836) contains dark hymns of a personified Death as "an unwelcome guest" who "has his millions slain" (Hymn 160) and who "is the consequence of sin" (Hymn 161). Notably, the child is not singled out, for punishment or exemption: "Young as I am, and free from pain, / I'm not too young to die …" (Hymn 163).

Tractarian hymns corroborate such theology, though their language is more poetic and metaphorical. Tractarian eschatology "was set within the framework of a seriousness shared with Evangelicalism and a sharp awareness that the drama of salvation was set against the ultimate choices of heaven and hell" (Rowell 90). Isaac Williams, in his *Ancient Hymns for Children* (1842), as discussed in Chapter 2, reminds his young readers of the Day of Wrath, the "trembling, the agony," that "Death and Time shall stand aghast" ("The Day of Judgment" 69). John Mason Neale, in his *Hymns for Children* (1842–1846) writes sparingly but pointedly of "that most dreadful Day":

---

a fact not readily known nor perhaps accurate. But these hymns on death and sin were almost all noted as having been written by Ann, a possibility corroborated by several severe hymns on death (10 and 11) in Ann Gilbert's *Hymns for Little Children* (1819).

> Then all in vain our prayers and cries;
>     One state alone remains;
> The worm whose torture never dies,
>     And everlasting chains. ("S. Matthew's Day," v. 7, 274)

Speaking of "the worm" as opposed to a personified Death, Neale yet shows the culpability of children who have known of God and yet choose not to believe: they will not "flee the wrath to come" (v. 1).

As Rowell explains, Tractarians reacted against the Evangelical focus on rewards and punishments, and created a more personal discussion often based on the lives of the saints (it is no surprise that this comes from a hymn commemorating St. Matthew); thus, the personal responsibility of his appeal. Yet Neale also entices his young readers with the glories of Heaven, as in his next, more famous, hymn:

> Around the throne of God, a band
> Of glorious Angels always stand ... (v. 1)

Eventually, the hymn promises, children will follow them:

> ... And we shall dwell, when life is past
> With Angels round Thy Throne at last. (v. 9, 375)

Some hymns continue to impart didactic messages of godly living with threats of hell and morbid portraits of death (recall "One day, dear children, you must die" [1862], the tune composed by J. B. Dykes, which describes limp limbs and stiff bodies in the grave ... God has "ruled that all on earth must die" [see Figure 3.4]).

But by mid-century another feature of hymns emerges such that hymns of death, though recognizing the final desired trajectory, yet often register a sadness for the moment when all earthly life is relinquished. Influenced by the sentimental literature of the day, perhaps, and a lightening of religion which was turning away from fire-and-brimstone doctrine, this trend also reveals the human reality in which semantic grief for the loss of this world overpowers the comfort (or fear) to be found in the dogma just explored. A little-known *Verses for My Children* (1849) by "E. C." shows this in striking terms as the author (hereafter "she" as several verses refer to "mother") attempts to deal with the actual death of her own child. She references hell in an earlier poem, that "Satan would his children doom, / To darkness, flames, and woe" if not for Jesus (31). Her verse titled "Written on the Anniversary of our Loss and their Gain," however, iterates instead theology of the godly life and the subsequent heavenly reward for the child ("their" appears to be used inconsistently as either the plural divine receiving the child or two deaths occurring on one day, as here):

> They liv'd their day—they saw the Lord;
>     On Him their souls believed;
> They lov'd his love, and works, and word,
>     And them He hath received. (v. 4, 33)

Writing personally about the reality of death, the author alludes to moments of personal grief, the pressure of "soft hands" she can never feel again, the sweet hymns chanted during life and "*How* beautiful" if only she could hear them again. But the hymn ends with praise:

> Lord! tune our fainting hearts to praise,
>     That when *our* day is come,
> We may with them unite, to raise
>     Glad hymns in heaven, our home! (v. 7, her italics)

Four years later, her hymn changes as the reality of grief amplifies and doctrine fails to comfort as before, in "On the Fourth Anniversary of our Loss and their Gain":

> Sweet child! I cannot see thy heavenward path …
> … Thy birthday comes
> So near thy heavenly birthday too, all sad,
> And drown'd in showers! Thy garden's treasured flowers
> Can scarce lift up their heads—my heart
> Is sad; and long it seems since that sweet smile,
> The sunshine of our dwelling, passed away. (45)

Though she is able to conclude her verse on a pat theological note—we "shall rise, like Him their head—then may we meet / To part no more"—the bulk of the poem is a heart-wrenching exposition of grief experienced in *this* world: the birth-day and death-day existing so close; the rain overwhelming the flowers; the loss of the child "sunshine" (with no religious pun on Son-shine). In contrast to the well-ordered "First Anniversary" poem in ABAB rhyme and common meter, easily sung to many tunes, this Fourth-Anniversary hymn crumbles in rhyme and meter as the writer is overcome with grief. It is a glimpse of personal anguish that no creed can comfort. The juxtaposition of these two verses, side by side, I suggest, represents many hymn writers of mid-century who seem unable to denounce their earthly home even as they attempt to preach Christian theology of the afterlife.

Jane Leeson's High Church *Hymns and Scenes of Childhood* (1842) is another example in this mode. Most of her "death" hymns are focused on the deaths of actual children and involve the earthly remembrances of their lives and mortal bodies; "The Last Prayer" (Scene VII) memorializes the final moments of Princess Anne, 4-year-old daughter of Charles I and Henrietta Maria, for instance. Similarly, "Little Leonard's Farewell" (Scene IV) is based on the death of a 2-year-old boy, its uneven narration symbolizing the grief of the family. It begins as if from the mother's point of view:

> The shade of death is o'er thee now,
>     My fair and cherish'd Child,
> His seal upon thy placid brow,
>     "Good night" thy lips have smiled. (v. 1)

Yet, as if Mother cannot accept the truth of the situation, the first-person perspective appears to shift to a child's (or another's) third-person point of view in the next lines:

> How strangely on thy Mother's ear
>> Those last, soft accents fell;
> The voice her bosom yearn'd to hear
>> But woke to breathe farewell! (v. 1)

It then ends in first-person plural, as if the entire family has joined the mother's grieving narration:

> With morn again we shall behold thee,
>> Till then, sweet Babe, Good night. (v. 3)

A scene of heightened heartache, the verse also reflects the unconscious desire of the narrator(s) to cling to worldly objects and details: Leonard's last words, the "dewy turf" which "must fold thee" (v. 3), the "early flowers" now fading and "storms coming on" (v. 2). Though clearly referenced in order to point to the "fadeless bowers" and "cloudless day" (v. 2) that Leonard will now enjoy, yet the speaker(s) is clearly lingering on these earthly moments, too.[9]

Likewise, *The Children's Hymn Book* (1854) provides hymns scattered throughout which allow for grieving schoolchildren to acknowledge the "Death of a Scholar" (189, 196, 264) and these, too, brim with the details of young children's living selves. Number 189 is that which Caroline Richards sang at the death of her classmate: "A mourning class, a vacant seat …" (Hymn 189, v. 1). However, the hymn lingers on details of this young girl: "the voice we loved to hear," "That welcome face," "that sparkling eye," and "sprightly form" (vv. 2–3). Its last verse is harshly didactic—"God tells us, by this mournful death, / How vain and fleeting is our breath" (v. 4)—but, notably, Caroline quotes only the first verse which seems to reflect the true semantic feelings of a class missing a friend.

Likewise, Hymn 264 contains vivid verses detailing the death of a little boy:

> One we loved has left our number
>> For the dark and silent tomb;
> Closed *his* eyes in deathless slumber—
>> Faded in *his* early bloom;
>>> Hear us, Saviour,—
>> Thou hast blest the lonely tomb. (v. 2, their italics) ….
> From our circle, little *brother*,
>> Early hast thou passed away!
> But the angels say,—Another
>> Joins our holy song to-day! (v. 5, their italics)

Visual cues (the italics) bring focus back upon this little brother while rhyming pairs (number-slumber, tomb-bloom, brother-another, away-today) keep alive the

---

9    For more on Leeson's hymn book, see my "Writing for, yet Apart."

tension between death and life, respectively in each pair (tomb and bloom, etc.). Yet by the end the Saviour has "blest the lonely tomb" and the angels rejoice when this brother joins them.

Honest doubts and authentic grief undergird a final, poignant hymn in an American hymn book, *Sabbath School* (New York, 1860), "Letters of Madgie to her Twin Sister, Minnie, Deceased" whose child speaker, Madgie, struggles to understand her sister's death:

> Minnie, Minnie! dearest sister!
>     Whither have you gone from me?
> Tell me—have you gone to heaven,
>     Little angel there to be? (v. 1)

Madgie cannot fully appreciate heaven either, using interrogative, not declarative, sentences:

> Are you happy up in heaven?
>     Is your home a pleasant place?
> Do they love you there as I do?
>     Do they kiss your angel face? (v. 3)

Here the child has learned the lesson—"where, they say"—but struggles to believe that anything good could come of the loss of her sister. Heavenly love is hard to envision without tangible reality, the kissing of faces. The only appeal heaven really has for Madgie is Minnie herself:

> Must you always live with Jesus?
> Then I want to live there, too! (v. 6)

As the hymn closes—and what a struggle for the child chorus to get through all seven verses, let alone their tragic content—Madgie really has only learned to parrot back the doctrine of adults:

> But meet in heaven with "Little Minnie,"
>     Who is "not lost, but gone before!" (v. 7)

Quote marks represent both the term of endearment ("Little Minnie") and the Sunday school lesson ("not lost, but gone before") but clearly the child speaker is wrestling with the latter.

This song is, admittedly, as sentimental a story as to be found in any Dickens novel, but this time it has been put in the mouth of a child herself who is struggling with genuine questions and attempting to feel the theological comfort expressed. This and other hymns of mid-century reveal modern skepticism alongside theological comfort found in the hymn literature. Ultimately, we are reminded that hymn writers were not just theologians of the caliber of Watts and Wesley but were mothers and fathers writing of the genuine grief in their lives, even if their hymns never became as widely read/sung. And the child singers were not always parroting back worn theology but were grappling with issues of faith and emoting true semantic grief, for a sister, for a classmate.

Skepticism would peak, of course, in the 1860s and 1870s, when evolutionary theory cast doubt on all aspects of Christian doctrine, from a heavenly afterlife to the immortality of the soul and whether human souls would have any privileged status over the animals from which they descended. By the 1880s and 1890s, the debate had died down, and furthermore, "As theology became more liberal the old Unitarian polemic against hell became reduced to the expression of incredulity that anyone had ever believed the doctrine" (Rowell 57).[10] Late-century hymns, left with the faith but not the fire, take on as much sentiment of the dying child, but without the earthly reality: these hymns, for the most part, delineate the glories of heaven even without the passage of death and certainly without God's Judgment. As Knight remarks, "As the hell-fire waned, a more optimistic strand within the religious consciousness began to assert itself [by the 1860s] ... This strand emphasised heaven as the eternal home of Christians, and was largely silent about the difficult questions concerning judgement and hell" (57–8). In hymns, especially, fire-and-brimstone fear-tactics were replaced by an all-out glorification of the immortal life in heaven as a persuasive injunction to believe.

Such can be seen in the "Heaven" sections of *The Methodist Sunday School Hymn- and Tune-Book* (1879), *Golden Bells* (1890), and *282 Hymns and Melodies* (1893). First to note is that these are anthologies of hymns, so earlier Evangelical hymns still reside in them. But the very fact that sections are created around the topic of "Heaven" but not of "Hell" clearly demonstrates changing theology across denominations. Tellingly, the Methodist hymn book uses the phrase "The Life to Come," as if heaven is the only option "to come." As Richard Helmstadter shows, focus on the Incarnation had taken priority over the Atonement for both Evangelicals and Anglicans (83), and this focus on Christ's holy life, not death, spilled over into eschatological approach. Furthermore, death "is redefined by hymn theology as victory rather than tragedy" and the arrival to heaven "is not only an ending, but the beginning of a new story," asserts Candy Gunther Brown (206).[11]

For children, heaven becomes a "next chapter," a "new story," almost guaranteed them, and it is truly an appealing tale. Whereas Henry Bateman (in his *Sunday Sunshine*, 1858) describes heaven vaguely as an "abode" lacking in sin, misery, pain, care, and strife (Hymn 102), now heaven is consistently located

---

[10]   Gladstone wrote that by the end of the century, the concept of hell had been "relegated ... to the far-off corners of the Christian mind ... there to sleep in deep shadow as a thing needless in our enlightened and progressive age" (qtd. in Rowell 212). That is, "The old assurances and the definite doctrines of orthodox Christian eschatology had become doubtful, not least because of the controversies over hell. Although the old language continued, in part, to be used, it was often in conjunction with a shadowy hope of a final apotheosis, expressed in terms of romantic yearnings" (Rowell 213).

[11]   Wheeler explores hymns mainly in the context of "Heaven," showing how hymns "exploit both the diachronic [historical] and the synchronic [present] potentialities of liturgical language in order to speak of heaven within the present act of worship" (136).

skyward with glowing descriptors of what it contains, not what it lacks: "Beautiful Zion built above ... Beautiful gates of pearly white" (*Golden* 445), "the beautiful city" with "bright mansions" (*Golden* 430) where inhabitants' "travel-stained garments" are replaced with "white raiment" (*Golden* 420) and "white robes for the righteous" (*Golden* 430).

These hymn-texts of course are biblical, many coming from Revelations 21–2, which also includes the reference to "a pure river of water of life, clear as crystal" (Rev. 22:1; King James Version), now distinguishing a place with life-saving water. Hymn writers embellish, and thus much water imagery is used to describe the passage from one world into the next: "Fording the river" (*Golden* 420), "by the side of the river of light" (*Golden* 426), "On the shores of the bright crystal sea" (*Golden* 425), "We are sailing o'er an ocean" (*Methodist* 456), "the beautiful stream that flows into the Father's land" (*Methodist* 463), "We are out on the ocean sailing ... to a home beyond the tide" (*Golden* 429), and the memorable gospel tune from America, "Shall we gather at the river" by Robert Lowry (1864) (see *282 Hymns* 230 and *Methodist* 464), with its haunting affirmative refrain with hypnotic sixteenth notes:

> Yes, we'll gather at the river,
>     The beautiful, the beautiful river,
> Gather with the saints at the river
>     That flows by the throne of God. (*282 Hymns*, Hymn 230)

Most majestic of all was the figure of God or Jesus waiting to receive the sanctified: "Around the throne of God in heaven" (*Methodist* 448), "We come before His throne" (*Golden* 434), "Beautiful temple, God its light! ... Beautiful seats at God's right hand" (*Golden* 445), "Bright home of our Saviour" (*Golden* 447), "Shall we meet with Christ our Saviour" (*Golden* 433), "seeing / My Saviour face to face" (*Golden* 439), and "at my Saviour's side" (*Golden* 440).

A major point of debate among Evangelicals in particular was whether the glory of heaven was defined solely by the presence of God or also the presence of earth's loved ones. The latter view tended to win out which "led to the heaven of much popular religious writing being conceived in very sentimental and anthropomorphic terms," writes Rowell (9). Sentimental, yes, but such assurances of meeting loved ones above brought comfort to children such as Franky, texts which expressed, "Shall we all meet...With the loved ones who long have been waiting? / What a meeting indeed it will be!" (*Golden* 425). Or, "think of the friends over there ... There my kindred and friends are at rest" (*Golden* 426). As ever, angels inhabit heaven, too: "white-robed angels" (*Golden* 432), "Beautiful angels clothed in white" (*Golden* 445), "angels bright and pure are there" (*282 Hymns*, Hymn 232).

Neale's translation of a medieval hymn by Bernard of Cluny, "Jerusalem the golden" (1861)[12] is especially rich with sensory imagery of heaven, imagined as the new Jerusalem:

---

[12]   "Jerusalem the Golden!" has a complex history, its text being a ballad translation of an intricate poem by twelfth-century monk, Bernard of Cluny. John Mason Neale, as

Jerusalem the golden,
    With milk and honey blest,
Beneath Thy contemplation
    Sink heart and voice oppressed.
I know not, O I know not
    What social joys are there,
What radiancy of glory,
    What bliss beyond compare! (Hymn 432, *Methodist Sunday School*)

Neale changed Bernard's intricate dactylic hexameter to 7.6.7.6 D meter with iambic stresses which "succeeds remarkably," according to J. R. Watson: "the images are held firmly in place in the line, and the whole hymn has a visionary quality" (*An Annotated* 48–9). A personal reflection is invoked and the mysteries of heaven are enjoyed a moment ("O I know not/What social joys are there") before verse 2 delineates heaven's scenes further with "halls of Zion," "jubilant with song" and "The Prince [who] is ever in them" (v. 2). Yet this seems more of an adult's fantasy of heaven; even the "jubilant song" is not attached specifically to children. It is therefore stunning to find it in 22% of children's hymn books. As explored in Chapter 3, there are two salient reasons for this phenomenon: Christian theology and comfort was extended to children and adults alike, children's "purity" notwithstanding. Furthermore, children loved Alexander Ewing's tune to the hymn (Neale in McCutchan 513).

However, by late century many of these hymns depict children as the main occupants of this glorious space, sentimentally described yet surely a comforting "next chapter" to children facing death themselves or experiencing the death of siblings and friends: "Yes, there are little ones in heaven; / Children like us around the throne" (*Golden* 431); "Bright crowns there are laid up on high, / Which youthful brows may wear" (*Golden* 434); "I know there's a crown for the young … The youthful shall stand in that beautiful land" (*Methodist* 449); and "Little Travellers Zionward" who come from all around the world, Greenland, India, Africa (*282 Hymns* 234). Undeniably to these hymn writers, as with many literary writers, "children were the guardians of virtue … For heaven was theirs by right, and not by God's mercy" (Sommerville 173).

A vital alternative to the static imagery of children on their deathbeds is the hymn's constant motif of children actively singing in heaven: "Children above are singing, with voices sweet and clear" (*Methodist* 446), "Ten thousand youthful tongues / Unite in Jesus' praise" (*Golden* 422), "Little children singing / Praises to Jesus there" (*Golden* 432), and "Children … Their sweet and everlasting song; / We hope to sing as loud as they" (*Golden* 431). Children are not stagnant any more but alive with melody and movement.

---

part of the Oxford Movement whose members sought to find and resurrect the hymns of the ancient church, translated part of this long poem, and from his translations, four hymns were made, "Jerusalem the Golden" being the most significant. Alexander Ewing composed the tune for a different part of Bernard's work in 1857, "For thee, O dear, dear Country," but when it was published in *Hymns Ancient and Modern* (1861), it was used also with "Jerusalem the Golden" (Hymn 142, "Part 3").

Clearly, the children on earth were singing these wonders of heaven with gusto and liveliness, too, as with "Jerusalem the golden." One aspect of these hymns of heaven of the late century is their penchant for lively choruses and tunes. "Shall we all meet at home in the morning" (*Golden* 425) ends with "Gathered home! ... gathered home ... On the shores of the bright crystal sea!" (their ellipses for musical pause); "Round the throne" ends with "They are clothed ... in spotless robes! (their ellipsis); and "I know there's a bright and a glorious land" concludes with "Will you be there and I?" asked four times in the chorus (*Golden* 448). "Press on! Press on!" is a phrase invoked throughout verses and refrain with a lively eighth-note-quarter-note combination; in the *Methodist Sunday-School Book*, it is enlivened even more by dividing up the verses between boys and girls, to sing "Press on! Press on! A glorious throng In heaven are watching o'er you" (Hymn 458). Some not only invoke the idea of marching, they exemplify it in their buoyant meters, as in "There is a glorious world of light" (*Golden* 422) whose chorus is: "We are marching through Immanuel's ground ... We hope to meet at Jesus' feet, and never, never part again...."

One "marching song" still very popular is "Come, ye that love the Lord," Robert Lowry's 1867 tune and added refrain ("Marching to Zion") greatly enhancing Watts's original text:

> Come, ye that love the Lord,
> And let your joys be known,
>     Join in a song with sweet accord,
>     Join in a song with sweet accord,
> And thus surround the throne,
> And thus surround the throne,
>     We're marching to Zion,
>     Beautiful, beautiful Zion;
>     We're marching upward to Zion,
>     The beautiful city of God. (*Golden Bells* 424)

Banerjee writes that for many Victorians, "Christianity had lost its power either to inspire or to console" by late century (34), but such songs belie this, showing what must have been inspiration and consolation for the many children who were grieving ... and a great deal of fun for those who were not.

It is not surprising, then, that five of the most frequently anthologized hymns about heaven (see Table 3.1), though written in the 1830s and 1840s, peaked in these hymn books of the last three decades: Anne Shepherd's "Around the throne of God in heaven" (1830s), Bilby's "Here we suffer grief and pain" (1832), Andrew Young's "There is a happy land" (1843), "Jerusalem the golden" (trans. J. M. Neale, 1840s), and Lyte's "Abide with me" (1847). Having analyzed most of these already, I would like to end with a close look at "There is a happy land" which is found in all three of these late-century collections and exemplifies many of the above points. (See Figure 6.2, from the *Methodist Sunday-School Book*.) An extremely popular hymn found in 38% of children's hymn books in my study, its tune in fact inspired the hymn. Andrew Young, a teacher in Scotland, heard

Figure 6.2    "There is a happy land." From *The Methodist Sunday-School Hymn and Tune-Book*, 1879. From the author's collection and in the public domain.

a friend play a rhythmic "Indian air" (Teluga, specifically) on the piano. He thereafter composed a hymn to be used in his own Edinburgh school, then allowed Rev. James Gall to use it in his popular *Sacred Song Book* (1843). In dactylic dimeter and a 6.4.6.4.6.7.6.4 hymn meter, its rhythm carries the lines, as do the unusual rhyme scheme (ABABCCCB) and refrains that "punch" the meaning:

> There is a happy land,
>     Far, far away,
> Where saints in glory stand,
>     Bright, bright as day,
> Oh, how they sweetly sing,
> Worthy is our Saviour King!
> Loud let His praises ring—
>     Praise, praise for aye. (v. 1)

A "bright" land with "saints in glory" and much sweet singing, this is a paradise where singers entice others to "Come to this happy land" and question them with "Why will ye doubting stand?" (v. 2). The tune (labeled "Happy Land") may be the most appealing aspect of this hymn, created by its use of two simple, repeated, yet invigorating melodic phrases. Further, a strong initial beat opens each measure while the alto and tenor notes hardly change, working to create a drum-like effect. A dotted quarter- and eighth-note rhythm clinches each phrase to produce sprightly rhythms. The lively tune masks—or makes more manifest—the serious discussion on heaven. According to Julian, by the turn of the century it was "heard in Sunday Schools all over the world," having been translated by various missionary organizations (1161). A story is told (by Mrs. E. R. Pitman, 1892) that William Makepeace Thackeray was brought to tears by hearing poor children singing it in the street (Pitman 47). Their dancing and singing about heaven when their poverty might more quickly send them there is perhaps the irony that caused Thackeray's emotional reaction. But the children had perhaps embraced the hymn simply because it was a joy to sing.

Modern readers might pity the children inundated with hymns of death, heaven, and hell, but memoirs suggest how hymns eased the transition for a dying child. *The Early Dead; Containing Brief Memoirs of Several Sunday-School Children who Died in 1846* (New York: Sunday School Union) details many moralistic and saccharine stories of child's deaths but one common element can be noted, if these accounts written by others are to be believed: children clung to hymns in their hour of need. One hundred and thirty years after Watts's *Divine and Moral Songs* was published, Sarah Matilda of New York transcribed his "There is an hour when I must die … There's no repentance in the grave" in her scrap-book only a few days before her death (33). Favorite hymns were included in the memoirs ("The following hymn was one which she [Eliza Bowen] often sung:—'My God is the Father of all'" 48); children sang favorite songs about heaven during their illness ("When I've been there ten thousand years" ["Amazing Grace"] or "There's nothing here deserves my joy" 64, 12) and sang them upon their deathbed: Juliette Kinney "broke out and sung, clearly and distinctly, a verse of the hymn, commencing, 'O, when shall I see Jesus, / And dwell with him above!'" (88). Little Nanette in *Brief Memoirs of Remarkable Children* (London, 1822), referenced earlier, showed her delight in songs by Watts ("I sing the almighty power of God" 88; "Let dogs delight" 100) and the Taylors ("When little Samuel awoke" 84), with almost complete verses cited of the latter two in her memoir. In her weakness, she "often repeated" their comforting words, such as the Taylors' "Great God! and wilt thou condescend" (which I examined in Chapter 2), whose lines about God's friendship must surely have reassured her:

> Great God! And wilt thou condescend
> To be my Father and my Friend;
> I, a poor child, and thou so high,
> The Lord of air, and earth and sky ... (85)

Similar stories are told in *Little Footprints on the Old Church Path: A Memoir of a Christian Child* (Oxford and London, 1854). To her 4-year-old son George, a mother "often spoke of heaven and of the holy angels, and he knew there was a place called hell" (19); thus, at his death, he is able to tell his mother that "I do love you better than any one on earth ... But I love Jesus Christ much more, for He died that I might live always with Him" (25–6). He "looked with pleasure on death," she writes, "repeating to himself the lines in his little hymn: 'We must not cry too bitterly / Over the happy dead'" (26). Engaging in semiotics of the deathbed—his "love so pure, hope so stedfast [sic], and faith so triumphant" (iv)—the scene is yet semantic in authentic grief and comfort-giving hymns.

One girl, in particular, knew and needed hymns, apparently, to see her through her final months. In the *Memoir of Mary Lothrop, Who Died in Boston, March 18, 1831, Aged Six Years and Three Months* (American Tract Society, 1832), a third-person female narrator (probably her mother) shares how much hymns played a part in Mary's holy living and dying. Concerned that readers might doubt its authenticity, in fact, she attaches words from their pastor that "nothing is exaggerated, or too highly colored" (9). As the narrator states: "The greatest alleviation that could be afforded to Mary under her daily sufferings was to sing hymns, or to read suitable passages of Scripture" (71), and a great many hymn-texts are quoted throughout the book. Gathering her sisters together before her death, Mary uses hymns to teach them the theology of her faith, both of hell and heaven:

> I've something I wish to say to you. I wish you to remember what that hymn says,
>
> > "There is a dreadful hell,
> >     And everlasting pains,
> > Where sinners must for ever dwell
> >     In darkness, fire and chains." (59)

Not too alarmed to quote these words of Isaac Watts (from Song XI), Mary urges her sisters in genuine concern that they "repent of all your sins" or "*you must* go there" (60; her italics). Her words are personal, conveying her belief in the re-acquaintance of loved ones in heaven, for she wants them "to meet me there" (60).

This Evangelical idea, just mentioned, of peopling heaven with loved ones was also used to prod the unbelievers into belief, much as Mary is doing with her sisters. Her last days were spent "reading ... Scripture, and singing hymns" with the last hymn recorded being Wesley's "Jesus, lover of my soul" (106). With his lines inviting the singer "to thy bosom fly" (v. 1) and providing "support and comfort ... Till the storm of life be past" to "receive my soul at last" (v. 2), surely Mary was comforted in her final hours.[13]

In short, hymns countered many of the problems associated with the cult of the deathbed. Rather than marginalizing the child in her pure death, hymns brought child and adult together as potential inheritors of both punishment and glory. They provided doctrinal answers but also betrayed hymn writers' human doubts and grief. Nevertheless, most also provide comforting "next chapters" to continue children's life stories beyond the deathbed. And rather than focusing on motionless bodies, hymns chronicle and allow for agency both in the life beyond and the life on earth. Ultimately, hymns sanctioned the child's *voice*. Beyond the staged scenes of death, such speaking and singing gave the child a prophet-like power to all around them; further, their singing would remain in others' ears afterwards, as one of the long-remembered actions which was worthy to be chronicled for many others to notice and "hear."

One problem with this analysis is, of course, that adults wrote the memoirs, possibly sentimentalizing, exaggerating, or purifying their children's final acts in semiotic gestures.[14] Admittedly, it is highly doubtful that they would fabricate entire actions such as hymn singing. Nevertheless, in this final section, to both chapter and book, I attempt to give children the final word: what they wrote, what they thought, what they sang, of hymns of death and also of hymn singing in general. What I have discovered is that children were full of life in their hymn singing, and hymns were an integral part of their *lives*.

## Part III
## Marginalia, Parodies, and Diaries:
## Child-*Life* within Children's Hymnody

Three final ways I ascertain children's thoughts about hymns, especially within the context of death, are through the marginalia they wrote in their hymn books

---

[13]    Mary had a vast repertoire of hymns, as noted in this memoir: "Now let me mount and join their song" (64); "Children of the heavenly King" (72; by John Cennick [1743]), found in 20% of children's hymn books); "I see the pleasant bed / Where lie the dying saint" (75); "Dear friend of friendless sinners, hear" (77); "Shall aught beguile us on the road" (81); "Do we not dwell in clouds below" (90); "Blessed Jesus, meet me on the road" (91); "Thine earthly Sabbaths, Lord, we love" (100); and "I cannot bear thine absence, Lord" (103).

[14]    For a discussion of the genre of autobiography—adults' reflections on their own childhood, which I have used on a limited basis throughout this book—as neither fiction nor history, see Luann Walther's "The Invention of Childhood in Victorian Autobiography."

in response to what they were reading and singing; through the extant parodies I have found, as they breathed life—even irony—back into their hymn singing; and, finally, through archival research of 25 English children's journals and diaries to ascertain their comments about hymn singing.[15] This final section will attempt to resurrect the empowered child singer.

## Marginalia

In this section, I will suggest the "play" to be found in children's nineteenth-century hymns based on the marginalia they left behind in their hymn books and cover inscriptions as they expressed delight and even witticism. Children did not always accept the bitter maxims being handed down to them, instead noting, questioning, and mocking "serious" truths in their marginal comments. M. O. Grenby analyzes the marginalia of over 5,000 children's books[16] in his *The Child Reader, 1700–1840* (2008), writing:

> Historians of early modern manuscripts and books often suggest that inscriptions and annotations indicate how valuable books were, in both monetary and intellectual or spiritual terms. To write in them was to assert ownership of a costly commodity and to acknowledge the importance of text's place in the owners' lives. Exactly the same might be said for eighteenth-century children, who also generally owned very few possessions. And the marginalia might best be regarded as a sign of an extremely interactive and engaged relationship with text.... (28–9)

These claims of value and ownership as demonstrated by marginalia could certainly be said of Victorian hymn books as well. One qualification that I make is that the marginalia I looked at may not have been a child's, for once again, the adult seemed to enjoy ownership of these hymn books as much as the child. As even Grenby admits, "there must always remain doubts about who was writing, when and why" (34). When in doubt, I will claim a child's hand since these *are* children's hymn books, but I will note adult marginalia when they appear obvious. Drawings, scribblings, ownership inscriptions, inserted texts—"most easily classifiable as graffiti" (Grenby 26)—tend to denote children's unimportant marks and yet have political meaning, "mak[ing] a bold though confused statement of accomplishment, selfhood and the attainment of citizenship, as well as simple ownership" (Grenby 29).

Another observation I make is to suggest that readers greatly respected hymn books over textbooks: only about 20 of the 200 hymn books I examined had any

---

[15] For a useful argument on how diaries are vital sites of public, not simply private, commentary, see Cynthia Huff's "Victorian Family Fictions." I also thank her for guidance in finding diary collections around the UK.

[16] My examination of children's hymn books for marginalia is not nearly as extensive: 200 hymn books to his 5,000, in part due to my more limited scope of genre and years (a century versus his century and a half).

markings, including any name identification in the cover. This is in sharp contrast to Grenby who found that "children wrote so much in their books" (28). This may be due to the difference in eras we researched; Kevin Sharpe and Steven N. Zwicker attribute less annotation to "the age of politeness" of the Renaissance but the same could be said of polite Victorian society (qtd. in Grenby 25). Furthermore, the genre of hymnody made a difference in that it might have felt sacrilegious to singers to write in "holy" books. Whereas children doing lessons would have had a writing utensil in hand, singers needed to sing hands-free without pens available. Finally, hymn-book users were not always the owners but merely "borrowers" of the books, using them in Sunday schools and school, and this awareness may have kept them from defacing another's property (and kept teachers enforcing this).

Of what marginalia is available, much is owner identification—"the assertion of possession" in a world where people owned few books if any at all (Grenby 27). Sometimes the public ownership is claimed against would-be thieves: "This book must not be taken from the church," most probably inscribed by the pastor (*Sunday-School Hymnal*, Reformed Church, Dayton, Ohio, 1899). A clever, pre-printed book plate, complete with an engraving of a bookcase, adorns the inside cover to *Studies in Worship-Music* (now in the Pratt Green Collection, Durham), the book itself suggesting an adult owner:

> A. R. Willey (sp?)
> Owns this Book
> If thou art borrowed by a friend,
> Right welcome shall he be
> To read, to study, not to lend,
> But to return to me.

Though witty, this book plate yet suggests the importance of retrieving valued and valuable books.

In most cases, private ownership is simply claimed by the owner's name and residence, as with: "W. G. Alexander, Temperance Cottages, Norfolk 1894" (*Psalms and Hymns*). The inside cover of an 1807 edition of Watts's *Divine and Moral Songs* reads in childish, though fancy, cursive: "Lucy Gallup's Book[,] Ledyard 1843," as Lucy reclaims an old book now almost 40 years old. When an 1802 edition of *Divine Songs* is inscribed with a signature ("K. Hemipoor" [sp?]) and dated 1897, one can especially appreciate the longevity and continuous circulation of this classic hymn book (now in the Lilly Collection, Indiana University).

Perhaps more often, though, these hymn books show their value as gifts to loved ones: "E. A. Ellinor with best wishes F. L. S. 1900" (*Wesley's Hymns*). Sometimes the gift-giver wishes to remain semi-anonymous, and the giver of *The Westminster Carol Book* cleverly uses the notes on the bass staff to indicate his/her initials, placing whole notes on the G, C, and E on the clef. I like to think a budding romance was percolating with the following gift to Henry Pearce: "With every good wish From his true and sincere friend Miss Charlotte Martyn Collyns (sp?) of the Mary Ansleigh Vicarage … September 9th, 1869."

Of course, Henry might have been a child and the gift was given by his Sunday school teacher; indeed, many hymn books were given as rewards for good work in school: *Pretty Poems for My Children* by Emma C. Somers was presented to "Mast[er] G. E. Whiting [sp?] for improvement in Reading." A copy of *Golden Bells* was "Presented to James Arthur Wilson for excellent attendance and conduct" from St. Edmunds Sunday School (1919). Other times, the gift is simply out of love for a child: "Mary Mosalie Dunn from her Great-Grandmamma who sends this to her Little Darling, January 1872"—a copy of Watts's *Divine and Moral Songs*, 1869. *Verses for My Children* (now housed at Cambridge), which contained the poems written on anniversaries of a child's death, analyzed above, was given to "Ellen Beatrice Wadsworth[,] a remembrance of Grandmama." Some of the notations are quite intricate as with the following text:

To/ Tom
on his/ Fifteenth Birthday.
From/ Douglas
With/ All good wishes

which cascades down the inside cover of the *Primitive Methodist Hymn Book* in lovely cursive and with the proper names underlined, dated and with his Manchester address given. Clearly this was an important gift from Douglas to Tom, and an interesting gift, to modern eyes, to give a 15-year-old. Notably, another owner, clearly of a later time era, "K. Bowden," has added his/her label of ownership, obscuring Tom's last name; such is the risk of multiple owners but it demonstrates the enduring importance of hymn books.

In several other cases, I am quite sure the gift-giver is a child: "Xmas 1896 From Polly" in childish cursive (*Sacred Songs and Solos*, by Sankey, n.d.) and certainly "To Daddy From His Dorrie" (*Wesley's Hymns with Tunes*, 1877), although the cost of both would suggest some adult monetary assistance. Marginalia suggests the value of these hymn books both as prized possessions and as treasured gifts, to show love and affection.

Other comments reveal the importance of the hymns themselves to the recipient. In the inside cover of *Songs for Little Ones*, a mother writes "The book I used to read through & through to my babies, especially to Mariechin (sp?)—in 1864 & 65 & 66. H. W. S." Or a favorite hymn might be recorded: "My Jesus I Love Thee 271" (*Victory Songs*) or several, as a series of numbers on the inside cover of *The Sunday School Hymnary* suggests.

Marginalia is, finally, a record of those now deceased, a record of their living hands touching pen to paper. This was not lost upon Victorians, as when a book inscribed by J. Spencer Curwen (son of John Curwen) is later marked thus: "This inscription is the handwriting of John Spencer Curwen, the author of this book. F. A. W." (*Studies in Worship-Music*; in the Pratt Green Collection). This tangible proof of *living* related to the *child* as well, as when Dorrie inscribes a message to her Daddy. I have also found imitation signatures, where it appears that a younger person decided to rewrite the owner's name in differing handwriting.

Sometimes, the child leaves a beautiful legacy, as on the inside cover of *The Day School Hymn Book* (1890) where a patriotic child writes down three verses of "God save our precious Queen" in elegant cursive.

Some examples are simply scribbles, moments when the book has been marked by a somewhat less reverent reader. Scribbles, for instance, cover music scores, possibly by bored children sitting through a church service. In the back of an 1857 *Divine and Moral Songs* copy, children practiced their letters and writing: many "W's" and "J's" cover the back page, along with different names (Simon, James, Jamie, Jimmi, and Woodhouse). The graffiti is so thick, written vertically and horizontally, every inch utilized, as a reminder of how precious paper could be to children (Grenby 28). The publication date is 1857 and one notation here reads "24th Dec 1867" attesting to at least 10 years' worth of scribbling that a book preserves. Another example shows children's doodling over the name of the original owner, including some math homework—playful imitation of the serious marks left by the adult.

Sometimes, though, these marks become comments back to the writers of the hymns, demonstrating the thought and even criticism children might make of the texts they sang. One example is found in *The Hymn-Book for the Use of Uppingham and Sherborne Schools* (1874), a copy of this boys' public school hymn book now found in the British Library, which suggests a schoolboy's response back to some of the stringent images found in "Rock of ages, cleft for me" (Hymn 72). Next to the gruesome image of verse 3, "When my eyestrings break in death, / When I soar through tracks unknown," the boy has underlined "eyestrings" and put an "X" mark on the right margin, as if to cross it out. Then, he appears to have added a visual image of a "track" next to the succeeding line. This entire verse being exorcised in many later nineteenth century hymn books, this school boy thus anticipates what editors themselves would finally realize was objectionable imagery marring an otherwise powerful hymn.

Though I have not found many such other markings, one hymn book—an American one, *The Sabbath School Bell*, 1856 (now owned by the University of Michigan Music Library)—exhibits playful parody throughout its pages, this time in direct commentary to the hymns there printed. I believe our scribbler is Hope Kelsy Odgen, as scrawled sideways on page 63. The handwriting looks very youthful, like one who is just learning to use cursive. Hope enjoyed adding to the titles of the hymns found here, contributing youthful annotations. Admittedly, some may be related to the music: circling difficult notes, labeling a singer. Yet others are clearly commentaries, like "yah" scribbled in answer to "Would you be as angels are?" (16). Even innocuous-looking scribbles are possibly used to scratch over the score of a less-favorite hymn, "Beautiful Zion" (94; not the better known hymn of this title just discussed). The hymn seems joyous enough—6/8 time and focus on Beautiful Zion—but the hymn *is* about dying to get there and Hope may not have been in the mood for such thoughts.

Many times, Hope contributes commentary by adding words to the titles. "Come, Ye Children, and adore Him" (72) is a hymn where children are preached to by teachers in a lesson-answer format by teacher, with very rote, saccharine verses:

Teacher: … Come, with humble hearts, expressing
    All your gratitude and praise
Children: On this holy day of gladness,
    We will join in praises meet;
    Every bosom free from sadness—
    All with happiness replete.

On the title, over the word "children," Hope writes "lovely." Or is it "lively"? Perhaps even more fitting. Clearly this child is trying to keep things light and less didactic, suggesting how lively children themselves could be in their responses.

One hymn (61) is about growing better every day: "lov[ing] our parents dear," living "in peace" with "friends and brothers" (v. 3), and never doing "willful wrong." Its melodic refrain reads: "Come take my hand, give yours to me, / And faithful we will try to be." Over the title of the same ("Come take my hand, give yours to me"), however, the child adds "and we will always happy be." This slight variant yet concludes the thought differently: from "And faithful we will *try* to be," she suggests "we *will* always happy be"—a more secular but also a more confident stance. Another example of her ingenuity is found with "I think when I read that sweet story of old" (46). To Jemima Thompson Luke's famous hymn, the little comic writes underneath the title, "about that wicked old tory." Given the difficulty of rhyming anything with "story," this added line is no small feat. Did the child only use "tory" to rhyme? Or is she making a political statement? Tories were, of course, English-loyalists, "wicked traitors" to some, during the American Revolution. Most probably, however, she was just having fun rhyming words.

Hope especially rebels against songs of death found in this hymn book. To the hymn, "The Angels told me so" (93) she writes, "Did they[?]" as she casts doubt on the existence of angels. A "Note" to the hymn delineates a sentimental story upon which this hymn was based about a young boy who was visited by two angels who told him his dead brother would return. Hope is thus commenting on a narrative intended especially for her: in the face of another child who believes in the visitation of earthly angels and ghostly returns, she doubts, and suspects the adult-world's sentimental "gimmicks" to entice her belief.

Hope's cheeky attitude is shown with another diatribe about sin and death entitled "'Tis not too soon" (79): "'Tis not too soon to … sicken and to die"; "… our guilt to be our own"; "the path to shun, That leads the soul astray." To the title, "'Tis not too soon," the child light-heartedly adds, as she might have heard at home on a daily basis: "to go to bed"! "Enough about dying!" she seems to say.

Perhaps the best example of animated children resisting the cult of the deathbed and sentimental hymns written in this mode is the marginalia on "Vital Spark of Heavenly Flame," subtitled "A Funeral Hymn" (74) (see Figure 6.3). This hymn is not as much a funeral hymn as a hymn which recounts, in overly dramatic terms, the actual moment of death from the dying person's point of view. Authored by Alexander Pope, its audience was surely not that of a child and its imagery is pure eighteenth-century poetic flourish:

2.

Hark! they whisper; angels say,
"Sister spirit, come away;"
What is this absorbs me quite?
Steals my senses, shuts my sight,
Drowns my spirit, draws my breath?
Tell me, my soul, can this be death?

3.

The world recedes; it disappears!
Heaven opens on my eyes; my ears
With sounds, with sounds seraphic ring.
Lend, lend your wings! I mount! I fly!
O grave! where is thy victory?
O death! O death! where is thy sting?

Figure 6.3    "Vital Spark of Heavenly Flame." From *The Sabbath-School Bell* (1856). Courtesy of the University of Michigan Library (Music Library).

Vital spark of heavenly flame,
Quit, oh quit this mortal frame,
Trembling, leaping, lingering, flying—
Oh, the pain, the bliss of dying!
Cease, fond nature, cease thy strife,
And let me languish into life. (v. 1)

The person then hears angels whisper, loses sight, and draws his breath (v. 2)—until the world recedes and the hymn is overtaken by poetic embellishments: "Lend, lend your wings! I mount! I fly!" (v. 3). It would be an incredibly difficult hymn for a child to sing without either tears or laughter. I suggest Hope chose the latter course. Alongside the title, as if in continuation of the title ("Vital Spark of Heavenly Flame"), Hope writes, "Stop burning." This may be an acknowledgement of the life spirit "stopping," as delineated in the hymn, or a clever comment on flames which do stop burning. Or it may be a comment back to the poet waxing sentimental: stop burning! It surely seems a tired reaction to the mawkish hymns of death in this hymn book, mocking them for their over-serious pretension and, ultimately, their attempts to "kill off" the child.

I would not suggest that any of this is malicious, but entirely playful, making interesting rhymes ("story" and "tory"), clever additions ("flame ... stop burning!"), and parroting back nagging reminders ("time to go to bed!") as a way to respond back to the dictates of adults. This hymn book gives some of the better examples of a child's rebellious desire to "play" even amidst the confines of adult didacticism and the cult of the deathbed. But not all marginalia reflected sarcastic views of hymns. Some noted the hymn singer's favorite hymn numbers, many reflected loving gifts to friends and parents. But the penchant to play cannot be ignored.

*Parodies*

I am convinced that the specific act of singing provided children great opportunity for play. Rather than reading words on the page, rotely and silently, singing is a physical act eliciting musical interpretation and bodily response. With singing, children may sing faster, louder, out of tune, with personal inflections, with passion and animated hand-gestures, with distraction and ambivalence, even with insolence and rebelliousness.

What I have found evidence of is that children often showed healthy wit with hymn lyrics, rewriting and parodying them to suit their own sense of "theology." E. H. W. [Eddie] Meyerstein, poet and writer, was wont to parody poems and hymns in his childhood; his autobiography (*Of My Early Life, 1889–1918*) gives several examples, including the following, which Eddie wrote for his tutor, nicknamed Lem:

> O, Divine and precious Lem,
> This is for you and not for them.
> For I will smile on you all day
> No matter what the others say.
> O, what a perfect day of joy
> For you to have your smiling boy,
> Who all day long will eat of cake
> And go to bed with a stomach ache. (34)

Though I have not found the exact hymn or religious poem that Eddie appears to be parodying, it is clearly in the Protestant hymn tradition in which he was raised (18), not unlike "O love divine, how sweet Thou art" (with the verse "my joy, my heav'n on earth, be this," v. 4) by Charles Wesley. Eddie cleverly co-opts divine apostrophes ("O love divine") into human ones ("O divine and precious Lem") and exploits religious language ("precious," "joy") for his own purposes, for the day of joy is not heavenly but earthly, and is not even Eddie's joy but his presumption of Lem's joy for him. Going quite against a Wattsian injunction for restraint, he will, in fact, eat cake all day, even knowing of the self-induced punishment, a stomach ache! Divine joy is now joy on earth, even including that of whimsical poetry-making and parody.

*The Life and Letters of Edmund J. Armstrong* (1877) gives another example of boyish irreverent creativity. Edmund's boyhood gang of friends regularly challenged themselves to compose "psalms[s] of devout thanksgiving" based on the "day's glorious ramble among the mountains"—with comical results:

> Give thanks, give thanks for hill and vale,
> Kippure's stern crag, and Dodder's dale,
> Where meet the brooks of Cot and Slade—
> Both of which the Lord hath made!

A loud burst of laughter greeted the puritanical whine. "Good, good," cried Armstrong: "go on, go on—here you are: —

> Praise-God Barebones, Leathern-coat Jack,
> Rotten slipper Jekur, and Old-Clo' Mack,
> Mullakin-Noles, and Lanty-from-Kent—
> These were the members of the Rump Parliament!" (31)

Using invented names or nicknames, the boys may have been inserting their own metered language into the Doxology ("Praise God from whom all blessings flow") or another long-metered psalm. Regardless, Armstrong recalls "those boyish poems" as "very delightful in their freshness and wild rhythmic cadences … Comic verses alternated with serious tales and apostrophes to the beloved hills; and often from the most solemn beginnings he would pass, when a sudden freak would seize him, into the wildest mockery" (30). Even years later, he could pull up their "wildest mockery" from memory:

> Bells: We tinkle for dinner, and—O careless sinner,
> We clatter to call you to Church!
> O, never neglect us, or you'll recollect us
> Some day when you're left in the lurch!
> Trumpets: We bray for the battle, and 'mid the last rattle
> We'll conquer the din of the bell—
> Take care, my good fellow, while thus we rebellow,
> That you're not sent posthaste to Hell! (30)

Alluding to various Christian admonitions regularly found in hymns—"O careless sinner" and "sent posthaste to Hell!"—the boys yet put the words in the "mouths" of nonthreatening, inanimate objects, so they can mock the admonitions they give. Creating words ("rebellow") and using internal rhyme ("neglect us/recollect us") showcase their verbal aptitude. Not only irreverent, the verse borders on the obscene (for who *is* tinkling if humans sing the verse?). It is exactly what you might expect from boys, then and now.

Perhaps the best example I have found of hymn parodying is a casual comment from a Nonconformist adult who, recalling days in "The Chapel," remembered "naughty boys" in a Yorkshire village who parodied the lyrics of "Here we suffer grief and pain" which began our chapter:

> Here we suffer grief and pain—
> Over the road they're doing the same,

Next door they're suffering more
Oh, won't it be joyful when we part to meet no more?
(qtd. in K. Young, *Chapel* 79)

Exorcising all reference to religion, hope of heaven, and joy in Jesus, the children yet diminish the earthly suffering bewailed in the original, too. Since everyone is suffering—poor neighbors, (potentially rich) folks down the road—the suffering of poverty, health, and heartache is all equalized. Or perhaps he who suffers most wins the prize. The clincher is the last line, which in the original concerned the joy "when we meet to part no more," alluding to eternity in heaven. Now, with a quick inversion of verbs, it becomes a satirical wish to be parted a bit more from annoying friends and neighbors. The charm of parody is that words are manipulated while the original, "unoffending" tune remains constant. Thus, the spritely tune which children loved with the hymn becomes a delightful, danceable tune to the parody, perhaps even more fitting. Which is the true child comment to this hymn? That of the dying Franky yet created by an adult who was herself mourning the death of her own child and offering a semantic situation true to many children dying during the century? Or is it that by children themselves, safe from death for the moment and enjoying the pleasure of playful parody and singing?

*Diaries*

The existence and survival of nineteenth-century children's diaries is sadly limited, as a new study I am conducting is revealing. When youthful diaries have been preserved and published, they are usually of the notable Victorians (*The Barretts at Hope End; The Early Diary of Elizabeth Barrett Browning*, edited by Elizabeth Berridge and published in 1974, is one such example). Others, thought to be worth less, must have been quickly tossed (though the Great Diary Project in London is attempting to rescue such diaries as descendants clear their attics). Those of the common child are much rarer. Literacy, availability of writing supplies, and actual time to write limited many working-class children's ability to keep journals. Other times simply the middle-class child's lack of motivation prevented the longevity of a diary: I have found several preprinted diary books clearly given to a child as a Christmas gift whose entries barely last two months.[17] When diaries do surface, they are often brief recordings of the day's events. But in a great many of them, these events will include hymn singing and these brief references are undoubtedly less frequent than the actual occurrences of hymn singing in their lives. What my study has thus far exposed is that hymn singing was an integral facet of nineteenth-century children's lives, and many children treasured it.[18]

---

[17] The diary of Arnold Whitehouse (1888, age 10) from the Gloucestershire Archives ends February 1; the diary of Annie Rothchild (later York), now housed at the British Library, runs barely four months (December 14, 1858–March 9, 1859).

[18] I am indebted to various librarians who aided me in retrieving about 22 children's manuscript-diaries during a research trip to the UK, May 2014: Sarah Aitken at the Gloucestershire Archives, Colin Harris, Special Collections Superintendent, Bodleian

For one, hymn singing brought families together. Adults may mention these moments (*My Children's Diary*, 1824, 159–60) but so do children. Ida Dean, 14-year-old daughter of lower middle-class hotel managers at St. Alban's, notes in almost every Sunday entry an important family tradition of visiting her Aunt Pod's on Sunday nights for singing, then reveals that they are singing "Sankey's Hymns" (November 10, 1901; journal housed at the Gloucestershire Archives). (Sankey's hymns were certainly gaining currency much earlier, as evidenced by a reference in Mary Ann Proust's 1882 diary [June 5]; see footnote 8 in my Introduction for more about Sankey.) Hymns were also a part of significant secular events. Hastings Rashdall, a precocious schoolboy at Harrow, 1871–1873, and future theologian, writes in his 1873 diary about the pomp and ceremony of the end-of-term Speech Day ceremony; this included "Two hymns ... [which] were sung one before and one after [the processional] by the School accompanied by the Band of the Soul's (?) Guard" (July 2, 1873 entry; journal in the Bodleian Special Collections). Hymn singing was not confined to land, either: a child (unnamed), taking a return boat from New Zealand to London after visiting her father, writes about sea-sickness, bands on board, church services ... and that "There were hymns in the evening on deck" (Sunday, October 16, 1882; British Library collection).

Not surprisingly, hymnody denoted sacred spaces as well. Alice Smith, age 9, begins her diary of 1876 by describing a "Bible class" conducted by her older brother: "We read part of the fifth chapter of St. Matthew. Then we wrote down the Blesseds. Then we sang some hymns and pretended that a chair was an organ. We sang the Ninty [sic] and Nine and what a friend we have in Jesus and Once for all and I forget the rest. Then we prayed" (Diary of Alyssa Whitall Smith, in the Lilly Library Collection, Indiana University). When hymn books are given as gifts, this might be important enough to record in a journal, as with Mary Ann Proust, her father's gift of "the Wesleyan Hymn Book with tunes" (noted on Friday [July] 4, 1882; journal owned by the Great Diary Project, Bishopsgate). And hymns mark the passage of family deaths; Ida May Berry records in her 1901 diary that the family sang "Abide with me" and "Rock of ages" with Grandma Berry before she died (January 15, 1902 entry; diary held by the Great Diary Project, Bishopsgate). Caroline Richards, quoted earlier, records the death of an important minister in her life and the hymns sung at his deathbed:

> December 1—Dr. Carr is dead. He had a stroke of paralysis two weeks ago and
> for several days he has been unconscious. The choir of our church, of which he

Libraries; Luke Parks and Stefan Dickers with the Great Diary Project at Bishopsgate Institute, London; and many librarians and staff at University College London, the National Archives, and the British Library. Five other diaries (three English, two American) were found at the Lilly Library, Indiana University, with help from librarian Isabel Planton, and the Newberry Library, Chicago. All are unpublished diaries except where noted. I will use the terms "journal" and "diary" interchangeably as per the Victorian convention: see, for example, the mother's explanation of their interchangeability (2–3) in *My Children's Diary or, The Moral of the Passing Hour* (1824).

was leader for so long, and *some of the young people* came and stood around his bed and sang, "Jesus, Lover of My Soul." They did not know whether he was conscious or not, but they thought so because the tears ran down his cheeks from his closed eyelids, though he could not speak or move. (December 1, 1861 entry; my italics)

The children feel they have something to offer even at the last by singing this hymn, not in sentimental fashion for a child but as a semantic gesture of true grief *by* children. Having quoted the lines to this hymn earlier, I suggest how it must have truly resonated with those grieving.

Clearly children are not passively singing these hymns, but often thinking through their meaning. Admittedly, that meaning could be misleading. Ten-year-old Catherine Havens admits to how confusing a "severe" Watts hymn, "Sleeper awake! For God is here" (which she quotes in its entirety), could be. Of its last line, "Like young Abijah may I see / That good things may be found in me," she whimsically writes that "my sister says when she was a little girl and learned it, she always thought that when Abijah died, they cut him open and found sugar plums in him" (August 6, 1849, *Diary of a Little Girl in Old New York* [1919]). Other times, hymn-texts are more transparent than other religious texts. Little 7-year-old Mary Chard, writing to her parents who were missionaries in India in 1883, must have been counseled by her father to listen to the sermons at church. She writes back, "Father darling I understand Mr. Ports (?) sermons but I do not understand Mr. Parishs. I can join in all the hymns in c[hurch?]. I can say some of them perfectly without a book" (November 10, 1883 entry). She struggles to comprehend the sermons but, significantly, the hymns come so easily to her that she has memorized several of them. Children debate about the ways to teach hymns, too, as 12-year-old Emily Shore discusses in her 1832 journal:

Every evening of Sunday, after tea, mamma hears us say a hymn of Watts', which we have previously learnt, each saying one verse … I believe none of us are taught anything which is not thoroughly explained, and I am afraid this is too unusual … If children are taught hymns and prayers before they can perceive anything of their meaning it is likely to produce a superstitious idea that they are to derive good from what they say, and will thereby please God, as the Roman Catholics do with their Latin prayers. But this is not my own idea; I learnt it from Whately, and must not pass it off as original. (27–8)

In this extended discussion, Emily evaluates her own family's practice of conversing about hymns' meanings and also the problems when families throw difficult hymns at young children who may mouth the words without understanding their import. These are salient points, showing both the use and misuse of hymns with young children, and an older child who values the significance of what she sings (Sunday, December 23, 1832 entry; *Journal of Emily Shore* [1891]).

Understanding the textual value of hymns could help children in life's struggles. Alice Smith's sister, Mary, writes in her journal (age 12, 1876) of a time when she was tempted to reveal a secret, "But I remember that hymn 'Yield not to temptation, For yielding is sin' so I will obey it!!" (October 19, 1876 entry, Mary W. Smith Diary, Lilly Library collection, Indiana University). The following New Year's, she made the resolution, among others, "not to dream so much[.] [B]etter to say over hymns or poetry," registering, of course, that hymns could often be antithetical to day-dreaming, but also recognizing that learning hymns and poetry would be more beneficial for her (January 1, 1877 entry). Mary Ann Proust, slightly older (age 21), finds comfort when desiring a friend to "tell my feelings too [sic]" because she does have a friend in Jesus, "all our griefs and sorrows to bear, what a privilege to carry everything to God in prayer" (Wednesday, May 8 entry), quoting the words (a bit inaccurately) to Joseph Scriven's popular 1855 hymn, "What a friend we have in Jesus."

Hymns could truly be pivotal to religious conviction and conversion. Prudence Jenkin leaves a record through her letters, diary entries, and friends' journals as compiled by her surviving sister (not named) in *The Triumph of Grace Exemplified in the Diary, Correspondence, Experience, and Happy Deaths of Prudence and Mary Jenkin* (London: J. Mason, 1836) of just such a moment. Having gone through a spiritual crisis at boarding school, Prudence returns home to friends and family. Once home, a friend records Prudence's conversion in part due to a hymn extolling Christ's sacrifice. Her friend writes:

> I shall not soon forget that night. Prudence was to sleep in my room ... and she opened to me all her heart; repeatedly saying, "I never can believe that Jesus does accept me" ... I spoke of that faith which justifies the ungodly ... I also repeated some expressive verses of hymns, among which were the lines,—
>
> "Thou hast by full ransom paid
>         And in thy wounds I rest";
>
> when she instantly sprang up, saying, "I can, I do believe; all my load is gone.
>
> I'll praise my Maker whilst I've breath;
> And when my voice is lost in death,
>         Praise shall employ my nobler powers." (17–18)

Though the former hymn is less recognizable, the latter is a famous one by Isaac Watts; both, apparently, had the full force to lead to Prudence's conversion. Both Prudence and her sister Mary, throughout the narrative and within their own journals and letters cited in this book, rely upon hymn-texts and religious verse to express the inexpressible depth of pious feelings that color their days and even their "holy deaths."[19]

In contrast, children also utilized hymns during times of play. Mary Chard recalls a delightful family practice of marching to hymn tunes, as she reminds her parents in one of her letters: "of course we won't be too dignified to have

---

[19]   Such verse and hymns are quoted on pages 20, 21, 22, 39, 41, 108, 112, 113, 119, 120, 121, 127, 129, 131, and 134.

processions round the table singing hymns like we used to do" (March 3, 1885 entry, age 9). Hymns were therefore not simply for imparting deep theology but a means of play and singing, something children did not feel "too dignified" to do.

Favorite hymn titles crop up in children's diaries as well. Ida May Berry, an avid singer and pianist, in her 1902 diary when she was 18, excitedly records that at the Devotional at the Guild, the attendees sang hymn favorites of four of her friends, carefully logging each hymn with the friend's name:

> Ruby Long "oh timely happy, timely wise"
> Queenie Wright "Christian seek not just repose"
> Harry Seed "When I survey the wondrous cross"
> Gertrude Bardsley "Oh how blest the hour Lord Jesus." (November 16, 1902 entry)

This list demonstrates that youth might corroborate the favorites of a culture; Harry's favorite is Watts's famous "When I survey the wondrous cross." However, hymns of more limited circulation could also hold personal meaning: Ruby's favorite is found in only four children's hymnals of my study, Gertrude's only in one, and Queenie's hymn ("Christians seek") is included in none.

Significant, too, is that youth contributed their enjoyment of hymn music to charities and services in their community: Ida's friend Ruby Long sang "Lead kindly light" for workhouse inmates (November 30, 1902 entry) and Ida herself "played the Hymns for them" at a Band of Hope Lantern Entertainment (November 17, 1902).

Most children's diaries are still in manuscript form; if published, it was, ironically, due to the child's death, and their family's wish to memorialize them (e.g., Prudence Jenkin, Emily Shore). But I give as a final statement words from a child who did *not* die but lived at least to age 65 when she wrote her own memoirs, Lucy Larcom whose words opened this book, and who writes about her hymn-singing younger self and the great value of hymns in her child-life:

> To learn hymns was not only a pastime, but a pleasure which it would have been almost cruel to deprive me of. It did not seem to me as if I learned them, but as if they just gave themselves to me while I read them over; as if they, and the unseen things they sang about, became a part of me. Some of the old hymns did seem to lend us wings, so full were they of aspiration and hope and courage. To a little child, reading them or hearing them sung was like being caught up in a strong man's arms, to gaze upon some wonderful landscape. (68)

Breaking down the barrier between young and old based on age only, Lucy concludes:

> There is something at the heart of a true song or hymn which keeps the heart young that listens. It is like a breeze from the eternal hills … a spiritual freshness, which has nothing to do with time or decay. (73)

And certainly nothing to do with death only, not when hymns keep the "heart young."

## Conclusion

Hymns formed the fabric of children's lives, woven into daily and weekly events, at times with great enthusiasm, at other times simply a part of living and dying. If Victorian children "should be seen and not heard," society yet sanctioned the child to be heard singing in powerful ways: during moments of learning, of church-going, of social agitating, even of dying. And the hymns themselves meant a great deal to children in this context. Early on in my research, I was touched to find a transcription that has fueled my dedication to this study ever since. In the back cover of a copy of *The Weston Hymnbook for Children* (1849) now owned by the John Rylands Library, Manchester, and written in a childish hand, are these arresting annotations:

> Steel [sic] not this Book for fear of shame for hear [sic] you See the oners [sic] name Mary Ann Hadfield 1852.

Next to the child's scrawl is another notation, in a different handwriting:

> Mary Ann Hadfield Died 13 of Dec. 1855 aged 11 years and 7 months. This being her Book and Given to her ant [sic] Maryann Swan Trevor (sp?) at her Death in Memory of the above.

Children do not bequeath to aunts at their deaths those books which were not of great importance to them during their lives. It is time not only to resurrect the Victorian child, as many scholars are doing, but to resurrect their hymns as well. We need to appreciate children's hymnody before we can ever fully understand children's lives. And though we cannot hear their actual voices singing the hymns anymore, we can imagine the joy and sincerity and impishness with which they sang them.

# Works Cited

**Primary Sources**

[Alexander, C. F.] *Hymns for Little Children*. 1848. 25th ed., illustrated. London: Joseph Masters, 1867. Print.

[Alexander, Cecil Frances.] *Hymns for Little Children*. 1848. 17th ed. London: Joseph Masters, 1858. Print.

Antliff, William, ed. *The Primitive Methodist Sabbath-School Hymn Book*. London: Richard Davies, 1864. Print.

Armstrong, Edmund J. *The Life and Letters of Edmund J. Armstrong*. London: Longmans, Green, 1877. Print.

Bacon, Dolores, ed. *Hymns That Every Child Should Know: A Selection of the Best Hymns of All Nations for Young People*. London: Doubleday, Page, 1907. Print.

*Band of Mercy Advocate*. Vols. 1–5. London: S. W. Partridge, 1879–1881. Print.

Barbauld, Anna Laetitia. *Hymns in Prose for Children*. 1781. London: John Murray, 1864. Internet Archive. Web. Accessed February 26, 2014.

Barrett, George S., ed. *A Service Book for Church and School*. London: Sunday School Union, 1891. Print.

Bateman, C. H., ed. *The Children's Hymnal and Christian Year for use at Children's Services*. London: John Hodges, 1872. Print.

———. *Sacred Melodies for Children, Selected Chiefly on the Ground of their Popularity with Children*. Edinburgh: Gall and Inglis, 1843. Print.

Bateman, Henry. *Sunday Sunshine: New Hymns and Poems for the Young*. London: James Nisbet, 1858. Print.

Benson, Joseph. *Hymns for Children and Young Persons, on the Principal Truths and Duties of Religion and Morality, Selected from Various Authors, and Arranged in a Natural and Systematic Order*. London: George Story, 1806. Print.

———. *Hymns for Children, Selected Chiefly from the Publications of the Rev. John and Charles Wesley and Dr. Watts and Arranged in Proper Order*. London: George Story, 1814. Print.

Betts, Henry John. *The Children's Hosannah: A Selection of Upwards of One Hundred and Twenty Hymns, Adapted for Sunday School and Family Use*. London: Jarrold and Sons, 1858. Print.

Blake, William. *The Songs of Innocence and of Experience* [Facsimile of the Original Outlines]. Intro. Edwin J. Ellis. London: Bernard Quaritch, 1893. Internet Archive. Web. Accessed July 30, 2013.

Bonar, James. *School Worship*. London: James Nisbet, 1876. Print.

Bonner, Carey, ed. *The Sunday School Hymnary: A Twentieth Century Hymnal for Young People*. London: Sunday School Union, 1905. Print.

Booth, General, comp. *Salvation Army Songs*. London: Publishing Dept., n.d. Print.

Booth, George, ed. *The Primitive Methodist Hymnal with Accompanying Tunes*. London: James B. Knapp, 1889. Print.

Braine, W. R., comp. *Hymns for the Church or Home Circle: The Poetry sel. From the Keble, Bishop Heber, Milman, Mrs. Adams, Mrs. Steele, James Montgomery, Lyte, Grant, Alexander, Milton, etc*. London: Novello, 1861. Print.

*Brief Memoirs of Remarkable Children, Whose Learning or Whose Piety is Worthy the Imitation of those Little Boys and Girls Who Desire to Improve their Minds, to Increase in Wisdom, and to Grow in Favour with God and Man, Collected by a Clergyman of the Church of England*. London: James Nisbet, 1822. Google Scholar. Web. Accessed April 1, 2014.

[Brock, Mrs. Carey, ed.] *The Children's Hymn Book for Use in Children's Services, Sunday Schools, and Families*. Published under the Revision of the Right Rev.'s W. Walsham How, Ashton Oxenden, and John Ellerton. London: Rivingtons, Waterloo, 1878. Print.

Brownlow, John. *The History and Objects of the Foundling Hospital with a Memoir of the Founder*. 1865. 4th ed. London: C. Jaques, 1881. Internet Archive. Web. Accessed May 5, 2013.

Burke, Thomas. *Son of London*. London: Readers Union, 1948. Print.

Burnett, John. *Bands of Hope in Town and Village; How to Start and Work Them*. London: Elliot Stock, 1877. Print.

Button, H. Elliot, ed. *The Young People's Hymnal, Edition with Tunes*. London: Charles H. Kelly, 1896. Print.

Cameron, George. *Morning and Evening Hymns for Every Day of the Year, for the Family and Church with Appropriate Music*. Glasgow: Publishing Office, 1857. Print.

Capel, Adela. *A Victorian Teenager's Diary: The Diary of Lady Adela Capel of Cassiobury, 1841–1842*. Ed. and intro. Marian Strachan. Hertfordshire: Hertfordshire Record Society, 2006. Print.

*Capper's Temperance Melodist, Comprising Original Hymns and Songs, Suitable for Temperance Societies and Bands of Hope*. Salford: Knight and Turton, 1870. Print.

Carroll, Lewis. *Alice in Wonderland*. 1865. Norton Critical Edition. Ed. Donald J. Gray. 2nd ed. New York: W. W. Norton, 1992. Print.

Cavendish, Lady Frederick. *The Diary of Lady Frederick Cavendish*. Ed. John Bailey. With illustrations. 2 vols. London: John Murray, 1927. Print.

Chard, Mary. *The First Letters of S. M. C. [Sarah Mary Chard] Written to Father and Mother in India from 1880 to 1887 (Four to Eleven Years of Age)*. John Johnson Collection, Bodleian Library, Oxford. MS. Eng. let. E. 145. Fol. 22.

*The Children's Hymn and Chant Book*. London: John Marshall, 1873. Print.

*The Children's Hymn Book*. London: T. Nelson, 1854. Print.

*Children's Hymns*. London: SPCK, 1873. Print.

*Children's Hymns with Musical Directory, and School Prayers, Published under the Direction of the Tract Committee*. London: SPCK, 1876. Print.

*The Children's Liturgy and Hymn Book*. London: Rivingtons, 1865. Print.

*The Christian Mother's Hymn Book*. London: Wertheim and Macintosh, 1855. Print.

*Church Hymnal.* New Edition Revised and Enlarged by Permission of the General Synod of the Church of Ireland. Dublin: Association for Discountenancing Vice and Promoting the Knowledge and Practice of the Christian Religion, n.d. Print.

Church of England Temperance Society. "Exeter Hall Meeting Programme—Music Edition." Tuesday, April 26, 1898. Print.

Clark, Thomas, arr. *The Juvenile Harmonist: A Selection of Tunes and Pieces for Children.* London: Sunday School Union, 1843. Print.

Compston, Rev. J. *Lancashire Sunday-School Songs with Music: Being the Words and Music of One-Hundred-Twenty-Three Valuable and Popular Hymns, Original and Selected, for Use in Sunday Schools.* London: W. and F. G. Cash, 1857. Print.

Coward, George, comp. *The Child's Book of Praise.* Durham: J.H. Veitch, 1871. Print.

Crowell, Henry. Diaries, November 1872–September 1886. 2 vols. Transcript (only). Bodleian Library, Oxford University. Special Collections. MS. Eng. misc. c. 402/1–2.

Cullen, John. *The Hundred Best Hymns in the English Language.* London: George Routledge, n.d. Print.

Currie, James, ed. *Infant School Hymns and Songs with Appropriate Melodies.* Edinburgh: Thomas Laurie, 1865. Print.

Curwen, John. *The Children's Sabbath Hymn Book, Including The Child's Own Hymn Book.* London: Ward, 1851. Print.

———. *School Songs, Sacred, Moral, and Descriptive.* London: Ward, 1851. Print.

Dean, Ira. Unpublished Diaries, 1900–1906. Ages 13–19. Gloucester Archives. Catalogue No. D7889/2/1–4. Print.

Dickens, Charles. *The Old Curiosity Shop.* 1840–1841. Ed. Angus Easson. Intro. Malcolm Andrews. Illus. George Cattermole, Hablot K. Browne, Samuel Williams, and Daniel Maclise. London: Penguin, 1985. Print.

Dykes, Rev. John B., ed. *Accompanying Tunes to the 'Hymns for Infant Children'.* London: Jos. Masters, 1862. Print.

*The Early Dead; Containing Brief Memoirs of Several Sunday-School Children Who Died in 1846.* New York: Carlton and Porter (Sunday-School Union), 1847. Google Scholar. Web. Accessed January 5, 2013.

*Easy Hymns for the Use of Children in the National Schools.* London: SPCK, 1850. Print.

Eddy, Sarah J. *Songs of Happy Life for Schools, Homes, and Bands of Mercy.* London: George Bell and Sons, 1897. Print.

———. *Songs of Happy Life for Schools, Homes, and Bands of Mercy.* Providence, RI: Art and Nature Study Publ., 1897. Google Scholar. Web. Accessed July 20, 2012.

Ellerton, John, ed. *Hymns for Schools and Bible Classes.* Brighton: H. & C. Treacher, 1859. Print.

Ellis, Sarah Stickney. *The Daughters of England: Their Society, Character, and Responsibility.* New York: D. Appleton, 1843. Print.

Esterbrooke, John H. *Bands of Hope: Their Vast Importance, and How to Form and Sustain Them*. London: Job Caudwell, 1850. Print.

Farmer, John, ed. *Hymns and Chorales for Schools and Colleges*. Oxford: Clarendon Press, 1892. Print.

Farrington, Charlotte, ed. *Hymns for Children with Opening and Closing Services and Songs and Hymns for Bands of Mercy and of Hope*. London: Sunday School Association, 1894. Print.

*First Steps to Temperance, for Young Children in Schools, Families, or Bands of Hope*. London: National Temperance Publ., 1883. Print.

Foley, Winifred. *A Child in the Forest*. London: British Broadcasting Corporation, 1974. Print.

Gadsby, William, ed. *A Selection of Hymns from Various Authors for the Use of Sunday Schools*. Manchester: John Gadsby and London: John Bennett, 1836. Print.

Gaskell, Elizabeth. *North and South*. 1854–1855. Ed. Angus Easson. Oxford: Oxford UP, 1982. Print.

———. "The Three Eras of Libbie Marsh [sic]". 1847. In *Elizabeth Gaskell: Four Short Stories*. Intro. Anna Walters. London: Routledge, Pandora, 1983. Print.

*Golden Bells: Hymns for Young People*. 703 Pieces. New and Enlarged Edition. London: Children's Special Service Mission, n.d., c. 1925. Print.

*Golden Bells; or, Hymns for Our Children*. 1890. London: Children's Special Service Mission, n.d. Print.

*Gospel Temperance Songs Sung at Richard T. Booth's Temperance Meetings*. London: Morgan and Scott, n.d. Print.

Gregg, T. H., ed. *The Sunday-School Hymnal*. London: Marlborough, 1870. Print.

Griffiths, J. R. *The Bible Christian Sunday-School Hymnal with Tunes*. London: Bible Christian Book-Room, 1898. Print.

Gunn, E. H. Mayo, ed. *School Hymns: With Tunes. A Book of Praise for Teachers and Scholars, Guilds, Christian Bands, Christian Endeavor Societies*. London: James Clarke, 1883. Print.

H. P. H. [Hester Periam Hawkins] and Edwin Moss, musical editor. *The Home Hymn Book: A Manual of Sacred Song for the Family Circle*. 1885. 2nd ed. London: Novello, Ewer, 1890. Print.

Hall, Newman, comp. *Harmonised Hymns and Songs for Bands of Hope*. Harmonized by Rev. C. G. Rowe. London: William Tweedie, 1862. Print.

Hammond, Henry A. *Our National Temperance Hymn and Song Book*. London: Longmans, 1871. Print.

Hardy, Thomas. *Far from the Madding Crowd*. 1874. Ed. Suzanne B. Falck-Yi. Oxford: Oxford UP, 2002. Print.

———. *Mayor of Casterbridge*. 1886. Ed. Dale Kramer. Oxford: Oxford UP, 1987. Print.

———. *Tess of the d'Urbervilles*. 1891. Ed. Juliet Grindle and Simon Gatrell. Oxford: Oxford UP, 1988. Print.

———. *Thomas Hardy: The Complete Poems*. Ed. James Gibson. New York: Palgrave, 2001. Print.

[Harrison, Miss, ed.] *The Weston Hymn Book for Children*. London: Wertheim and Macintosh, 1849. Print.

Havens, Catherine Elizabeth. *Diary of a Little Girl in Old New York*. New York: H. C. Brown, 1919. Print.

Hogarth, George, arr. and John Curwen, ed. *The Child's Own Tune Book: Hymns and Chants, and Sacred Songs for Sunday Schools, Arr. For 3 Voices*. London: T. Ward, 1846. Print.

Hopkins, J. W., comp. *Book of Odes, with Tunes, for Juvenile Temples, Senior Temples, and Junior Lodges*. Birmingham: Templar Printing Works, n.d. Print.

Horsley, William. *A Collection of Hymns and Psalm Tunes: Sung in the Chapel of the Asylum for Female Orphans*. London: Clements, 1820. Print.

Hoyle, William. *Temperance Offering; One Hundred and Twenty Melodies for Bands of Hope*. London: W. Tweedie, 1863. Print.

Hubbard, Alfred J. *The Children's Tune-Book: Containing the Treble and Alto Parts of the Wesleyan Sunday-School Tune-Book*. London: John Mason, 1860. Print.

Hughes, Mary Vivian [Molly]. *A Victorian Family, 1870–1900*. London: Guild, 1990. Print.

Hughes, Thomas. *Tom Brown's School Days, by An Old Boy (Thomas Hughes)*. 1857. London: J. M. Dent, 1911. Print.

*Hymn-Book for the Use of Uppingham and Sherborne Schools*. London: Novello, Ewer, 1874. Print.

*Hymn-Book for the Use of Wellington College*. Ed. Edward White Benson. 1st ed. London: David Nutt, 1860. Print.

*Hymns and Bible Songs for Use in Sunday Schools*. 4th ed. Manchester: General Sunday School Committee of Churches of Christ, 1895. Print.

*Hymns and Carols for the Children of the Church*. London: Church Sisters Homes, 1871. Print.

*Hymns and Choral Songs for Whitsuntide and Anniversary Services for Bands of Hope and Temperance Meetings; Together with Hymns and Carols for Christmas and the New Year*. Manchester: Manchester District Sunday School Union, 1899. Print.

*Hymns and Poems for Very Little Children*. By Hon. M. E. L. [Margaret Elizabeth Leigh Child-Villiers, Countess of Jersey, 1849–1945]. London: Religious Tract Society, 1875. Print.

*Hymns and Rhymes for Children: By the Daughter of a Clergyman*. London: Ward, Lock, and Tyler, 1871. Print.

*Hymns and Songs for Bands of Hope, Containing One Hundred and Seventy-Six Pieces*. London: United Kingdom Band of Hope Union, 1894. Print.

*Hymns and Tunes for Church Sunday School*. Bradford, 1899. Print.

*Hymns for Children Selected with a View of Being Learnt by Heart*. Oxford and London: John Henry and James Parker, 1856. Print.

*Hymns for Factory Children, Original and Paraphrased; to which are added, Three Songs and a Short Heroic*. Leeds: T. Inchbold, 1831. Print.

*Hymns for Infant Children.* London: Joseph Masters, 1852. Print.

*Hymns for Schools, Missions, and Bible Classes.* London: Church Press and
  G. J. Palmer, 1866. Print.

*Hymns for Sunday Schools, Arranged According to the Order of the Ecclesiastical
  Year.* London: Rivingtons, 1866. Print.

*Hymns for the Chapel of Harrow School.* 3rd ed. Harrow: Crossley and Clarke,
  1866. Internet Archive, from Harvard University collections. Web. Accessed
  June 4, 2013.

*Hymns for the Chapel of Harrow School.* 4th ed. Harrow: Wilbee, 1881. Internet
  Archive, from Harvard University collections. Web. Accessed June 6, 2013.

*Hymns for the Use of Rugby School.* Rugby: W. Billington, 1876. Internet Archive,
  from Harvard University collections. Web. Accessed June 6, 2013.

*Hymns for the Use of the Providence Sunday Schools Selected from Various
  Authors.* Keighley: R. Ahed, 1821. Print.

*Hymns for Use in the Sunday School and the Guild and at Children's Services in
  the Congregation.* Halifax: Womersley, Exchange Printing Works, 1891. Print.

*Hymns of Childhood for Primary and Junior Grades.* Ed. I. H. Meredith, Arthur
  Grantley, and Edith Sandford Tillotson. Princeton, NJ: Tullar Meredith,
  1939. Print.

*Hymns to be Sung at City Road Chapel, near Finsbury Square, on Sunday,
  November 27, 1825 by the Children of the Methodist Sunday Schools.* London:
  W. Tyler, 1825. Print.

*Hymns to be Sung by the Children of the Sunday School at the Methodist Chapel,
  Frome, on Sunday, May 30th, 1813.* Frome: A. Crocker and Sons, 1813. Print.

*Infants' Songs for Home and School.* London: Wesleyan Methodist Sunday School
  Union, 1876. Print.

Inglis, J. Gall and E.W. *282 Hymns and Melodies for School and Family Use.*
  Edinburgh: Gall and Inglis, 1893. Print.

Jackson, Annabel. *A Victorian Childhood.* London: Methuen, 1932. Print.

Jones, Joseph. *Cottage Verse: A Collection of Hymns and Spiritual Songs; Chiefly
  Intended for the Use of Cottagers and Young Persons.* London: Hamilton,
  Adams, 1852. Print.

Jones, L. E. *A Victorian Boyhood.* London: Macmillan, 1955. Print.

*Joyful Songs for Sunday School and Home, Being a Selection of Two Hundred
  Hymns.* London: SSU, 1890. Print.

Kendon, Frank. *The Small Years.* Intro. Walter de la Mare. Cambridge: Cambridge
  UP, 1930. Print.

Kingdom, Frank. *Jacob's Ladder: The Days of My Youth.* New York: L. B. Fischer,
  1943. Print.

Lamont, Thomas. *My Boyhood in a Parsonage: Some Brief Sketches of American
  Life Towards the Close of the Last Century.* New York: Harper, 1946. Print.

Larcom, Lucy. *A New England Childhood Outlined from Memory.* Boston:
  Houghton, Mifflin, 1889. Print.

Leach, A., ed. *The Methodist Band of Hope Hymnal.* London: H. Webber,
  1876. Print.

Leeson, Jane E. *Hymns and Scenes of Childhood, or A Sponsor's Gift*. London: James Burns, 1842. Print.

[Lewis, H. K.] *Little Children's Hymns and Songs*. London: Simpkin, Marshall, Hamilton, Kent, 1895. Print.

*Little Footprints on the Old Church Path: A Memoir of a Christian Child*. 2nd ed. Oxford and London: John Henry Parker, 1854. Google Scholar. Web. Accessed December 12, 2013.

Ludbrook, Walter, comp. *The Temperance Meeting Melodist; Containing Hymns and Songs for Temperance and Maine Law Meetings, and Bands of Hope*. London: Job Caudwell, 1861. Print.

MacCarthy, Mary. *A Nineteenth-Century Childhood*. Intro. John Betjeman. London: Hamish Hamilton, 1924. Print.

MacDonald, Greville. *Reminiscences of a Specialist*. London: George Allen, 1932. Print.

Major, S. D., sel. and arr. *A Book of Praise for Home and School*. London: Book Society, 1869. Print.

Mann, John. *Original Hymns: Adapted for Social Prayer-Meetings, Missionary Services, Sunday-Schools and Christians in General*. London: n.p., 1828. Print.

Manning, Leah. *A Life for Education: An Autobiography*. London: Victor Gollancz, 1970. Print.

Martin, Edward. *The Family Altar, a Collection of the Most Favorite Psalms and Hymns*. London: D'Almaine, 1843. Print.

May, Robert. *The Children's Hymn Book; Being a Selection of Hymns from Various Authors, Including Watts' Diving Songs for Children, and Doddridge's Principles of the Christian Religion, Designed for the Use and Instruction of the Rising Generation*. Philadelphia: Thomas and William Bradford, 1811. Print.

Mayo, Elizabeth. *A Selection of Hymns and Poetry for the Use of Infant Schools and Nurseries*. London: E. Suter, 1838. Print.

McManus, Blanche. *Childhood's Songs of Long Ago, Being Some of the Divine and Moral Songs Writ by Rev. Isaac Watts, D. D.* With Picturings by Blanche McManus. New York: E. R. Herrick, 1897. Print.

*Memoir of Mary Lothrop; Who Died in Boston, March 18, 1831, Aged Six Years and Three Months*. New York: American Tract Society, 1832. Web. Accessed January 5, 2013.

*The Methodist Sunday-School Hymn and Tune-Book*. London: Wesleyan Methodist Sunday School Union, 1879. Print.

Miller, John C. *A Hymn Book for Church of England Sunday Schools and Children's Services; Arranged in the Order of the Church's Year*. Birmingham: H. Barclay, 1862. Print.

*A Missionary Catechism for the Use of Children; Containing a Brief View of the Moral Condition of the World and the Progress of Missionary Efforts Among the Heathen*. New Haven: S. Converse, 1821. Print.

"Mogg's New Picture of London." 1844. *The Dictionary of Victorian London*, online. Web. Accessed June 2013.

Monk, William Henry. *The Children's Hymnal with Accompanying Tunes*. London: T. Nelson and Sons, 1876. Print.

———, ed. *Hymns Ancient and Modern for Use in the Services of the Church with Accompanying Tunes*. London: Novello, 1861. Print.

Morgan, Joseph Brown. *Selections from the Christian Endeavor Hymnal: Junior Rallies*. London: Andrew Melrose, 189-. Print.

Mundella, Emma, ed. *The Day School Hymn Book*. London and New York: Novello, Ewer, 1896. Print.

Murphy, G. M. *Popular Melodies and Hymns for Temperance, Band of Hope, and Social Meetings*. London: Tweedie, 1871. Print.

*My Children's Diary, or The Moral of the Passing Hour*. London: Darton and Harvey, 1824. Print.

Neale, John Mason. *Collected Hymns, Sequences, and Carols of John Mason Neale*. Intro. Mary Sackville Lawson. London: Hodder and Stoughton, 1914. Print.

Newman, John R. *Hints on Working Senior and Junior Bands of Hope*. London: Church of England Temperance Society, 1897. Print.

Ogden, W. A. *Silver Songs: Consisting of One Hundred and Eighty Beautiful Melodies for the Sunday School and Sacred Use*. London: W. Nicholson, 1876. Print.

Okey, Thomas. *A Basketful of Memories: An Autobiographical Sketch*. London: J. M. Dent, 1930. Print.

Pacis, Oliver, ed. *Arrows for Temperance Bows, Being One Hundred Readings and Recitations, Suitable for Bands of Hope, Temperance Meetings, and Family Use*. London: Wesleyan Methodist SSU, c. 1888. Print.

Palmer, Herbert E. *The Mistletoe Child: An Autobiography of Childhood*. London, 1935. Print.

Parr, Thomas. *The Sabbath School Reciter, Juvenile Harmonist, and Missionary Advocate*. London: T. Jepps, 1860. Print.

Peabody, Andrew Preston. *Portsmouth Sunday School Hymn Book: Compiled for the Use of the South Parish Sunday School*. Portsmouth: John W. Foster, 1840. Google Scholar. Web. Accessed June 10, 2013.

Pelly, John Kendrick. *The Ragged-School Hymn Book*. London: J. Snow, 1848. Print.

Pitman, Mrs. E. R. *Lady Hymn Writers*. London: T. Nelson and Sons, 1892. Print.

Pollock, Alice. *Portrait of My Victorian Youth*. London: Johnson, 1971. Print.

*Praise and Service Songs for Sunday Schools*. Ed. Gordon D. Shorney and G. Herbert Shorney. Chicago: Tabernacle, 1927. Print.

*The Primitive Methodist Sunday School Union*. London: James Knapp, 1879. Print.

Proust, Mary Ann. Unpublished diary of 1899. Owned by the Great Diary Project, Bishopsgate Institute, London.

*Psalms and Hymns for the Use of Clifton College*. Bristol: J. Leech, 1863. Print.

*Psalms and Hymns for the Use of the Congregation of Rugby School Chapel*. Rugby: Crossley and Billington, 1857. Print.

*Psalms and Hymns with Supplement for Public, Social, and Private Worship.* London: Psalm and Hymn Trust, 1895. Print.

*Psalms, Hymns, and Anthems Used in the Chapel of the Hospital for the Maintenance and Education of Exposed and Deserted Young Children.* London, 1774. Print.

*The Public School Hymn Book.* 1903. Ed. Committee of the Headmasters' Conference. London: Novello, c. 1918. Print.

*Ragged School Hymns by a Ragged-School Teacher.* London: R. B. Shaw, 1848. Print.

Rashdall, Hastings. 1873 Diary. Bodleian Library, Oxford University. Special Collections. MS. Eng. misc. e 361.

Reid, Forrest. *Apostate.* Boston: Constable, 1926. Print.

Rhodes, Benjamin. *Hymns and Divine Songs for Young Persons.* Birmingham: J. Belcher, 1796. Print.

Richards, Caroline Cowles. *Village Life in America, 1852–1872, Including the Period of the American Civil War as Told in the Diary of a School-Girl, by Caroline Cowles Richards.* Intro. Margaret E. Sangster. New York: H. Holt, 1913. Print.

Rogers, Charles. *The National Hymns and Hymn-Writers.* London: Longman, 1861. Google Scholar. Web. Accessed June 3, 2012.

Rothchild, Annie (later York). Unpublished diary, December 14, 1858–March 9, 1859. British Library. Pattersea Papers. Vol. LVI. Add MS 47964. Print.

*The Sabbath-School Bell.* Comp. Horace Waters. Rochester, NY: Adams and Dabney, 1856. Print.

Sankey, Ira D. *Sacred Songs and Solos with Standard Hymns Combined.* London: Morgan and Scott, c. 1896. Print.

*School Hymn Book of the Methodist Church.* London: Methodist Youth Dept., 195-? Print.

*The Scottish Psalter, 1929: Metrical Version and Scripture Paraphrases with Tunes.* London: Oxford UP, 1929. Print.

*Select Music for the Young; 55 Hymns with Tunes.* London: Sunday School Union, 1858. Print.

Sharwood, Mrs. *The Juvenile Missionary Manual; Containing Hymns and Prayers.* London: J. Hatchard and Son, 1843. Print.

Sherwood, Mrs. [Mary Martha]. *The History of the Fairchild Family or, The Child's Manual.* 1818. London: T. Hatchard, 1853. Internet Archive. Web. Accessed August 7, 2014.

Shore, Emily. *Journal of Emily Shore.* Ed. and intro. Barbara Timm Gates. Charlottesville and London: UP of Virginia, 1991. Print.

Smart, Christopher. *Hymns for the Amusement of Children.* 1770. Oxford: Luttrell Society reprint of 3rd ed. London: T. Carnan, 1775. Print.

Smith, Alys Pearsall. Unpublished journal of 1876. H. W. Smith Collection, Lilly Library, Indiana University. Print.

Smith, Mary. Unpublished journal of 1876–1877. H. W. Smith Collection, Lilly Library, Indiana University. Print.

Smith, Rev. W. T. *Missionary Concerts for the Sunday-School: A Collection of Declamations, Select Readings, and Dialogues.* Cincinnati: Walden and Stowe, 1881. Print.

*Soft Showers on the Opening Bud; or, Easy Scripture Lessons for Young Children, with Questions, and Practical Instructions, and an Appropriate Hymn for Each Lesson.* Halifax: Milner and Sowerby, 1859. Print.

*Songs for the Little Ones at Home.* London: Ward, Lock, and Tyler, 1868. Print.

*Songs of Gladness: A Hymn Book for the Young.* London: Old Bailey, 1871. Print.

*Songs of Love and Mercy for the Young: A Hymn Book for Children's Services and Sunday Schools.* London: Morgan and Scott, 1878. Print.

Stead, W. T., ed. *Hymns That Have Helped, Being a Collection of Those Hymns, Whether Jewish, Christian, or Pagan, Which Have Been Found Most Useful to the Children of Men.* London: Stead's Publishing, 1912. Print.

Stone, S. J., comp. *The Penny Hymn Book for Temperance Societies, Designed for the Use at Weekly Meetings, Anniversaries, Children's Gatherings.* London: S. W. Partridge, 1867. Print.

Sturge, H. J., ed. *Texts and Hymns Selected for Children.* London: Hamilton, 1857. Print.

Sturrock, Thomas. *The Sabbath School Tune-Book and Service of Praise for the Sanctuary.* Edinburgh: A. Fullerton, 1855. Print.

Sullivan, Sir Arthur. *Church Hymns with Tunes.* London: SPCK, 1894. Print.

*The Sunday-Scholar's Companion; Being a Selection of Hymns, From Various Authors, for the Use of Sunday Schools.* 7th ed. London: Committee of Silver Street Sunday Schools, 1822. Print.

*The Sunday Scholar's Hymn Book Consisting of Five Hundred Hymns, with Tones for Use in Sunday Schools.* London: Sunday School Union, c. 1880. Print.

*The Sunday School Hymn Book.* Manchester: Sidney Smith, 1871. Print.

*Sunday-School Hymns, Prepared by Direction of the Annual Assembly of the United Methodist Free Churches.* London: W. Reed, 1870. Print.

*The Sunday School Union Hymn-Book.* London: J. Ryder, 1835. Print.

[Sykes, E.] *Temperance Band of Hope Melodies, Original, and Selected.* London: William Tweedie, 1860. Print.

[Taylor, Ann and Jane.] *Hymns for Infant Minds.* 1809. 2nd ed. London: T. Condor, 1810. Print.

*Temperance Band of Hope Melodies, Original and Selected.* Revised by a Conductor. London: W. Tweedie, 1860. Print.

Thomson, A. D. and W. Sugden. *The Training-School Song-Book.* Glasgow: William Hamilton, 1849. Print.

[Thrupp, Dorothy Ann, ed.] *Hymns for the Young Selected for the Purpose of Being Committed to Memory.* London: Religious Tract Society, 1839. Print.

Tilleard, James. *A Collection of Sacred Music for the Use of Schools.* London: J. Alfred Novello, 1849. Print.

*The Triumphs of Grace Exemplified in the Diary, Correspondence, Experience, and Happy Deaths of Prudence and Mary Jenkin*. London: J. Mason, 1836. Print.

*The Union Tune Book with Supplement*. London, 1879. Print.

*The Voice of Praise: For Sunday School and Home with Tunes in Old Notation and Tonic Sol-fa*. London: SSU, 1887. Print.

Walker, J. H., ed. *Psalms and Hymns for the Use of the Congregation of Rugby School Chapel*. Rugby: Crossley and Billington, 1849. Print.

Watts, Isaac. *Divine and Moral Songs, Attempted in an Easy Language for the Use of Children, Revised and Corrected. By Isaac Watts, D. D.* 1715. Boston: Manning and Loring, 1803. Print.

———. *Divine and Moral Songs for Children by Isaac Watts, D. D.* 1715. Illus. incl. four color plates. London: Religious Tract Society, 1869. Print.

———. *Divine and Moral Songs for Children by Rev. Isaac Watts, D. D.* 1715. New Edition. London: S. W. Partridge, 188-. Print.

———. *Divine and Moral Songs for Children by the Rev. Isaac Watts, D. D.* 1715. London: T. Nelson and Sons, 1857. Print.

———. *Divine and Moral Songs for Children by the Rev. Isaac Watts, D. D.* 1715. London: Ward and Lock, 1857. Print.

———. *Divine and Moral Songs for Children by the Rev. Isaac Watts, D. D. Illustrated by Anecdotes and Reflections, Embellished with Beautiful Woodcuts* [by Lossing]. Philadelphia: Presbyterian Board, c. 1850. Print.

———. *Divine and Moral Songs for Children by the Reverend Isaac Watts, D. D.* 1715. Pictured in Colours by Mrs. Arthur Gaskin. London: Elkins Mathews, 1896. Print.

———. *Divine and Moral Songs for the Use of Children by Isaac Watts*. 1715. Thirty Illustrations Drawn on the Wood by C. W. Cope and Engraved by John Thompson. London: John Van Voorst, 1848. Print.

———. *Divine Songs Attempted in an Easy Language for the Use of Children, Ornamented with Cuts, by I. Watts, D. D.* 1715. London: Booksellers and Stationers, c. 1800. Print.

———. *Divine Songs for Children, by Isaac Watts, D. D.* 1715. London: Darton and Harvey, 1802. Print.

———. *Divine Songs, in Easy Language for the Use of Children. By I. Watts, D. D.* 1715. From Ross's Juvenile Library [Illus. attrib. Thomas Bewick.] Glasgow: I. Lumsden, 1814. Print.

———. *Dr. Watts's Divine Songs, for Children*. 1715. Banbury: J. G. Rusher: c. 1835. Print.

———. *Songs, Divine and Moral, for the Use of Children, by I. Watts, D. D.* 1715. Stereotyped and Printed by W. Davison [Wood Engravings]. Alnwick: W. Davison, 184-. Print.

[Wesley, Charles.] *Hymns for Children, and Others of Riper Years*. Bristol: E. Farley, 1763. Print.

Wesley, Charles. *Hymns for Children, and Others of Riper Years*. 1790. 5th ed. London: John Mason, 1842. Print.

Wesley, John. *A Collection of Hymns for the Use of People Called Methodists With a New Supplement.* London: Wesleyan Conference, 1876. Print.

———. *A Collection of Hymns for the Use of People Called Methodists With a New Supplement.* Edition with Tunes. London: Wesleyan Conference, 1877. Print.

*Wesleyan Sunday Schools, Priory-Place, Doncaster, Hymns Appointed to be Sung by the Children on Sunday, April 30th 1848.* Doncaster: T. Brooke, 1848. Print.

Weston, James, comp. *Recitations and Concerted Pieces for Bands of Hope and Sunday Schools.* London: S. W. Partridge, c. 1892. Print.

Whitehouse, Arnold. 1888 unpublished diary. Gloucestershire Archives. Catalogue No. D6035/7/1. Print.

Whittemore, W. M. *The Infant Altar or, Hymns and Prayers for Children.* London: George Stoneman, 1889. Print.

[Wightman, W.] *Try Your Best; or, Proof Against Failure: A Complete Entertainment for Bands of Hope and Juvenile Temples.* London: John Kempster, 1878. Print.

[Williams, Isaac]. *Ancient Hymns for Children.* London: James Burns, 1842. Print.

Wilson, J. H., ed., *Hymns for Children.* N.p., 1866. Print.

[Wilson, Lucy.] *Short and Simple Prayers, with Hymns, for the Use of Children, by the Author of "Mamma's Bible Stories"... etc.* 1844. London: Griffith and Farran, 1882. Print.

Wilson, Sarah. *Hymns for Children.* Music by Sir Arthur Sullivan. Illus. Jane M. Dealy and Fred Marriott. London: Eyre and Spottiswoode [1888]. Print.

Winskill, P. T. *Winskill's Band of Hope Melodist.* London: Tweedie, 1870. Print.

Winters, William, ed. *Sunday School Hymnal for Schools and Private Use.* London: Robert Banks, c. 1892. Print.

Woods, M. A., comp. *Hymns for School Worship.* London: Macmillan, 1890. Print.

Woodward, M., ed. *The Children's Service Book, with Hymns, Litanies, Carols, and Prayers for Public, Private, and School Use.* 1889. Music arr. C. J. Ridsdale. 5th ed. London: Skeffington and Son, 1898. Print.

Woodward, O. P. *The Domestic and Social Harp: A Collection of Tunes and Hymns Intended for Family and Chapel Use.* Hartford: D. R. Woodford, 1848. Print.

Yates, John. *Harrington-School Hymns.* Liverpool: F. B. Wright, 1818. Print.

Yonge, Charlotte. *Henrietta's Wish; or, Domineering: A Tale.* 1850. 2nd ed. London: Joseph Masters, 1853. *Victorian Women Writers Project: An Electronic Collection.* Perry Willett, General Editor. Web. Accessed July 10, 2010.

———. *Leonard, the Lion-Heart.* 1856. Republished in *Village Children.* Intro. Gillian Avery. London: Victor Gollancz, 1967. Print.

[Yonge, Mrs. Frances M., ed.] *The Child's Christian Year: Hymns for Every Sunday and Holy-Day. Compiled for the Use of Parochial Schools.* With contributions by herself, John Keble, and Joseph Anstice. Oxford: J. H. Parker, 1841. Print.

*Young Men's Hymn-Book for Use in Bible Classes and Devotional Meetings.* London: Seeley, Jackson, and Halliday, 1857. Print.

*The Young People's Mission Hymn Book for use in Sunday Schools, Bible Classes, Mission Services, and Temperance Societies.* 1911. London: Sunday School Committee of the Metropolitan Association of Strict Baptist Churches. Print.

## Secondary Sources

Adey, Lionel. *Class and Idol in the English Hymn*. Vancouver: U of British Columbia P, 1988. Print.

———. *Hymns and the Christian "Myth."* Vancouver: U of British Columbia P, 1986. Print.

Allen, Cecil J. *Hymns and the Christian Faith*. London: Pickering and Inglis, 1966. Print.

Altick, Richard D. *Victorian People and Ideas*. New York: W. W. Norton, 1973. Print.

Ariès, Philippe. *Centuries of Childhood: A Social History of Family Life*. Trans. from the French by Robert Baldick. New York: Vintage, 1962. Print.

———. *The Hour of Our Death*. Trans. from the French by Helen Weaver. New York: Oxford UP, 1981. Print.

Arscott, Caroline. "Childhood in Victorian Art." Roundtable: Victorian Children and Childhood. *Journal of Victorian Culture* 9.1 (Spring 2004): 96–106. Print.

Auerbach, Sascha. "'Some Punishment Should Be Devised': Parents, Children, and the State in Victorian London." *Historian* 71.4 (Winter 2009): 757–79. Print.

Avery, Gillian. *Nineteenth Century Children: Heroes and Heroines in English Children's Stories, 1780–1900*. London: Hodder and Stoughton, 1965. Print.

Bailey, Albert Edward. *The Gospel in Hymns: Backgrounds and Interpretations*. New York: Charles Scribner, 1950. Print.

Baker, Steve. *Picturing the Beast: Animals, Identity and Representation*. Manchester: Manchester UP, 1993. Print.

Banerjee, Jacqueline. "Dying Young: A Social Problem and Its Repercussions in the Victorian Novel." *Kobe College Studies* 39.1 (1992): 15–40. Print.

"Be Kind: A Visual History of Humane Education, 1880–1945." National Museum of Animals and Society (Los Angeles). Web. Accessed July 20, 2012.

Beers, Diane L. *For the Prevention of Cruelty: The History and Legacy of Animal Rights Activism in the United States*. Athens: Ohio UP, 2006. E-text.

Benson, Louis F. *The English Hymn: Its Development and Use*. 1915. Richmond, VA: John Knox P, 1962. Print.

Berry, Laura C. *The Child, the State, and the Victorian Novel*. Charlottesville: U of Virginia P, 1999. Print.

Blessington, Francis C. "'That Undisturbed Song of Pure Conceit': *Paradise Lost* and the Epic-Hymn." *Renaissance Genres: Essays on Theory, History, and Interpretation*. Ed. Barbara Kiefer Lewalski. Cambridge, MA: Harvard UP, 1986. 468–95. Print.

Blouet, Olwyn M. "Missionaries." In *Victorian Britain: An Encyclopedia*. Ed. Sally Mitchell. New York: Garland, 1998. 508–9. Print.

Boone, Troy. *Youth of Darkest England: Working-Class Children at the Heart of Victorian Empire*. New York: Routledge, 2005. Print.

Bottigheimer, Ruth B. *The Bible for Children: From the Age of Gutenberg to the Present*. New Haven and London: Yale UP, 1996. Print.

Bradley, Ian. *Abide with Me: The World of Victorian Hymns*. Chicago: GIA and London: SCM, 1997. Print.

———. "The Theology of the Victorian Hymn Tune." *Music and Theology in Nineteenth-Century Britain*. Ed. Martin V. Clarke. Farnham, UK: Ashgate, 2012. Print.

Bradley, Laura. "From Eden to Empire: John Everett Millais's *Cherry Ripe*." *Victorian Studies* 34. 2 (Winter 1991): 179–203. Print.

Bratton, J. S. *The Impact of Victorian Children's Fiction*. London: Croom Helm, 1981. Print.

Brawley, Benjamin. *History of the English Hymn*. New York: Abingdon P, 1932. Print.

Breton, Rob. "Diverting the Drunkard's Path: Chartist Temperance Narratives." *Victorian Literature and Culture* 41 (2013): 139–52. Print.

Briggs, Julia, Dennis Butts, and M. O. Grenby, eds. *Popular Children's Literature in Britain*. Aldershot, UK: Ashgate, 2008.

Brown, Candy Gunther. "Singing Pilgrims: Hymn Narratives of a Pilgrim Community's Progress from This World to That Which Is to Come, 1830–1890." In *Sing Them Over Again to Me: Hymns and Hymnbooks in America*. Ed. Mark A. Noll and Edith L. Blumhofer. Tuscaloosa: U of Alabama P, 2006, 194–213. Print.

———. *Word in the World: Evangelical Writing, Publishing, and Reading in America, 1789–1880*. Chapel Hill: U of North Carolina P, 2004. Print.

Brown, Marilyn R., ed. *Picturing Children: Constructions of Childhood Between Rousseau and Freud*. Aldershot, UK: Ashgate, 2002. Print.

Brown, Penny. *The Captured World: The Child and Childhood in Nineteenth-Century Women's Writing in England*. New York: St. Martin's P, 1993. Print.

Carroll, Yvonne. *A Hymn for Eternity: The Story of Wallace Hartley, Titanic Bandmaster*. 2002. Stroud, UK: The History P, 2011. Print.

Clapp-Itnyre, Alisa. *Angelic Airs, Subversive Songs: Music as Social Discourse in the Victorian Novel*. Athens: Ohio UP, 2002. Print.

———. "The Contentious 'Figure' of Music in the Poetry of Thomas Hardy." *The Hardy Society Journal* 2.2 (Summer 2006): 26–34. Print.

———. "Nineteenth-Century British Children's Hymnody: Re-Tuning the History of Childhood with Chords and Verses." *Children's Literature Association Quarterly* 35.2 (2010): 144–75. Print.

———. "Writing for, yet Apart: Nineteenth-Century Women's Contentious Status as Hymn Writers and Editors of Hymnbooks for Children." *Victorian Literature and Culture* 40.1 (2012): 47–81. Print.

Clarke, Martin V., ed. *Music and Theology in Nineteenth-Century Britain*. Farnham, UK: Ashgate, 2012. Print.

Cleall, Esme. *Missionary Discourses of Difference: Negotiating Otherness in the British Empire, 1840–1900*. New York: Palgrave/Macmillan, 2012. Print.

Cunningham, Hugh. "Childhood Histories." Roundtable: Victorian Children and Childhood. *Journal of Victorian Culture* 9.1 (2004): 90–96. Print.

————. *Children and Childhood in Western Society Since 1500*. 1995. 2nd ed. Harlow, UK: Pearson, Longman, 2005. Print.

————. *The Children of the Poor: Representations of Childhood since the Seventeenth Century*. Oxford: Blackwell, 1991. Print.

Cunningham, Hugh and Joanna Innes, eds. *Charity, Philanthropy and Reform, from the 1690s to 1850*. New York: St. Martin's P, 1998. Print.

Curtis, Gerard. *Visual Words: Art and the Material Book in Victorian England*. Aldershot, UK: Ashgate, 2002. Print.

Curtis, Heather D. "Children of the Heavenly King: Hymns in the Religious and Social Experience of Children, 1780–1850." In *Sing Them Over Again to Me: Hymns and Hymnbooks in America*. Ed. Mark A. Noll and Edith L. Blumhofer. Tuscaloosa: U of Alabama P, 2006. 214–34. Print.

Cutt, Margaret Nancy. *Ministering Angels: A Study of Nineteenth-Century Evangelical Writing for Children*. Herts, UK: Five Owls P, 1979. Print.

Danahay, Martin. "Sexuality and the Working-Class Child's Body in Music Hall." *Victorians Institute Journal* 29 (2001): 102–31. Print.

Darton, F. J. Harvey. *Children's Books in England: Five Centuries of Social Life*. 1932. Cambridge: Cambridge UP, 1970. Print.

Davie, Donald and Robert Stevenson. *English Hymnology in the Eighteenth Century: Papers read at the Clarke Library Seminar, 5 March 1977*. Los Angeles: University of California, 1980. Print.

Davies, Rupert A., Raymond George, and George Rupp, eds. *A History of the Methodist Church in Great Britain*. 5 vols. London: Epworth P, 1978. Print.

Davin, Anna. *Growing Up Poor: Home, School and Street in London 1870–1914*. London: Rivers Oram, 1996. Print.

DeJong, Mary. "'I Want to be Like Jesus': The Self-Defining Power of Evangelical Hymnody." *Journal of the American Academy of Religion* 54.3 (1986): 461–93. Print.

————. "'Theirs the Sweetest Songs': Women Hymn Writers in the Nineteenth-Century United States." In *A Mighty Baptism: Race, Gender, and the Creation of American Protestantism*. Ed. Susan Juster and Lisa MacFarlane. Ithaca, NY: Cornell UP, 1996. 141–67. Print.

Dekker, Jeroen J. H. "Transforming the Nation and the Child: Philanthropy in the Netherlands, Belgium, France, and England, c. 1780–c. 1850." In *Charity, Philanthropy and Reform from the 1690s to 1850*. Ed. Hugh Cunningham and Joanna Innes. Houndmills, UK: Macmillan, 1998. 130–47. Print.

Demers, Patricia, ed. *A Garland from the Golden Age: An Anthology of Children's Literature From 1850 to 1900*. Toronto: Oxford UP, 1983. Print.

————. *Heaven upon Earth: The Form of Moral and Religious Children's Literature, to 1850*. Knoxville: U of Tennessee P, 1993. Print.

Demers, Patricia and Gordon Moyles, eds. *From Instruction to Delight: An Anthology of Children's Literature to 1850*. Toronto: Oxford UP, 1982. Print.

Denisoff, Dennis. *The Nineteenth-Century Child and Consumer Culture*. Aldershot, UK: Ashgate, 2008. Print.

Douglas, Winifred. *Church Music in History and Practice*. New York: Charles Scribner, 1937. Print.

Drain, Susan. *The Anglican Church in Nineteenth Century Britain: Hymns Ancient and Modern (1860–1875)*. Texts and Studies in Religion, vol. 40. Lewiston, NY: Edwin Mellen P, 1989. Print.

Duckworth, Jeannie. *Fagin's Children: Criminal Children in Victorian England*. London and New York: Hambledon and London, 2002. Print.

Dvorak, Wilfred P. "Charles Dickens's *The Old Curiosity Shop*: The Triumph of Compassion." *Papers on Language and Literature* 28.1 (1992): 52–71. MLA Bibliography. PDF file.

Eaton, Anne Thaxter. "Illustrated Books for Children Before 1800." In *Illustrators of Children's Books, 1744–1945*. Ed. Bertha E. Mahony, Louise Payson Latimer, and Beulah Fomsbee. Boston: Horn Book, 1965. 3–24. Print.

Effeny, Alison. *Cassatt: The Masterworks*. New York: Portland House, 1991. Print.

"Emblematica Online: Resources for Emblem Studies." University of Illinois, Urbana-Champaign. Web. Accessed March 11, 2014.

"English Emblem Book Project." Pennsylvania State University. Web. Accessed March 11, 2014.

Ernest, Edward, ed. *The Kate Greenaway Treasury: An Anthology of the Illustrations and Writings of Kate Greenaway*. Intro. Ruth Hill Viguers. Cleveland: World Publ., 1967. Print.

Escott, Harry. *Isaac Watts: Hymnographer: A Study of the Beginnings, Development, and Philosophy of the English Hymn*. London: Independent, 1962. Print.

Fahey, David M. "Temperance Movement." In *Victorian Britain: An Encyclopedia*. Ed. Sally Mitchell. New York: Garland, 1998. 788–90. Print.

Feaver, William. *When We Were Young: Two Centuries of Children's Book Illustration*. London: Thames and Hudson, 1977. Print.

Flegel, Monica. *Conceptualizing Cruelty to Children in Nineteenth-Century England: Literature, Representation, and NSPCC*. Farnham, UK: Ashgate, 2009. Print.

———. "'How Does Your Collar Suit Me?': The Human Animal in the RSPCA's *Animal World* and *Band of Mercy*." *Victorian Literature and Culture* 40.1 (2012): 247–62. Print.

Fyfe, Aileen. "Commerce and Philanthropy: The Religious Tract Society and the Business of Publishing." *Journal of Victorian Culture* 9.2 (Autumn 2004): 164–8. Print.

Galbraith, Gretchen R. *Reading Lives: Reconstructing Childhood, Books, and Schools in Britain, 1870–1920*. New York: St. Martin's P, 1997. Print.

Gallagher, Susan VanZanten. "Domesticity in American Hymns, 1820–1870." In *Sing Them Over Again to Me: Hymns and Hymnbooks in America*. Ed. Mark A. Noll and Edith L. Blumhofer. Tuscaloosa: U of Alabama P, 2006. 235–52. Print.

Gathorne-Hardy, Jonathan. *The Public School Phenomenon, 597–1977*. Harmondsworth, UK: Penguin Books, 1977. Print.

Gentry, Helen. "Graphic Processes in Children's Books." In *Illustrators of Children's Books, 1744–1945*. Ed. Bertha E. Mahony, Louise Payson Latimer, and Beulah Fomsbee. Boston: Horn Book, 1965. 157–72. Print.

Gillman, Frederick John. *The Evolution of the English Hymn*. London: George Allen and Unwin, 1927. Print.

Ginsburg, Michal Peled. "Sentimentality and Survival: the Double Narrative of *The Old Curiosity Shop*." *Dickens Quarterly* 27.2 (2010): 85–101. Print.

Golden, Catherine J., ed. *Book Illustrated: Text, Image, and Culture, 1770–1930*. New Castle, DE: Oak Knoll, 2000. Print.

Goldman, Paul and Simon Cooke, eds. *Reading Victorian Illustration, 1855–1875: Spoils of the Lumber Room*. Farnham, UK: Ashgate, 2012. Print.

Goldstrom, J. M. *The Social Content of Education, 1808–1870: A Study of the Working Class School Reader in England and Ireland*. Shannon, Ireland: Irish UP, 1972. Print.

Green, William John Cooper. *The Development of Musical Education in the Public Schools from 1840 to the Present Day*. Durham theses, Durham University, 1990. *Durham E-Theses Online*. Web. Accessed June 10, 2013.

Grenby, M. O. *The Child Reader, 1700–1840*. Cambridge: Cambridge UP, 2011. Print.

Gryllis, David. *Guardians and Angels: Parents and Children in Nineteenth-Century Literature*. London and Boston: Faber and Faber, 1978. Print.

Gubar, Marah. *Artful Dodgers: Reconceiving the Golden Age of Children's Literature*. Oxford: Oxford UP, 2009. Print.

Hall, Catherine. *Civilising Subjects: Colony and Metropole in the English Imagination, 1830–1867*. Chicago: U of Chicago P, 2002. Print.

Harrison, Brian. *Drink and the Victorians: The Temperance Question in England 1815–1872*. Pittsburgh: U of Pittsburgh P, 1971. Print.

———. *Peaceable Kingdom: Stability and Change in Modern Britain*. Oxford: Clarendon P, 1982. Print.

Hawn, C. Michael and June Hadden Hobbs. "'Thy Love … Hath Broken Every Barrier Down': The Rhetoric of Intimacy in Nineteenth-Century British and American Women's Hymns." In *Music and Theology in Nineteenth-Century Britain*. Ed. Martin V. Clarke. Farnham, UK: Ashgate, 2012. 61–77. Print.

Helmstadter, Richard J. "Orthodox Nonconformity." In *Nineteenth-Century English Religious Traditions: Retrospect and Prospect*. Ed. D. G. Paz. Westport, CT: Greenwood P, 1995. 57–84. Print.

Heywood, Colin. *A History of Childhood: Children and Childhood in the West*. Cambridge: Polity, 2001. Print.

Hilton, Boyd. *The Age of Atonement: The Influence of Evangelicalism on Social and Economic Thought, 1795–1865*. Oxford: Clarendon P, 1988. Print.

Hobbs, June Hadden. *'I Sing for I Cannot Be Silent': The Feminization of American Hymnody, 1870–1920*. Pittsburgh: U of Pittsburgh P, 1997. Print.

Hoiem, Elizabeth. "Chartist Children: Re-thinking Middle-Class Definitions of Play and Work in Early Children's Literature." Presented at the 41st Annual Children's Literature Association Conference. June 20, 2014.

Holdsworth, Sara and Joan Crossley. *Innocence and Experience: Images of Children in British Art from 1600 to the Present*. Published in conjunction with the exhibition September 19–November 15, 1992, Manchester City Art Galleries. With an essay by Christina Hardyment. Manchester: Pale Green P, 1992. Print.

Holt, Jenny. *Public School Literature, Civic Education and the Politics of Male Adolescence*. Ashgate Studies in Childhood, 1700 to the Present. Farnham, UK: Ashgate, 2008. Print.

Höltgen, Karl Josef. *Aspects of the Emblem: Studies in the English Emblem Tradition and the European Context*. With a Foreword by Sir Roy Strong. Kassel: Edition Reichenberger, 1986. Print.

Hopkins, Eric. *Childhood Transformed: Working-Class Children in Nineteenth-Century England*. Manchester: Manchester UP, 1994. Print.

Hopkinson, David. "Education, Secondary." In *Victorian Britain: An Encyclopedia*. Ed. Sally Mitchell. New York: Garland, 1998. 245–7. Print.

Horn, Pamela. *Children's Work and Welfare, 1780–1880s*. Studies in Economic and Social History. Basingstoke, UK: Macmillan, 1994. Print.

———. *Pleasures and Pastimes in Victorian Britain*. Gloucester: Sutton, 1999. Print.

———. *The Victorian and Edwardian Schoolchild*. Gloucester: Alan Sutton, 1989. Print.

———. *The Victorian Country Child*. 1974. Gloucester: Sutton, 1997. Print.

———. *The Victorian Town Child*. Washington Square, NY: New York UP, 1997. Print.

Hotz, Mary Elizabeth. *Literary Remains: Representations of Death and Burial in Victorian England*. Albany: State U of New York P, 2009. Print.

Huff, Cynthia. "Victorian Family Fictions." *Auto/biography Studies* 19.1–2 (2004): 89–99. Print.

Hunt, Tamara L. "Education of Women." In *Encyclopedia of the Victorian Era*. Ed. James Eli Adams. Danbury, CT: Grolier Academic Reference, 2004. 31–5. Print.

*Hymnary.org*. Sponsored by Christian Classics Ethereal Library, Calvin College, the Hymn Society of the United States and Canada, and the National Endowment for the Arts. Web. Accessed August 2012–August 2014.

Jackson, Mary V. *Engines of Instruction, Mischief, and Magic: Children's Literature in England from Its Beginnings to 1839*. Lincoln: U of Nebraska P, 1989. Print.

Julian, John, ed. *A Dictionary of Hymnology*. 1907. Rev. ed. 2 vols. London: J. Murray, 1915. Print.

Kelly, Karen A. "*The Young Christian Soldier* and the Domestic Missionary Army." *Anglican and Episcopal History* 79.3 (September 2010): 20. Internet PDF.

Kete, Kathleen. *The Beast in the Boudoir: Petkeeping in Nineteenth-Century Paris*. Berkeley: U of California P, 1994. Print.

Kincaid, James R. *Child-Loving: The Erotic Child and Victorian Culture*. New York: Routledge, 1992. Print.

Knight, Frances. *The Nineteenth-Century Church and English Society*. Cambridge: Cambridge UP, 1995. Print.

Knoepflmacher, U. C. *Ventures into Childland: Victorians, Fairy Tales, and Femininity*. Chicago: U of Chicago P, 1998. Print.

Knuth, Rebecca. *Children's Literature and British Identity: Imagining a People and a Nation*. Lanham, MD: Scarecrow, 2012. Print.

Kolodziej, Benjamin A. "Godfrey Thring: Victorian Hymnwriter of the Via Media." *The Hymn* 64.2 (2013): 29–37. Print.

Kooistra, Lorraine Janzen. *Christina Rossetti and Illustration: A Publishing History*. Athens: Ohio UP, 2002. Print.

Laqueur, Thomas Walter. *Religion and Respectability: Sunday Schools and Working Class Culture, 1780–1850*. New Haven: Yale UP, 1976. Print.

Larsen, Timothy. *A People of One Book: The Bible and the Victorians*. Oxford: Oxford UP, 2011. Print.

Larson, Judy L. *Enchanted Images: American Children's Illustration, 1850–1925: Catalogue Essay*. Santa Barbara: Santa Barbara Museum of Art, 1980. Print.

Lenti, Vincent A. "*Hymns for Little Children*: The Life and Legacy of Cecil Frances Alexander." *The Hymn* 50.3 (1999): 32–6. Print.

Lerner, Laurence. *Angels and Absences: Child Deaths in the Nineteenth Century*. Nashville: Vanderbilt UP, 1997. Print.

Lesnik-Oberstein, Karín. *Children's Literature: Criticism and the Fictional Child*. Oxford: Clarendon P, 1994. Print.

Lightwood, James T. *The Music of the Methodist Hymn-Book*. 1935. Ed. and rev. Francis B. Westbrook. London: Epworth P, 1955. Print.

Linkman, Audrey. *Photography and Death*. London: Reaktion, 2011. Print.

Lovelace, Austin C. *The Anatomy of Hymnody*. New York: Abingdon P, 1965. Print.

Lundin, Anne. *Victorian Horizons: The Reception of the Picture Books of Walter Crane, Randolph Caldecott, and Kate Greenaway*. Lanham, MD, and London: Children's Literature Association and Scarecrow P, 2001. Print.

MacCulloch, Laura. "'Fleshing out' Time: Ford Madox Brown and the *Dalziels' Bible Gallery*." In *Reading Victorian Illustration, 1855–1875: Spoils of the Lumber Room*. Ed. Paul Goldman and Simon Cooke. Farnham, UK: Ashgate, 2012. 115–35. Print.

Mahony, Bertha E., Louise Payson Latimer, and Beulah Fomsbee, eds. *Illustrators of Children's Books, 1744–1945*. Boston: Horn Book, 1965. Print.

Manwaring, Randle. *A Study of Hymn-Writing and Hymn-Singing in the Christian Church*. Texts and Studies in Religion, vol. 50. Lewiston, NY: Edwin Mellen P, 1990. Print.

Marks, Harvey B. *The Rise and Growth of English Hymnody*. New York: Fleming H. Revell, 1938. Print.

Marsh, Joss. "Dickensian 'Dissolving Views': The Magic Lantern, Visual Story-Telling, and the Victorian Technological Imagination." *Comparative Critical Studies* 6.3 (2009): 333–46. Print.

Marshall, Madeleine Forell and Janet Todd. *English Congregational Hymns in the Eighteenth Century*. Lexington: UP of Kentucky, 1982. Print.

Mavor, Carol. "Dream-Rushes: Lewis Carroll's Photographs of the Little Girl." In *The Girl's Own: Cultural Histories of the Anglo-American Girl, 1830–1915*. Ed. Claudia Nelson and Lynne Vallone. Athens: U of Georgia P, 1994. 156–92. Print.

McCutchan, Robert Guy. *Our Hymnody: A Manual of the Methodist Hymnal*. 2nd ed. New York: Abingdon P, 1937. Print.

McDonald, Ruth K. *Literature for Children in England and America from 1646 to 1774*. Troy, NY: Whitson P, 1982. Print.

McGavran, James Holt, Jr., ed. *Romanticism and Children's Literature in Nineteenth-Century England*. Athens: U of Georgia P, 1991. Print.

McGillis, Rod. "Editor's Comments: That Great Writer in the English Language." *Children's Literature Association Quarterly* 13.4 (1988): 162–4. Print.

McGuire, Charles Edward. *Music and Victorian Philanthropy: The Tonic Sol-fa Movement*. Cambridge: Cambridge UP, 2009. Print.

Meigs, Cornelia, Anne Thaxter Eaton, Elizabeth Nesbitt, and Ruth Hill Viguers, eds. *A Critical History of Children's Literature: A Survey of Children's Books in English, Prepared in Four Parts Under the Editorship of Cornelia Meigs*. 1953. Rev. ed. London: Macmillan, 1969. Print.

Melnyk, Julie. "The Congregational 'We': Women's Hymns and the Poetry of Community." Unpublished study.

———. *Victorian Religion: Faith and Life in Britain*. Victorian Life and Times Series. Westport, CT: Praeger, 2008. Print.

Mills, Arthur E. *Children's Hymns and Hymn Writers*. London: Epworth P, 1950. Print.

Morse, Deborah Denenholz and Martin A. Danahay, eds. *Victorian Animal Dreams: Representations of Animals in Victorian Literature and Culture*. Farnham, UK: Ashgate, 2007. Print.

"Mrs. Arthur Gaskin and *The Travellers*." Exhibitions of Early Children's Literature at Exeter Central Library and the University of Exeter. Web. Accessed March 11, 2014.

Neill, Stephen. *A History of Christian Missions*. 1964. 2nd ed. London: Penguin, 1986. Print.

Nelson, Claudia. "Drying the Orphan's Tear: Changing Representations of the Dependent Child in America, 1870–1930." *Children's Literature* 29 (2001): 52–90. Print.

———. *Precious Children and Childish Adults: Age Inversion in Victorian Literature*. Baltimore: Johns Hopkins, 2012. Print.

Nodelman, Perry. *The Hidden Adult: Defining Children's Literature*. Baltimore: Johns Hopkins UP, 2008. Print.

―――. "Pleasure and Genre: Speculations on the Characteristics of Children's Fiction." *Children's Literature* 28 (2000): 1–14. Print.

―――. *Words about Pictures: The Narrative Art of Children's Picture Books.* Athens: U of Georgia P, 1988. Print.

Noll, Mark A. "'All Hail the Power of Jesus' Name': Significant Variations on a Significant Theme." In *Sing Them Over Again to Me: Hymns and Hymnbooks in America.* Ed. Mark A. Noll and Edith L. Blumhofer. Tuscaloosa: U of Alabama P, 2006. 43–73. Print.

Noll, Mark A. and Edith L. Blumhofer, eds. *Sing Them Over Again to Me: Hymns and Hymnbooks in America.* Tuscaloosa: U of Alabama P, 2006. Print.

Norcia, Megan. "Playing Empire: Children's Parlor Games, Home Theatricals, and Improvisational Play." *Children's Literature Association Quarterly* 29.4 (2004): 294–314. Print.

Novo, Laura. "Education, Elementary." In *Victorian Britain: An Encyclopedia.* Ed. Sally Mitchell. New York: Garland, 1998. 241–3. Print.

Nutter, Charles S. and Wilbur F. Tillett. *The Hymns and Hymn Writers of the Church: An Annotated Edition of the Methodist Hymnal.* New York: Eaton and Mains, 1911. Print.

*The Oxford Dictionary of the Christian Church.* 1957. Ed. F. L. Cross. 2nd ed. Ed. F. L. Cross and E. A. Livingstone. Oxford: Oxford UP, 1974. Print.

Palmer, Sally B. "Projecting the Gaze: The Magic Lantern, Cultural Discipline, and *Villette.*" *Victorian Review* 32.1 (2006): 18–40. Print.

Paul, Lissa. *The Children's Book Business: Lessons from the Long Eighteenth Century.* New York: Routledge, 2011. Print.

Paz, D. G., ed. *Nineteenth-Century English Religious Traditions: Retrospect and Prospect.* Contributions to the Study of Religion, No. 44. Westport, CT: Greenwood P, 1995. Print.

Perkins, David. *Romanticism and Animal Rights.* Cambridge: Cambridge UP, 2003. Print.

Pickering, Samuel F., Jr. *Moral Instruction and Fiction for Children, 1749–1820.* Athens: U of Georgia P, 1993. Print.

Pierce, A. J. and D. K. *Victorian and Edwardian Children from Old Photographs.* London: B. T. Batsford, 1980. Print.

Pinchbeck, Ivy and Margaret Hewitt. *Children in English Society.* 2 vols. London: Routledge and Kegan Paul, 1969. Print.

Plotz, Judith. *Romanticism and the Vocation of Childhood.* New York: Palgrave, 2001. Print.

Pollock, Linda A. *Forgotten Children: Parent-Child Relations from 1500–1900.* Cambridge: Cambridge UP, 1983. Print.

Porter, Andrew. *Religion versus Empire? British Protestant Missionaries and Overseas Expansion, 1700–1914.* Manchester: Manchester UP, 2004. Print.

Rainbow, Bernarr. *Land Without Music: Musical Education in England 1800–1860 and Its Continental Antecedents.* London: Novello, 1967. Print.

Randel, Don Michael, comp. *Harvard Concise Dictionary of Music.* Cambridge, MA: Harvard UP, 1978. Print.

Reed, John R. "The Public Schools in Victorian Literature." *Nineteenth-Century Fiction* 29.1 (1974): 58–76. Print.

Ritvo, Harriet. *The Animal Estate: The English and Other Creatures in the Victorian Age*. Cambridge, MA: Harvard UP, 1987. Print.

Rivers, Isabel and David L. Wykes, eds. *Dissenting Praise: Religious Dissent and the Hymn in England and Wales*. Oxford: Oxford UP, 2011. Print.

Robson, Catherine. "The Ideal Girl in Industrial England." *Journal of Victorian Culture* 3.2 (1998): 197–233. Print.

Rogal, Samuel J. *The Children's Jubilee: A Bibliographical Survey of Hymnals for Infants, Youth, and Sunday Schools Published in Britain and America, 1655–1900*. Westport, CT: Greenwood P, 1983. Print.

———. "Isaac Watts' London printers, publishers, and booksellers (1700–1748)." *Library Gazette* 46 (1972): 167–75. Print.

Rogers, Helen. "'Oh, what beautiful books!' Captivated Reading in an Early Victorian Prison." *Victorian Studies* 55.1 (2012): 57–84. MLA Bibliography. PDF file.

Rogers, Jacquelyn Spratlin. "Picturing the Child in Nineteenth-Century Literature: The Artist, the Child, and a Changing Society." *Children and Libraries* (2008): 41–6. Print.

Routley, Erik. *Christian Hymns Observed*. London and Oxford: Mowbray, 1982. Print.

———. *Hymns and Human Life*. 1952. 2nd ed. London: John Murray, 1959. Print.

———. *The Musical Wesleys*. London: Herbert Jenkins, 1968. Print.

———. *A Panorama of Christian Hymnody*. Chicago: G.I.A., 1979. Print.

———. *A Short History of English Church Music*. 1977. With Additional Material by Lionel Dakers. Carol Stream, IL: Hope Publ., 1997. Print.

Rowell, Geoffrey. *Hell and the Victorians: A Study of the Nineteenth-Century Theological Controversies Concerning Eternal Punishment and the Future Life*. Oxford: Clarendon P, 1974. Print.

Ryden, E. E. *The Story of Christian Hymnody*. Philadelphia: Fortress P, 1959. Print.

Saltman, Judith, ed. *The Riverside Anthology of Children's Literature*. 6th ed. Boston: Houghton Mifflin, 1985. Print.

Sánchez-Eppler, Karen. *Dependent States: The Child's Part in Nineteenth-Century American Culture*. Chicago: U of Chicago P, 2005. Print.

Schorsch, Anita. *Images of Childhood: An Illustrated Social History*. 1979. Pittstown, NJ: Main Street, 1985. Print.

Schupf, H. W. "Education for the Neglected: Ragged Schools in Nineteenth-Century England." *History of Education Quarterly* 12.2 (1972): 162–83. Print.

Schwarzbach, F. S. "Twelve Ways of Looking at a Staffordshire Figurine: An Essay in Cultural Studies." *Victorians Institute Journal* 29 (2003): 7–60. Print.

Scotland, Nigel. *Squires in the Slums: Settlements and Missions in Late-Victorian London*. London: I. B. Tauris, 2007. Print.

Scrivener, Michael. *Poetry and Reform: Periodical Verse from the English Democratic Press, 1792–1824*. Detroit: Wayne SUP, 1992. Print.

Semple, Rhonda Anne. *Missionary Women: Gender, Professionalism and the Victorian Idea of Christian Mission*. Suffolk: Boydell P, 2003. Print.

Shavit, Zohar. *Poetics of Children's Literature*. Athens: U of Georgia P, 1986. Print.

Shaw, John Mackay. "Poetry for Children of Two Centuries." In *Research About Nineteenth-Century Children and Books: Portrait Studies*. Urbana: U of Illinois P, 1980: 133–43. Print.

Shea, Victor. "Education Act of 1870." In *Encyclopedia of the Victorian Era*. Ed. James Eli Adams. Danbury, CT: Grolier Academic Reference, 2004. 30–31. Print.

Shiman, Lilian Lewis. "The Band of Hope Movement: Respectable Recreation for Working-Class Children." *Victorian Studies* 17.1 (1973): 49–74. Print.

———. *Crusade against Drink in Victorian England*. New York: St. Martin's P, 1988. Print.

Shuttleworth, Sally. "Victorian Childhood." Roundtable: Victorian Children and Childhood. *Journal of Victorian Culture* 9.1 (Spring 2004): 107–13. Print.

Sigler, Carolyn. "Wee Folk, Good Folk: Subversive Children's Literature and British Social Reform, 1700–1900." Diss. Florida State U, 1992. Print.

Smith, John T. *Methodism and Education, 1842–1902: J. H. Rigg, Romanism, and Wesleyan Schools*. Oxford: Clarendon P, 1998. Print.

Sommerville, C. John. *The Rise and Fall of Childhood*. Beverly Hills: Sage, 1982. Print.

Stanley, Brian. *The Bible and the Flag: Protestant Missions and British Imperialism in the Nineteenth and Twentieth Centuries*. Leicester, UK: Apollos, 1990. Print.

———, ed. *Christian Missions and the Enlightenment*. Grand Rapids, MI: Wm. B. Eerdmans, 2001. Print.

Stolte, Tyson. "'And Graves Give up Their Dead': *The Old Curiosity Shop*, Victorian Psychology, and the Nature of the Future Life." *Victorian Literature and Culture* 42.2 (2014): 187–207. Print.

Stone, Lawrence. *The Family, Sex and Marriage in England, 1500–1800*. New York: Harper Colophon, 1979. Print.

Tamke, Susan S. "Hymns: A Neglected Source for the Study of Victorian Culture." *Journal of Popular Culture* 9 (1975): 702–8. Print.

———. "Hymns for Children: Cultural Imperialism in Victorian England." *The Victorian Newsletter* 49 (1979): 18–22. Print.

———. *Make a Joyful Noise Unto the Lord: Hymns as a Reflection of Victorian Social Attitudes*. Athens: Ohio UP, 1978. Print.

———. "Separating the Sheep from the Goats: Victorian Didactic Hymns." *Albion: A Quarterly Journal Concerned with British Studies* 8.3 (1976): 255–73. JSTOR. Web. Accessed September 2, 2011.

Temperley, Nicholas. "John Wesley, Music, and the People Called Methodists." In *Music and the Wesleys*. Ed. Nicholas Temperley and Stephen Banfield. Urbana: U of Illinois P, 2010. 3–25. Print.

———. *The Music of the English Parish Church*. 2 vols. Cambridge: Cambridge UP, 1979. Print.

———. *Studies in English Church Music, 1550–1900*. Variorum Collected Studies. Farnham, UK: Ashgate, 2009. Print.

Temperley, Nicholas and Stephen Banfield, eds. *Music and the Wesleys*. Urbana: U of Illinois P, 2010. Print.

Thomas, Greg M. *Impressionist Children: Childhood, Family, and Modern Identity in French Art*. New Haven: Yale UP, 2010. Print.

Thomas, Julia. "Happy Endings: Death and Domesticity in Victorian Illustration." In *Reading Victorian Illustration, 1855–1875: Spoils of the Lumber Room*. Ed. Paul Goldman and Simon Cooke. Farnham, UK: Ashgate, 2012. 79–96. Print.

———. *Pictorial Victorians: The Inscription of Values in Word and Image*. Athens: Ohio UP, 2004. Print.

Thorne, Susan. *Congregational Missions and the Making of an Imperial Culture in Nineteenth-Century England*. Stanford: Stanford UP, 1999. Print.

Travisano, Thomas. "Of Dialectic and Divided Consciousness." *Children's Literature* 28 (2000): 22–9. Print.

Turner, James. *Reckoning with the Beast: Animals, Pain, and Humanity in the Victorian Mind*. Baltimore and London: Johns Hopkins UP, 1980. Print.

Vallone, Lynne. "'A humble Spirit under Correction': Tracts, Hymns, and the Ideology of Evangelical Fiction for Children, 1780–1820." *The Lion and the Unicorn* 15.2 (1992): 72–95. Print.

Vicinus, Martha. *The Industrial Muse: A Study of Nineteenth-Century British Working-Class Literature*. New York: Barnes and Noble, 1974. Print.

Waggoner, Diane. "Photographing Childhood: Lewis Carroll and Alice." In *Picturing Children: Constructions of Childhood Between Rousseau and Freud*. Ed. Marilyn R. Brown. Aldershot, UK: Ashgate, 2002. Print.

Wallace, Eileen. *Children of the Labouring Poor: The Working Lives of Children in Nineteenth-Century Hertfordshire*. Hatfield, UK: Hertfordshire Publications, an Imprint of the U of Hertfordshire P, 2010. Print.

Walther, Luann. "The Invention of Childhood in Victorian Autobiography." In *Approaches to Victorian Autobiography*. Ed. George P. Landow. Athens: Ohio UP, 1979. 64–83. Print.

Watson, J. R., ed. *An Annotated Anthology of Hymns*. Oxford: Oxford UP, 2002. Print.

———. *The English Hymn: A Critical and Historical Study*. Oxford: Clarendon P, 1997. Print.

Webb, R. K. "The Gaskells as Unitarians." In *Dickens and other Victorians*. Ed. Joanne Shattock. New York: St. Martin's P, 1988. 144–71. Print.

———. "Quakers and Unitarians." In *Nineteenth-Century English Religious Traditions: Retrospect and Prospect*. Ed. D. G. Paz. Westport, CT: Greenwood, 1995. 85–115. Print.

Weinberg, Ian. *The English Public Schools: The Sociology of Elite Education*. New York: Atherton, 1967. Print.

Wheeler, Michael. *Death and the Future Life in Victorian Literature and Theology.* Cambridge: Cambridge UP, 1990. Print.

———. *The Old Enemies: Catholic and Protestant in Nineteenth-Century English Culture.* Cambridge: Cambridge UP, 2006. Print.

Wicke, Jennifer. *Advertising Fictions: Literature, Advertisement, and Social Reading.* New York: Columbia UP, 1988. Print.

Williams, Leslie. "The Look of Little Girls: John Everett Millais and the Victorian Art Market." *The Girl's Own: Cultural Histories of the Anglo-American Girl, 1830–1915.* Ed. Claudia Nelson and Lynne Vallone. Athens: U of Georgia P, 1994. 124–55. Print.

Winter, Sarah. "Curiosity as Didacticism in *The Old Curiosity Shop.*" *Novel* 34.1 (2000): 28–55. MLA Bibliography. PDF file.

Wolosky, Shira. "Rhetoric or Not: Hymnal Tropes in Emily Dickinson and Isaac Watts." *The New England Quarterly* 61.2 (1988): 214–32. Print.

Young, Carlton, ed. *The Book of Hymns: Official Hymnal of the United Methodist Church.* 1964. Nashville: United Methodist Publishing House, 1979. Print.

———. *The United Methodist Hymnal: Book of United Methodist Worship.* Nashville: United Methodist Publishing House, 1989. Print.

Young, Carlton R. *Companion to the United Methodist Hymnal.* Nashville: Abingdon P, 1993. Print.

Young, Kenneth. *Chapel: The Joyous Days and Prayerful Nights of the Nonconformists in their Heyday, circa. 1850–1950.* London: Eyre Methuen, 1972. Print.

Zelizer, Viviana A. *Pricing the Priceless Child: The Changing Social Value of Children.* New York: Basic Books, 1985. Print.

Zipes, Jack. *Sticks and Stones: The Troublesome Success of Children's Literature from Slovenly Peter to Harry Potter.* New York: Routledge, 2001. Print.

# Index

Note: Page numbers in bold indicate
    figures; page numbers in italics
    indicate tables.

Adams, Sarah Flower 52, 91, 98, 102, 117,
    134
Adey, Lionel 5, 11, 16, 17, 21, 22, 38, 49,
    51, 94, 98
advertising in hymn books 97–8
Alexander, C. F. 12, 26, 30, 32–3, 49, 51,
    71, 77, 84, 93, 94, 96, 97, 98, 99,
    29, 134, 150, 217
American
    children xv, 13, 30, 83, 239, 264
    holy dying stories 252, 253
    hymn books for children 13, 66n12,
        80n26, 82, 90n1, 135n37, 165,
        186n10, 196n20, 246, 258. *See also*
        *Songs of Happy Life*
    hymn composers or writers 83, 118,
        121n30, 123n31, 161, 206, 267
    hymn tradition 13n10, 13–14, 50
    periodicals 12n9
Anglican/Anglican Church 16, 18, 19,
    21–3, 32, 35, 41, 45, 51, 59, 77, 96,
    107, 109, 133, 143, 185, 240, 247
animal
    cruelty 183, 184, 210, 220–22
    death 238–9
    in children's literature 210n29
    legislation: Lacey Bird and Game Act
        (1900) 222
    references in hymns 75, 149, 167,
        169–70. *See also* Bands of Mercy
        hymn and song titles
    rights and welfare 210–12, 222–4.
        *See also* Royal Society for the
        Prevention of Cruelty to Animals
        (RSPCA)
animal studies 212n30, 224
Ariès, Philippe 1, 18, 227, 231, 232

Ascension Day 139
Atonement 84, 98, 99, 230, 241, 247
autobiographies (of Victorian childhood)
    Burke, Thomas, *Son of London* 133,
        159
    Foley, Winifred, *A Child in the Forest*
        141
    Hughes, Molly, *A Victorian Family* 31
    Jones, L. E., *A Victorian Boyhood* 33,
        200
    Kendon, Frank, *The Small Years* 51
    Kingdom, Frank, *Jacob's Ladder* 31
    Lamont, Thomas, *My Boyhood in a
        Parsonage* 30
    Larcom, Lucy, *A New England
        Girlhood Outlined from Memory*
        14, 26, 31, 83, 133, 267
    MacCarthy, Mary, *A Nineteenth-
        Century Childhood* 33
    MacDonald, Greville, *Reminiscences
        of a Specialist* 133
    Okey, Thomas, *A Basketful of
        Memories* 133
    Palmer, Herbert, *The Mistletoe Child* 133
    Pollock, Alice, *Portrait of My Victorian
        Youth* 28, 30
    Reid, Forrest, *Apostate* 31, 132
    Shaw, Charles, *When I was a Child* 34,
        41, 141

*Band of Mercy Advocate* 213n31, 214–15,
    216, 224
Bands of Hope
    American 196n20
    English 3, 10, 159, 182, 183, 197–201
    hymns and songs 201–9
Bands of Hope hymn- and songbooks
    *Capper's Temperance Melodist* 196n20
    *Harmonised Hymns and Songs for
        Bands of Hope* (Hall, 1862) 205,
        205n27

*Hymns and Songs for Bands of Hope*
    (UK, 1894) 205, 205n27
*Hymns for Children ... for Bands of*
    *Mercy and of Hope* (Farrington,
    1894) 85n32, 208, 215
*Our National Temperance Hymn and*
    *Song Book* (Hammond, 1865) 208
*Popular Melodies and Hymns*
    (Murphy, 1871) 205, 206
*Temperance Meeting Melodist*
    (Ludbrook, 1861) 196, 202, 206, 207
*Winskill's Band of Hope Melodist*
    (Winskill, 1870) 202, 203, 204, 206
Bands of Hope hymn and song titles *202*
    "Band of Hope hymn" 208
    "Dare to do right" 201, 202
    "Drops of crystal water" 201, 203
    "Give me a draught from the crystal
        spring" 201, 203
    "I love water pure and bright" 206
    "Kind words can never die" 201, 206
    "Lift up the Temperance standard" 206
    "Little drops of water" 149, 201, 203
    "Maggie's Trials" 204
    "The Pride of the Village" 204
    "Teetotal Charlie" 203, 206
    "Temperance Hymn" 208
    "There is a happy time" 206
    "Who will go for Father now?" 204
Bands of Mercy
    American 213–14
    English 18–23, 194, 209–10, 213–25
    hymns and songs 211–13, 215–24. *See*
        *also Songs of Happy Life*
Bands of Mercy hymn and song titles
    "Band of Mercy Anniversary" 217
    "Bells of Mercy" 216
    "A Cry for Liberty" 223
    "Don't Kill the Birds" 219
    "God bless our native land" 223
    "Lift aloft our banner" 223
    "The Little Bird's Nest" 220
    "Little Hands" 219
    "The Little Maiden [or Child] and the
        Little Bird" (Lydia Maria Child)
        213, 223
    "True Freedom" (James Russell
        Lowell) 224
    "The Voice of the Helpless" (Carlotta
        Perry) 220–22, **221**

"We are marching from the mountains"
    223
Barbauld, Anna Laetitia, *Hymns in Prose*
    *for Children* 5n8, 63–4
Berry, Laura C. 8, 181–2
Bewick, Thomas 146, 152, 165, 167, 168,
    169, 172, 173
Bible
    Acts 2 150
    Acts 5:3–5 166
    Deuteronomy 4:28 187
    Genesis 22:5–8 235
    Genesis 28:10–22 102
    John 1:5 161
    John 8 150
    John 14:26 76
    2 Kings 2:23–5 167
    Luke 16:19–31 41
    Luke 24:29 119
    Matthew 5:16 161
    Matthew 19:14 75, 91, 102, 147
    Revelations 15:2 132
    Revelations 21–2 248
    1 Samuel 1 150
    1 Samuel 3:1–18 85
    1 Samuel 17 150
Bilby, Thomas 15, 50–51, 52, 99, 228–9,
    250
Blake, William 33, 79, 80, 139–40, 151–2
Bodleian Library, Oxford xviii, 11, 21,
    107n16, 263n18, 264
Boys' Brigades 40–41
Bradley, Ian 5, 50, 101, 106–7, 109, 122,
    123, 128, 205, 206
British Library xviii, 4, 11, 201n26, 258,
    263n17, 264
Broad Church 11, 82–3
Brock, Mrs. Carey 3, 89, 92, **130**
Brontë, Charlotte, *Jane Eyre* 12, 227, 235
Brothers Dalziel 146
Browning, Elizabeth Barrett, "The Cry of
    the Children" 1, 43n23, 44, 181–2,
    224, 263
Burns, Rev. James Drummond 85–7, 102

Caldecott, Randolph 142, 151–2, 174
Calvinism/Calvinist 26, 29, 32, 39, 58–9,
    60, 62n8, 67, 92–3, 106n10, 164,
    167, 176, 239–40

Cambridge University Library xviii, 11, **27**, 165n28, 174n30, 190n16, 257

Carroll, Lewis, *Alice in Wonderland* (1864) 1, 55, 79, 81, 144, 158, 165, 166

Cassatt, Mary 154n16, 158

chapbooks 62–3, 66, 146, 151, 165, 205

child legislation
    Factories Acts/Factory Acts (1833–1878) 2n5, 43n23
    Factories and Workshops Amendment Act (1871), Miners and Colliers Act (1842), and Ten Hours Act (1833) 181n1

child reform, philanthropy for children 181–2

child reform of the adult world ("reverse reform") 10, 182–3, 197, 210

childhood death/death rates 3, 10, 14, 15, 42, 48, 59, 168, 176, 181, 203, 204, 227–54, 259–60

childhood disease 231

childhood studies 1, 182

children's diaries 3, 10, 11, 13, 14, 184, 255, 263–7

children's services 32–3

chromoxylography 152

Clapp-Itnyre, Alisa
    *Angelic Airs, Subversive Songs* 11–12, 106, 128n34
    "The Contentious 'Figure' of Music in the Poetry of Thomas Hardy" 107n15
    "Writing for, yet Apart" 12, 29n12, 33n14, 49, 73n20, 245n9

class divisions of hymns 16–18

congregational singing xv, 20, 105, 106–14, 133

Congregationalism/Congregationalist 16, 36, 62, 65, 67, 99, 109, 185, 240n7

cottage industry 17, 34, 35
    hymns for 44

Crane, Walter 142, 151–2

crossover hymns 9, 94–5, 101, 136

Croswell, Rev. Henry 107–8

Cruikshank, George 144

cult of the child 1–2, 9, 151

cult of the deathbed 10, 227–38

Cunningham, Hugh 1n3, 2

Curtis, Heather D. 14n11, 82

Curwen, John 37, 89, 109–10, 127–8, 199–200

Curwen, John Spencer 199, 257

Cutt, Margaret 63

Darton, F. J. Harvey 4, 7, 146–7

Darwin, evolutionary theory 82, 211, 217

death hymns. *See* hymns about death

deaths of children. *See* childhood death/death rates

Degas, Edgar 158

Dekker, Jeroen J. H. 183

Demers, Patricia 50, 55, 59, 63, 73

diaries, children's. *See* children's diaries

Dickens, Charles 1n2, 181, 213, 230, 235–7
    *David Copperfield* (1849–1850) 165
    *The Old Curiosity Shop* (1840–1841) 227, 235–7

Dissenter/Dissenting 58, 62, 83, 106, 107. *See also* Nonconformist

*Divine and Moral Songs for Children. See* Watts, Isaac

Duncan, Mary Lundie 29, 50, 79, 101, 121

Durham University (Fred Pratt Green Collection) xviii, 11, 19n6, 256

Dykes, John Bacchus 117, 123, 126–33, **127**, **130–31**, 243

Edmeston, James 101, 150, 194, 208

Elementary Education Act (Forster Education Act) of 1870 2, 36, 214

Eliot, George 11
    *The Mill on the Floss* 235

Ellerton, John 82–3

Ellis, Sarah Stickney 28

emblem books 145–6, 149, 150, 165, 177

engravings. *See* wood engravings

eschatology 8, 227–8, 238–9, 242, 247

Evangelical/Evangelicals 3, 4, 6, 9, 21, 23, 31, 35, 39, 40, 55, 56, 58, 62–72, 73, 74, 75, 79, 80, 82, 86, 87, 98–9, 119, 168, 178, 183–96, 210, 235, 238–43, 247–8, 254

Evans, Edmund 152

Ewing, Alexander 118, 128, 249

Factory Acts. *See* child legislation

factory hymns: *Hymns for Factory Children* (1831) 44–5

Flegel, Monica 3, 211, 213, 219, 223, 225n38
Foundling Hospital 45–8
foundlings. *See* orphans
fundraising 40, 46, 139–41, 185–6

Gaskell, Elizabeth 11, 228, 230
    "Libbie Marsh's Three Eras" 227–31
    *Mary Barton* 235
    *North and South* 127
Gaskell, William 83
Gaskin, Mrs. Arthur 154–6, **155**
gendering
    of hymns/hymn-singing 17, 28–9,
        40–41
    lack of (within hymn context) 3, 36,
        49–50
    within illustrations 170–71
gift books 145
Gilbert, Ann. *See* Taylor, Ann and Jane
Girls' Friendly Societies 41
Golden, Catherine 144, 150
Golden Age of Children's (Literature)
    Illustration 142, 151–5
Golden Age of Illustration 143–51
*Golden Bells. See* Hymn Index
Goldman, Paul and Simon Cooke 142, 147
Grant, Sir Robert 99–101, 105, 107
Great Diary Project, London 263, 264
Green, William John Cooper 19–20
Greenaway, Kate 142, 151–2, 154, 155,
    174
Grenby, M. O. 255–6, 258
Gubar, Marah 1n2, 2, 6, 56, 81n28,
    158n21, 182, 236

Handel, George Frideric 45, 98, 111
Hankey, Katherine 102–3, 104, 105, 134
Hardy, Thomas 11
    *Far from the Madding Crowd* (1874)
        89, 92, 128
    *Jude the Obscure* (1895) 235
    *Mayor of Casterbridge* (1886) 118n27
    poetry 107n15
    *Tess of the d'Urbervilles* (1891) 15–16,
        51, 235
Harrow School 18, 19, 20, 24, 264
heaven 10, 42, 56, 63, 69, 91–2, 98, 99,
    103, 125, 128, 135–6, 161–3,
    168–9, 176, 194, 227–54, **251**, 263

Heber, Reginald 23, 24, 29, 51, 52, 83,
    90, 92, 93, 98, 99, 129–32, 133,
    188–90
Hickson, W. E. 109, 223
high-art depictions of children 143, 155–64
High Church 13, 21, 23, 58, 72–7, 107,
    121, 178, 244
holy death (joyful death) stories 57, 230,
    232–3
Hopkins, Eric 2, 5, 16, 30–31, 38, 181
Horn, Pamela 25, 34, 36, 37, 200, 210,
    225, 231
Hullah, John 109
hymn books and hymn titles. *See* Hymn
    Index
Hymn Society in the United States and
    Canada xv, xvi, xvii
Hymn Society of Great Britain and Ireland
    xv, xvii, 92
hymns about death 21, 39, 41–2, 48, 59,
    61, 67, **68**, 74–5, 78, 84, 98, 102,
    103, 110–11, 118–21, 127, 203,
    227– 9, 238–54, **251**, **260**
*Hymns Ancient and Modern* (1861) 22,
    93, 97, 101–2, 104, 105, 108, 111,
    117–20, 128–9, 134

illuminated printing 151
illustrated hymn books 147–51, **148**,
    153–5, **153**, **155**, 164–79, **176**, **177**,
    **178**, **191**, 256, 264, 266
illustration studies 142, 144
Impressionism/Impressionists 142, 157–8
Indiana University xvi–xviii, **68**, 84n31, **153**,
    **155**, 165n28, **176**, **191**, 256, 264
infant hymn books 7, 17, 25–7, 65–72
Infant Schools and hymns 35, 36, 37, 51,
    65, 228–9

Janeway, James, *A Token for Children*
    (1672) 59, 232
Julian, John 38, 61, 72, 74, 79, 229, 252

Keble, John 24, 51, 52, 72–4, 79, 83, 90,
    92, 98, 101–2, 104, 121
Ken, Thomas 24, 32, 52, 83, 90, 92, 99,
    101, 124, 149, 202
Kincaid, James 157n18, 235, 237
Knight, Frances 144, 227, 240, 247

Kooistra, Lorraine Janzen 142, 143–4, 145, 165, 166

Laqueur, Thomas 35, 40, 62, 140
Larcom, Lucy, *A New England Girlhood Outlined from Memory. See* autobiographies
Leeson, Jane 71n18, 244–5
Lerner, Laurence 229–32, 235n3, 236
Lesnik-Oberstein, Karín 2, 57
Locke, John 60
London Missionary Society 185
Low Church 31, 58, 62, 75
Luke, Jemima Thompson 50, 51, 76, 83, 90, 91, 95, 134–6, 190, 259
Luther, Martin 75, 114, 122
Lyte, Henry Francis 24, 83, 90, 98, 118, 119–21, 250

magic lantern shows 9, 141–3, 159, 163–4, 179, 214
magic lantern slides
    "Abide with me" 233–4, **234**
    "Gentle Jesus meek and mild" 160–61
    "I think when I read that sweet story" 161, **162**
    "Jesus bids us shine" 161–3
marginalia in hymn books 230, 254–61
Marsh, Joss xvii, 159
McCutchan, Robert 29, 50, 85, 103, 111, 114, 117, 119, 128, 129, 135, 188, 233, 249
McGuire, Charles xvi, 109, 196, 199–200
Melnyk, Julie xvii, 53, 62n8, 65, 75, 82, 185
Methodism/Methodist xv, xviii, 9, 16–17, 24, 29, 30, 31, 35, 36n19, 38, 40, 60, 62, 72, 77– 9, 106–7, 127, 133, 184, 197, 198, 241
Methodist hymn books 60–62, 77–9, 96, 111. *See* Hymn Index for specific titles
meter
    hymn 59, 64, 69, 76–7, 85, 100, 105, *116*, 124, 129, 135, 189, 244, 249, 252
    poetic 59, 68–9, 71, 76–7, 86, 90, 100, 135, 252
middle-class children's hymn singing 25–33

Midlane, Albert 91
Millais, John Everett 146, 157
mission work/missionaries (British) 184–5
    and children 23–4, 184–6, 188, **191**
missionary
    hymn books for children 186, 190–94
    hymns 23, 92, 136, 183, 186–90, 194–6, 220
Monk, William Henry 98, 108, 110, 118, 119–21, 123, 133
Moody and Sankey 13, 97, 102, 205, 257, 264
most frequently occurring hymn titles
    adult 95–7, *96*, *97*
    children's 89–93, *90–91*, 95–105
musical education 19–20, 109–10

National Society for the Prevention of Cruelty to Children (NSPCC) 219–20, 225
nature in hymns 64, 153, 168–70
Neale, John Mason 24, 74–5, 99, 128, 242–3, 248–9
Neill, Stephen 184, 188
Nelson, Claudia xviii, 2, 94
Newbery, John 4, 151, 210
Newman, John Henry 72, 74, 92, 128
Nodelman, Perry 2, 7, 8, 57, 94n4, 152
Nonconformist 11, 62n8. *See also* Dissenter/Dissenting
Nutter, Charles and Wilbur Tillett 87, 117, 134, 188

orphans 17, 18, 45–9, 139–40
    hymn books 45–7
    hymns 45–9, 51, 220–22
Oxford Movement 57, 72–4, 249n12

parodies of hymns 106n13, 165–6, 202, 205–6, 230, 258–63
the Passion 75, 84, 92–3, 99, 149, 235
photography 144, 152n15, 158–9, 170, 233
pictures in hymn books. *See* illustrated hymn books
Pitman, Mrs. E. R., *Lady Hymn Writers* (1892) 28, 252
popularity of hymns. *See* most frequently occurring hymn titles
postmortem portraits 230, 233–4
Pre-Raphaelites 144, 157

Presbyterianism/Presbyterian 16, 60n6, 62n8, 115
psalmody 21, 44, 45, 46, 59, 106–8, 114, 118n27, 122, 123, 262
public school hymn books 18–24. *See* Hymn Index for specific titles
public schools 8, 17, 18–24, 35
publishing technology 144–5

Queen Victoria 109, 117

Ragged School hymns and hymn books 41–3
Ragged Schools 8, 17, 36
Religious Tract Society (RTS) 12, 37, 63, 153
Renoir, Pierre-Auguste 157–8
Ritvo, Harriet 211–12
Rivière, Briton, *Sympathy* (1877) 157
Romantic child 9, 40, 55–8, 72, 79–87, 154, 174, 178–9, 231
Routley, Erik 5, 7, 38, 94, 100, 106, 108, 134
Royal College of Music xviii, 11
Royal Society for the Prevention of Cruelty to Animals (RSPCA) 183, 212, 219, 220
Rugby School 18, 19, 20

St. Paul's Cathedral 45, 139–40
semantic 230, 233, 243, 245, 247, 253, 263, 265
semiotic 230, 233, 254
sentiment/sentimentality 48, 233, 235, 237, 247
Shaw, Charles, *When I was a Child. See* autobiographies
Shepherd, Anne 91
Sherwood, Mary, *The History of the Fairchild Family* (1818–1847) 63, 64n10, 235
Shiman, Lilian Lewis 196–200, 207, 209
Smart, Christopher 211
Society for the Promotion of Christian Knowledge (SPCK) 37, 38, 45, 63, 145, 184
Society for the Propagation of the Gospel (SPG) 184
Sommerville, C. John 2, 72, 235–6, 249

*Songs of Happy Life* (ed. Sarah J. Eddy, 1897) 215, 217–24, **221**
Stanley, Brian 184–8, 195n18
Stead, W. T. 95, 104
Sternhold and Hopkins's "Old Version" 106n10, 114
stock images 148–50
Sullivan, Arthur 85–6, 117, 123, 126, 154
Sunday School Anniversaries 40, 140–41, 179
Sunday school hymn books. *See* Hymn Index
Sunday School Union (SSU) 35n17, 37, 63, 132
Sunday schools 3, 15–18, 31, 35–41, 51–2

Tallis, Thomas 116, 122, 124, 126
Tamke, Susan S. 3, 5, 227
Taylor, Ann and Jane 25–6, 28, 29, 37, 49, 51, 52, 65–72, 75–6, 78, 79, 83, 85–6, 91, 94, 99, 118–19, 128, 187–8, 190, 214–12, 253
temperance hymns, songs, hymn- and songbooks. *See* Bands of Hope
temperance movement 196–9
Temperley, Nicholas xviii, 45–6, 77, 96, 106–7, 111n22, 121–4, 139n1
Thomas, Greg M. 157–8
Thomas, Julia 165–6, 234, 237
Thorne, Susan 36, 184–6, 193, 195
Thring, Edward 18n5, 19, 23–4
Thring, Godfrey 19n7
Titanic 95n6, 118
*Tom Brown's School Days* (1857) 20
Tonic Sol-fa 37, 50, 109–10, 114, 196n19, 199–200
Toplady, Augustus 20, 24, 29, 32, 40, 52, 83, 90, 92–3, 115, 121
Tractarian. *See* Oxford Movement

*Union Tune Book* 115, 132
Unitarianism/Unitarian 35n17, 83, 117, 118, 247
University of Cardiff Library, Wales xviii, 11
University of Illinois, Urbana-Champaign xv, xvii, xviii, 59n3, 146n7, 165n28, **178**
University of Manchester xviii, 11, 45n25, 268
University of Michigan 80n26, **260**

Uppingham 18n5, 19–20, 24

Vallone, Lynne 5n8, 56n2, 63–4

Watson, J. R. xvii, 5–6, 26, 81, 94, 117, 119, 121, 129, 249
Watts, Isaac 7, 52, 58, 60, 240
  *Divine and Moral Songs for Children* (1715) 4, 6, 26, 29, 52, 57, 58–60, 61–2, 65–7, 72, 73–4, 78, 80, 82, 83, 87, 90–92, 94–5, 96, 99–101, 104, 106, 115, 117, 122, 136, **176**, **177**, **178**, **191**, 211, 219, 240, 250, 252, 253, 256, 257, 265, 266, 267
  nineteenth-century illustrated editions 10, 143, 146, 147, 154, **155**, 163, 164–79, **176**, **177**, **178**, 186–8, 190, **191**, 193
website (to this book) xvi, xviii
Wesley, Charles 20, 24, 29, 32, 40, 52, 60, 65, 83, 90, 91, 92, 99, 106, 110–11, **112–13**, 123, 133, 136, 160, 241, 254, 254, 257, 261, 264
  *Hymns for Children, and Others of Riper Years* (1763) 4, 6, 60–62, 67, 160, 241

Wesley, John 57, 60–61, 65, 72, 77, 79, 80, 106, 111, 134, 136
Wesley, Samuel Sabastian 85n33, 123, 127
Wesley Chapel and Museum xviii
Wesleyan. *See* Methodism/Methodist
Whit-Walks/Whitsuntide 140–43, 179
Williams, Isaac, *Ancient Hymns for Children* (1842) 58, 74–7, 83, 85, 242
Williams, Ralph Vaughan 20, 123, 124
Winkworth, Catherine 22, 51, 110n20
wood engravings **27**, **68**, 143, 144, 146–7, **148**, 149, 150, **153**, **155**, **176–8**, 165–9
woodcuts **39**, 62n9, 145–6, 150, 151, 165, 167, 169, 172, 173, 190, **191**

Yonge, Charlotte 72–3, 79, 87, 235
  *Henrietta's Wish; or, Domineering* (1850) 73
  *Leonard, the Lion-Heart* (1856) 55, 73
Yonge, Frances M. *The Child's Christian Year* (1841) 73–4, 83
Young, Carlton 111
Young, Kenneth, *Chapel* 140, 141, 198, 263

# Hymn Index

Note: Page numbers in bold indicate figures.

## British Nineteenth-Century Hymn Books for Children

*282 Hymns and Melodies* (1893) 115, 161–2, 186n11, 194, 229, 240, 247–9

*Accompanying Tunes to the 'Hymns for Infant Children'* (1862; Dykes) 126–7, **127**

*Bible Christian Sunday-School Hymnal with Tunes* (1898; Griffiths) 132

*The Child's Book of Praise* (1871; Coward) 80, 84n32

*The Child's Own Hymn Book* (1841, 1851; Curwen) 89, 109, 127

*Childhood's Songs of Long Ago* (1897; McManus) **cover**, 80n27, 163, 165n28, 175

*The Children's Hosannah* (1858; Betts) 38

*The Children's Hymn Book* (1811; May) 242

*The Children's Hymn Book* (1854) 47, 145, 186n11, 189n14, 245

*The Children's Hymn Book for Use in Children's Services, Sunday Schools, and Families* (1878; Brock) 3, 92n2, 117, **130**

*The Children's Hymnal and Christian Year* (1872; Bateman) 32

*The Children's Hymnal with Accompanying Tunes* (1876; Monk) 98, 108

*The Children's Liturgy and Hymn Book* (1865) 32

*The Children's Service Book* (1897; Woodward) 32, 51, 85n32

*The Christian Mother's Hymn Book* (1855) 29

*Cottage Verse: A Collection of Hymns and Spiritual Songs* (1852) 44

*Divine and Moral Songs for Children. See* Watts, Isaac

*The Domestic and Social Harp* (1848; Woodward) 98, 104, 122

*Easy Hymns for the Use of Children in the National Schools* (1850) 37

*The Family Altar* (1843) 108

*The Family Hymn-Book* (1864) 25

*Golden Bells* (1890) 58, 80, 83–6, 97, 102, 114, 240, 247–50, 257

*The Home Hymn Book* (1885) 25, 48

*Hymn-Book for the Use of Uppingham and Sherborne Schools* (1874) 19n7, 20, 258

*Hymn-Book for the Use of Wellington College* (1860) 20, 21

*Hymns and Divine Songs for Young Persons* (1796; Rhodes) 97

*Hymns and Poems for Very Little Children* (1875; M. E. L.) 149, **153**

*Hymns and Rhymes for Children, by the Daughter of a Clergyman* (1871) 97, 149–50, 156, 212

*Hymns and Scenes of Childhood* (1842; Leeson) 71n18, 244–5

*Hymns for Children* (1842–1846; Neale) 74, 242–3

*Hymns for Children* (1888; Wilson; Dealy and Marriott; Sullivan) 126, 149, 154

*Hymns for Children, and Others of Riper Years* (1763; Wesley) 4, 60–61, 110, 134, 160, 241

*Hymns for Children and Young Persons* (1806; Benson) 38, 77, 78n24, 110

*Hymns for Children, Selected with a View of Being Learnt by Heart* (1856) 26

*Hymns for Children with Opening and Closing Services* 71, 85n32, 208, 215

*Hymns for Infant Children* (1852) 25

*Hymns for Infant Minds* (1809; Taylors) 25–6, 28, 29, 58, 65–72, **68**, 74, 92–3, 96, 104, 187–8, 241–2

*Hymns for Little Children* (1848; Alexander) 33n14, 49, 51, 77, 84, 93, 96, 99, 150

*Hymns for School Worship* (1890; Woods) 21, 22, 24, 80, 97

*Hymns for Schools and Bible Classes*
(1859; Ellerton) 82–3
*Hymns for the Church or Home Circle*
(1861; Braine) 98, 124
*Hymns for the Use of Rugby School* (1876)
20–23, 24, 52
*Hymns for the Young* (1839; Thrupp) 26,
47, 71n18
*Hymns for Use in the Sunday School and
the Guild* (1891) 83, 85n32
*Infant Altar* (1889; Whittemore) 150
*Infant Amusements* (1867) 25–6
*Infant School Hymns and Songs with
Appropriate Melodies* (1865;
Currie) 7
*Juvenile Missionary Manual* (1843)
190–94
*Lancashire Sunday-School Songs with
Music* (1857; Compston) 117
*Little Children's Hymns and Songs* (1895,
Lewis) 80, 81, 85n32
*The Methodist Sunday-School Hymn and
Tune-Book* (1879) 78–9, 92n2, 93,
100, 102, 108, 110–11, **112–13**,
114, 115, 116, 186n11, 188–9, 124,
135, 241, 247–8, **251**
*Morning and Evening Hymns* (1857;
Cameron) 25, 115
*Primitive Methodist Sabbath-School Hymn
Book* (1864; Antliff) 77–8, 257
*Psalms and Hymns for the Use of Clifton
College* (1863) 20
*Psalms and Hymns for the Use of the
Congregation of Rugby School
Chapel* (1867) 21
*The Public School Hymn Book* (1903) 23
*Ragged-School Hymn Book* (1848; Pelly) 43
*Ragged School Hymns by a Ragged-School
Teacher* (1848) 41–3
*Sabbath School Tune-Book* (1855;
Sturrock) 98, 110, 128
*Sacred Melodies for Children* (1843;
Bateman) 108, 126, 132
*School Hymns: With Tunes* (1893; Gunn)
108, 132
*A Selection of Hymns and Poetry* (1838;
Mayo) 37, 51, 65, 71n18
*A Selection of Hymns from Various Authors
for the Use of Sunday Schools*
(1836; Gadsby) 38, 39–40, 242

*A Service Book for Church and School*
(1891; Barrett) 32
*Short and Simple Prayers* (1844; Wilson)
**27**, 145
*Songs for the Little Ones at Home* (1868)
154
*Songs of Gladness* (1871) 80, 84n32, 145,
186n11
*Songs of Love and Mercy for the Young*
(1878) 50, 80, 102
*The Sunday-Scholar's Companion* (1822)
26, 65, 71n18
*The Sunday Scholar's Hymn Book* (c. 1880;
Tonic Sol-fa) 109n18, 117
*Sunday School Hymn Book* (1871) 84n32
*Sunday School Hymnal* (1892; Winters)
30, 52
*The Sunday-School Hymnal* (1870; Gregg)
38, 40
*Sunday-School Hymns* (1870; Free
Methodist) 78
*The Sunday School Union Hymn-Book*
(1835) 38, **39**, 145
*Sunday Sunshine* (1858; Bateman) 27, 30,
80, 84, 247
*Texts and Hymns Selected for Children*
(1857; Sturge) 147, **148**
*Young People's Hymnal* (1896; Button) 51,
90, 124–6, **125**
*The Weston Hymn Book* (1849; Harrison)
71n18, 92, 268

**Hymn Titles**

"Abide with me" (Lyte/Monk) 24, 41, 90,
90n1, 92, 95, 96, 97, 104, 118,
119–21, **120**, 133, 233–4, **234**, 250,
264
"All hail the power of Jesus' name"
(Perronet) 50, 78, 90, 96, 97, 99,
110, 133n36
"All people that on earth do dwell" (Kethe)
91, 97, 99
"All things bright and beautiful"
(Alexander) 26, 93, 99, 134
"Among the deepest shades of night"
(Taylors) 69
"Around the throne of God in heaven"
(Shepherd) 91–2, 99, 243, 248, 250

"Awake, my soul, and with the sun" (Ken)
32, 52, 83, 90, 92, 96, 97, 98, 149

"Christ in the manger" (Williams) 75

"Christ the Lord is risen today" (Wesley)
29, 41, 44, 61, 83, 99, 110–14,
**112–13**, 133, 229

"Come, Thou creating Spirit blest"
(Williams) 76–7

"Come, Thou long-expected Jesus"
(Wesley) 32

"Come, ye that love the Lord" (Watts) 250

"Death has been here, and borne away"
(Taylors) 118–19, 121

"Father, in high heaven dwelling"
(Jackson) 124, **125**

"For all the saints" (How) 123

"From Greenland's icy mountains" (Heber)
23, 29, 44, 51, 52, 90, 92, 96, 97,
188–90

"Gentle Jesus, meek and mild" (Wesley)
29, 40, 61, 115, 117, 159–60

"Glory to Thee, my God, this night" (Ken)
90, 92, 98, 101, 124, 201

"God entrusts to all" (Edmeston) 150, 208

"God is in heaven, Can He hear?" (Taylors)
99, 101n8

"Great God, and wilt Thou condescend"
(Taylors) 66, 70–71, 91, 92

"Happy the home" (Ware) 29–30

"Hark, the herald angels sing" (Wesley) 52,
61, 83, 90, 92, 102n9, 123

"Hark! The Voice of Jesus Crying"
(March) 195

"Here we suffer grief and pain" (Bilby) 15,
22, 40, 50, 51, 52, 99, 182, 227–9,
250, 262–3

"Holy, holy, holy" (Heber/Dykes) xvi, 24,
51, 52, 83, 90, 93, 96, 97, 99, 123,
129–32, **130–31**, 133

"Hosanna, laud Hosanna" (Threlfall) 102

"Hushed was the evening hymn" (Burns)
85, 86–7, 102

"I heard the voice of Jesus say" (Bonar)
91, 96, 101

"I love to tell the story" (Hankey) xv,
102–3, 104, 105, 134

"I sing the almighty power of God" (Watts)
29, 78, 90, 92, 99, 100, 115, 164,
168–9, 173, 253

"I thank the goodness and the grace"
(Taylors) 51, 52, 66–7, 69n14, 79,
92, 187–8

"I think, when I read that sweet story of
old" (Luke) xvi, 50, 51, 52, 76, 80,
90, 91, 93, 96, 102, 115, 134–6,
159, 161–2, **162**, 190, 206, 259

"Jerusalem the golden" (Neale) 40, 74, 97,
99, 118, 128, 133, 248–50

"Jesus bids us shine" (Warner) 161–3

"Jesus, lover of my soul" (Wesley) 29, 61,
95, 96, 111, 241, 254, 265

"Jesus loves me! This I know" (Warner)
84, 205

"Jesus shall reign where'er the sun"
(Watts) 52, 90, 92, 97, 99

"Jesus, tender Shepherd, hear me"
(Duncan) 50, 79, 101, 121

"Joy to the world" (Watts) 58

"Joyful, joyful, we adore thee" (Van Dyke)
123

"Just as I am, without one plea" (Elliott)
24, 29, 91

"Lead, kindly light" (Newman) 89, 92,
123, 128–9, 267

"Let us with a gladsome mind" (Milton) 7,
90, 99

"Little drops of water" (Carney) 149, 202, 203

"Little travelers Zionward" (Edmeston)
194, 249

"Lo! He comes with clouds descending"
(Wesley) 91

"Lord, dismiss us with Thy blessing"
(Fawcett) 91

"Lord, how delightful 'tis to see" (Watts)
175–9, **176**, **177**, **178**

"Lord, I have passed another day"
(Taylors) **21**, 22, 27–8

"Lord, we thank Thee for the pleasure"
(Jex-Blake) 22–3

"Nearer, my God, to thee" (Adams) xv, 52,
90n1, 91, 96, 97, 102, 104, 117–18

"Now condescend, Almighty King"
(Taylors) 69–70

"Now the day is over" (Baring-Gould) 101

"O God our help in ages past" (Watts) 58,
64n10, 122

"O I love to think of Jesus" (Cushing) 102

"O Love, Who formedst me" (Silesius/
Winkworth) 22, 51

"O worship the King" (Grant) 99, 100–101, 107

"One day, dear children, you must die" (anon.) 126, **127**

"One there is above all others" (Newton) 99

"Onward, Christian soldiers" (Baring-Gould) 123, 205

"Our blest Redeemer, ere He breathed" (Auber) 32, 91, 104

"Rock of ages" (Toplady) 20, 24, 29, 32, 40, 41, 52, 83, 90, 92, 95, 96, 97, 99, 121, 258, 264

"Saviour, breathe an evening blessing" (Edmeston) 101, 194

"See! the blood is falling fast" (Taylors) 67

"Shall we gather at the river?" (Lowry) 248

"Sun of my soul" (Keble) 73, 83, 90, 92, 96, 97, 101, 104, 121, 202

"Take my life" (Havergal) 201

"Tell me the stories of Jesus" (Parker) 103–5

"The church's one foundation (Stone) 123

"Th' eternal God will not disdain to hear an infant sing" (Watts) **155**

"There is a fountain filled with blood" (Cowper) 84, 99, 201

"There is a glorious world of light" 250

"There is a green hill far away" (Alexander) 84, 96

"There is a happy land" (Young) 29, 40, 90, 99, 202, 206, 250–52, **251**

"There is a land of pure delight" (Watts) 99

"There's a Friend for little children" (Midlane) 83, 91, 93, 115

"This is a precious book indeed" (Taylors) 29, 66, 67

"'Tis to Thy sovereign grace I owe" (Watts) 187

"To God be the glory" (Crosby) 84

"Vital spark of heavenly flame" (Pope) 259–60, **260**

"We are but little children weak" (Alexander) 32–3

"We are little friends of Jesus" (Lowry) 194

"We thank Thee, Lord, for this fair earth" (Cotton) 52

"When I survey the wondrous cross" (Watts) 52, 91, 96, 97, 99, 267

**Hymn Tunes**

Abridge 116, 122, 192, 205
Aurelia 123
Bedford 116, 122
Bethany 118
Dix 116
Dublin 100
Easter Hymn 111–14, **112–3**, 116, 122
Ellacombe 100, 115
Evening Hymn 116, 122, 124
Eventide 118, **120**, 121
Ewing 118, 128, 249
Farrant 116
Forest Green 123
French (Dundee) 116
German Hymn 116, 122
Glory 116
Greek Air 115, 135, 161
Hankey 103
Hanover 100, 116
Happy Land 116, **251**, 252
Harts 116
Horbury 117–18
Hosanna 116
Hursley 121
Innocents 115, 116, 122, 160
Joyful 229
Kingsfold 123
Lux Benigna 128
Mainzer 115, 116
Marching to Zion 250
Martyrdom 116, 119
Melcombe 116
Morning Hymn 116
Nicaea 129, **130–31**
Old Hundredth 122
Portsmouth New 193
Rockingham 116
Royal Oak 122
St. Ann [St. Ann's] 116, 122
St. Gertrude 123
Sine Nomine 123
Stories of Jesus 103
Stutgard 116
Tallis's Canon 116, 122
Toplady 121n30
Vienna 116, 122
Westminster 116